The Perfectly Simple Triune God

The Perfectly Simple Triune God

Aquinas and His Legacy

D. Stephen Long

To Lily,
With deep gratitude
and joy for your presence
in our life. May the God
of the "traditional answer"
always haunt you.
Steve

Fortress Press
Minneapolis

THE PERFECTLY SIMPLE TRIUNE GOD

Aquinas and His Legacy

Cover image: Mei, Bernadino (1615-1676)

Cover design: Tory Herman

Library of Congress Cataloging-in-Publication Data

Print ISBN: 978-1-4514-9239-2

eBook ISBN: 978-1-5064-1687-8

The paper used in this publication meets the minimum requirements of American
National Standard for Information Sciences — Permanence of Paper for Printed
Library Materials, ANSI Z329.48-1984.

Manufactured in the U.S.A.

This book was produced using Pressbooks.com, and PDF rendering was done by
PrinceXML.

For Lindsey and Adam

Contents

Teach me to seek you, and as I seek you, show yourself to me, for I cannot seek you unless you show me how and I will never find you unless you show yourself to me.

Anselm, Proslogion 2.155

Preface

The following work challenges modern criticisms of what I have called the "traditional answer" to the question of God. I do not like that term, but it is better than alternatives such as "classical theism" or "substance metaphysics." I argue that some of these criticisms are wrong, some are caricatures, some are important and require supplementation to the traditional answer. I assume theologians can make, and have made, mistakes, and those mistakes have consequences. I also assume our knowledge of God can advance. I make an apology for the "traditional answer" in this work, but I do so attentive to the progress that has been made in the doctrine of God. The apology is to theologians and especially clergy and laity whose task is to teach by word and deed who God is. We cannot comprehend God; no one has exhaustive knowledge of who God is other than God. Nonetheless theology assumes we can know God. It is a knowledge that never comes to an end. No one "masters" divinity. My apology for the "traditional answer" is not that it is a definition of God. Nor does it say all that needs to be said. It is, as Thomas noted in his prologue to the first part of his *Summa Theologiae*, a beginning. Knowledge of God is a journey, and we are always on pilgrimage.

What follows is a generalist approach to theology that will undoubtedly stick in the craw of those who are comfortable with the academic life defined by commitment to specific disciplines, subdisciplines in those disciplines, sub-subdisciplines in those subdisciplines, and so on. The need to make an original contribution to a specified discipline in academic life forces scholars to know more and more about less and less and then guard that less and less against generalists (as well as other specialists) who will never know all the details of those committed to a small slice of history or to the knowledge and dissemination of a specific theologian or movement. Ranging across historical periods and academic disciplines, bringing them into conversation, and constructing large narratives has increasingly been called into question in the modern academy. To attempt, as I do here, to have a conversation on the doctrine of God that draws on Thomas Aquinas; Augustine; Dionysius; Scripture; the Reformers; Protestant Scholastics; process, open, and analytic theists; liberation and postcolonial theologians; and antimetaphysical Barthians will seem to some a ridiculous act or possibly an act of hubris. Many scholars work their entire vocation to make a contribution to a minute historical or theological aspect of such thinkers or theologies. We need this kind of scholarship, and I have been enriched by it. If it were not for it, I could not be a generalist. A generalist does not have the time to know Augustine, Thomas, the Reformers or analytic theology with the same thoroughness that historical specialists or devoted practitioners of the analytic method know their subject matter. It has become impossible even for the specialist to keep up on all the relevant literature in her or his subdiscipline. Given that reality, the generalist appears as a dilettante. The difficulty with the specialist, however, is that he or she speaks increasingly with the same people in her or his subdiscipline, failing to see how the subdiscipline fits with the *universus* that should be part of scholarship and the academy if the university is to be something other than a trade school. For that reason, I am an unapologetic generalist, while at the same time recognizing the limitations it brings. The limitations are these: dangers of not understanding the nuances of a specific discipline from the inside, misrepresenting it, and thus forcing its insights into a framework so alien to it that those who practice it no longer discover what they practice in its representation. The danger is a lack of charity.

Yet charity is not indifference; every theologian or historian errs and must be accountable to others. In fact, there should be such a thing as "theological malpractice." If theology cannot make errors, it would never be falsifiable. But how do we determine theological error, and what do we do about it? Here things get complicated because of our history. Identifying theological errors conjures images of anathemas, inquisitions, blasphemy laws, ecclesiastical prisons, and other sordid events from our past. Most of those events are, thank God, *history* in the sense that they are behind us, and I hope never to return. We have made "progress" in dealing with theological error. Some of the theological movements I will critique have had institutional power brought against them; theologians have lost jobs or otherwise been ostracized and excluded from faith communities for their teaching. Others have used institutional power to safeguard them from critique. I find no comfort or satisfaction in such actions. Coercive actions based on institutional power should not define how we resolve theological disagreements.

If theology is to be a discipline that is not only about power, then it has to engage in seeking to resolve disagreements, and that requires first identifying where those disagreements lie. The task of scholarship is not to defend one's self but to present a position and have it tested by those who have a stake in the subject matter. This task is why time for research is so crucial to scholarship, and one cannot be a good teacher, despite how entertaining one is, if one has not published positions for public accountability.

I would be pleased if the following work were free of error and all those, specialists and generalists, whose disciplines or subdisciplines I draw on affirmed my presentation of them, even when we disagree. If so, then we could discuss the disagreements and their theological significance rather than the presentations. I know, however, scholarship seldom works this way, so although I an unapologetic in my generalist approach, I am apologetic to any who do not find themselves adequately represented in my interpretation of them, whether I affirm or critique them. I invite corrections along with the significance that those corrections would bear on the position I take in this work. If I misrepresented your position and we actually agree that the perfectly simple Triune God should be affirmed by modern theologians, then I rejoice. If I misrepresented the reasons why we disagree that the perfectly simple Triune God should be affirmed, then I welcome the further clarification. If I represented well the position and the reasons as to why we disagree, and those committed to a position other than the one I defend here consider me wrong, then I hope they will continue publicly to display those disagreements. Charity and truth require ongoing conversation. St. Augustine's words that I cite in the second chapter should also preface this and every theological work:

> Therefore let everyone who reads these pages proceed further with me, where he is as equally certain as I am; let him make inquiries with me where he is equally hesitant as I am; wherever he recognizes the error as his, let him return to me; wherever it is mine, let him call me back. Thus let us enter together on the path of charity in search of Him of whom it is said: "Seek his face forevermore."[1]

This work has been a long time in process. I would say it began in graduate school over lunches with my friend Fritz Bauerschmidt. He taught me a great deal about how to read Thomas Aquinas and be a theologian. I remain grateful for the Latin group Robert Pasnau initiated when we both taught at St. Joseph's University. I was allowed to teach a doctoral seminar on Thomas Aquinas at Garrett-Evangelical, and many of the ideas for this work began to germinate in that seminar. George Kalantzis and I put together a yearlong discussion on divine impassibility at the seminary when we both taught there, and it has been invaluable for me to figure out the complexity of modern teachings on God. I have benefited many times over from George's collaborations and knowledge. I was asked to teach a Protestant Doctrine of God course at Marquette; we begin by carefully reading through the first forty-three questions of Thomas's *Summa Theologiae*.

---

1. St. Augustine, *The Trinity*, in *The Fathers of the Church*, trans. Stephen McKenna, CSSR (Washington, DC: Catholic University of America Press, 1988), 8.

The students in that course formed this work in ways they may not have known. I am in the debt of Glenn Butner, Nick Elder, Jonathan Heaps, Ryan Hemmer, Chris Lilley, Matthew Olver, Gene Schlesinger, Tyler Stewart, and Jim Vining for all the assistance they provided. Anne Carpenter and David Luy assisted me in this project as well. I remain grateful for their friendship and scholarship. I have always had excellent colleagues who made me a better scholar than I otherwise would have been. Mark Johnson and Mickey Mattox pointed me in the direction of important sources and helped me understand Thomas and Luther. None of the above, of course, are to blame for my inadequacies. Conversations with the faculty from the Marquette Department of Theology were invaluable. To move from Marquette to Southern Methodist University, as I did toward the end of this project, was a difficult decision, but I am honored and pleased to have been invited to join its faculty. Without the sabbatical SMU provided I would not have had the time to finish this work in a timely manner.

I am grateful for those with a vocation to preach and teach in local parishes. I hope this work will benefit them as much as I hope it will call theologians not to accept the plethora of revisions to the perfectly simple Triune God on offer today. Nothing is more central to theology than the core constitutive practice of worshiping and glorifying God. It is where theology matters most. For that reason, I dedicate this book to my daughter Lindsey, a Methodist preacher who has my deepest admiration, and her husband, Adam, whose own calling as a lay theologian makes substantive differences in daily life. Their life together, and the common vocation they pursue, is a source of great joy for all who know them.

D. Stephen Long
Southern Methodist University

Abbreviations

ad	to, or toward
art.	article
CD	Karl Barth, *Church Dogmatics*. 4 vols. in 14 parts. Edited by T. F. Torrance and Geoffrey W. Bromiley. Translated by Geoffrey W. Bromiley. Edinburgh: T&T Clark, 1956–75
CCSL	Corpus Christianorum, Series Latina
obj.	objection
otc.	on the contrary
proem.	*proemium*, preface or introduction
prol	prologue
rep.	reply
resp.	response
sc	*sed contra* (on the contrary)
SCG	Thomas Aquinas, *Summa contra Gentiles*
ST	Thomas Aquinas, *Summa Theologiae*
WA	*Weimar Ausgabe* (Weimar edition) of Luther's Works

Introduction

Who is God? Below is the traditional Christian answer, or better its necessary beginning. This answer does not resolve every theological question; it generates further questions that call for more theological investigation. It is not a definition but an invitation to a journey, for theology is always *in via*. The answer comes from Thomas Aquinas, who set it forth in the first forty-three questions of his *Summa Theologiae*. His first twenty-six questions lead us into God's essence or nature: God is simple, perfect, immutable, impassible, infinite, eternal, and one; the next seventeen into God's processions: the one essence is revealed in three persons, Father, Son, and Holy Spirit. Because the essence or nature is the processions, the two parts, following the pattern of the Nicene Creed, signify the one God. The following is a summary of the traditional answer:

> God is simple, perfect, immutable, impassible, infinite, eternal and one, who is revealed in three persons, Father, Son and Holy Spirit. God's essence is one, yet each person is the essence. The Father is the essence. The Son is the essence and the Spirit is the essence. The Father, Son and Spirit are also the essence. Nonetheless, there is only one essence and three persons. The persons are distinguished by their relations.

Aquinas did not invent this answer; he developed it from authorities, especially Holy Scripture, Augustine, Dionysius, Hilary, John of Damascus, Boethius, Lombard, and others. He also drew on philosophers such as Aristotle, Plotinus, and Proclus. The answer is found throughout the Christian tradition, among Catholic, Orthodox, and Protestant theologians and confessions, but that alone does not yet tell us much. To discern the importance of this answer we must ask, "What kind of answer is this, what questions gave rise to it, and to what questions does it give rise?"

Like all answers, this answer makes good sense within the context of some questions and less so in the context of others. The argument in this work will be that the context within which the answer makes best sense is the question, "How do we speak well of the mystery of the Holy Trinity?" Divine simplicity and perfection make most sense when they are an answer to that question. They are also used as an answer to questions such as "What can be known of God by reason independent of faith or nature independent of grace?" and "How does God predestine all things to God's own glory?" When the answer is to the latter questions, so my argument will suggest, it generates difficulties that are not as troubling as when it answers the first question.

Notice how the different contexts subtly shift the answer:

Question 1: How do we speak well of the mystery of the Holy Trinity?

Answer: God is the perfectly simple Triune God.

Question 2: What can be known of God by nature and reason, and what by faith and grace?

Answer: Nature or reason tells us God is perfectly simple; faith or grace that God is Triune.

Question 3: How does God predestine all things to God's own glory?

Answer: God predestines them as the perfectly simple God whose knowledge is the cause of all things.

The answer to all three questions is not wrong per se, but the terms *perfectly* and *simple* have different functions in each of these contexts. In the first question, the terms function to speak as well as we can of the Triune mystery. In the second question, the answer is divided into two parts to address epistemological concerns. In the third question, the terms *perfectly* and *simple* function not to address the Triune mystery but God's relationship to creation as a causal power.

Although all three answers may be accurate, the meanings of *simple* and *perfection* shift. My argument in what follows is that the first question is the most proper, and any role remaining for the next two questions must come by way of it. I also hope to show that this is the best, albeit not the only way, to interpret Thomas's first forty-three questions in the *Summa*. When they are not interpreted through that question, then the affirmation of the "perfectly simple Triune God" will lose something significant. A tacit assumption running through my argument is that the "counters" of Counter-Reformation and countermodernist theologies on both the Catholic and Protestant sides took the common answer and used it to address questions for which it was not primarily made, seeking to drive a wedge between opponents. What should unite people of faith, the knowledge and identification of the Holy Trinity as the object worthy of our worship, was turned into an instrument of battle to gain victory over others.[1] If Reformed theologians placed the answer in a new context emphasizing predestination, Catholic Counter-Reformation theology often placed it in a new context of argument, emphasizing theological epistemology. The answer then supposedly demonstrates that Catholicism maintains reason against Protestant and modern fideism.

When the answer is placed in the context of the relation between reason and faith or grace and nature, then it requires parsing it other than Aquinas presented it. That happened: Thomas's answer became divided into two treatises and were given titles he did not use. Rather than his own terms of the essence of God and the "Triune persons *in divinis*" (see *ST* I 27 proem.), they became known as *de deo uno*, or God's oneness, and *de deo trino*, or the divine Trinity. The first supposedly sets forth what metaphysical reason can know of God without revelation, and the second how revelation further specifies who the one God is without reference to metaphysics or philosophy. Such a division,

---

1. I use the term *object* intentionally, drawing on Katherine Sonderegger's convincing argument that God is the subject who in his love is also object. See Katherine Sonderegger, *Systematic Theology*, vol. 1, *God* (Minneapolis: Fortress Press, 2015), 441–45.

however, distorts how the answer names the Triune God. Far from creating two separate treatises, one based on philosophy and the other on revelation, the terms used to identify God's oneness are necessary to express well divine Trinity, and vice versa. In other words, simplicity does not name an "attribute" or "property" of God known by reason alone; it is what allows theologians to identify the persons as the essence of God without positing four essences, or making creation a fourth divine hypostasis. Likewise, the divine Trinity is not a further specification of God after metaphysical reason has completed its task; the Triune persons reveal what simplicity means so that it can be applied to God, who is known to have real distinctions, which at first glance appears to deny simplicity. If we are to use the terms, then *de deo uno* must always be read from the perspective of *de deo trino*, and *de deo trino* must always be read from the perspective of *de deo uno*. They must be read simultaneously. But creaturely human language does not permit their simultaneous expression in either written or oral form; it always fails, which is also what this answer affirms, and this is the cause of much theological confusion in contemporary theology.

The confusion comes in two main forms. One form finds the *de deo uno* as the necessary metaphysical supposition for the *de deo trino*. Convinced that metaphysical reason properly identifies *that God is*, this first form confuses the *de deo uno* with an objective metaphysical foundation on which the divine Trinity must be expressed. The result is often a loss of the dramatic character of God's existence in God's self and for us. In other words, an "abstract" metaphysics renders God impersonal.[2] A second form emphasizes the *de deo trino* and

---

2. Although I will defend "abstraction" and metaphysics throughout this work, I also recognize there are presentations of them that are problematic. I think they are much more feared than they should be, but the concern is not misplaced. See Hegel, *Science of Logic*, trans. A. V. Miller (Amherst, NY: Humanity Books, 1969), for a discussion of Hegel's difficulty with Anselm's ontological proof for God's existence and how it leads to "abstract being" that cannot distinguish between being and nothing. Hegel writes, "When reality, taken as a determinate quality as it is in the said definition of God, is extended beyond its determinateness it ceased to be reality and becomes abstract being; God as the *pure* reality in all realities, or as the sum total of all realities, is just as devoid of determinateness and content as the empty absolute in which all is one" (113). I have serious reservations about theologians' use of Hegel's critique of "substance" metaphysics, as will become evident in what follows. However, I would agree with Cyril O'Regan's affirmation of Hans Urs von Balthasar's work that "although Hegel's own metaphysical articulation proves problematic for Balthasar, Hegel's critique both of the abstraction of the classical metaphysical

acknowledges God's dramatic character, but finds the *de deo uno* static, restrictive, and unnecessary. This form results from the Trinitarian and christological turns in modern theology, turns as we shall see that follow rules established by Karl Barth and Karl Rahner. The consequence has been repeated calls for revisions to the traditional language of the *de deo uno*.

The following work is an exposition, defense, and, in part, critical revision of Aquinas's synthesis of the traditional answer to the question "Who is God?" noted above, attending to the good and not-so-good reasons for the two forms of confusion. To accomplish this task, the work divides into three parts. The first part is exposition. Engaging with Thomas Aquinas, the first part explains how the (so-called) *de deo uno* and *de deo trino* entail each other. Each of the terms expressing God's unified essence—*existence, simplicity, perfection, immutability, infinity,* and *eternity*—are explained in terms of their key role in expressing divine Trinity. I recognize some might find this reading of Thomas Aquinas a Protestant reading. Although there are Catholic theologians who would confirm it, I no longer contest the charge. There are important "Protestant" reasons for engaging Thomas and reading him against much of nineteenth- and twentieth-century antimodern Catholic thought.

In his 1941 seminar on the Council of Trent, Karl Barth stated that every generation of Protestant theology must "engage the phenomenon of Roman Catholicism" in order to recognize where it does and does not require reform.[3] For the sake of our own self-understanding, Protestant theologians must engage Thomas. Our generation is not the first to do so. As will be demonstrated, many of the significant Protestant theologians of the sixteenth and seventeenth centuries cited Thomas for their doctrine of God. They were part of a Thomistic renaissance. They may even provide a reading of Thomas that became obscured by the "counters" that came to define those

tradition and its commitments to a static ontology are not entirely misplaced"; Cyril O'Regan, *The Anatomy of Misremembering: Von Balthasar's Response to Philosophical Modernity*, vol. 1, *Hegel* (New York: Crossroad, 2014), 117.

3. See D. Stephen Long, *Saving Karl Barth* (Minneapolis: Fortress Press, 2014), 243.

generations after the fact. The perfectly simple Triune God was never a source of division for the Reformers or Protestant Scholastics.

Since Leo XIII's 1879 encyclical *Aeterni patris* set forth Thomas as the philosopher who could restore philosophy against modernity's criticisms, Thomas's work has been a bulwark for Catholic engagements with the doctrine of God against modern (Protestant) trends, both in philosophy and theology. Such an engagement led to the antimodernist oath and the reduction of Thomas's thought to twenty-four theses set forth by Pius X in his 1914 *Postquam sanctissimus*. It was, in part, the dissatisfaction of some of this engagement that led Catholic theologians such as Henri de Lubac, Hans Urs von Balthasar, Bernard Lonergan, Karl Rahner, Joseph Ratzinger, and others to reread Thomas and provide a different engagement with modernity that led to Vatican II. Protestant theology must ask what relationship it has to these diverse Catholic engagements. As we will see in what follows, many Protestant theologians have now set their doctrine of God against Thomist answers to the question "Who is God?" Thus what was not at stake in the Reformation, the teaching on God's essence or nature, has now become one more point of division in the "enigmatic cleft" dividing Protestants and Catholics. Should it be? I think not. It matters that we worship the same God, a God everyone recognizes across our divides.

A great deal is at stake here. If we can only name, love, and worship what we know, and if we have differing doctrines of God, then the only way forward for theology is to identify the grave errors on the other side and require conversion. But if, despite the significant differences on authority and ecclesiology that divide Protestants from Catholics as well as Protestants from Protestants and Catholics from Catholics, we are still able to recognize that each tradition names, identifies, and worships the same God, then the importance of those differences will be relativized. In other words, if each tradition claims that its understanding of authority and ecclesiology is necessary for a proper doctrine of God and yet nonetheless also recognizes the same Triune God is the object of worship in the other tradition, then with respect to what matters most—our chief end—those differences cannot be decisive. The following argument sets forth a Thomist answer to the question "Who is God?" and shows the breadth of acceptance it found among Protestant theologians, and among church confessions prior to the eighteenth century.

Although Thomas Aquinas gave a formative answer to the question "Who (and what) is God?" in the thirteenth century, his presentation of it was neither unique nor original. He found it in the Bible, and in most of the church fathers, in Augustine, Dionysius, John of Damascus, Anselm, and Peter Lombard. Thomas also drew on philosophy and non-Christian authorities for his answer. The first chapter takes the reader through the first forty-three questions of his *Summa*. The focus is on those questions because they have become the source of division. The second chapter examines Thomas's sources for those divisions, arguing that he found them particularly in two central church fathers, Augustine and Dionysius, as well as in sacred Scripture. The point of this chapter is to show the breadth of authorities for the traditional answer. Thomas was not being innovative or making a unique contribution to the doctrine of God. These two chapters constitute the first part of the work.

The second part of this project shows how Protestant traditions inherited Thomas's answer. The heart of the traditional answer was not challenged by the Reformation, for it is found with some modifications in Reformed thinkers such as Philipp Melanchthon, Martin Luther, John Calvin, Girolamo Zanchi, Peter Martyr Vermigli, John Owen, Richard Hooker, and John Wesley. The second part includes, then, an exposition of the broad consensus this language had, a consensus that is instantiated in most Protestant confessions.

The third part describes how the answer became questioned in the modern era from a variety of theologians and theological movements. Many, if not the majority, of contemporary theologians would agree with Barry Smith: "Even though enshrined in historical Articles of Faith, the simplicity doctrine in the modern period has faded from prominence that it formerly enjoyed, sometimes being judged to be a piece of scholastic arcanity."[4] Or, as John Sanders notes, "Modern theology has witnessed a remarkable reexamination of the divine-human relationship as well as of the attributes of God."[5] This "remarkable reexamination" does not fit any prescribed theological or political programs. It occurs among evangelicals, Roman Catholics, Orthodox, liberal and magisterial Protestants. It can be found among theologians who delight in the scandal of heresy as well as theologians who affirm the core teachings of Chalcedon and Nicea. Most calls for revision arise from the perceived inability of the traditional answer to address questions of evil, freedom, liberation, logical analysis, or biblical interpretation. This third part seeks to accomplish two goals. The first is to present and take seriously the challenges each of the theologians and theological movements critical of the traditional answer pose to it. The point of this work is not simply to repeat past formulas but to bring them into conversation with modern, postmodern, and postcolonial challenges. The second is to ask whether the traditional answer can accommodate these critiques. It will do so by suggesting where the challenges misunderstand and/or misstate the traditional answer, where they require an either-or judgment, where they make an important point that the traditional answer cannot, or has not yet, addressed, and where they raise something completely new, which will call for supplementation. Doctrine develops and makes progress. Defending the "traditional answer" is not an act of nostalgia, nor a call for a return to an era to which we cannot, and should not, return.

---

4. Barry D. Smith, *The Oneness and Simplicity of God* (Eugene, OR: Pickwick, 2014), 84.
5. John Sanders, *The God Who Risks* (Downers Grove, IL: InterVarsity, 2007), 160.

PART I

Exposition

1

The Simple, Perfect Triune God

Language presenting God as simple, perfect, immutable, impassible, infinite, eternal, and one, revealed in three persons, can readily be found from early church fathers, West and East, through Augustine, Dionysius, Anselm, Lombard, Aquinas, and into the Reformers. Aquinas was the great synthesizer of the traditional language, building on the central term used by the fathers that God is simple.[1] As many theologians and philosophers have noted, once God's simplicity is granted, the other terms logically follow. To say that God *is* simple makes a number of important claims that will be examined below, but at its heart it affirms that God is "to be," which is also to say God's essence is God's existence; in other words, *what* God is is identical to *that* God is. God's essence answers the question, what is God (*quid est*)? while God's existence answers the question, whether God is (*an sit*)? For every creature from tadpoles to stars, what it is is not equal to that it is. Each creature's existence does not exhaust its essence. A

---

1. Simplicity is not a single teaching; it has many facets that I hope to present below. Andrew Radde-Gallwitz has shown how, early in the tradition, simplicity had to be "transformed" to express the mystery of the Triune processions. It is this tradition that Thomas inherited. See Andrew Radde-Gallwitz, *Basil of Caesarea, Gregory of Nyssa and the Transformation of Divine Simplicity* (Oxford: Oxford University Press, 2009).

single star does not identify all stars, and whether or not one particular tadpole exists would not call into question the essence of tadpoles. For God alone existence equals essence, which also means that God is not contained in a genus. God is simple, then, because God is not composed of parts as creatures are. We cannot divide God's essence and existence, nor apply to God other creaturely distinctions such as potentiality and actuality, form and matter, genus and difference, or substance and accidents. Nor can God's "attributes" finally be distinguished from one another, even though their mode of appearance to us requires such distinctions.[2] Although many, if not most, patristic and medieval theologians affirm this teaching about God's attributes, it was Thomas Aquinas, in questions 2 through 11 of his *Summa Theologiae*, who synthesized it and suggested, in contrast to Peter Lombard's *Sentences*, that the passing on of the knowledge of God should begin with these terms.

The first twenty-six questions of Thomas's *Summa* set forth God's essence; questions 27 through 43 discuss the divine persons. Thomas did not name these treatises, but at least since Cajetan (1469–1534) the first twenty-six questions have been called *de deo uno* (*On the One God*), and the following twenty *de deo trino* (*On the Triune God*).[3] Those names make sense and capture much of what is present in the *Summa*, but this division also carries with it Counter-Reformation polemics. Protestant teachings on total depravity supposedly lost the positive significance of nature, reason, and philosophy, leading to a modernity that only knows history, relativism, and fideism. Catholics preserve nature and reason, and Thomas Aquinas's work is the bulwark to defend them against Protestant and modern historicism. The first treatise, *de deo*

---

2. The key term here is *finally*. Thomas does not teach, for instance, that wisdom is goodness per se. They differ, but how they differ matters if we are not to make each of them really distinct and thus turn them into processions. Revelation would not permit such a move. More will need to be said on this below.

3. In the prologue to question 27 Thomas writes, "Having considered what belongs to the unity of the divine essence, it remains to treat of what belongs to the Trinity of the persons in God" (*ST* I 27 prol). In what follows, all Latin citations for the *Summa Theologiae* come from corpus thomisticum.org. English translations primarily come from the New English Translation by Alfred J. Freddoso at http://www3.nd.edu/~afreddos/summa-translation/TOC.htm. Even when I offer my own English translations, I consulted Freddoso's as well.

uno, is what reason alone can accomplish in achieving knowledge of God. The second, *de deo trino*, is knowledge of God given in faith.[4] Reason lets us know what can be demonstrated of God's existence and essence; faith supplements that demonstration with the knowledge of revealed mysteries insofar as they can be known. This distinction between reason and faith, however, like the distinction between *de deo uno* and *de deo trino*, leads to the misunderstanding that somehow Thomas's first twenty-six questions were about something other than divine trinity. Such a division requires a "mis-remembering," since Thomas made explicit his opposition to such an understanding in the first question of the *Summa*. It often gets neglected. Sixteenth- and seventeenth-century Protestant theologians read Thomas's teaching less in terms of a distinction between philosophy and theology and more in terms of the Nicene Creed and the economy of Scripture; God is one essence in three persons.

In what follows I will argue that Thomas's work cannot be easily divided between knowledge produced by reason and that produced by faith. Perhaps this works against Catholic readings of Aquinas. It appears to oppose Vatican I's *Dei Filius*, which affirmed a natural knowledge of God. Although there are Catholic theologians who question any interpretation of *Dei Filius* that sets forth a sharp distinction between faith and reason (de Lubac, Balthasar, Gerald McCool, David Burrell, Janet Soskice, Frederick Bauerschmidt), there are others who for a variety of reasons defend this distinction, or some version of it (Garrigou-Lagrange, John F. Wippel, Thomas Joseph White, Alasdair MacIntyre, Steven A. Long, Jean Porter, Denys Turner).[5] Is

---

4. This distinction is then read back into the tradition. Take, for instance, Stephen McKenna's introduction to Augustine's *The Trinity*. In distinguishing Augustine from "the Greeks," McKenna argues St. Augustine found it "better to begin with the unity of the divine nature, since this is a truth that is demonstrated by reason." See *The Trinity*, trans. Stephen McKenna, CSSR (Washington, DC: Catholic University of America Press, 1970), xiv. McKenna continues, "The logic of this arrangement is today commonly recognized, and in the textbooks of dogma the treatise *De Deo Uno* precedes that of *De Deo Trino*" (xiv).

5. I see strong continuities with my argument here and the work of Jean-Pierre Torrell, OP, and Gilles Emery, OP. The latter, commenting on the work of the former, states, "[Thomas] has no treatise 'of the one God' separated from the treatise of the Trinity, but simply two approaches to the same God depending on whether one considers in him what is common to the three persons or what is proper to each of them"; "Preface," in Gilles Emery, *Trinity in Aquinas* (Ypsilanti, MI: Sapientia Press of Ave Maria College, 2003), xx. Emery rejects dividing the two treatises between

calling this distinction into question a Protestant reception of Aquinas? The latter group of thinkers might have their suspicions. But my point is not to defend a "Protestant" reading of Thomas against a Catholic one. It is to argue that the "enigmatic crack" between Protestants and Catholics should not be unnecessarily widened either by a defense of Thomas as providing what Protestantism lacks on the Catholic side—a metaphysical demonstration of God's oneness as a foundation for Trinity—or as a criticism by Protestants (and some Orthodox) that Catholic theology fits God into an abstract, rationalist, metaphysical framework that then hinders an adequate doctrine of God. Some Protestants are too willing to jettison foundational terms from the traditional teaching on God such as simplicity, whereas some Catholics argue that such terms function as a necessary philosophical basis for an adequate theology. If, as I hope to show, Thomas's defense of simplicity is best understood from the perspective of the Triune processions, then this debate will be recognized as misplaced. Neither a sharp distinction between reason and faith nor a collapsing of one into the other suffices to capture the beauty of the twists and turns Thomas takes his readers on in his greatest *Summa*.

Beginning Where Thomas Begins: "Beyond Philosophy": *ST* I Q. 1

Thomas's teaching is best understood as a pilgrimage; he is taking us somewhere drawing on earlier teachings to explain later ones, and later ones to clarify earlier ones. To understand requires being led along a way. After a brief prologue to the entire *Summa*, Thomas begins the journey into our knowledge of God by asking in his very first question whether we need a discipline beyond philosophy (*praeter philosophicas disciplinas*) to know God. He answers yes for two reasons. First, because human creatures are ordered to God, and such an ordering "exceeds rational comprehension."[6] Reason qua reason, as

---

"a philosophical approach and a theological approach." He states, "The totality of the treatise of God concerns God the Trinity under the aspect of revelation" (ibid., 133).

6. *ST* I 1 resp., *quia homo ordinatur a Deo ad quemdam finem qui comrehensionem rationis excedit.*

important and necessary as it is in knowledge of God, does not suffice as the means for the completion of our creaturely journey, which has its end in God who exceeds human rationality. Second, even in those things *de Deo* that human reason can investigate, Thomas argues, "it is necessary for man to be instructed by divine revelation." Notice what Thomas has stated here and what he has not. He has not said that human reason can investigate *de deo uno* but not *de deo trino*, nor that faith provides knowledge of *de deo trino* but not *de deo uno*. Nor has he divided his treatise into two: *de deo uno* and *de deo trino*. He refers to the entire treatise as *de Deo* and has explicitly stated that even that aspect of *de Deo* that human reason can investigate will require "divine revelation."[7] In the first question of the *Summa* Thomas not only denies any sharp distinction between *de deo uno* and *de deo trino* based on reason and faith, but he tells us that knowledge of God's essence requires revelation as much as knowledge of God's persons will. The reason God's essence requires revelation, he states, is that what can be known *de Deo* through reason qua reason can only come "to a few" (*a paucis*), "after a long time" (*per longus tempus*), and "mixed with many errors" (*cum admixtione multorum errorum*).

None of this, of course, is new or surprising to Thomas scholars, even those who would distinguish sharply between the *de deo uno* and the *de deo trino*. What I want to suggest, which may be controversial, is that philosophical and theological knowledge cannot be easily disentangled in Thomas. Such an argument would be opposed by a Thomist such as John Wippel, who argues that Thomas's "self-contained philosophical discussions" in the *prima pars* can be freed "from their theological context and the biblical and patristic references found in their *videturs* and *sed contras*," and then used independently "as valuable sources for Thomas's thought."[8] Likewise it would conflict with Robert Pasnau's

---

7. Gilles Emery finds a sharper distinction between sacred science and philosophy than I have noted here. He writes, "Effectively, Trinitarian epistemology involves two distinct orders of knowledge: that which concerns the divine essence (oneness), which natural reason can reach to a certain extent, and that which concerns the distinction of persons (Trinity), to which only faith gives access"; Emery, *Trinity in Aquinas*, 25.
8. John F. Wippel, *Metaphysical Themes in Thomas Aquinas* (Washington, DC: Catholic University of America Press, 1984), 28.

philosophical interpretation of Thomas.[9] Of course, purely philosophical arguments can be ripped out of their context in the *Summa* and made to function as "self-contained," but they will not be Thomas Aquinas's arguments. If, as I will argue, Thomas is taking us on a journey where the limitations of philosophy, despite its importance for manifesting revelation, require theology, then nicely distinguishing the philosophical from the theological will turn that journey into atomistic steps that lose the sense of the whole.

To be more specific: the language of simplicity and its necessary correlates is not a piece of philosophical reasoning known by reason alone. It is *both* a species of philosophical knowledge known only by a few after much labor and mixed with many errors *and* revealed wisdom that manifests how God is Triune. Simplicity and perfection allow Thomas, following primarily Augustine and Dionysius, to account for Triune agency.[10] For that reason, simplicity will only be rightly understood when placed within theological knowledge, or *sacra doctrina*. Thomas does not affirm "simplicity" *per se*; he rejects some interpretations of it. The simplicity he affirms is that which helps us understand what matters most, divine Trinity, and for that it must be correlated with perfection. Sacred doctrine is open to philosophy, but never out of necessity or because it lacks something. Instead, it is hospitable to using philosophy to manifest sacred doctrine's truth about God.[11] Philosophy does not condition sacred doctrine. It helps sacred doctrine manifest its truth.

Too often, I fear, readers of Aquinas fail to take seriously question 1 as a guide for reading the *Summa*. Instead, questions 2–26 are read as self-contained philosophical arguments that are either necessary to make sense of divine Trinity or dismissed as metaphysical speculation that hampers an adequate presentation of the Trinity. However, if we

---

9. Robert Pasnau, *Thomas Aquinas on Human Nature* (Cambridge: Cambridge University Press, 2002). For an interpretation of Aquinas to which my argument would be much less controversial see Frederick Bauerschmidt, *Thomas Aquinas: Faith, Reason and Following Christ* (Oxford: Oxford University Press, 2013).

10. This point will be developed more fully in chapter 2.

11. In *ST* I 5 rep. obj. 2, Thomas writes *haec scientia accipere potest aliquid a philosophicis disciplinis, non quasi ex necessitate eis indigent, sed ad majorem manifestationem eorum quae in hac scientia traduntur. Non enim accipit sua principia ac aliis scientiis sed immediate a Deo per revelationem.*

keep in mind what Thomas has told us about the relationship between philosophy and theology as we move from question 26 to the opening question 27 on the divine processions, then we will gain richer insight into what we had been doing all along. What must be kept in mind are these claims: First, sacred doctrine is necessary for any philosophical presentation of God, including what can be known by reason. Second, what reason alone presents of God will easily mislead because it is always "mixed with many errors." Thomas presents simplicity as something that can be known about God by reason, but if it is only known by reason God will not be properly known, for simplicity can also mislead. Divine Trinity establishes the context to know how God is, and is not, simple, immutable, perfect, and so on. These two insights do not deny a proper philosophical knowledge of God. They do, however, set the context for the surprising turn that occurs in question 27, which gives us—for the first time—a proper understanding of God's existence, simplicity, perfection, immutability, infinity, eternity, and unity. If they are not to mislead, their meaning must be placed within the divine processions, and readers must be patient with where they are being led.

Thomas tells us that the knowledge we are seeking will not easily be obtained. It is a "science," but it is a science whose first principles are not "known by the natural light of the intellect." They are found in "God and the blessed in heaven" (*ST* I 1.2 resp.). Our access to this occurs through divine revelation and this revelation makes sacred doctrine a "single science." It takes the "formal characteristics of its object," who is God (*ST* I 1.3 resp.). It is nonetheless more a speculative than practical science. This distinction and the relation between the two sciences will be essential for what follows. Sacred doctrine as a speculative science concerns God's self-knowledge. Sacred doctrine as a practical science concerns God's work. The former focuses on God in God's self. The latter on God's relation to creatures. Thus we find three important distinctions that will require speaking about different relations. First is speculative sacred doctrine; it seeks knowledge that only God has, knowledge of God's essence and Triune relations. Second is practical sacred doctrine; it seeks knowledge of God through God's relation to creatures. It will consist of two parts that should not be equated because of the doctrine of analogy. First is God's relation to creatures, and second is creatures' relation to God. God knows what God makes. Creaturely access to that knowledge can never be identical to God's knowledge, for our knowledge is from the perspective of the made, not the maker. Although theology is primarily speculative, our access to it is only through the second part of practical sacred doctrine (ST I 1.4 resp.). I will refer to these three aspects of theology in terms of three different relations. The first, "speculative theology," concerns God's relationship to God's self. "Practical theology 1" concerns God's relationship to creatures. "Practical theology 2" concerns creatures' relations to God. Whatever knowledge we have of speculative theology and practical theology 1 only comes about because of practical theology 2. Herein lies the difficulty of theology as a science.

For Thomas, these three aspects of sacred doctrine remain a "single science." Laying it out through these distinctions lets the reader know how difficult attaining this most "noble, human wisdom" will be. Notice how Thomas explains how sacred doctrine makes us wise.

> Now it is sacred doctrine that most properly makes determinations about God insofar as He is the highest cause. For it does so not only with respect to that which is knowable through creatures—this the philosophers have discovered, as it says in Romans 1:19 ("That which is known of God is manifest to them")—but also with respect to that which He alone knows about Himself and which has been communicated to others by revelation. Hence, sacred doctrine is called wisdom in the highest sense. (ST I 1.6 resp.)

The wisdom of sacred doctrine aims at the speculative task—what God "knows about Himself"—but it never has direct access to this knowledge; the knowledge is always mediated "through creatures" and by what "has been communicated to others by revelation." God, then, is the subject of this "science," either as God is in Godself (speculative theology) or as God is the "origin and end" of creatures (practical theology 1) (ST I 1.7 resp.). These important distinctions must be kept in mind as Thomas takes us into the mystery of God's essence and persons.

Intending God through the Way Jesus Is: *ST* I Q. 2

The prologue to question 2 sets forth the itinerary for the journey toward God that Thomas sets before us in his *Summa*, a journey that we have already been told exceeds our rational comprehension. Thomas nevertheless tells us that the primary *intentio* ("intention" or literally "stretching to") of sacred doctrine is nothing less than "to transmit knowledge of God." The word *intentio*, and the verb to which it is related, *tendere*, is used three times in this short but all-important prologue. The first use lets the reader know that the "intention" of sacred doctrine is the knowledge of God, both as God is in God's self and as God is the beginning and end of all things. In other words, Thomas will explain both who God is in God's essence and how that matters for creatures.[12] Because God is the "end" of human existence, and because this end exceeds rational comprehension, the completion of sacred doctrine's intention will not be easy. Thomas's second use of the term appears when he lays out the threefold structure of the *Summa* and its goal: *ad huius doctrinae expositionem intendentes* ("for the purpose of setting forth an exposition of this doctrine"). Now Thomas uses the participle form of the verb *intendere* (to stretch forth) and sets forth the exposition of sacred doctrine, first treating *de Deo*, second "of the movement of rational creatures to God," and third *de Christo, qui secundum quod homo, via est nobis tendendi in Deum* ("of Christ, who as human, is the way of our tending to God"). These three expressions constitute the three parts of the *Summa*. Here we find the third use of *tendere*, which is explicitly related to Christ as the way for the journey. The movement from *intentio* through *intendentes* to *tendendi* shows how a term gains richness in Thomas's thought; what comes later helps us see better what came first. A seemingly innocuous phrase, "the intention of sacred doctrine," which the *Summa* "intends" to exposit,

---

12. Thomas begins his discussion of God's existence by arguing we cannot know God's essence, but that he does so in a treatise on God's essence should not be lost on the reader.

gains a richer significance because of the "tending" to God that Jesus is. The "intention" of sacred doctrine finds its fulfillment in the "tending to God" that Jesus is as our *via* ("way") to God.

The prologue shows how biblical, and especially Johannine, Thomas is, even when he is being philosophical. Jesus is the "way, truth and life" (John 14:6). This revealed knowledge never leaves Thomas, not even when he exposits God's "essence," for it will be exposited as "truth" (*ST* I 16) and "life" (*ST* I 18). Thomas will not always state it explicitly, but even when we are discussing God's essence from a philosophical perspective, he is at the same time manifesting God's Triune life to us.[13] We see a glimpse of this in the first sentence of the prologue, where we are told that the purpose of sacred doctrine is not only to guide us into knowledge of God *secundum quod in se est* ("as God is in Godself"), but also *secundum quod est principium rerum et finis earum* ("as God is the beginning and end of things").[14] Thomas returns to God as God is in Godself in question 12, as will be noted below.

The Divine Names:
God's Existence and Philosophy's Limits: *ST* I Q. 2

In question 2 Thomas begins with philosophy's significant but limited accomplishments. Philosophy provides a skeletal knowledge that God exists, but that knowledge is not yet of the living God. In fact, if divine simplicity is correct, then "that God is" cannot be separated from "what God is." Thomas seems to argue that he can have the former without the latter in question 2 and then denies the two can be divided in question 3. Is he being careless? Or is something else going on

---

13. Gilles Emery makes a convincing case that it is because Thomas begins with the relations and persons that he must start with God's essence. If he began with the Father qua Father and explicated the Father in the first moment, then he would have presented the Father "before having grasped the Father in his relation to the Son"; Emery, *Trinity in Aquinas*, 196.

14. Wayne Hankey finds in these two statements a synthesis between Aristotle and Proclus. Aristotle is present in *secundum quod in se est* and Proclus in *secundum quod est principium rerum et finis earum.* Hankey writes, "It is a Christian understanding of sacred doctrine involving a positive revelation of the divine nature, and a humanity raised to receive this through its reasonings about physical things, which is able to unite as never before these two aspects of divinity and these two opposed theologies in one science under a most comprehensive conception of the *ratio Dei*"; *God in Himself: Aquinas's Doctrine of God as Expounded in the* Summa Theologiae (Oxford: Oxford University Press, 1987), 68. More will be said about Thomas's complex use of "sources" below.

in what could amount to a confused argument? Addressing those questions requires asking what kind of knowledge of God question 2 provides when it tells us we can demonstrate "that God is."

Thomas argues that God's existence is *per se nota* ("self-evident"), but only to God, which of course does not help human creatures, since we have no direct access to God's self-evident knowledge of God's self. Because we have no direct access to who God is in God's own being, Thomas rejects Anselm's ontological argument, "God is that than which nothing greater can be conceived," on the grounds that some do not understand that God is what Anselm suggests but think instead that God is composed. The extent to which Aquinas understands what Anselm has done with his argument is questionable.[15] He is applying Aristotle's understanding of "demonstration" to Anselm's prayer, which forces Anselm's argument into an alien structure. Thomas assumes that for Anselm's argument to work creatures would not only need to know *that God is*, but also *what God is*—God's essence. The essence provides the definition necessary for a demonstration of God's existence. Anselm assumes the definition without telling us how he arrives at God's essence, and for Thomas not everyone agrees with the definition. Some think God is composite rather than "that than which nothing greater can be thought." Thomas himself, of course, will agree with Anselm's definition, for it is based on divine simplicity, in which God's existence is God's essence, but he will disagree on how we arrive at this knowledge and what must be demonstrated before we arrive at it.

Because we do not know God's essence, and therefore the definition of who God is, a demonstration of God's existence would seem to be impossible. Thomas's understanding of demonstration comes from Aristotle's *Posterior Analytics*. Aristotle suggests there are two kinds of demonstration, *demonstratio propter quid* and *demonstratio quia*. The first is the stronger form of demonstration because it moves from cause to effect. If we know what something is, its *quid*, with certainty,

---

15. It might be significant that he does not name Anselm at this point. Perhaps it is his way of acknowledging that his critique is not necessarily what Anselm opposes?

then we can trace its effects with a high level of certainty. Aristotle states, "Assuming then that my thesis as to the nature of scientific knowing is correct, the premises of demonstrated knowledge must be true, primary, immediate, better known than and prior to the conclusion, which is further related to them as effect to cause."[16] For a *demonstratio propter quid*, then, we would need to know *per se nota* God's *quid* or whatness such that we can say "God is X." Then we could follow it out to its logical conclusion. The argument would look like this:

> "God is X" where X is God's essence, *quid est*, or the definition.
> "X's exist and are the unassailable reason for Y's."
> Therefore God exists.

But we do not know God's essence, so we cannot have a *demonstratio propter quid*. However, all is not lost; there is a lesser form of demonstration known as *demonstratio quia* that traces effects back to causes. It has less certainty than a *demonstratio propter quid*, but it is nonetheless a demonstration based on the rather uncontestable ontological claim that nothing causes itself.

Thomas then discusses his well-known five *viae* leading from effects to God as their cause.[17] It is according to his Aristotelian principles a weaker form of demonstration, but it nonetheless points to God as the source and end of being. Before presenting the five ways demonstrating God's existence, however, Thomas lodges two important possible objections against it. The first has to do with evil. If God is good and infinite, as he has not yet but will argue, and evil is also infinite, then something is wrong, for two metaphysical "infinites" that contradict each other cannot both exist. Evil does exist, so God cannot. As with much of the journey that this first part of the *Summa*

---

16. Aristotle, *Posterior Analytics* 1.2 (71b9–25), trans. G. R. G. Mure, in *The Works of Aristotle*, ed. W. D. Ross and J. A. Smith (Oxford: Clarendon Press, 1928).

17. I agree with Janet Soskice about the function of Thomas's five ways. They are too brief and undeveloped to serve an apologetic function, as if Thomas were trying to convince unbelievers that God exists. Instead, they serve as an entrance point into the journey to God's name(s). She writes, "Indeed I suggest that to focus solely on their efficacy as proofs (always somewhat unaccountable in virtue of their brevity) and to fail to see that they open up Aquinas's discussion of naming God is to get the *Summa* wrong from the outset"; Janet Soskice, "Aquinas and Augustine on Creation and God as 'Eternal Being,'" *New Blackfriars* 95, no. 1056 (2014): 197.

invites its reader to take, Thomas's brief argument here depends on later arguments. For Thomas, evil is real in everyday life, but it is not metaphysically infinite; only God's goodness and perfection is. Evil then can at most be permitted by God, and it cannot be permitted without serving in some sense that which is metaphysically infinite—God's goodness. Evil can only be a privation from what is perfect and good. It does not possess metaphysical existence in the same way God's goodness does.

The second objection is that creation does not need explanation. It suffices as an explanation in itself. Once again Thomas anticipates his later argument concerning God's immutability. Unless we can be content with sheer contingency as self-explanatory, which Thomas thinks is absurd, then everything changeable needs to look to something other than what is changeable for its existence. Otherwise its existence is unintelligible. God as the simple, perfect, immutable, infinite eternal being renders contingent beings intelligible. Although Thomas's terms seek to name God as best we can, they always serve his interest in identifying the proper relation between God and creation as well, but he will tell us explicitly that we cannot move from God's essence to a discussion of creatures without first passing through God's processions. "God" is not an affirmation of some original moment of creation, a moment that merely begins everything; God is the eternal, infinite source of all that is as the processions of wisdom and love.

After addressing these two objections, Thomas then proceeds to his five ways and claims that the first mover, who puts all things into motion without being moved, everyone "understands" (*intelligunt*) to be God; that the necessity of a first efficient cause, everyone "names" (*nominatur*) God; and that the necessary cause, the cause being perfect and good, and governor of all things, everyone "calls" (*dicunt*) God. Thomas does not yet say, as he will when he nears the end of his discussion of God's attributes with God's unity in question 11, "This is God" (*Et hoc est Deus, ST* I 11.3 resp.). He says something less. In question 2 Thomas offers a weak *demonstratio quia* that God exists and concludes that the arguments for "God" are what people understand, name, or call God, but he does not yet make the stronger, later claim, "This is God."

Thomas's five ways are philosophical arguments, and like all such arguments they have validity as long as we remember they are always mixed with errors. Thomas does not explain how they are mixed with errors at this point; in fact, he never does. The argument for God as the efficient cause is particularly troubling, as numerous philosophers and theologians have pointed out. "Cause" assumes a motion to something that exists in order to have an effect on it. The common example of billiard balls colliding demonstrates the difficulty. God is not a cause that puts preexisting material into motion (except, as we shall see, for process theologians, who more than any other modern theology adopt God as cause). If creation is not eternal, then the term *cause* is being used in an odd way. The world was eternal for Aristotle, so it made more sense for him to think of God as a "cause" than it does for Aquinas, who affirms *creatio ex nihilo*. The Latin Western tradition too often adopts God as Absolute Cause and makes this one of God's attributes. Victor Preller identifies this error, especially as it became normative among neo-Scholastic Thomists. Preller argues that if we begin with the claim "God is the 'cause of the world'" and assume we know what this means, and then "predicate certain 'perfections' of God in a mode appropriate to the 'cause' of the world," we are already involved in bad circular reasoning.[18] We lose the ability to make sense of creation out of nothing, for it cannot make sense of *x* caused *y*. The only Thomist response is to argue that the use of *cause* with respect to God is unique and unlike its uses in any other discipline, including metaphysics. For Preller, this response is unhelpful. Having attempted to tie our language of God to the language of causality, we must then so thoroughly equivocate on the language of causality that our language about God fails. David Hart has made a similar indictment of the Thomist use of causality and identifies it as generating serious problems in Western teachings on providence and predestination.[19]

---

18. Victor Preller, *Divine Science and the Science of God: A Reformulation of Thomas Aquinas* (Princeton, NJ: Princeton University Press, 1967), 19.

Thomas's argument for God's existence from efficient causality bears no relation to his presentation of divine attributes. God's essence is not defined as cause or power in the first eleven questions of the *Summa*. This simple point will have a crucial role in the development of the argument below. Once cause or power become a name or attribute of God's essence, neither a speculative theology that addresses God's essence nor a practical theology that addresses God's relation to creation can be sustained. The two become collapsed into one.

Too much should not be made of Thomas's five ways. They have limited use in his work; he refers to them again in his later questions, but not with the frequency to which he appeals to divine simplicity and perfection. The five ways are also supplemented even in these first eleven questions; they are framed by sacred doctrine. Thomas begins his exposition by first responding to his objections, citing Exod. 3:14, where God names God's self as *ego sum qui sum* ("I am what I am") (*ST* I 2.3). He returns to Exod. 3:14 when he comes to the end of the discussion of the divine attributes and our knowledge of them in question 13, "On the Names of God," when he tells us *qui est* is the *maxime proprium nomen Dei* ("most proper name of God") (*ST* I 13.11). Exodus 3:14 brackets his presentation on God's existence and attributes.[20]

Thomas also begins his discussion on God's existence by an explicit reference to a maximal natural theology by citing John of Damascus in his first objection. The objection states, "The knowledge of God is

---

19. David Hart, "Providence and Causality: On Divine Innocence," in Francesca Murphy and Philip Ziegler, eds., *Providence of God: Deus Habet Consilium* (London: T&T Clark, 2009), 40.

20. Thomas also cites Exod. 3:14 in an objection and reply as a way to interpret Isa. 65:1, placing the words, "I am who I am" as the Son speaking to Moses. Thomas defends the "holy fathers" assigning the "essence" to the persons. While in the other two contexts noted in the text above Thomas refers to the divine name as most proper to God qua God, here he finds it appropriate to the Son because of the "liberation" the Son effects in history. In other words, the divine name is not only a metaphysics but also a historical accomplishment of the Son. Thomas writes, "Now *He Who Is* is appropriated to the person of the Son not according to its proper meaning, but rather by reason of something added to it, viz., that the liberation of the human race, which is accomplished through the Son, is prefigured in what God says to Moses. Still, insofar as 'Who' is taken as a relative pronoun, it could sometimes refer to the person of Son and so be taken for a person—as, for instance, if one were to say, 'The Son is the Begotten Who Is,' in the same way that 'God Begotten' is the name of a person. However, 'He Who Is,' taken without modification, is a name of the essence"; *ST* I 39.8 rep. to obj. 5.

naturally implanted in all." He cites this as an objection against his own argument that God's existence is not self-evident to us. Keeping faith with the need for something beyond philosophy for our knowledge of God, Thomas counters this objection by stating knowledge of God that "exists in a general way, under a certain confusion is naturally inserted in us, inasmuch as God is the beatitude of human creatures for a person naturally desires beatitude." But this is not to know God *simpliciter*. What is "natural" to the human creature is not knowledge of God per se but God's effects in us that make us seek happiness. We know something of God because we desire happiness as our end, but we do not yet know God as God is in himself, which is the purpose of sacred doctrine. The five ways only begin us on our journey toward our true end. They are "ways," and we have already been told Jesus will be *the* way.

What kind of knowledge for God's existence can we derive from the five ways? Vatican I, and the modernist oath, interpreted Thomas's arguments through a maximal natural theology. Vatican I states "that God the beginning and end of all things, may be known for certain by the natural light of human reason, by means of created things." A careful reading of Thomas would raise a question about such certitude. How does Thomas's avowedly "confused and general knowledge" that God is the beginning and end of all things become one grounded on the certainty of natural human reason? Thomas does, of course, claim his five ways result in "everyone" understanding, naming, or calling the first cause "God," but who is meant by "everyone"? Is Thomas making a maximal natural theology argument that all right-thinking people in any context can arrive at certain knowledge that God exists?

Lutheran theologian Robert Jenson finds such a maximal natural theology problematic, but also finds Thomas himself less guilty of such a theology than those who came after him. The seeds for a mistaken overreaching of metaphysical accomplishment in Thomas's five ways emerge in later Catholic, Protestant, and philosophical arguments that take Thomas's ways out of their historical context and turn them into an ahistorical metaphysics. The problem lies in later interpretations of

Thomas's appeal to "everyone." Thomas's concluding comment in each of his five ways—"and all understand this to be God"—suggests Jenson, was intended for Jews, Christians, and Muslims. It originally occurred within a "specifically biblical apprehension already in place" based on "historically particular divine dispositions," but the audience shifted in the Enlightenment. After the Enlightenment it became something else:

> The "natural" knowledge encompassed in it was thought to be a body of knowledge about God and his intentions not intrinsically dependent on historically particular divine dispositions, and therefore properly the common property of humanity. In fact, however, this body of theology was as historically particular as any other set of theological proposals: it comprised a part of the theology that Greek religious thinkers, pondering the revelations claimed for Homer and Parmenides, had provided for the cults of Mediterranean antiquity as it became religiously homogenous, the part that the church's fathers also found themselves able to affirm.[21]

Jenson does not find arguments for such a natural knowledge of God compelling. Knowledge of God is always historically mediated, for God addresses creatures in history. To abstract from it and seek a putatively neutral, universal reason that can demonstrate God is to abandon the church's sacred wisdom. Moreover, it neglects that all such arguments serve some *historical* presentation of deity. The difficulty with Aquinas's arguments as they were received is that they hide the potential conflict between the "historically particular theological proposals" of the Greeks with that of Scripture. Jenson raises the metaphysical question, a question we will see below that numerous contemporary theologians raise against Thomism. For that reason, he is open to some significant revisions of the traditional answer especially with respect to divine simplicity. Jenson has identified a later deformation in the Thomistic tradition, but does it require the revisions he suggests? Should we heed his warning? A reasoned response requires significant attention be given to the purpose for "divine simplicity."

---

21. Robert Jenson, *Systematic Theology* (New York: Oxford University Press, 1997), 1:7.

Divine Simplicity: To What End? *ST* I Q. 3

The skeletal knowledge that God is in question 2 gains substance as Thomas takes us through his treatise on God's essence, adding to what we know of God by a way of not-knowing, which he tells us in an ambiguous expression is the purpose of questions 3–11. Question 2 addressed whether God exists (*an Deus sit*), but beginning with question 3 until a discussion of our knowledge of God in question 12, Thomas sets forth the "manner" of God's existence. Here once again he runs up against the limits of philosophy, for he addresses this "manner" with the use of an ambiguous expression, *quomodo sit, vel potius quomodo non sit* ("in what manner God exists, or rather in what manner God does not exist"). The expression is powerful in its ambiguity. Thomas seems uncertain, at this point, exactly what our knowledge of the "manner" of God's existence is. Is it positive (*quomodo sit*)? Or is it negative (*quomodo non sit*)? If it were purely a negative theology, there would be no reason for the first positive expression. If it were purely a positive theology, there would be no need to qualify it with the second negative expression. Thomas leaves the ambiguity as to what questions 3–11 are. We could assume he is confused, uncertain as to what he is doing. He begins by telling us "in what manner God is," but then becomes uncertain and changes his mind telling us instead "in what manner God is not." If the latter renders the former void, should he not have gone back and revised the expression, doing away altogether with the original, "in what manner God is"? It is better to see his ambiguous expression as intentional. He does not yet resolve it for a specific reason. It cannot yet be resolved; we are only at the beginning of a journey. It will require patience to see the end more clearly, to see in what manner God is from a discussion of in what manner God is not. In fact, Thomas will wait until the prologue to question 12 to tell us what we are accomplishing in questions 3–11, restating what he already told us he would do in the prologue to question 2. In question 12 he tells us that we have been considering nothing less than *qualiter Deus sit secundum se ipsum* ("God as God is in Godself"), but we have not yet arrived at that knowledge. We can only get there by attending to "in what manner God is not."

On our way to considering God in Godself, Thomas begins with simplicity. It follows on God's existence; for simplicity is another way of saying "God is" where God's essence or *quid* does not differ from God's existence. In other words, bringing "God" and "is" together does not bring together two different parts into a composite whole. Being is not a category larger than God for which God is one of the members. Nor is God a larger category than being in which being is one of the members. No such logical arguments for predication based on the analysis of sentences will make sense of the metaphysical claim that God's essence is God's existence. Divine simplicity works against any predication that attributes parts to deity. It already conveys the limitations of our language, for it requires bringing two different terms together—*God* and *is*. What appears as parts of a whole is being used to deny God has parts belonging to a whole. Language confuses us, but it need not mislead us. We can use it to express God by showing how what we mean by saying "God is" is not limited by the material means used to express it. In order to do so, care must be exercised in the use of language. For Thomas, terms build on each other, limiting possible meanings and opening up better combinations of terms that convey meaning even when the means by which it is conveyed are inadequate.

Once simplicity is granted, then, *as Thomas develops them*, all the other terms—*perfection, immutability, infinity, eternity, unity*—must follow. One term cannot be revised or rejected without revising or rejecting all, but the key qualification in that statement is "as Thomas develops them." The terms are not properties that have a set definition, which is then predicated of a subject. Each of them could be misunderstood or misused and neglect the whole that his *de Deo* is. For instance, God is simple, but God also has real distinctions. God is immutable, but God has the necessary motion that the operations knowledge and will entail. God is infinite, but God also has an "origin" and "end" that allow us to make sense of divine processions. Defenses of each of these terms that neglect the later Trinitarian argument could easily defend something other than what Thomas defends. It is insufficient to argue "God is simple" if it does not contribute to God's unitary essence manifested in the real distinctions of the three persons; we are, after all, considering God as God is in himself—even in questions 3–11.

God's simplicity, as we have seen in Jenson and shall see in other theologians, has been challenged from diverse theological and philosophical quarters. It also has its defenders. James Dolezal rightly notes how central it is in Thomas.[22] He recognizes that the Reformers neither rejected nor diminished its central role. He writes, "The Protestant Reformers and their scholastic heirs did not alter Thomas's account of the DDS [doctrine of divine simplicity] in any significant way except to make the biblical motivations for the doctrine more explicit."[23] Dolezal offers a powerful defense of simplicity, one that finds great sympathy with the argument set forth here. However, there is one significant difference between his defense and the present argument. Dolezal defends simplicity as "the ontologically sufficient condition for God's absoluteness."[24] His focus is on God's "absoluteness," which distinguishes God from creaturely reality as the omnipotent sovereign over creation. In Dolezal's defense of simplicity it primarily serves the "traditional understanding of doctrines such as God's aseity, unity, infinity, immutability and eternity."[25] While his argument is convincing, especially against the analytic theologians and philosophers of religion he cites, he has not yet stated the most important thing. Nowhere does Dolezal suggest that simplicity primarily renders Trinity intelligible. Instead, it becomes intelligible based on God's relation to creation. But Thomas refuses to move from divine simplicity to creation without first using simplicity to make sense of divine processions. This, I shall argue, is its primary use in

22. "The doctrine of God's simplicity reaches the zenith of expression and sophistication in the thought of Thomas Aquinas. He regards the DDS as the centerpiece of the Creator-creature distinction and he makes recourse to the doctrine both explicitly and implicitly throughout the vast corpus of his theological and philosophical writings"; James Dolezal, *God without Parts: Divine Simplicity and the Metaphysics of God's Absoluteness* (Eugene, OR: Pickwick, 2011), 6.

23. Ibid., 8.

24. Ibid., 2.

25. Ibid., 67.

Aquinas. Simplicity allows theologians to posit real distinctions in God without losing God's unity or dividing God into three parts. Without it, divine Trinity is unintelligible. Only after that has been established can divine simplicity be used to address the relationship between God and creation.

Thomas's development of divine simplicity is not as concerned with God's "absoluteness" as is Dolezal. Simplicity does not serve the interest of establishing God's power over creatures, although Thomas nowhere doubts God's omnipotence and in fact has a strong doctrine of predestination. Nevertheless, simplicity, and all that flows from it, serves the surprising purpose of making sense of divine Trinity, but to see this the reader must be patient, recognizing that all those indications Thomas provides in his argument connecting his questions together help us see how the terms he uses are fitting for God, as well as how they might not be fitting because they always have the potential of being mixed with error. We are pilgrims (*viatores*) in the *Summa* following a way (*via*). As with any pilgrimage, the journey brings with it surprises; later events render earlier ones intelligible, and what we thought we were doing at first gains a richer, deeper knowledge as we travel along the way. Such is especially the case with divine simplicity.

In his first presentation of simplicity in question 3, Thomas tells us something about who God is not and therefore who God is. We know God has no body, and no distinctions of matter/form, potentiality/act, essence/nature, essence/existence, genus/difference, or substance/accidents. Nor is God in composition with created things. By knowing God is not composed of these distinctions, we know something of God's manner of existence, but what it is remains ambiguous. We could easily misunderstand it to think God has no distinctions at all, which would work against the knowledge of our true end: the beatific vision of the divine Trinity. We could also misunderstand simplicity as bare existence, as a kind of imperfect substratum of pure potentiality or prime matter, which would be a less perfect form of existence than more complex entities. Such an interpretation of simplicity can be found in Proclus, as will be discussed below. Then we might be speaking of "simplicity," but it would not be divine simplicity. In order to make sure we do not misunderstand simplicity along these lines, Thomas immediately follows it up with perfection. Simplicity without perfection invites misunderstanding, just as perfection without simplicity would convey a false sense of perfection.

Perfection: *ST* I Q. 4–6

Perfection follows from simplicity. God does not actualize a potential and become perfect (a problematic theogony found from Valentinianism to Hegelianism). Because God's essence is God's existence, God cannot become more God than God already is. No such "more" exists. Moreover, the perfection of creatures cannot add to God's perfection. Instead, God's perfection entails that all perfection, even creaturely perfection, preexists in God, an argument Thomas explicitly makes, drawing on Dionysius. God's existence as perfect being, as *ipsum esse*, is, however, not a bare existence. Thomas points ahead in his argument to God's immanent operations of "living" and "wisdom" to help us see what it means for God to be; for, as Dionysius also taught, because the divine essence is *ipsum esse subsistens* it includes the immanent operations of "living" and "wisdom" (see *ST* I 4.2 otc.). Living and wisdom do not add something to God's *esse*. Because God is simple, they are one in God's essence. But they will entail that God's one essence contains immanent operations, especially knowledge and will, which is an early glimpse of divine Trinity. Thomas will show us this only after we enter into his treatise on the divine processions. Because God's perfection is not just bare existence but also contains immanent operations of knowledge and will, perfection is also goodness. Goodness does not contradict God's essence, as evil or potentiality would. It can be "infinite" with God because it is infinite as God. In God, being, wisdom, knowledge, perfection, and goodness are one; God is simple.

Infinity: *ST* I Q. 7–8

Infinity poses significant problems as a term for God. It can be applied to imperfect things composed of material and parts or with magnitude or matter and form (*ST* I 7.1–3). Thomas insists that divine infinity is not this kind of infinite but is infinity *simpliciter*. He is willing to concede that other things, such as angels or certain magnitudes, have a kind of infinity. However, only God is infinity *simpliciter*, because only God's essence is God's existence. In other words, simplicity allows us to see how God can be infinite without assuming God's infinity is the "spurious infinite" of Hegel, where it is merely that which is opposed to the finite.[26] God's infinity is a participable infinity, just as God's being is a participable being and God's perfection a participable perfection. God and creation are not merely juxtaposed against each other, as if what we know of God is only the negation of what we know of creation. God is the donating source of everything in creation such that it is both like and unlike God, which is how a term like *infinity* functions. It allows for God to be "in all things" without displacing them or being composite with them.[27] In other words, if God's infinity were merely the opposite of finitude, it would only make God other than finite creatures. Likewise, if God were finite, then God and creatures would exist in a "competitive relation" where for God to know or will, creatures would be forced to cease to know or will. Infinity is God's lack of limitation so that God and creatures can inhabit the same space and time because God's essence is not *in* space or time; God is not one more item or object that can be cataloged along with creaturely objects. Finite creatures can participate in infinity without divine infinity displacing them. For this reason, Thomas brings infinity, God's unique existence, and creaturely existence together in an interlude between infinity and immutability by asking how God can be infinite in all things without displacing them. He states, "God exists in all things not as a part of essence (*essentiae*) or as an accident, but as an agent present

26. G. W. F. Hegel, *Science of Logic*, trans. A. V. Miller (Amherst, NY: Humanity Books, 1969), 137.
27. An argument found in David Dinant that Thomas refers to as "very stupidly claimed" (*ST* I 3.8 resp.).

to that in which he acts" (*ST* I 8.1 resp.). This primary agency does not evacuate a free, secondary creaturely agency. Because of God's infinity, the two agencies are not competitive, as if God acts 75 percent and the creature 25 percent. Infinity functions to avoid any such misunderstanding.

Immutability: *ST* I Q. 9

Based on all the premises he has so far affirmed, Thomas moves in his prologue to question 9 to immutability and points ahead to eternity. Immutability, he argues, leads ineluctably to eternity. For three reasons "God is altogether immutable." His argument builds on previous questions: question 2 that God is the first being, question 3 that God is simple, and questions 4 and 7 that God is perfect and infinite. First, because God is the "first being," who is "altogether actual," God cannot change. Second, in order to move "something must have potentiality." Thomas restates his claim that "God is simple." Mutability implies composition, which God cannot have. Third, things in motion "acquire something they did not have." As perfect and infinite, God does not acquire things. Thomas states that God is *infinitus comprehendens in se omnem plenitudinem perfectionis totius esse* ("infinity comprehending in himself the whole plenitude of perfection of all being"). This statement could easily be seen as a complicated midrash on the divine name. It is reasonable to think Thomas has God's "proper" name in mind (Exod. 3:14), for, as we have seen, he brackets this entire conversation with the revelation to Moses. Here we also see how Thomas is not predicating properties, attributes, or characteristics to God, but each of these terms is used with qualification explaining how divine names can be said of God so that the inevitable errors found in such terms are limited as far as possible. An analytic approach to what he is doing will not suffice without the importance of a hermeneutic one as well. The qualifications used in one term provide a context by which the next one can be used, and the use of the next one further clarifies the previous one.

Eternity: *ST* I Q. 10

Unlike infinity, only God is immutable. All creatures are mutable, which means they are only sustained by God's gift of being. God, Thomas states, *semper eis esse dando* ("is always giving being to them"). God is then the one who gives being not only at the beginning of things but "always." God is not causal, like a big bang that generates all things with an initial impetus acting on something that already is. God is the constant donating source of being, which requires that God always be "before," "during," and "after" creaturely being. Eternity follows. To discuss God's eternity, Thomas begins with a definition from Boethius, asking whether it properly defines eternity. The definition includes explicit references to immutability and perfection, and of course presumes simplicity. The definition is: *aeternitas est interminabilis vitae tota simul et perfecta possessio* ("Eternity is the simultaneous whole and perfect possession of interminable life"). Thomas then raises several important objections. Is it proper to speak of God's eternity as the negation of a life that can be terminated? If God's essence were defined in terms of a "negation," it could imply "the negation is part of the essence." In other words, God would not be defined as the fullness of being but a being who is known in terms of what it is not. Negation does help us identify many things. This rock is not that tree. Such negation does not work with God. "This infinite God is not that infinite God" makes no sense. Then God would not be able to be a determinate, living being without negation; God is God because God is *not* that. Thomas responds that this misunderstands how "negations" are used in speaking of God. They are not used of God's essence; they only negate creaturely composition. In other words, God is not known only as the negation of creation. Thomas has already told us we know God from creatures. The God who is known from creatures, however, is know by "remotion," removing what is unfitting to God in creaturely existence such as composition. Of course, to know what is to be removed already assumes some positive knowledge of God.

Thomas next asks whether the word *vita* is properly used of God.

So far, in the first ten questions of the *Summa*, Thomas has primarily spoken of God's being; he has not discussed at length God's "life." With God's eternity, *living* must be added to the term *being*, and we are pointed toward the necessary discussion of God's operations. *Vita* implies immanent "operations" within God's existence that entail God is more than a bare *esse*. God's eternity does not cordon God off from temporal existence; it is what allows God to act without being reduced to a being among beings, or a potentiality that must actualize something in order to create, sustain, or redeem. God acts eternally as the one who perfectly possesses life.

Unity: *ST* I Q. 11

If God is living, that is to say, if God is acting being, then God must also be one. Thomas's discussion of terms used for God concludes with God's *unity*, a term of course that has a biblical foundation. Thomas cites Deut. 6:4, "Hear, O Israel, the Lord our God is one." But how can we speak of God's oneness without making God a being among beings, for unity places something within a genus? He acknowledges the problem in the way he poses the question: *utrum unum addat aliquid supra ens* ("whether one adds something beyond being"). His first objection is a warning about the difficulty of using *one* to name God. Everything in a "determinate genus" adds something to being. One is in such a genus of quantity. Unity brings a collection of things together, giving them an identity as a unity. But, because of divine simplicity, perfection, immutability, infinity, and eternity, unity should not be misunderstood in such terms. God is not in a genus. To speak of the "one God," then, is not to place God in a category. Fortunately, *one* refers to beings in two ways. It refers to simple being, as designating its indivisibility; here it is convertible with *ens*. It also refers to complex being, as whole to parts; here it would not be convertible with *ens* and would add something to being by placing it within a unifying genus. God, of course, can only be called "one" in the former sense.

So we must speak of God's oneness as Scripture demands, and we can do so only as we understand it designates God's indivisibility and is convertible with God's being. Thomas then argues we can speak of God's unity for three reasons: First, *ex ejus simplicitate* ("from his simplicity"). Second, *ex infinitate ejus perfectionis* ("from the infinity of his perfection"). This second reason already points both to God's operations and the procession of the Son from the Father. For Thomas, God comprehends the whole of being in himself, and in comprehending himself God knows, wills, and loves himself. If God were not one this would make no sense. Third, *ab unitate mundi* ("from the unity of the world"). One world requires one cause: *Cum igitur illud quod est primum sit perfectissimum et per se non per accidens, oportet quod primum reducens omnia in unum ordinem sit unum tantum.* **Et hoc est Deus** ("Therefore, because that which is first is most perfect and [exists] *per se* and not *per accidens*, it is necessary that the first which restores or brings back everything to one order is only one. **And this is God**" [*ST* I 11.3 resp., emphasis added]). Thomas makes the bold claim "this is God," something he had not yet stated. We can now move to the prologue in question 12 and be told that we are considering God as God is in himself. This one God, who leads everything back to himself, is not merely "called, named or understood" as God. "This is God" (*Et hoc est Deus*).

The above all-too-brief discussion of God's simplicity, perfection, and so on suggests the following. Each of the terms cannot be read in isolation from the others. They are fitting to God not as "properties" but as analogous names that qualify, and depend on, one another. If they are not read in relation to one another, we might speak of simplicity, perfection, infinity, and unity, but it would not be *divine* simplicity, perfection, infinity, and unity. We gain insight into God's existence, simplicity, and perfection by understanding God's unity and vice versa. As true as this is with each of the terms, it is even more so as we follow Thomas through a discussion of God's operations and processions.

God as God Is in Our Knowledge and Language: *ST* I Q. 12–13

Question 12 marks an important transition in the way on which

Aquinas leads us. In the preface to the question, he tells us what we have been discussing up to this point: "having considered God as God is in himself" (*qualiter Deus sit secundum se ipsum*), we now move into a discussion of "God as God is in our knowledge" (*qualiter sit in cognitione nostra*). Question 12 informs us that something other than our knowledge of God has been occurring in the previous eleven questions. It could be seen as marking a transition between "speculative" and "practical" theology. In question 1 Thomas argued sacred doctrine is both speculative and practical. In an objection to the claim that it is primarily a practical rather than a speculative science, he cites Aristotle: *Finis enim practicae est operatio* ("For the end of practical science is an operation"). Practical sciences are concerned with operations; they attend to things that are made. Because he already told us God is the "end" of the human creature, theology, it would seem, is primarily "practical." It deals with the relation between God and creation. Because God makes something—creation—and it is the condition that makes possible our knowledge of God, theology would seem to be primarily practical. However, he raises questions about this in his *sed contra: omnis scientia practica est de rebus operabilibius ab homine* ("every practical science is concerned with things performed/worked by a human being") (*ST* I 1.4 resp.). God is not something humans make.

Speculative theology differs from practical theology in that it is not concerned with human operations. Because God is not something made by human operations, theology cannot primarily be practical. It is speculative inasmuch as it concerns God in Godself and neither human operations toward God nor God's operations toward creatures. It is practical because it also includes God's operations toward creatures and vice versa and thus assumes God is the end of creatures. For Thomas, then, if theology were only practical, it would entail that its only concern was the creature's relationship with God or God's relationship with creatures. These concerns would make the God-creature relationship the sole foundation for theology. But God is not a work of human creatures, and God does not depend on creatures for God's existence. For that reason, theology must be primarily speculative and secondarily practical. Theology attends to God as God is in himself and not only God as God is related to creatures. In questions 12 and following, Thomas takes up sacred doctrine as a practical science. First he examines "our knowledge" of God. Then he looks at how our language addresses God. After examining these two topics, he takes up God's "operations." By telling us in question 12 that up until this point we were considering God *qualiter Deus sit secundum se ipsum*, he marks a transition from theology as a speculative to a practical discipline. If we did not have the former, we could not have the latter. God cannot be an "object" made by human operation, but our knowledge and language of God, even in its speculative mode, cannot be had without human operations.

This distinction between speculative and practical sacred doctrine, and its importance for Thomas's *de Deo*, warrants further investigation. Because Thomas told us we cannot know God's essence, what is the status of the "speculative" knowledge we have been pursuing? What does it mean to confess that God is, simple, perfect, infinite, immutable, eternal, and one? These terms do not first describe God's operations toward creatures, even though we only know them from creaturely existence. A delicate balance has been formed. We know God as God is in Godself from God as God is in our knowledge and language because of God's operations toward us. In other words, only in our historical, creaturely existence can we arrive at knowledge of, and language for, God. But that does not entail such knowledge, and language is only "practical," a statement not about God but only our relationship to God. Questions 12 and 13 help us see how we have done what we have done and why it can be speculative and practical. The language used for God to this point, especially simplicity, allows for a speculative science of God that grounds its practical aspect as well. An examination of the first article in questions 12 and 13 suffices to show that divine simplicity also makes possible theology as a practical science.

The question that drives the thirteen articles in question 12 is whether creatures can see God in God's essence. Thomas returns us to a theme previously discussed to help us see what speculative theology accomplishes. More so than any other thinkers, Dionysius and Augustine assist Thomas in answering this question. Of the sixty-seven explicit references to Dionysius in the first forty-three questions of the *De Deo*, eight occur in question 12, followed by ten in question 13. The only reference to Dionysius's *Mystical Theology* occurs in question 12. Augustine is cited twenty-one times in question 12 and four times in question 13.[28] In contrast, Aristotle only receives seven explicit references in these two questions. Dionysius and Augustine are the authorities Thomas draws on to move us from the perfectly simple unified essence of God to God's relation to creatures.

Perfection and simplicity are central for our knowledge and language of God. They provide the heart of his argument in both questions. In his preface to question 12 Thomas tells us we are moving from considering *qualiter Deus sit secundum se ipsum* ("God in God's self") to *qualiter sit in cognitione nostra* ("God in our knowledge"). The practical knowledge of God, God as known and spoken by us, assumes simplicity and perfection for its intelligibility. His first article draws on simplicity to inquire whether God can be known by the created intellect. Because simplicity tends toward an apophatic theology, it seems to pose a barrier to our knowledge of God. What we know is what God is not—a composite creature—more than what God is.

Thomas raises four objections to our possible knowledge of God. The first objection is biblical. John 1 teaches that no one has seen God, and Dionysius's theology also affirms God cannot be seen and therefore God cannot be known. The second refers back to Thomas's teaching on infinity. If God is infinite, then not even God can know God's self, for the infinite exceeds comprehension. The third draws on Dionysius's theology that states God is beyond being and therefore unknowable. The fourth responds to what seems to be Aristotle's argument for proportionality—"A knower must have some proportion to what is known." The finite is disproportionate to the infinite, so God cannot be known. Thomas begins his counterarguments with Scripture. First

---

28. More will be said below in chapter 2 in terms of the importance of Augustine and Dionysius in Thomas's theological epistemology.

John teaches that we shall see God as God is. He then supports this initial argument by his teaching on simplicity. Everything is known to the extent that it has actuality. If it is only potential, then it cannot be known, because it is not yet actual. All created existence is composed of potentiality and actuality. If it were pure potentiality, it would not actually be, and could not be known. The more something is actual the more it can be known. God as Creator is not composed of potentiality and actuality. God is pure act and thus "maximally knowable." God is the most knowable of all that can be known. God is so knowable, in fact, that knowledge of God exceeds our limited, creaturely knowledge. God as pure act overwhelms our cognition, rendering knowledge of God nearly impossible. It is not because God is distant, static, and aloof that we do not know God; it is because God is so purely actual it overwhelms us. Thomas refuses to concede the point that knowledge of God is impossible, however, because we know from faith that God is humanity's "beatitude." If God is the end of creaturely existence, then God must be able to be known. We also know from reason that creatures have "a natural desire to know the cause" when they "perceive an effect; and it is from this desire that wonder originates." As we shall see below, the origination of wonder is the source for metaphysics. Because a "natural desire" is never in vain, it must be able to be satisfied. It is satisfied by the beatific vision (*ST* I 12.1).

Thomas returns to a discussion of simplicity in the first article to question 13 on naming God as well. We can only name what we know, so naming God follows on knowing God. Just as simplicity made it both difficult and possible to know God, it also makes it both difficult and possible to name God. Concrete names, names that would signify particulars, are not fitting to God, because they assume composition, formed matter. They cannot express divine simplicity. Abstract names can express simplicity because they do not refer to particulars, but they fail to identify God as *perfectum subsistens*. The logical consequence would be that no name is appropriate for God. Thomas acknowledges all our names fall short of God's essence. Our names, like our knowledge, are our operations. But language is not a prison house of finitude. We can use both concrete and abstract names in order to name God, recognizing that in doing so more will need to be said than simply attributing a name to God. A concrete name must be supplemented with an abstract one, and an abstract one with a concrete. After establishing that we can know God and use language to name God, Thomas then turns from our operations to God's.

Divine Operations: *ST* I Q. 14–26

God's operations are threefold: knowledge (questions 14–18), will (questions 19–24), and power (25–26) The first two are immanent operations; they will be "internal" to God, which is an inadequate and easily misunderstood claim because God has no limits (per God's infinity) in which something could be internally contained. Had we not discussed the previous terms, the discussion on God's operations would be riddled with error. God's third operation, power or *potentia*, is God's "external" operation, which is God's living activity flowing from God's knowledge and will toward creatures. God does not exercise power over God's self; power is an operation related to what is not God. The expressions "internal" and "external" are not about space or location; they signify what God must be to be God (internal operations) and what God can do in God's freedom as God (external operations).

Discussion of divine operations in terms of "knowledge, will, and power" is risky. These are, after all, human acts that assume potentiality, imperfection, finitude, and temporality. Had we not first been shown how to speak of God's essence, we might even think Thomas is doing nothing more than giving a "psychological analogy" from creaturely agency to divine agency. But something much more interesting than that is going on here. Thomas presents God's dynamic, living agency without trespassing the divine/creaturely distinction that such language could easily trespass. The terms laid out in questions 2 through 11 help us make sense of God's knowledge and will without any threat of univocally ascribing to God a creaturely agency and making God the kind of determinate being that would be nothing but a being among beings. Throughout his discussion of God's operations, Thomas acknowledges the difficulty. Knowledge for us is a habit; it is midway between potentiality and act. It is also discursive, speculative, and practical, and tends to move toward what is outside the subject. None of this applies to God, and yet Thomas argues *in Deo perfectissime est scientia* ("knowledge is most perfect in God"). He refers back to his discussion of infinity to make his argument. The more immaterial something is, the more it is infinite. Matter constricts form, limiting that form to the other forms in which it could participate. But God as simple and infinite is not so limited. Thus God can "contain" the form of all knowable things without limit. For this reason, in loving God's self, God loves all things; in knowing God's self, God knows not only Godself but all things; and as knowing and loving all things God is also their constant, donating source.

The terms *direct* and *indirect* are inadequate to explain God's knowledge and love of all things. The point is not that God knows God's self directly and only that which is not God indirectly. Instead, in knowing God's self, God also knows creatures more intimately than they know themselves. Their knowledge and will share some similarity to God, who gives them life, but such similarity exists within the ever-greater dissimilarity of the perfect eminence that God's knowledge and will always are.

Speaking of divine will raises similar difficulties to speaking of divine knowledge. Will, for Thomas, following Aristotle, naturally follows intellect. What the intellect knows the will either possesses, finding itself at rest, or seeks after until it rests. The will moves the intellect until it rests, but how can this be fitting to God, who is immutable and simple? Thomas's analogy from his Aristotelian argument for the natural will and intellect to the divine will and intellect is too sketchy. He moves from this claim: *Unde in quolibet habente intellectum, est voluntas; sicut in quolibet habente sensum, est appetitus animalis* ("Hence in anything having intellect there is will just as in anything having sense there is an animal appetite") to this claim: *Et sic oportet in Deo esse voluntatem, cum sit in eo intellectus* ("Thus it is proper/necessary that will exists in God since intellect is in him"). Thomas does not tell us how we move from natural appetites to God, or how we can move so directly from creaturely descriptions of will and intellect to divine descriptions of the same. The argument is too sparse, but we should assume he does not intend to contradict what he has already discussed concerning analogical predication of terms to God, nor the attributes identified so far. He does give us a brief reminder of his earlier argument by once again implicitly appealing to simplicity: *Et sicut suum intelligere est suum esse, ita suum velle* ("Just as his understanding is his *esse*, so also is his will") (*ST* I 19.1). God's knowledge and will are God's *esse*; they do not divide up into composite parts, even if knowledge and will are not the same operation. For this reason, God wills who God is necessarily, but God wills all other things only with a conditional necessity that does not deny God's freedom. The conditional necessity arises because once God has willed something, since it will be a perfect, eternal, immutable act, God cannot will otherwise (*ST* I 19.2).

The difficulties simplicity generates for God's knowledge and will are many. If both divine knowledge and will are the divine essence, and they are all the same eternal, immutable, simple, pure act, then how do we avoid the claim, first, that there is no difference between God's knowledge and will, and second, that what God knows God must will? Thomas, like the Reformed theologians we will examine below, distinguishes God's knowledge from God's will. That God knows future contingents does not mean God must will them. That God indirectly knows evil does not mean God wills it. But how can this be if we accept the traditional answer as to who God is? These legitimate concerns drive process, open, and analytic theologians to question whether the traditional answer generates problems it cannot answer. They ask whether this distinction can be sustained given divine simplicity. They think it cannot, and thus simplicity raises serious theological concerns. Does it make God the author of evil? Does it evacuate human freedom of meaning? Is it illogical? Those questions will be explored at length in part III of this work; the present exposition only presents Thomas's use of simplicity so that we can later determine whether the traditional answer generates the problems modern theologians seek to remedy. To this point, simplicity does not serve the function of describing God's relation to creation. Its primary purpose has been in a speculative theology that seeks to know who God is in God's self. The two "internal" operations of knowledge and will are not yet concerned with creation. They will soon be correlated with the two divine processions of the Son and the Spirit, Wisdom and Love. These are "real relations," so Thomas asserts a distinction between them, but within the simple, unified essence. Knowledge is not will any more than the Son is the Spirit. But the one essence is knowledge is will is Son and is Spirit. The purpose of divine simplicity is not to solve a logical problem but to set forth the mystery of how God's one essence is simultaneously three persons.

God also has the operation of "power," which is directed "externally." The third operation, divine power, is discussed in question 25, after Thomas discusses God's knowledge, including the divine ideas, truth, falsity, and the life of God; and then God's will, including God's love, justice, mercy, providence, predestination, and the book of life. The difficulties simplicity faces arise acutely in Thomas's discussion of predestination and reprobation, so we will examine question 23 in more detail.

Providence and Predestination: *ST* I Q. 22–23

Providence (question 22) and predestination (question 23) are discussed in terms of the joint operation of divine knowledge and will. Although they come prior to divine power, they would seem better suited to be discussed after it. However, for Thomas, like the Reformers, providence and predestination are present in God prior to the act of creation. Before discussing them, Thomas affirms that God is love. Some of the criticisms of the traditional answer claim it creates a God who cannot love. Often those criticisms altogether neglect question 20, a question committed to presenting God's will as love. Thomas later affirms "Love" as another name for the Holy Spirit.

Thomas addresses the question whether God loves everything God creates. This question is important, especially for theologians like

Thomas who teach a strong doctrine of predestination that includes reprobation. If God reprobates part of God's creation, how can God be said to love it? As we shall see, some Thomistic Reformed theologians take this question head-on and assert that God does not universally love all creation. God hates what God reprobates. Their answer to this question leads to the controversial thesis, adopted at the Synod of Dort, that Christ did not die for all; he only died for the elect or for those whom God loves. Thomas may very well have laid the seeds for that teaching, as Peter Martyr Vermigli argued,[29] but it is not quite what he taught.

Thomas locates predestination primarily, albeit not exclusively, in God. He states,

> Thus, it is clear that predestination is a plan, existing in God's mind, for ordering certain persons to eternal salvation. On the other hand, the execution of this ordering is something passive that exists in those who are predestined, whereas it exists in God as something active. Now this execution of predestination is a *calling* (*vocatio*) and *glorification* (*magnificatio*) according to the Apostle in Romans 8:30: "And whom He predestined, them He also called. And whom He called . . . them He also glorified." (*ST* I 23.2 resp.)

Predestination exists in God's providential ordering; it is internal to God's knowledge and will, which is why it is discussed prior to divine power.

Thomas draws on simplicity for this teaching on predestination. However, in Thomas's case it will be because creatures cannot share in simplicity that some are elect and some damned. The lengthy quote below sets forth his position.

> But it is necessary for God's goodness, which is one and simple in itself, to be represented in a multitude of ways in things, since created things cannot attain to God's simplicity. And so diverse grades of things are required for the completion of the universe—with some things occupying high places and others the lowest places in the universe. And as was explained above (q. 2, a. 3 and q. 22, a. 2), in order for this multiplicity

29. Peter Martyr Vermigli, *Commentary on the Book of Judges*, in Patrick Donnelly, SJ, ed., *The Peter Martyr Reader* (Kirksville, MO: Truman State University Press, 1999), 178.

of grades to be conserved among things, God permits certain evils to be effected, lest many goods should be impeded. So, then, suppose that we think of the whole human race as a complete collection of things. God willed that some men, whom He predestines, should represent His goodness in the mode of mercy, by sparing them; and He willed that other men, whom He reprobates, should represent His goodness in the mode of justice, by punishing them. And this is the reason why God chooses some and reprobates others. . . . However, there is no explanation other than God's will for why He chose these *particular* men for glory and reprobated those *particular* men. Hence, in *Super Ioannem* Augustine says, "As to why He draws this one to Himself and not that one—do not dare to judge if you do not want to be mistaken." (*ST* I 23.5 rep. obj. 3)[30]

Simplicity's incommunicability coupled with perfection or goodness's communicability leads to predestination and reprobation. God communicates God's goodness to creatures, but God cannot communicate simplicity to them. Because creatures are not simple, the universe's "completion" requires that goodness must be received through multiplicity. God permits evil, God does not directly will it, in order to attain that completion or perfection. The result is that God elects some through God's mercy and damns others through God's justice, both of which were discussed under the will of God in question 21. Although this looks like a contradictory divine operation, it is not, because both result from the communication of God's goodness through God's will.

The argument that divine simplicity requires a hierarchy of multiplicity including the damnation of God's creatures is odd and objectionable. It easily underwrites injustice. It had unsavory consequences. If some are reprobated for God's glory, such as heretics, then it will be easy to argue, as Thomas did, that they can be executed. It tells us what is "necessary" without telling us why. Nor are we told what the "completion" or perfection of the universe is. It shares in God's goodness through all the multiple ways creatures can participate in it. Some of those ways are through damnation. Damnation as a participation in God's goodness strikes us moderns as vulgar, and it should. It struck some sixteenth-century Protestant theologians that

30. Thomas quotes Rom. 9:22–23 and 2 Tim. 2:20 to support his teaching.

way as well. While some Thomistic Protestant theologians take Thomas's teaching on predestination and emphasize simplicity as God's absolute power (Vermigli, Zanchi, Owen), others will stress God's communication of goodness without finding it leads to absolute predestination (Arminius).

Thomas does not say as much as later Reformed theologians will say. He does not devote an entire treatise to explain some of his odd arguments here, but he has said too much. He has given a theodicy in which evil now has an intelligible place. The fact that he has given it this place within God's internal operations is deeply troubling and vexing. He has used simplicity to justify this place, but he has not done what he will later do—draw on simplicity to set forth God's processions as the necessary precondition for discussing creation and redemption. That later use of simplicity corrects this earlier objectionable one.

If God is love, can God will reprobation? Thomas rejects reprobation as God's "antecedent" will. God creates willing that "all should be saved." But God does not will this absolutely; God wills it "in a certain respect." Thus what God wills "antecedently," God does not will "consequently."[31] How does this distinction between God's antecedent and consequent will not violate simplicity? As will be seen, critics of the traditional answer will raise these kinds of distinctions found in Thomas as evidence that not even he could sustain what he intended to sustain, divine simplicity.

Just as God antecedently wills the salvation of all, God loves all God's creatures. Here is a more consistent use of divine simplicity. Thomas sets this forth in his discussion whether or not God loves some creatures more than others. He states that there are two ways in which love can will the good of another. "First, on the part of the very act of the will, which can be more or less intense. And in this sense God does not love some things more than others, since He loves all things by the single and simple act of His will, which always remains the same

---

31. "As was explained above (q. 19, a. 6), God wills *antecedently* that all men should be saved—which is not to will it absolutely speaking, but only in a certain respect. However, He does not will this *consequently*, i.e., He does not will it absolutely speaking"; *ST* I 23.4 rep. obj. 3.

(*semper eodem modo se habente*)" (*ST* I 20.3 resp.). But Thomas has to explain reprobation, so he continues.

> Second, on the part of the good that one wills for the thing loved. Thus, we are said to love someone more than another because we will him a greater good—even if we do not love him with a more intense act of will. And in this sense one must claim that God loves some things more than others. For since, as has been explained (a. 2), God's love is the cause of goodness in things, one thing would not be better than another if God did not will a greater good to the one than to the other. (*ST* I 20.3)

Like the Reformed theologians who come after him, Thomas teaches that God's eternal act of willing a "greater good" to one rather than the other is the basis for predestination.

Divine Power: *ST* I Q. 25

After these internal operations are explored, Thomas turns to divine power. Divine power, or *potentia*, poses difficulties. Thomas's presentation of who God is began with simplicity denying that the distinction between actuality and *potentia* was fitting for God. Yet in question 25 he affirms God's *potentia* as one of God's operations. He acknowledges the potential objection; it would appear inappropriate now to attribute *potentia* to God. But God is living, and as living God must have something like the power of self-movement, even though God has no potentiality nor mutability (see *ST* I 18.1 and 3, where Thomas defines life by the power of movement and argues God as pure act has this most perfectly). In order to attribute *potentia* to God, Thomas makes a distinction between an active and a passive *potentia*. God has "active power," but not "passive." Such an active power does not stand in a dialectical relationship to potentiality; it does not "contrast" with it or actualize it. Divine power knows no lack; it is an abundance that makes possible that which is not God without diminishing God. God does not need to withdraw or limit God's self to make room for creation. Divine power is an external operation that makes possible that which is not God, creating, preserving, and redeeming it. But this external operation is not correlated to any procession; it arises only from the perfectly, actual, simple essence found in the real distinctions of Son and Spirit, Wisdom and Love (*ST* I 28.3). Divine simplicity, then, does not prohibit the real distinction of processions or the corresponding multiplicity of participable life and being that they generate in creation. Is this mere assertion? How can God be simple and have real distinctions?

Divine Processions: *ST* I Q. 27–43

After he has addressed God's essence through God's operations, Thomas turns to God's processions. Before entering into the Triune processions in question 27, we should pause and recognize what has occurred so far. Beginning with philosophical terms and showing us how they do and do not apply to God, Thomas begins our journey into the mystery of God. The names build on each other until we come to the important confession "God is one." After affirming God's unity, Thomas states for the first time, "This is God." Yet more needs to be done, which he begins to do by showing how the terms used for God's essence assist us in making sense of God's operations. Had we not had those terms, we would easily have mixed our analysis with the error that God's agency is univocal to creaturely agencies. Had we not arrived at the knowledge that God is one, we would easily have mixed our analysis with the error that God is not an agent at all. God would be an impersonal being to which no dramatic action could be attributed. His argument has taken twists and turns in which simplicity has been affirmed, negated, and demonstrated in order to be more than we could have imagined from the bare starting point of a *demonstratio quia* "that God is."

We should have been prepared for these twists and turns, for Thomas forewarned us of philosophy's limitations concerning the subject matter of God; it points in a proper direction, since God is our beatitude and all our actions intend happiness, but it always comes mixed with error. We learn much about who God is not in questions 3–11, and in learning who God is not we gain clarity as to who God is. We have gained sufficient clarity that Thomas can make the somewhat bold assertion in the prologue to question 12, especially given the more ambiguous claim found in the prologue to question 3, that we have indeed been discussing nothing less than God as God is in himself, which is of course God's "essence," something Thomas said we could not know of God by reason qua reason in question 2. But even with question 12 we have not yet found ourselves in a clearing where vision is easy. For instance, in question 12 Thomas raises the question whether God can be known at all, since Boethius teaches that the human creatures cannot know "simple form" (*ST* I 12. obj. 1). He had already established the centrality of divine simplicity, and now, as he moves to our "natural" knowledge of God, he questions whether God is knowable at all. Things look bleak. His response is not reassuring. Natural reason knows that a simple form is (*ut sciat an est*) but not what it is (*ut sciat de ea quid est*). What good would such knowledge do? Very little, for if this is all that can be known, our journey would be little more than groping in the dark for something unidentifiable. We do not yet see as we should.

We have moved from what everyone calls, names, or understands to be God through a more and more detailed discussion of God's essence, culminating in a discussion of God's unity that sets forth the startling claim "This is God," into a risky discussion of God's dramatic operations that dares to affirm that the one personal and living God involves "internal" and "external" operations of knowledge, will, and power. God knows, wills, and loves God's own life and in so doing shares being with creatures. These "operations" are not operations *on* God because they are God's very *esse*. God's *esse* is knowing, loving, and willing. In knowing and willing God's own *esse*, God knows, wills, and loves all things, but here Thomas also says too much. He seeks the answer to evil and can only find it by viewing reprobation as a form of participation in divine goodness. In order to do so he begins to make distinctions such as God's antecedent and consequent will, God's intense universal and partial specific love. He sets the stage for teachings on absolute predestination that sixteenth-century Reformed theologians will adopt. Question 23 came too early. It works against Thomas's better insight, as we shall see, that creation cannot be addressed prior to discussion of God's processions.

Before moving from the divine operations to the processions, Thomas takes up the question of beatitude once again and returns to the argument that God is the proper end of happiness for human creatures. God is this end because God is beatitude in his essence. Clarity has been gained, even if we cannot yet state sufficiently who God is in God's self. Beatitude is the "perfect good of an intellectual nature" that knows itself as such (*ST* I 26.1). As such, God contains the beatitude of all creaturely perfections. After this discussion, Thomas gives the following direction to his reader before moving on to the divine processions: *Et haec dicta sufficant de his quae pertinent ad divinae essentiae unitatem* ("And these remarks suffice/are enough/lay a foundation concerning what belongs to the unity of the divine essence"). He explicitly tells us that the questions coming before question 27 concerned the divine essence. Thomas has not said everything that needs to be said, and on some matters he has said too much, but he has said enough about the divine essence that he can now speak of the divine processions, which we will discover is nothing other than speaking again of the divine essence.

For the first time, in question 27, we come into a clearing where we see more fully where we were being led in the previous questions; for, despite appearances, Thomas was never presenting to us only God's unity but always at the same time the divine Trinity. There is no *de deo uno* independent of a *de deo trino*; that would be heretical, as if the divine essence were not the Triune persons and the Triune persons the essence. Thomas's argument all along was thoroughly Nicene, even when he was using philosophy to manifest it. The terms used in questions 2–11, which challenged whether we could know God at all, now gain a living substance, taking us on a surprising journey that represents something of a reversal and yet at the same time brings what has been accomplished to this point into a new light. His first article in question 27 asks, "Whether there is procession in God?" To our surprise, we discover that the very terms he used to identify God seem to stand in the way of affirming divine processions. They now function as objections against divine processions. If God is immutable and infinite, then it makes little sense to speak of divine procession. *Processio*, he argues, "signifies motion without (*extra*)." How can that which does not move (immutability) and does not contain an end (infinity) be signified by motion toward something? Thomas uses his own words from his previous questions against divine processions. *Sed in divinis, nihil est mobile neque extraneum.* Not only immutability and infinity render divine processions unthinkable, but even more so does simplicity. His second objection acknowledges that if there are divine processions, then they will require diversity in God. Something proceeding is diverse from that from which it proceeds, but in God there is no diversity because God is *summa simplicitas* ("the most simple"). His third objection points back to his five ways. If God is the *primum principium*, as he says, "has been shown," then he cannot be a God who is processed to a place (*locum*). For God cannot be both the first principle and at the same time the terminus of a movement. Everything we have accomplished to this point moves in the direction of rejecting divine processions. Nonetheless, Thomas knows God has processions, for he cites Jesus' words in John 8:42: "Our Lord said, 'I proceed from God.'"

What then follows not only shows how those terms can express this mystery, but it also lets us know we were always already involved with expressing that mystery even when it appeared we were doing nothing more than setting forth what cannot be said of God. His answer shows that he was identifying the Triune God throughout his first treatise. Thomas answers: *quod divina Scriptura, in rebus divinis, nominibus ad processionem pertinentibus utitur* ("divine Scripture uses names pertaining to procession in divine things") (*ST* I 27.1). He refers to the tradition of the divine names, which he had already developed in question 13, and affirms that names signifying procession, like those signifying unity and essence, must be used. They have not, however, always been used well, which occurs when causality is misunderstood. Arius thought of procession as effect proceeding from a cause (*quod effectus procedit a causa*), and Sabellius as cause proceeding to the effect (*quod causa dicitur procedere in effectum*). The very terms used for a weak demonstration "that God is" in question 2 are now raised as a potential obstacle to understanding divine processions. The problem with both is that they take procession to name a movement *ad aliquid extra*. Now we begin to see how Thomas's earlier terms norm Trinitarian language to avoid speaking poorly of God. Because God is perfectly simple and infinite, there is no *extra* to which God moves. "Hence," he argues, "neither posits procession *in ipso Deo*." The processions Arius and Sabellius posit are not "in" God himself but only causal arguments from a cause to an effect. They speak too creaturely, making the Triune relations more like the God-creation relationship.

However, we must speak of God's processions as Scripture demands, and that will imply speaking of a kind of movement "in" God. In order to do so, Thomas now adds more substance to the divine operations. There is such a thing even among creatures, he argues, as an inner procession, which is *in intellectu, cuius actio, scilicet intelligere manet in intelligente* ("in the intellect, whose act, namely to understand, remains in the understanding"). Thomas immediately qualifies any univocal attribution of this internal procession in creatures to God. He states,

> *Cum autem Deus sit super omnia, ea quae in Deo dicuntur, non sunt intelligenda secundum modum infimarum creaturarum, quae sunt corpora; sed secundum similitudinem supremarum creaturarum, quae sunt intellectuales substantiae; a quibus etiam similitudo accepta deficit a repraesentatione divinorum* ("Since however God is above all things, those things said of God are not understood according to the mode of weak creatures, which are corporeal, but according to the similitude of the highest creatures, which are intellectual substances, from which also the similitude taken lacks a representation of divine things"). (*ST* I 27.1)

Only if God is perfectly simple is it intelligible to posit procession "in" God without mixing error with the use of such a term. The "movement" internal to God is not from one place to another. God is infinite. It is not from one substance to a different one; God is simple. It is not from something lesser to something more, or vice versa; God is perfect. It is not from a beginning to an end; God is eternal. It is an immutable movement of "internal" processions, which he will go on to argue, are only two—the processions of the Son and the Spirit. The Son's procession will be related to the operation of divine knowledge. The Spirit's procession will be related to the operation of divine will and love. There is no third procession based on divine *potentia*, for it is an "external" operation by which God is the source, power, and end of all creatures. If it too were a procession, then creation would be a fourth person and would not be other than God. Creation would be divine. For this reason, Thomas must argue that the Triune processions are "real relations," but the relation between God and creation is not a "real relation," even though the relation between creation and God is. In other words, creation is not divine essence, for each relation from God to God is the divine essence. There is no essence behind the relations; they are the essence. Thomas states this explicitly. Only an uncharitable reading could argue otherwise. Its interesting result is that knowledge and will define God as God is in God's self, but power only defines God's relation to what is not God. God is not in God's self "power." It is not an immanent operation. Thomas had Abelard's attribution of "power" to the Father as a possibility, but he did not use it as such.[32] Power is not *in divinis* in the same way knowledge and will or the Son and Spirit are.

Question 27 article 1 shows us how to read questions 2–11. Had we stopped at question 11 or ripped his philosophical arguments out of the theological context in question 27, they would have been misleading. He has taken a turn in our journey into the mystery of God and shown us how what we thought we had already accomplished now gains depth, but we are not yet done. The twist in the argument at question 27 continues as Thomas draws on his previous terms for God to express divine Trinity and draws on divine Trinity to clarify those terms. The very next article takes us through a similar surprising twist to affirm that not only can the procession of the Son be called "generation," but now we can also speak of God's "received being." Thomas begins

---

32. See Emery, *Trinity in Aquinas*, 4–9, 124; and Timothy L. Smith, *Thomas Aquinas's Trinitarian Theology: A Study in Theological Method* (Washington, DC: Catholic University of America Press, 2003), 126–29.

questioning how such a term could possibly be used to speak of God, since generation requires change. He lodges a fascinating objection to the possibility of generation based on God as *ipsum esse subsistens*. Every *genitum* ("thing generated"), he argues, receives *esse a generante* ("being from the one generating"). Thus it would be an *esse receptum*, which is not possible *per se subsistens* (*ST* I 27.2 2). If God is pure act and *ipsum esse subsistens*, then God cannot "receive being." Thomas went lengths to affirm that God is pure act and *ipsum esse subsistens* in his earlier discussion of God's essence. Why and how, then, is it possible to use such a strange term for God as *esse receptum*?

Consistent with the biblical writers and the church fathers, Thomas draws on Ps. 2:7, "Today I have begotten thee," as a counterargument. Scripture names one procession as generation, so even though it risks misunderstanding we must speak of one procession as generation. We can do so, he suggests, if we use generation *dupliciter*. We use it in a first way that would be inappropriate to name the Son's generation; we use it *communiter ad omnia generabilia et corruptibilia* ("generally for everything generable and corruptible"). But we also use it in a second way: *proprie in viventibus* ("properly of living things"). Here generation signifies the "origin of something living connected to the principle of living." We have already been told that God is "living," so "generation" will apply to God, but more eminently than it applies to any creaturely reality. Simplicity guards the difference. What proceeds from potentiality to actuality includes both uses of generation, but if there were something living and simple, then generation would be possible without assuming a movement from potentiality to actuality. Thomas states, *Si autem sit aliquod vivens cuius vita non exeat de potentia in actum, processo, si qua in tali vivente invenitur, excludit omnino primam rationem generationis; sed potest habere rationem generationis quae est propria vivenentium* ("If however, there is something living whose life does not go out from potentiality to act, procession, if found in such a living thing, altogether excludes the first meaning of generation, but is able to have the meaning of generation which is proper to living things") (*ST* I 27.2). For in God *idem est intelligere et esse*. So does God have *esse receptum*? In another surprising twist, for Thomas never would have acknowledged this in the first twenty-six questions, Thomas now says yes. God does not have "received being" in the sense that it comes from one being that generates a diverse being that is generated. Instead, it is only because the person who generates and who is generated share in the one, simple essence that received being can be attributed to God. In fact, Thomas argues, this received being of the Word is a divine perfection. In other words, God is in God's self gift and reception of being, and reception is a perfection, not a potential that is actualized. This "movement" constitutes God's perfection.

The surprising turns in the first two articles of question 27, in which terms that first looked inimical to divine Trinity are discovered after careful reflection to be necessary for it, continue throughout Thomas's treatise on the processions. Take, for example, Aquinas's transition from his discussion in questions 27 and 28 concerning what should be "known beforehand" of the persons and relations to question 29, in which he addresses the persons themselves. He begins with a definition of *person* taken from Boethius: *Persona est rationalis natura individual substantia* ("A person is an individual substance of a rational nature"). Here we find an explicit use of the term *substance*, to which, as we shall see, many contemporary theologians object, and for good reason. Boethius's definition of person could easily mislead, especially if we think Thomas's argument ends with his first article. The problem is this: How can we use Boethius's definition when it posits a "singular" in the "genus of substance"? Thomas admits in his *respondeo* that Boethius's definition does this. "Individual," he states, places "person" in the "genus of substance," and "with a rational nature" further signifies the substance within which "person" is placed. Such a definition of "person" would require composition. It could not be applied to God. To this point, however, Thomas has done nothing more than explain Boethius's definition. He has not yet applied it to divine persons, so we have not yet arrived at a *divine* person. Only in article 3 does Thomas address how *person* can be applied to God, and once again we see him draw on his previous questions from the treatise on God's essence to do so.

Thomas already acknowledged *person* requires composition in article 2 in his reply to his second objection, so attentive readers will know another twist is forthcoming before the term can be spoken of God. It occurs in article 3, when Thomas makes two steps in his argument. The first is that *person* as an individual substance in a rational nature is what is most perfect in nature. God contains all perfections, so such a perfection could not be absent in God. However, how it is "in" God cannot be univocally read off from how it exists among other persons. He writes, *Non tamen eodem modo quo dicitur de creaturis, sed excellentiori modo; sicut et alia nomina quae, creaturis a nobis imposita, Deo attribuuntur; sicut supra ostensum est, cum de divinis nominibus ageretur* ("Yet not in the same mode by which it is spoken of creatures, but in a more excellent mode, just as other names which, imposed by us on creatures, are attributed to God, as was shown above when we dealt with the divine names"). Thomas acknowledges that our language uses the same terms for God by which we speak of creatures, but they cannot be used in the same way. What norms their use? His answer is found in the objections, when he distances the use of Boethius's terms from any hint that it implies composition such as substance/accidents (*ST* I 29.3 rep. obj. 3). In the previous article he offered three definitions of the term *substance*: (1) It means it exists in its own right. (2) It "stands under" a common nature. (3) It "stands under" accidents. Any use of the term *substance* for God can only use the first definition; the other two would jeopardize simplicity. Thomas develops this more in his fourth objection, in which he tells us *rational* only applies to God if it removes "discursive reasoning"; *individual* only applies if it refers to "incommunicability" and not individuation by matter, as it would in composite creatures; and *substance* only applies if it refers to the fact he "exists per se."

In question 30 Aquinas shows how God's simplicity helps us understand the Triune relations. Having developed Boethius's understanding of *person*, Aquinas now defends it as it applies to the

Triune persons, but herein is the problem. If the "person" is individual, how can there be "three" of them without positing three substances or essences? If there are "three" substances or essences, then we violate the teaching on simplicity laid out in previous questions. Not only that, but because every other attribute assumes simplicity, the doctrine of the Trinity would stand in opposition to everything Thomas had written to this point. Aquinas's response draws on the earlier questions to show how they illumine the Triune relations and in turn are illumined by them. God is three persons because a "person signifies in God a relation as subsisting in the divine nature. It was also established that there are many real relations in God. Hence it follows that there are many realities subsistent in the divine nature, which means that there are many persons in God" (*ST* I 30.1 resp.). Had Aquinas begun here we could easily misunderstand this claim and posit number or composition in God, thereby violating simplicity and underwriting tritheism or modalism. Because he already identified simplicity as essential to divinity, he can affirm "person" and avoid any attribution of number or plurality without losing the real relations. Thus he writes, "The supreme unity and simplicity of God exclude every kind of plurality taken absolutely, but not plurality of relations; for relations are predicated relatively, and thus they do not imply composition in that of which they are predicated" (*ST* I 30.1 ad 3). Notice how the argument works. Simplicity supplements Boethius's definition of *person* to show the uniqueness of divine relations. Simplicity rules out any absolute plurality in God, but not plural relations "predicated relatively." Because the persons are subsistent relations, they are not three items, individuals, or things that can be quantified. They are defined relatively. The Son is the Son *of the Father*, and the Father is the Father *of the Son*. The Spirit is the Spirit *of the Father and Son*.

Simplicity now qualifies Boethius's definition, for an "individual substance" does not mean a separate, individuated substance, as it would with creatures. The Trinity does not have three of them (which some social doctrines of the Trinity come perilously close to suggesting).[33] This revised understanding of relation also explains how

God can have real relations within himself but without number. The two treatises are tightly woven together, and only in their unity can we properly speak (inasmuch as we can) of the Triune mystery.

We could continue through each question on Thomas's treatise on the divine processions to show how he uses the treatise on God's essence to qualify divine Trinity, and the treatise on processions to qualify divine essence. Both treatises should be read simultaneously, even though such a reading is impossible for finite creatures. We are caught between them, but God is not. The one God who is simple, perfect, immutable, impassible, infinite, and eternal is revealed in three persons, Father, Son, and Holy Spirit. The language used to express God's essence is, for Aquinas and nearly every Christian theologian prior to the modern era, never an end in itself. It is not the basis or foundation on which one can then build, adding the mystery of the Trinity to a doctrine of God already known by reason alone. Such a division of intellectual labor between reason and faith, philosophy and theology, was at best a neo-Scholastic innovation, a Catholic reaction against modernity that oddly enough mirrored the division of intellectual labor found in much of modern philosophy. For Aquinas, however, the language used to express God's oneness is always in service to, and only gains its intelligibility from, the divine processions and vice versa.

What is Aquinas doing with this language? David Burrell explains it by discussing how simplicity functions in Aquinas's argument. He writes, "This assertion does not function like a description, or even an analogical description. It is rather a shorthand way of establishing a set of grammatical priorities designed to locate the subject matter as precisely as possible." Here this means "God exhausts divinity," where a predication "is" to "God" does not imply a subject-predicate

---

33. For instance, note how William Alston also affirms Boethius's definition of a *person* but then goes on to argue for real relations between God and creation and against God "as pure act, free of any potentiality, and as unaffected in his being by relations to us, and hence not as purely simple as Augustine and Aquinas would have it." This means that his account of "person" cannot be the same as what Aquinas means when he used it, even though they both affirm Boethius's definition. See William P. Alston, "Substance and the Trinity," in Stephen T. Davis, Daniel Kendall, and Gerald O'Collins, eds., *The Trinity* (Oxford: Oxford University Press, 1999), 187, 195.

relation such that the predicate "outreaches a subject as it usually does," for example with the expression "Socrates is human."[34] These terms establish the "grammar" within which we can speak well of the two great mysteries of the faith—the Trinity and the incarnation. If we lose this grammar, then we may very well lose the ability to speak well of these mysteries, and if we lose them we lose the ability to speak well of creation.

With the cautions in place that the traditional language can easily mislead, and that it is used as a "grammar" to identify a subject matter that always exceeds rational comprehension, we can conclude this first chapter by first expanding on the answer to the question "Who is God?" that began this work.

Trinity

God's essence as simple, perfect, immutable, infinite, and eternal is one, and that one essence is revealed in three persons. Each person is the essence. The Father is the essence. The Son is the essence, and the Spirit is the essence. The Father, Son, and Spirit are also the essence. Nonetheless, there is only one essence. The essence does not generate the essence or the persons. Trinitarian agency does not operate with an essence working behind or before the persons; as we saw above, there is no such space or time, no temporal differentiation *in divinis*. No orthodox theologian ever taught there is an essence prior to the persons or that the persons each had distinct essences or substances. Such accusations are uncharitable readings. The internal relations of the Triune persons (what came to be called the immanent Trinity) are "processions." These are "substantial relations," which is to say that one cannot be without the other—they subsist in one another. Although creation has analogous relations, God's substantial relations are not identical to any other, creaturely relation.

In Catholic (or Latin) theology, there are two processions in God and four relations. The two processions are first the ungenerate Father,

---

34. David Burrell, *Aquinas: God & Action* (London: Routledge & Kegan Paul, 1979), 5.

who eternally generates the Son, and second the Father and the Son, who eternally process the Spirit. Each of these processions has a principle (an originating point) and a term (a culminating point) that leads to four relations in the Trinity. There are two relations of origination: *paternitas* or generating (The Father generates the Son), and *spiratio* or spirating/processing (The Father and the Son spirate the Spirit). There are two relations of procession: *filiatio* or being generated (the Son is generated by the Father), and *processio* or being processed/ spirated (the Spirit is processed by the Father and the Son). The names *being, simple, perfect, immutable, infinite, eternal,* and *one* are not to be attributed to a person in distinction from the others but to the essence. In that each person is the essence, these names also identify the same essence each person shares with the other. They guard the fact that God is not a creature and thus prevent any violation of the first table of the Ten Commandments. We should not speak of God such that we turn God into a creature. They also ensure that we speak properly of each person's being the same essence.

There is also a relation of the Trinity to creation that will later be called the "economic Trinity." The economic Trinity is the "mission" of the persons toward creation. The Son becomes incarnate in Jesus of Nazareth, is born of the Virgin Mary, lives, teaches, is crucified and resurrected, and then ascends to the Father, where he is "Lord." The Spirit authorizes and commissions the Son's ministry and is also poured out by the Son on the disciples at Pentecost, constituting the church, the first fruits of God's reign, in order to continue Jesus' ministry until he returns. We only know God is the "immanent Trinity" because we know God as "economic Trinity." An important question in theology is the relationship between the immanent and economic Trinity. Here matters get even more complicated. If we say the immanent and economic Trinity are identical, which we must, then we are liable to tie God necessarily to creation, which we must not. Then creation would be necessary for God's being, making creation a "fourth hypostasis" of the Trinity and requiring that God, like creation, has a history, including past and future. Some find Hegel responsible for such a "historicizing" of the Trinity. Left-wing Hegelians affirm this interpretation and find in it an origin for a theological atheism in which God is literally poured out into secular history. The traditional language for God, language such as simplicity, eternity, infinity, impassibility, and pure act, blocks historicizing God. Creation has no effect on God; it does not contribute something to God that God otherwise lacks.

If we divide the immanent and economic Trinity decisively, then we are liable to posit a "God" behind the God revealed in Christ who might have an "absolute power" that is independent of the "ordained power" we find in the economic Trinity, which tells us God is love. Power becomes determinative of God as an immanent operation, a position Thomas rejects. Some find this to be an implication of "nominalism," where even though no theologian would ever intend it, the God "behind" the revealed God becomes a capricious, arbitrary will, what Michael Gillespie calls "the transrational God of will."[35]

Incarnation

We have already seen how central the traditional language is for the doctrine of the Trinity, both to understand and to avoid misunderstanding. A brief discussion of its role for the incarnation is also in order. If God already has a "real" relation to creation, then the incarnation brings nothing new in the creation-God relation. At most, it illustrates something that always already was and is. It will not be a free act of God, for God will of necessity have a "potential" that relates God to the creation.

Thomas Weinandy explains well how Aquinas draws on immutability to set forth the doctrine of the Incarnation:

> Because the Son as God in his *esse personale* is a subsistent relation fully in act, he does not have any self-constituting relational potential to enact in order to establish further relations. Being fully relational in himself [as the Second Person of the Trinity] when, in the incarnation, the humanity is ontologically united/related to him, by the power of the Holy Spirit,

35. Michael Gillespie, *Nihilism before Nietzsche* (Chicago: University of Chicago Press, 1995), 41.

it is united to him as he actually is as Son and so he is able to exist as man. Thus it is the Son's immutable and unchangeable actuality as a person (a subsistent relation) fully in act that enables him to establish an incarnational relationship. Far from being a detriment to the incarnation, immutability, as Aquinas well knew, is an absolute prerequisite for allowing, empowering and warranting the incarnational "becoming" with its consequent incarnational "is."[36]

If the Son "changes" in the incarnation, if he becomes something other than really related to the Father and the Spirit, fully sharing in the common essence in this relation, then it will not be the Son who is incarnate but some *tertium quid*. Thus just as we saw with the Trinity, so we see with the incarnation. It is present from the beginning of the *Summa*, and the grammar used to present God in the treatise on the common essence is for the purpose of helping us understand (albeit not comprehend) this great mystery. The language we use for God assumes and directs us to the only one who gives us true knowledge of God, the Son (John 1). This should come as no surprise to careful readers of Thomas, for he told us this explicitly in the prologue to question 2; Jesus is the *via*.

Creation

The two mysteries, Trinity and Incarnation, are necessary, according to Thomas, to make sense of creation. Gilles Emery emphasizes that Thomas's treatise does not have two parts, God's essence and persons, but three. The third part of the *de Deo* is God's work of creation.[37] Without the mystery of the Trinity, we cannot speak well of the practical knowledge that deals with God's relation to creation and vice versa.

One of the most disconcerting and easily misunderstood claims that

36. Thomas Weinandy, "The Marvel of the Incarnation," in *Aquinas on Doctrine*, ed. Thomas Weinandy, David Keating, and John Yocum (London: T&T Clark, 2004), 87.
37. Emery, *Trinity in Aquinas*, 28. For a fuller discussion of the Trinitarian causality in Aquinas and how he inherits it from Albert, see Emery, "Trinity and Creation," chap. 2 in *Trinity in Aquinas*, 33–70. See also his important reminder that when Thomas sets forth his structure for *de Deo* in *ST* I 2, he does so by considering it in three—not two—parts: *consideratio autem de Deo tripartite erit*. The three parts are God's essence, processions, and the processions of creatures. See Emery, *Trinity in Aquinas*, 176.

Aquinas makes is that no real relation exists between God and creation. What Aquinas means by "real relation" must first be acknowledged before this can be critiqued. We have already seen that Thomas primarily uses the term "real relation" to refer to the Triune persons. By *real*, he means sharing in a common essence or something ontologically necessary for something else. If he stated that God has real relations to creation, then he would either divinize creation or mythologize God by turning God into a creature. A "real relation" in God is a procession that cannot be *extra*, for no *extra* exists. For this reason, he must say that God does not have a real but only a "logical" relation with creation. He is not saying that God is unrelated to creation. He is building on a threefold understanding of relation; it is logical, real, or mixed.[38]

Real relations imply ontological similarity and dependence. I am really related to my father and mother as well as my children. God is not this except in the incarnation, and then the humanity of Christ is really related to his divinity, while the divinity is logically related to his humanity. Logical relations imply no change in the terms related.[39] Real relations usually imply change (one exception is the immutable common essence of God). If God were really related to the created order, then God would be affected by it and thus on the same plane of being. God would be a creature, a mythological being, or creation would be God. If God were on the same plane of being, then there would be no need for the incarnation; God would already be incarnate. There would be no divine drama. God would not need to become human without ceasing to be God, for contained within God would be creatureliness or humanity. The incarnation is a mixed relationship because humanity and divinity are not on the same plane of being. It affects a real change in humanity without changing God. Moreover, if God and creation were on the same plane of being that a real relation signifies, then they would exist in a competitive relationship. One could act only at the expense of the other.

38. See Weinandy, "Marvel of the Incarnation."
39. Ibid., 76.

Some theologians still find the claim that God has no real relations to creation objectionable because it leads to the claim that God loves us because God loves himself. On the face of it, that claim does seem objectionable. If I said I loved my children only because I loved myself, people would rightly think of me as a narcissist. But only if we adhere to a doctrine of univocity can we move from this claim directly to an understanding of God's love. Thomas does not have such a doctrine, and therefore God's love is not to be measured solely by the mediated forms of love we possess. For Aquinas this claim comes from faith in the Holy Trinity.

> Knowledge of the divine persons was necessary for us in two ways. First, it was necessary in order for us think correctly about the creation of things. For by holding that God made all things by His Word, we exclude the error of those who claim that God produced things by a necessity of nature. And by positing the procession of the Love in God, we show that God produced creatures not because of any need on His part or because of any other extrinsic cause, but because of the love of His own goodness. . . . Second, and more importantly, knowledge of the divine persons was necessary in order for us to think correctly about the salvation of the human race, which is perfected through the Incarnate Son and through the gift of the Holy Spirit. (ST I 32.1 ad 3)

The doctrine of the Trinity, although primarily speculative, is also practical. It demonstrates God's relationship to creatures. If God loves creatures solely because of what they are in themselves, then God needs them to perfect God's love. The love of creatures and the love of God would be greater than God's love alone, and God would not be the perfection of being and goodness. That God loves creatures because God loves God's self does not mean that God does not genuinely love creatures, even as they exist in themselves, but they are not ends in themselves; they are means to be loved because they participate in something that is perfect, God's own being. Thus while God does not need creatures in order for God to be love, creatures do need God to enjoy the perfection of love. God's love of creatures through God's self means God loves creatures from and into God.

God then does not create out of any lack in God's own being that needs to be satisfied from something outside God. God loves his own goodness and, as Dionysius taught, such a goodness communicates itself. Creation is an utterly free gift that has no necessary reason for it other than the communicability of God's goodness. As previously mentioned, for Thomas, God is *semper eis esse dando* ("always giving being to them"). This gift is the basis for *creatio ex nihilo*. Unlike ancient creation myths where the deity comes on a preexisting matter and has to fashion it into existence (as in Plato's *Timaeus* and its return in process theology), Aquinas follows the later trends in the Old Testament, the witness of the New Testament, and the church fathers to argue that God creates even the matter (potentiality) that will then be the basis for things that are. Matter or potentiality does not exist outside God in some eternal space. If it did, then God would be in a constant state of competition with it. No such competitive relation exists. The doctrine of *creatio ex nihilo* is the only way to maintain a nonviolent ontology in which something other than strife and agonism forms the fundament of being. With *creatio ex nihilo*, no such violent fundament exists.

That God creates us out of God's love for God's own goodness does not imply God fails to love us. This would only be the case if God and creatures competed in space and time. They do not. As Rowan Williams puts it, God is not a power over creation, and "creation is not an exercise of divine power." In explaining why Aquinas follows the witness in Isaiah 40–55, in which *creatio ex nihilo* comes to prominence in the Bible, Williams states,

> Power is exercised *by x over y*; but creation is not power, because it is not exercised *on* anything. We might, of course, want to say that creation presupposes a divine potentiality, or resourcefulness, or abundance of active life; and "power" can sometimes by used in those senses. But what creation emphatically isn't is any kind of imposition or manipulation; it is not God imposing on us divinely willed roles rather than the ones we "naturally" might have, or defining us out of our own systems into God's. Creation affirms that to be here at all, to be a part of this natural order and to be the sort of thing capable of being named—or of having a role—is "of God"; it *is* because God wants it to be.[40]

If matter or potentiality exists prior to God's act of creation, then it cannot be God's love that is the full cause of creation, and God will inevitably be a "power over," even if the cause of that power is God's partial ability to lure creation by God's love to God's self. But if nothing is prior to the act of creation (and this nothing is not a nothing that is in a meontological sense), then all of creation is caused solely by God's love. To say that God loves us because God loves God's self is also to say that God creates solely because God is love. God's love of God's own goodness is at the same time the most perfect and profound love of creation.

If we lose the language of *creatio ex nihilo* and posit real relations between God and creation, then we will inevitably lose the importance of God's intimate relation to creation via its "emanation." We will not be able to fully express how God is love. As David Burrell notes,

> Yet the fact that a cause of being, properly speaking, is not affected by causing all-that-is does not imply remoteness or uncaring; indeed, quite the opposite. For such a One must cause in such a way as to be present in each creature as that to which it is oriented in its very existing. In that sense, this One cannot be considered as *other* than what it creates, in an ordinary sense of that term; just as the creature's *esse-ad* assures that it cannot *be* separately from its source.[41]

That God loves us in God's own self-love means that our end is not found in ourselves, but in God alone. We have a supernatural destination. For Burrell, similar to Rowan Williams, this recognition of an end that exceeds our natural abilities should "divert us from imaging the creator over-against the universe, as an entity exercising causal efficacy on anything-that-is in a manner parallel to causation within the universe." Burrell notes that theologians, such as William Hasker, who construe God and the universe as competing causes lose the importance of this "emanation" scheme and the immediate intimacy of love between God and creation it implies.[42] We shall see

---

40. Rowan Williams, "On Being Creatures," in *On Christian Theology* (Oxford: Blackwell, 2000), 68–69.
41. David Burrell, "Act of Creation with Its Theological Consequences," in Weinandy, Keating, and Yocum, *Aquinas on Doctrine*, 39–40.
42. Ibid., 44.

that this is a constant temptation to analytic theologians, although some do not fall prey.

The first step in my argument must now come to an end. In the above argument I have examined six theological moves Thomas makes that some theologians find troubling. The first move, a rigid division between *de deo uno* and *de deo trino*, I have argued, is not present in Thomas, and thus the criticism (the second move) that he subordinates theology to an overarching metaphysics is found wanting. *De deo uno* is not a metaphysical foundation for *de deo trino*. It identifies God's essence, which is always at the same time an identification of the divine persons even if both cannot be done simultaneously through the composite reality of language. The next four troublesome moves are present in Thomas. He defines God as pure act; argues that no real relation exists between God and creation; teaches that God creates us because God knows, wills, and loves God's self; and insists on *creatio ex nihilo*. These moves, however, do not emerge from a metaphysics alien to the biblical drama. Instead, they preserve that drama, for without them neither the Trinitarian missions—the incarnation of the Son and the gift of the Spirit—nor creation makes sense.

I have not yet addressed criticisms modern theologians bring against Aquinas's doctrine of God. I hope the accusation that he cannot sustain the central biblical claim that God is love has been at least in part answered. Certain caricatures can be dismissed outright, especially that he presents an abstract, static God who cannot love. I recognize, however, that no response has yet been made to charges that he cannot account for human freedom, that he cannot answer the problem of evil, that his position lacks analytical rigor, that his teaching diverts us from what matters most—liberation from injustice—or that his metaphysics is not sufficiently normed by the biblical drama. Responses to those charges must wait until the third step of the argument. Before making that step, a second is in order. The second step is important because it demonstrates how Thomas's teaching on God is not unique. It is built from a tradition of important authorities who came before him, especially St. Augustine and Dionysius. Thomas never sought originality, relevance, or uniqueness; he sought truth. His teaching on God did not slavishly follow what came before him, or he would have been content to have his students read Peter Lombard, but he never intended any break or rupture with previous authorities. He sought clarity and brevity in stating what mattered most about the perfectly simple Triune God. Those who came after him, including most Reformation theologians, affirmed that teaching. Thomas rejects some earlier positions and develops others. Likewise, those who came after him did the same, as should we. Yet prior to the late eighteenth century, no theologian suggested that the basic shape of this teaching required radical revisions. The common assumption found in Thomas and those who preceded and followed him was that this doctrine of God served the core, constitutive practice of the church—to worship Jesus as God without conflating divinity and humanity. The following chapter, then, shows the authorities that flowed into Thomas's teaching.

2

―――

Authorities for Thomas's Traditional Answer

Thomas did not invent the language that expresses the answer to the question "Who is God?" He inherited it and sought to express it as clearly and briefly as possible, saying neither too much nor too little. His presentation is as much an exercise in humility as it is in truth. He did not return to original sources to critique his peers and present a revised doctrine of God. As a theologian, his primary authorities were Scripture mediated through church fathers in conversation with his peers. Those "sources" merge into each other such that the question of "sources," which animates a great deal of Thomist research, finds little agreement. Some have suggested that Thomas was influenced early by Augustine but then left him behind once Dionysius became more central to his work.[1] Others turn to Aristotle as Thomas's chief source, finding in Thomas an ontological existentialism and logical

---

1. See D. Juvenal Merriell, *To the Image of the Trinity: A Study in the Development of Aquinas's Teaching* (Toronto: Pontifical Institute of Mediaeval Studies, 1990), for a defense of Augustine's influence. Merriell argues against M.-J. de Beaurecueil's thesis that Aristotle and Dionysius provide the key sources. He writes, "We must reject de Beaurecueil's thesis that Augustine's influence waned as Thomas grew older and fell increasingly under the spell of Aristotle and Dionysius" (242).

analysis that combats the historical emphasis in the modern era. Still others find him committed to Neoplatonism, especially Proclus and Porphyry.[2] Some find Thomas providing a unique "metaphysics of Exodus" drawn primarily from Scripture.[3] Some interesting recent research looks to Arabic philosophy for significant sources of his thought.[4] All of this work is illuminating and demonstrates the richness of Thomas's "sources." Without denying the importance of this research, Mark Jordan has made a compelling case that the search for Aquinas's sources is misplaced.

If the term *sources* signifies elements or building blocks in the construction of a system, then the term does not fit well Thomas's synthesis of Christian tradition. He did not approach the Bible as a "source" independent of the patristic authorities through whom he received it. He had no critical editions of primary works to fashion together a constructive theology. In fact, theology was not about "sources" but the common faith passed down from and through multiple trusted authorities. Trying to separate out his Augustine from Peter Lombard's Augustine, or his use of Scripture from the Fathers, is not only difficult but also distorting, because Thomas's "sources" are not separable criteria. They are multilayered. As Mark Jordan notes, "Many of Thomas's authorities, often the most important, come to him through other authorities, including theological works of reference."[5] His sources are always set within a received tradition in order to illuminate an aspect of the Christian journey where one author passes on the teaching of another. They are, suggests Jordan, "multiple languages" that are more akin to Wittgenstein's notion of language as an ancient city. Wittgenstein writes, "Our language can be seen as an ancient city: a maze of little streets and squares, of old and

2. For the latter see Wayne Hankey, *God in Himself: Aquinas's Doctrine of God as Expounded in the* Summa Theologiae (Oxford: Oxford University Press, 1987).

3. See Etienne Gilson, *The Christian Philosophy of St. Thomas Aquinas* (South Bend, IN: University of Notre Dame Press, 1994).

4. See David Burrell, *Knowing the Unknowable God: Ibn Sina, Maimonides, Aquinas* (South Bend, IN: University of Notre Dame Press, 1992). See also Richard Taylor, Aquinas and "the Arabs" project, International Working Group, www.AquinasAndTheArabs.org.

5. Mark Jordan, "The Competition of Authoritative Languages and Aquinas's Theological Rhetoric," *Medieval Philosophy and Theology* 4 (1994): 77.

new houses, and of houses with additions from various periods; and this surrounded by a multitude of new boroughs with straight regular streets and uniform houses."[6] What is the "source" of the city? Can its houses, boroughs, and streets be clearly distinguished and identified, attempting to trace the present back to an original source? Only by razing the city could a clearly identified original source be had. Thomas reads Scripture through Augustine (among others) through Lombard. Each reading emerges from multiple authorities overlaid on each other like the houses in Wittgenstein's ancient city. Because of this Jordan asks readers of Aquinas to "relinquish, at last, the troublesome category of 'sources.'"[7] Rather than thinking of "sources" on which Thomas builds, Jordan presents Thomas as a doxographer.

Doxography acknowledges a hierarchy of authorities, beginning with the earliest but recognizing that historical change brings new questions and formulations, albeit not new answers, for the faith has a unity through space and time if the same God is to be identified and worshiped even amid new questions and formulations. Jordan writes,

> The doxographer is responsible for making the unity of faith manifest through the history of changing articulations. Since changes will never end so long as history continues, the multiplicity of theological articulations will continue to grow. Moreover, the doxographer's task is not to cancel the earlier formulations, but to save them. Theology ought never to be an *abolitio memoriae*. It ought to be an act of gratitude to one's predecessors acted out as charitable attention to them.[8]

What follows in this work seeks to heed Jordan's advice by examining key authorities for the perfectly simple Triune God, interpreting them charitably and then extending their teaching by attending to modern changes.

Thomas forms his doctrine of God in the first forty-three questions of the *Summa* based on the scholastic method of *ordo disciplinae* ("order of learning"). It was not the only method he used; his biblical

---

6. Ludwig Wittgenstein, *Philosophical Investigations*, trans. G. E. M. Anscombe (New York: Macmillan, 1968), 8.

7. Jordan, "Competition of Authoritative Languages," 77. See also Mark Jordan, *Rewritten Theology* (Oxford: Wiley-Blackwell, 2005).

8. Jordan, "Competition of Authoritative Languages," 84.

commentaries exposited line by line. The two methods, however, had the same end—to present the truth of God and its significance for creatures—but *ordo disciplinae* did so with a specific purpose. Its purpose is to "teach beginners." Whether or not the *Summa* was intended for teachers who would teach the beginners or for the beginners themselves is inconsequential; either way it presents what matters most in a coherent form by countering potential objections and misunderstandings of previous authorities with Thomas's responses.

As Jean-Pierre Torrell notes, Thomas was most likely dissatisfied using Peter Lombard's *Sentences* for the instruction of basic Christian doctrine during his four years teaching at Orvieto (1261–65). In 1265 he was instructed to move to Rome and begin a *studium* at St. Sabina "for the formation of chosen friars from the various priories of the Roman province."[9] Thomas's *Summa*, as he tells us in its prologue, had two motivations. The first was to teach the friars what is necessary for "the things belonging to the Christian religion" in order to convey them to others. The second was to avoid teaching "superfluous" matters that "hampered" learning through unnecessary repetition and a confusing order. Instead, he will teach "according to the order of learning" (*secundum ordinem disciplinae*).[10] The treatise *De Deo*, then, like the remainder of the *Summa*, does not say everything that could or should be said about God. It says what matters most, as "clearly" and "briefly" as possible, and it does so by intentionally beginning with what is most elemental. Thomas begins the *Summa* by citing Paul in 1 Cor. 3:1–2, "As unto little ones in Christ, I gave you milk to drink, not meat." Thomas's purpose should be kept in mind as we enter into a discussion of his authorities. That God is perfectly simple is elemental; it is a teaching so basic that it is milk, not meat. That God is perfectly simple and Triune is the meat of the faith. The former without the latter could hardly sustain life.

Thomas did not begin the *Summa* de novo. He had commented on

---

9. Jean-Pierre Torrell, OP, *Saint Thomas Aquinas*, vol. 1, *The Person and His Work*, trans. Robert Royal (Washington, DC: Catholic University of America Press, 1996), 142.
10. *ST* prol, *prima pars*.

Holy Scripture, written important works addressing the doctrine of God, such as *De Potentia* and *Summa Contra Gentiles* (1259–64);[11] the latter, Gilles Emery suggests, contains much of the biblical basis for the *De Deo* in the *Summa*.[12] He had put together a rich source of patristic quotations, the *Catena Aurea*. He began it in 1262 or 1263 and finished it between 1265 and 1268, as he was beginning the *Summa*.[13] The *Catena Aurea* offers sentences from the church fathers on each of the verses of the four Gospels. The verses themselves are not noted but assumed, and the sentences are not commented on.[14] The quotations are strung together like beads on a chain; thus they are a "chain of gold" (*Catena Aurea*).

Unlike the *Summa Theologiae*, the *Catena* was not Thomas's idea. Pope Urban IV requested it.[15] Thomas dedicated it to him.[16] It does, however, provide insight into Thomas's "multiple languages." Scripture is read through the Holy Fathers, and it is assumed that their comments offer a harmonious witness to its truth. That Thomas produced the *Catena* shortly before or during the time he began composing the *Summa* is significant. Scriptural quotation plays a central role throughout *De Deo*; it appears, especially at those moments where it matters most, in order to illumine beginners as to the things pertaining to the Christian religion. When it is not explicitly present, it is nonetheless in the background, available to the beginner in the *Catena*, the commentaries, or the *Summa Contra Gentiles*.

Scripture

Thomas crafts his *de Deo* from Scripture. No philosopher or church father is cited as much as Scripture.[17] In the first two parts of the *de*

---

11. Torrell, *Saint Thomas Aquinas*, 1:102.
12. "Thomas's conception of theological research on the Trinity is entirely based around Scripture"; Gilles Emery, *Trinity in Aquinas* (Ypsilanti, MI: Sapientia Press of Ave Maria College, 2003), 119. For Emery the biblical basis is found most extensively in *SCG* and then assumed in *ST*.
13. Torrell, *Saint Thomas Aquinas*, 1:136.
14. See Aquinas, *Catena aurea in quatuor Evangelia Expositio in Matthaeum*, www.corpusthomisticum .org/cmt01.html.
15. Torrell, *Saint Thomas Aquinas*, 1:136.
16. *Sanctissimo ac reverendissimo patri domino Urbano, divina providentia Papae quarto, frater Thomas de Aquino, ordinis fratrum praedicatorum, cum devota reverentia, pedum osculo beatorum.*

Deo, which we examined in chapter 1, Thomas explicitly cites the Old Testament 148 times[18] and the New Testament 191 times[19] for a total of 339 citations. Paul receives the highest number of citations, at 110 (including Hebrews, to which Thomas refers eleven times, attributing authorship to Paul). In citing individual books, Psalms receives the most references (forty) followed by the Gospel of John (thirty-nine) and then Romans (thirty-five). The closest authority to Scripture in terms of the sheer number of citations is St. Augustine, whom he cites 240 times. Next comes Aristotle, at 114, followed by Dionysius at sixty-seven.

Someone might object that the previous paragraph overstates how central Scripture is for Thomas. Although he frequently cites it, Thomas nonetheless quotes Aristotle more than any single scriptural book by a factor of three. He makes no explicit reference to the Gospel of Mark, refers to Luke on only eight occasions, and Matthew on only eighteen. Even Paul is cited less than Aristotle, and no one approaches Augustine, especially his *De Trinitate*, in terms of sheer quantity of citations. Do these statistics lend support to those who find Thomas's doctrine of God subordinating theology to philosophy? Has he built up a doctrine of God from philosophical sources more so than from Scripture?

The statistics and tables noted above easily mislead. More important than the quantity of citations is how an authority is used. One hundred and twelve times Thomas uses Scripture as the "on the contrary" in his argument.[20] One-third of his explicit uses of Scripture occur in the

---

17. Thomas does not put the fathers on par with Scripture. He explains the distinction he uses between them for sacred doctrine by appealing to Augustine: "Still, even though sacred doctrine uses citations of the sort in question as extraneous and probable arguments, it properly uses citations from the canonical Scriptures when arguing from necessity, whereas it uses citations from other doctors of the Church as if arguing from what is properly its own, though with probability. For our Faith is based on the revelation made to the Apostles and Prophets who wrote the canonical books and not on any revelation that might have been made to the other doctors. Thus, in a letter to Jerome, Augustine says, 'It is only to those books of the Scriptures called canonical that I have learned to give the honor of believing with utter confidence that none of their authors has erred in anything. In contrast, I read other authors in such a way that no matter how distinguished they might be in holiness and learning, I do not think something true simply because they have thought it or written it'" (*ST* I 8 rep. obj. 2).
18. See appendix.
19. See appendix.

sed contra. Nearly half of the articles in the first forty-three questions cite Scripture in their *sed contra* (112 of 233).[21] Aristotle only appears in the "on the contrary" on nine occasions. These statistics matter because the "on the contrary" is where Thomas begins his argument. The objections set forth inaccurate answers to questions. They are sometimes simply wrong, sometimes insufficiently nuanced, sometimes misunderstandings, on rare occasions correct. As Thomas leads the initiate on the way to knowledge of God, the errors, insufficiencies, and misunderstandings are, in the vast majority of articles, first corrected with the "on the contraries." The *sed contra* does not say all that needs to be said, so it is followed up with an extended response, often, although not always, clarifying the truth found in the "on the contrary" by careful distinctions and arguments. Thomas clearly follows Aristotle in his method of making distinctions and arguments, but the purpose is to clarify and manifest sacred doctrine. Only after those clarifications and manifestations can the misunderstandings, insufficiencies, and errors be adequately addressed. Scripture is not the only authority found in the *sed contra*, but it is the overwhelming authority in the first forty-three questions of the *De Deo*; it is the entrance into the clarification of the question. Thomas does not, however, confine Scripture to one part of his argument. It also appears in objections, responses, and replies. Scripture has a variety of uses; they are best understood by observing specific uses of two key passages.

Two central passages in Thomas's doctrine of God are Exod. 3:14 and John 14:6. They appear at crucial places on the journey into God; each of them appears in question 2, on the existence of God, and in question 39, on the relationship between the Triune persons and the divine essence. The relationship he finds between them is as telling of Thomas's use of Scripture as his use of each passage individually. Thomas's overriding concern is with divine agency. Thomas is less

---

20. He uses Old Testament quotations fifty-nine times and New Testament fifty-three: Matthew, three; Luke, one; John, twelve; Paul, twenty-six; Hebrews, three; James, two; and 1 John, six.
21. There are 233 *sed contras* in the first two parts of *De Deo*. Forty-eight percent of the *sed contras* then are Holy Scripture.

interested in making God a character in the biblical story and more in understanding God as its author. When God acts and/or speaks in Scripture, who is it who acts and speaks? For instance, Thomas initiates his five ways by God's self-attestation of God's existence in Exod. 3:14. But if God addresses Moses, who is it who addresses him? It is not the divine essence, for the divine essence does not act; the persons do. For the persons to act, however, and not turn them into competing actors, each acts as the essence. Triune processions and God's perfect simplicity render divine agency intelligible.

Exodus 3:14

Thomas explicitly cites Exod. 3:14 twice in the *de Deo* and implicitly once. The two explicit citations are both in a *sed contra*, and, as I noted above, they bracket Thomas's analysis of how we speak of God, providing an entry into a demonstration of God's existence in the five ways (*ST* I 2.3) and then culminating in the affirmation that God bears a proper name (*ST* I 13.11). The first use of Exod. 3:14 is undeveloped but foundational to all that follows, as *ST* I 13.11 shows. Having discussed how knowledge of God is not *per se*, despite what John 14:6 might lead one to think (*ST* I 2.1), and how God's existence can be demonstrated despite what Heb. 11:1 might lead one to think (*ST* I 2.2), Thomas then discusses the question for which these previous two articles prepare the reader: does God exist (*ST* I 2.3)? He begins with two objections that assume what will come later in the argument. The first objection refers to the "name God" (*in hoc nomine Deus*) as a "certain infinite good" (*quoddam bonum infinitum*). Here Thomas associates the name *Deus* with infinity and goodness, although he has not yet discussed infinity, goodness, or God's names. His associations work proleptically. As we saw in the previous chapter, the objection states that if God were infinite goodness, evil would be inexplicable. Two contraries cannot both be infinite, but evil and good appear to be contrary infinites. If God exists, there would be no evil. There is evil. Therefore there is no God. The second objection states God's uselessness in accounting for creation. Everything in nature can be accounted for in terms of natural causes or human reason and will. God is unnecessary.

Sandwiched between these objections and Thomas's response to them is Exod. 3:14. Before he begins to explain the five ways for God's existence or answer the above objections, Thomas cites this key passage as an authority. He does not tell us what kind of authority it is or how it is related to the five ways. He only affirms that we have a witness *ex persona Dei, ego sum cui sum.* From God's own person we have God's self-attestation, "I am who I am." God affirms God's own existence by conveying it to Moses, but that is all the reader is told, leaving open several questions. Is God a person? Does *esse* (the infinitive form of *sum*) name God? How does God as *person* bear witness to God's existence? All of these questions will be addressed in later articles. Question 13, article 11 explains how the name *Qui est* ("He who is") is God's proper name *maxime* ("in the highest degree"). Question 20, article 3 argues affirmatively that *person* should be said of God. Question 2 prepares the reader for further articles that will need to address who this God is who attests to his own existence. Not all that needs to be said has yet been said. While those later arguments are assumed in question 2, their fuller articulation will have to wait. For now, it suffices that Thomas knows God exists from God's self-attestation to Moses. It authorizes the rational pursuit of God's existence; it also places limits on that pursuit. Because we know God attests to God's existence, some knowledge of God is possible even to reason, but with the qualifications Thomas laid out in his first question—only to a few, after a long time, and with many errors. The first and final authority for God's existence is God. As creator of all that is, however, that authority finds itself involved in multiple authorities, found in Scripture, the holy Fathers, and among philosophers.

When Thomas returns to Exod. 3:14 in question 13, article 11, he not only appeals to revelation to argue that *Qui est* is God's most proper name, but he also seeks to give reasons in order to manifest why it is so. He finds three, each consistent with what he previously developed. The first is based on simplicity, the second on infinity, and the third on eternity. First, *Qui est* signifies God above all other names because it does not signify a particular form but *ipsum esse*. He then states that every thing is "denominated" from its form and concludes that *ipsum esse* best names God. Isolated to this question alone, the argument would have significant gaps. It is a stronger argument than appears, however, because Thomas assumes what he has already stated in the question on infinity (*ST* I 7) but does not repeat here. *Ipsum esse* is *maxime formale omnium* ("the most formal of everything"). Because God is form without matter, *esse* signifies God in a way that it cannot signify composite creatures, who are matter limited by form. *Esse* alone is God's form because it is not limiting. Second, *esse* as a finite term has a "universality" to it that does not "determine" God in the way other more determinate terms would. All terms, because they are finite, tempt users and hearers to an overdetermination of God, but *esse* does so less than others. If God were *a* being, rather than being itself, then we would misunderstand God. The name *esse* prevents misunderstanding because it is "less determinate" and "more common and absolute." Third, *esse* is always present. It does not imply past or future. (Thomas cites Augustine's *De Trinitate*, book five, for this argument.)

One other intriguing reference to Exod. 3:14 occurs in question 39, article 8. Here Thomas brings together Exod. 3:14 and John 14:6 to discuss Triune agency. Thomas asks whether the "sacred doctors" unfittingly (*inconvenienter*) assign essential attributes to the persons. This question poses a difficulty for Thomas, one he readily acknowledges. If the "unity of the essence" is known to some extent by reason, as he suggests in previous articles (*ST* I 32.1 and 39.7), and essential predicates must be appropriated by the persons, as he also argues, then how are the persons not known by reason alone, a position Thomas consistently rejects? Two of the texts he uses to explain how the essential predicates (or names) are appropriated to the persons are John 14:6 and Exod. 3:14. He states, "Now *He Who Is* is appropriated to the person of the Son not according to its proper meaning, but rather by reason of something added to it, viz., that the liberation of the human race, which is accomplished through the Son, is prefigured in what God says to Moses" (*ST* I 39.8 rep. obj. 5). Thomas argues that the Son is not *Qui est* in its proper signification, for its proper signification defines the essence. He also argues the essence is no fourth "thing" behind the persons and that each person is the essence. The divine essence does not have agency; only the persons do, but the persons each have agency as the essence. These arguments raise the question, Who says *ego sum qui sum* when God makes God's self-witness to Moses? Who is the *persona* in the *ex persona Dei* that could make such a statement?

Thomas labors to answer the question because of the distinction he makes in both question 32, article 1 and 38, article 7: "By natural knowledge we can know what belongs to the unity of essence and not that which belongs to the distinction of persons" (*ST* I 32.1 resp.). How can Thomas make this distinction without assuming the essence is an actor independent of the persons? Thomas himself identified the difficulty:

> To anyone who considers God's simplicity, the truth regarding this question is evident. For it was shown above (q. 3, a. 3) that God's simplicity requires that in God the essence is the same as a *suppositum*, which in intellectual substances is nothing other than a person. But a difficulty seems to arise because the essence retains its oneness even though the divine persons are multiplied. (*ST* I 39.1 resp.)

How can we maintain the unity of the essence and the multiplication of the persons when the person is the same as the essence? Thomas answers that the persons are relations "subsisting in the divine nature," so that they are only distinguished from the essence conceptually, even though they are really distinct from each other; his answer bears directly on divine agency.

Thomas addresses the difficulty by examining God's agency in Scripture. He implicitly asks the question, Who tells Moses *ego sum qui sum*? Who is the person who attests to God's own existence? Is it the essence, the Father, the Son? He asks whether the essence can be appropriated to the Son and answers yes because of the Son's mission to liberate the human race. The essence is appropriated properly to the

Son when the difference between the Son and the Father is maintained. Thomas states, "Still, insofar as 'Who' is taken as a relative pronoun, it could sometimes refer to the person of Son and so be taken for a person—as, for instance, if one were to say, 'The Son is the Begotten Who Is,' in the same way that 'God Begotten' is the name of a person. However, 'He Who Is,' taken without modification, is a name of the essence" (*ST* I 39.8 rep. obj. 5). The persons appropriate essential predicates. Each person is the essence, but each person is the essence through its unique relation, and it is as person that God speaks, acts, redeems, liberates, etc. *Qui est*, like *Deus*, then, can be appropriated to the Son as long as we recognize the real distinction among the persons and the identity between each person and the essence. The difference between each person and the essence is a conceptual, not a real distinction. The Begotten *Qui est* speaks, who is distinct as Begotten from the Unbegotten, and yet is the same *Qui est* as the Unbegotten and the Spirit. The *qui* refers to both a relative person and the essence at the same time. For this reason, the *esse* is not only God's nature; it is also God's activity. What the "I am" shows is not only who God is but also what God does. They cannot be separated because of God's simplicity. When the Son says "I am," it also refers to the Son's activity in liberating humanity from its captivity.

Thomas's intriguing use of Exod. 3:14 answers modern historical critics who rush to judgment that the ancients and Scholastics were more interested in abstract, metaphysical speculation than God's dramatic historical action. Take, for instance, Gerhard von Rad's criticism of unnamed theologians' interpretation of Exod. 3:14. He states that the revelation of God's name

> has from the very beginning keenly attracted the interest of theologians, because they believed that here at last was a reference giving a comprehensive and fundamental account of the nature of the revelation of Jahweh, and reducing it, so to speak, to a final axiomatic formula (Ex. 3.14), but caution has to be exercised at this point; for nothing is farther from what is being envisaged in this etymology of the name of Jahweh than a definition of his nature in the sense of a philosophy (LXX ἐγώ εἰμι ὁ ὤν)—a suggestion for example of his absoluteness, aseity, etc. Such a thing would be altogether out of keeping with the Old Testament. The whole

narrative context leads right away to the expectation that Jahweh then intends to impart something—but this is not what he is, but what he will show himself to be to Israel.[22]

Von Rad does not tell us which theologians he critiques, but Thomas is not as poor an interpreter of Scripture as von Rad suggests some theologians might be. Thomas affirms God's being as absolute and *a se* (by which he means that God is not caused by anything other than God), and he finds it in the Old Testament, but as previously noted, the names he uses are not a "definition," for a definition of God's essence is not possible. Thomas finds it necessary to locate the subject "God" in language as well as it can be located. If Scripture does not provide such an account, we could not identify God as its author. Thomas, unlike von Rad, finds God revealing to us not only God's historical agency as an identity but also the divine nature. Thomas does not, however, do what von Rad does; he does not divide God's nature from God's agency. He does not divide "what he is" from "what he will show himself to be." Had von Rad understood the importance of divine simplicity, he would not have made such an obvious theological blunder, a blunder that cannot but hinder identifying God's agency in the Scriptures by importing temporality and composition into it, an error all too common in modern theology. Thomas finds the "what he will be" in the presence of "what he is," so the *ipsum esse* that identifies God is at the same time the Son who liberates the human race.

John 14:6

No other passage from John is cited by Thomas in the *De Deo* as much as John 14:6; Thomas cites it five times.[23] No passage from Romans or the Psalms, two other books Thomas often cites, are quoted as much. John 14:6 appears in the context of the following crucial theological questions:

---

22. Gerhard von Rad, *Old Testament Theology* (New York: Harper & Row, 1962), 1:180.
23. He cites John 17:3 four times, John 1:18 three, John 5:19 three, John 1:3–4 twice, and John 15:26 twice. The remaining twenty-two references to John are cited once.

1. *ST* 2.1 Is it known *per se* that there is a God? (as objection)
2. *ST* 3.3 Is God the same as his essence or nature? (as *sed contra*)
3. *ST* 16.5 Is God truth? (as *sed contra*)
4. *ST* 39.8 Have the Holy Doctors correctly assigned the attributes of the essence to the person? (twice, as objection and reply)

The first use of John 14:6 occurs in the context of God's relation to truth. For Aquinas truth is known *per se*, that is, "in itself." If the "definition" is known and universally acknowledged, then what is defined is *per se notum*. Truth is *per se notum* because it cannot be rejected without contradiction. If someone denies the existence of truth, she or he must assume its existence in order to make the denial. Suppose someone says, "There is no truth." Then the next question would be, "Is it true that there is no truth?" If someone answers yes, then truth is acknowledged to exist. If the answer is no, then the original statement makes little sense and was not worth uttering in the first place.

Scripture complicates this argument by correlating God and truth. Jesus says in John 14:6, "I am the way, the truth and the life." Because Jesus is God, his self-description correlates truth with God. Scripture, then, could be used for the following syllogism:

1. Truth is known *per se* by us (Aquinas agrees).
2. Scripture teaches God is truth (Aquinas agrees).
3. Therefore, God is known *per se* by us (Aquinas disagrees).

Thomas presents a version of the above argument as his third objection to the question whether God's existence is *per se notum*. Scripture would seem to affirm that it is, but Aquinas denies that the consequence follows from the major and minor premises. His argument makes sense once the "truth" used in 1 and 2 is understood not to be univocal. If we are forced to use univocal predication in our interpretation of Thomas, then his argument makes no sense.

That truth is unavoidable does not entail God is *per se notum* as the first truth, because for something to be *per se notum* two conditions must be fulfilled. It must not only be *secundum se* but also *secundum se et quoad nos*. These two conditions reflect two different relations; the first assumes God's relation to God's self (speculative theology), the second God's relation to us (practical theology). Thomas does not collapse them, even though they identify a single science of God. For something to be "known in itself and for us," its predicates would need to be contained in its subject and everyone acknowledge it, such as the fact that truth exists. It is *per se notum* but *in communi* ("in general"). We cannot think, speak, or act without assuming a generic understanding of truth, but the specific truth "God is" is not contained within the generic truth our speech and action entail. John 14:6 cannot be used to argue from our *per se* knowledge that truth is to the conclusion that God's existence is *per se notum*. We must be led to God. Jesus is *via, veritas et vita* ("way, truth and life").

The first reference Thomas makes to John 14:6 is to God as truth. The second is to God as life, and the argument hinges once again on divine simplicity. The question asks whether God is the same as deity? Thomas uses John 14:6 as the *sed contra* in order to defend God's simplicity. God is the same as God's essence (*essentia*) or nature (*natura*). The essence or nature of God is God's "deity" (*deitas*). The question relates well to Thomas's previous use of John 14:6, for just as we cannot move seamlessly from our generic knowledge "that truth is" to the specific knowledge "that God is truth," neither can we move from a putative knowledge of deity and relate it to God as a particular instantiation of that essence. This inability makes knowledge of God different from other forms of discursive knowledge. For instance, we can move from our generic knowledge of *humanitas* to recognize that the particular Socrates fits the generic form. We know that the specific human person fits within the genus *humanitas*. Although specific features of *humanitas* differ from person to person, for instance, some are black and some white (Thomas uses the example), neither is decisive for the definition of humanity. Black and white folk are both human, so their humanity is not determined by blackness or whiteness *per se* any more than it would be determined by height or weight or length of years. Each particular human individual differs from every other and yet shares in the definition of humanity. What makes each one differ does not determine the definition, the *quid est*.

Should we expect the same for God? Is *deitas* a category like *humanitas*? If we know *deitas*, can we then fit God within it? Once again, if we are forced to use univocal predication, we will not understand Thomas. He argues *deitas* is not the same as *humanitas* because God is simple. God is *deitas*; the latter is not a genus that contains God as an individual species. Here is a key biblical argument for simplicity. To begin his argument, he refers again to John 14:6. "It is said *de Deo* (of God) that he is *vita* (life) and not just that he is *vivens* (living)." Thomas draws from John 14:6 the conclusion that God is God's life, and God's life is *deitas*. This conclusion renders it impossible for Thomas to construct a method whereby we first identify "deity" and then further define it to make it fit the Triune God, as if we could have a generic *de deo uno* and then specify it as *de deo trino*. Any interpretation of the first forty-three questions that suggests as much must be in error; it would violate simplicity. We do not begin with a generic discussion of God known to all (*deitas*) in the first treatise and then fit the Triune God within it; Thomas argues explicitly against such a method.

Thomas refers to John 14:6 in the question on truth (*ST* I 16). Once again, the passage occurs in the *sed contra*. Much as the claim that God is living draws on simplicity, Thomas's argument for God as truth does the same. The *sed contra* initiates a discussion as to how God is truth. It is a counterintuitive claim, for Thomas argues elsewhere that truth is a discursive practice of the intellect. The first objection states truth is the "intellect's composing and dividing," but God's simplicity would not allow for such a discursive practice. That God is life and truth signifies that truth is not only in God's intellect but also is God's intellect. It is not "conformed" to God's *esse* but is God's *esse* (*ST* I 18.3 resp.).[24]

---

24. Readers might expect Thomas to make a specific reference to John 14:6 in the question on God's life (*ST* I 18); he does not. He does, however, develop the argument begun in his second use of the passage in question 3. God is the most living of beings because God's "nature is its very act of understanding" (*ST* I 18.3 resp.).

The final two references to John 14:6 are found in question 39, article 8. As was the case with Exod. 3:14, John 14:6 is used to discuss the Son's appropriation of the divine name and identify the Triune God's agency. Objection 5 argues the divine name should be proper to the Son, not appropriated to him because of John 14:6. If Jesus says, "I am the way, truth and life," then the divine name "I am" and its corollaries—way, truth, life—belong most properly to him. Thomas does not reply to the objections in this question. He has a lengthy response that does, however, explicitly mention objection 5. It brings Exod. 3:14 and John 14:6 together. Both inform the other. The divine name does not name a relation but the essence. Yet the essence is appropriated to each of the persons such that essential predicates like truth and life are appropriated to the person's distinct identity while they are at the same time common to the essence. We must have means to speak both of God's essence and persons without positing an essence other than the persons. Language fails to do this precisely, but it is in acknowledging its failure that we can know "God as God is in himself."[25]

Thomas uses Scripture to begin his responses. Scripture is not, however, perspicuous. It can be misunderstood, so it can be found as an objection as well as a *sed contra*, response, or reply to objections. To alleviate misunderstanding, Thomas interprets Scripture through the church's teaching—especially the doctrines of the Trinity and incarnation. Thomas allows the faith of the church to guide his reading of Scripture. He also finds in Scripture the faith of the church. The pairing of Exod. 3:14 and John 14:6 is illustrative. Together they identify God's nature and agency. One cannot be had without the other.

---

25. Aquinas makes specific reference to God's truth (*veritas*) and life (*vita*) in questions 2 and 3 of *De Deo*. He also dedicates entire questions to both truth (*ST* I 16) and life (*ST* I 18). Given the importance of John 14:6 for him, the question arises, Why is there no corresponding question on *way*? He does mention *via* in the preface to question 2, where the reader is reminded that Jesus is the "way" of our movement toward God, and he develops "five ways" in his question on God's existence. He also returns to this theme in the *tertia pars*. Its preface states that Jesus "demonstrated the way of truth to us in himself" (*viam veritatis nobis in seipso demonstravit*). Perhaps no single question is devoted to "way" because it brackets the entire *Summa* from the preface to *de Deo* to the preface to Christology in the *tertia pars*? Way, truth, and life are more important for Thomas's argument than the Neoplatonic triad—being, life, and intelligence—although the latter seems to have generated much more interest among Thomist scholars than the former. The latter is clearly present, but has it not been reinterpreted through way, truth, and life?

This use of Scripture and the church's faith may appear circular, but if so it is no vicious circularity. The church's faith guides the reading of Scripture because that faith is drawn from Scripture. Scripture locates, as much as it can be located (meant metaphorically, of course, because God has no location), God's nature and agency. The church's faith preserves the authorities who assist in that "location" and in turn help us understand better what lacks perspicuity. God speaks to Moses in Exod. 3:14. What could such speech be? Does it imply God has the bodily organs necessary for speech? Does it suggest composition, temporality, passibility, and other finite categories necessary for proper acts of speech? Because of the multiple authorities that help us read Scripture well—the holy fathers and philosophical reason manifesting the faith—Thomas avoids such idolatrous identifications of the God who *ex personae* witnesses to his own existence. Simplicity leads the reader to understand well that when God speaks, no distinction between God's nature and action results. The perfectly simple Triune God who authors Scripture communicates through it.

Despite his dissatisfaction with the structure of Lombard's *Sentences*, Thomas does not seek to develop a new doctrine of God relevant for his times by using the latest philosophical system, a theological method that would be anathema to him. Thomas's doctrine of God differs very little from what Lombard presented in his *Sentences*. Nor does Thomas seek to retrieve a past, either apostolic or patristic, to correct errors that occurred since then. Thomas assumes continuity in identifying God's nature and agency throughout the church's history; divine eternity and the operation of providence demand it. His teaching on God is not novel; earlier authorities should be trusted but not followed blindly. Two of the most important for his doctrine of God are St. Augustine and Dionysius, an interesting combination because these two are often pitted against each other, the former representing either the strength or weakness of Western Christianity and the latter doing the same for the East. Aquinas draws on both of them for the arduous theological task of naming God. They are central authorities for Thomas in that they assist in two key tasks: identifying God as perfectly simple and predicating terms for the Triune God. As was already noted above in discussing Scripture, for Thomas these two tasks require each other.

Augustine

Augustine (and Pseudo-Augustine) appears 247 times in the first forty-three questions of the *De Deo*. Interestingly, he is cited more in the treatise on the divine essence (141 times) than he is in the treatise on the persons (106 times).[26] The vast majority of citations, eighty-one, come from *De Trinitate*. The next-closest work cited is *De Civitas Dei*, twenty-two; *De diversis quaestionibus LXXXIII*, twenty; and *Super Genesim ad Litteram*, fourteen. No other work has more than nine citations. Clearly Thomas, like Lombard, is preoccupied with *De Trinitate*. When Thomas cites Augustine, he cites *De Trinitate* 33 percent of the time. He uses it for 13 percent of his Augustine citations in the first treatise on the divine essence, but 56 percent in the second on the Triune processions. Thomas's use of *De Trinitate* is broad, although he makes no reference to books 8, 10, 11, and 13. He cites book 7 the most—twenty times—followed by book 15 seventeen times, book 6 thirteen times, book 4 eleven times, and book 5 eight times. The other books are cited from one to six times.[27]

Whether or not he has a complete grasp on Augustine's corpus, Aquinas finds his way into theology as a science from Scripture and Augustine's *De Trinitate*. The first two articles in question 1 of the *Summa* bear this out. Scripture is the authority for the *sed contra* in the first article, which explains why sacred doctrine beyond philosophy is necessary; Augustine's *De Trinitate* is the authority for the *sed contra* in the second article, which begins the argument that sacred doctrine is a science. The importance of Augustine should not be surprising. As Gilles Emery notes, Augustine's work *De Trinitate* "set the tone for Trinitarian research during the golden age of scholasticism."[28] Peter

26. See appendix.
27. See appendix.
28. Emery, *Trinity in Aquinas*, 1.

Lombard's *Sentences*, especially book 1 on the Trinity, was composed of extended quotations from Augustine. He provided the content and the form for Trinitarian teaching.

Augustine set an important precedent by neither saying too much nor saying too little about the Triune God. He encouraged others to do the same. In his first book Augustine wrote,

> Therefore let everyone who reads these pages proceed further with me, where he is as equally certain as I am; let him make inquiries with me where he is equally hesitant as I am; wherever he recognizes the error as his, let him return to me; wherever it is mine, let him call me back. Thus let us enter together on the path of charity in search of Him of whom it is said: "Seek his face forevermore." This is the sacred and safe compact into which I, in the presence of the Lord our God, shall enter with those who read what I am writing in all my writings, and especially in the present one where we are investigating the unity of the Trinity, of the one Father, the Son and the Holy Spirit. For nowhere else is the error more dangerous, the search more laborious and the results more rewarding.[29]

Peter Lombard placed a version of this quote as a caution to readers when he began his teaching on the Trinity.[30] Aquinas cited it as well, both in his commentary on the *Sentences* and in the *Summa*.[31]

Augustine's "sacred compact" stems from his opening statement in *De Trinitate*: "The reader of this treatise on the Trinity should know

29. St. Augustine, *The Trinity*, in *The Fathers of the Church*, trans. Stephen McKenna, CSSR (Washington, DC: Catholic University of America Press, 1988), 8. English translations primarily come from McKenna's translation. I will cite book and chapter and also note the page number. Latin comes from Corpus Christianorum, Series Latina, with the standard designation CCSL.

30. Emery, *Trinity in Aquinas*, 1. Josef Pieper described Lombard's *Sentences* as "a systematically organized Augustinian breviary"; cited in Wayne Hankey's "Reading Augustine through Dionysius," in Michael Dauphenais, Barry David, and Matthew Levering, eds., *Aquinas the Augustinian* (Washington, DC: Catholic University of America Press, 2007), 246.

31. In his commentary on Lombard's *Sentences*, Thomas makes reference to Augustine's "social compact" at the same place Lombard does, at the beginning. In the *Summa*, however, he does not cite it until question 31, in his response to whether the Son is other than the Father. Thomas states, "For as Augustine says in *De Trinitate* 1, 'There is no other place where error is more dangerous, where questions are asked more rigorously, or where anything more fruitful is found.'" Question 31 marks another important turn in Thomas's journey into the mystery of God. He prefaces it with the statement that it is an "inquiry" into "things that pertain to the oneness or to the plurality in God." Thomas asks whether there is a Trinity in God. His task, which has been his task all along, is to explain how what appears to be multiple—Trinity—is in fact unity. He also cites a version of it in *ST* I 32.4 as obj. 1, as to whether "contrary opinions about the notions are permissible." The objection is that they are not, but he then argues that, unlike the persons and relations, they are.

beforehand that our pen is on the watch for the sophistries of those who consider it beneath their dignity to begin with faith, and who thus are led into error by their immature and perverted love of reason."[32] This perverted love of reason produces three classes of errors. The first two move univocally from the creature to God: the first in terms of the body and the second of the soul. Errors arise either because God is conceived in terms of corporeal objects known from senses or from the "nature and affections" of the incorporeal (soul). A third class emerges from those who acknowledge God's transcendence but do so from "preconceived ideas" they cling to without openness to the "purification" of the soul in Christ.[33] Augustine acknowledges errors are easily made in setting forth the central mystery that God is Triune, and thus the inquirer should "at last realize how wholesome is the medicine that has been entrusted to the holy Church for the faithful."[34] For this reason he is "not reluctant" to inquire or have others inquire into his possible errors. He asks his reader in charity to do the same. From this invitation and its attendant cautions emerges his "sacred compact."

Augustine reminds his readers that the doctrine of the Trinity is not known from philosophical reason. He is less interested than Thomas in demonstrating God's unity from philosophy; he does not begin with any demonstration of God's existence. Like Thomas, however, he finds reason capable of manifesting the truth about God and defending it against errors. Although Augustine has less place for a demonstration of God's existence by reason than Thomas, Thomas uses quotes from Augustine to suggest the Triune persons can be known by natural reason in the first two objections to his question 32. The first objection suggests that the Triune persons can be rationally demonstrated because Trinity can be found in the "books of the Platonists." The second affirms the possibility of knowing the Trinity from the *imago Dei*; the procession of the word and love in our minds can lead us to the Triune God. These objections, Thomas then argues, misunderstand

---

32. Augustine, *De Trinitate*, trans. McKenna, bk 1.1, p. 3.
33. Ibid., bk 1.1, p. 6.
34. Ibid., bk 1.1, p. 7.

Augustine. He affirms neither position. The misunderstanding could have been generated from Lombard's use of Augustine, for, as we shall see below, Lombard has a more positive yet nonetheless limited appraisal of reason's ability to move from creatures to the Triune God because of the *imago Dei*. Thomas does not emphasize the *imago Dei* as a possible theological epistemology, as Lombard does when he discusses the Trinity. On this point Thomas may be the better Augustinian.

Augustine seeks to say what must be said about the Triune God without saying too much based on reason alone or too little through a lack of faith. His work is ruled by his "Christological epistemology."[35] His "social compact" acknowledges that saying too much or too little is not easy, and so the one presenting the teaching, like the one receiving it, must be open to correction. As he presents his teaching on the Trinity, Thomas has Augustine's caution in mind.

Thomas draws from the fruit of Augustine's teaching not only in the treatise on divine persons but also the divine essence. As previously mentioned, Augustine is the authority cited in the *sed contra* to begin the argument that sacred doctrine is a science. Augustine also assists him in his argument that sacred doctrine is wisdom.[36] He appears at crucial places in Thomas's argument for God's existence, simplicity, perfection, goodness, immutability, and eternity. In all these citations Augustine is used affirmatively. Curiously, citations also appear to Augustine in arguing for God's infinity, but all the citations appear as objections.[37] The majority of references to Augustine occur in questions of theological epistemology: our knowledge of God (twenty references to Augustine are present in question 12), God's knowledge of God's self (twelve references appear in question 14), and God's knowledge of creatures (five on the divine ideas in question 15, ten on God's will in 18, and eight on predestination in 23). Thomas builds on these Augustinian themes once he moves directly into the treatise on

---

35. See Lewis Ayres, *Augustine and the Trinity* (Cambridge: Cambridge University Press, 2010), 6, 142–73.
36. As we shall see, it is unclear that Thomas made a careful inquiry into Augustine's use of these terms as he adopts them within his Aristotelian framework.
37. See *ST* I 8.1 and 4; I 25.2, where Augustine is cited in an objection in the question on God's infinite power.

the Triune persons. Augustine gets used to a great extent to explain predication in the Triune nature and agency. In particular, Augustine's theological predication assists Thomas in showing how the relations are the essence, how God is three persons, and how the Father is the source of the Trinity (unlike Luther, for Thomas the essence does not generate as essence), and to make sense of the Trinitarian missions. In the sections that follow only Aquinas's use of Augustine to argue for theology as science and wisdom, divine simplicity, perfection, and predicating terms for the perfectly simple Triune God will be examined.

Theology as Science and Wisdom

Aquinas's use of Augustine begins with his questions on whether or not sacred doctrine is science and wisdom. His first question in the *Summa* asked whether something more than philosophy was necessary; he does not stipulate necessary for what. The argument assumes it would be necessary not just for our knowledge of God but also for God in relation to creatures. He begins his affirmative answer in his *sed contra* in article 1 with Scripture, 2 Tim. 3:16, "All scripture, inspired of God, is profitable to teach, to reprove, to correct, to instruct in justice." Scripture leads the way into sacred doctrine; Augustine is our next guide. Thomas's first use of Augustine is his "on the contrary" in the second article of his first question, whether sacred doctrine is a science. It is the only time he refers to book 14 of *De Trinitate* in his first forty-three questions. He cites Augustine as an authority who affirms that sacred doctrine is a science because it alone has "the means by which saving faith is begotten, nourished, defended, and strengthened."

Finding Thomas's Augustinian citations in Augustine is not easy. *De Trinitate* book 14 does not contain a statement that fits Thomas's quote well. Book 13 and book 1, chapter 2 come closer. In it Augustine addresses those who reject beginning with faith and seek to comprehend God through their reason without purification. It cannot be accomplished, states Augustine, "because the weak eye of the human mind cannot be fixed on a light so dazzling unless it has been nourished and become stronger by the justice of faith."[38] Book 13 has something remotely similar, but it is by no means as precise as Thomas's quotation. In book 14 Augustine refers back to book 13, where he parses the differences between "wisdom" and "science." He refers to Christ as both "our wisdom" and "our science" because he "plants" and "manifests" faith in us.[39] For Augustine, the two terms *wisdom* and *science* are not easily distinguished. "According to a wider usage of speech," he writes, both terms refer to temporal and divine things. However, St. Paul named each as a distinct gift in 1 Cor. 12:8: "To one is given through the Spirit the utterance of wisdom, and to another the utterance of knowledge according to the same Spirit" (RSV). Augustine seeks to honor Paul's distinction by finding wisdom to refer to eternal, divine matters and knowledge (*scientia*)[40] to human ones.[41] Augustine explains the distinction: "For it is one thing merely to know what a man must believe in order to gain the blessed life, which is none other than eternal life, but another thing to know how this may help the godly, and be defended against the godless, which the Apostle seems to call by the proper name of science."[42] Wisdom appears to be saving knowledge of eternal matters; science is the temporal demonstration of that saving knowledge to assist the "godly" and counter the "godless."

Thomas likewise distinguishes between science and wisdom in question 1, but his distinction is closer to Aristotle than Augustine. Wisdom is the Aristotelian virtue of *phronesis*. Thomas speaks of wisdom as "ordering" and "judging." Wisdom is not contemplation of the eternal qua eternal but God's work as architect of all that is. Science refers to knowledge *per se nota*, which would more closely approximate Augustine's "wisdom." Thomas's first reference to Augustine does not

---

38. Augustine, *De Trinitate*, trans. McKenna, bk 1.2.

39. Ibid., bk. 13.19, p. 406.

40. Augustine, *De Trinitate*, CCSL, 423.

41. Augustine, *De Trinitate*, trans. McKenna, bk 14.1, p. 413.

42. Ibid. He also explained the distinction earlier, in bk 12, chap. 14, "But there is a difference between the contemplation of eternal things and the action by which we use temporal things well; the former is called wisdom, the latter science" (p. 363).

offer much evidence that he studied the *De Trinitate* carefully. His first reference to Augustine is similar to a statement found in his *Commentary on the Sentences* in a question on whether some doctrine beyond natural philosophy is necessary (I 1). Thomas answers yes, and then addresses a *quaestiuncula* as to whether or not this discipline would be a science. Augustine is the authority who provides an affirmative answer, for Augustine purportedly states that *theologia est scientia de rebus quae ad salutem hominis pertinent. Ergo est scientia.*[43] Thomas has framed Lombard's *Sentences* with his own question; his question is not found in Lombard's first distinction. He then answers his question with a quotation from Augustine that is also not found in Lombard's book 1 of the *Sentences* in the form Thomas quotes it.

Lombard begins teaching the Trinity through Augustine's use/enjoy distinction. He then moves into a discussion of the Trinity and states:

> And so, as Augustine says, *On The Trinity*, book 1, this is to be held with true and pious faith, that "the Trinity is the one and only and true God, namely Father, Son, and Holy Spirit. And this Trinity is said, believed, and understood to be one and the same substance, or essence, which is the highest good discerned by the most purified minds. For the weak sharpness of the human mind is not fixed in this highest light without being cleansed through the justice of faith."[44]

Thomas's questions are not Lombard's, but their answers seldom contradict each other. Like Thomas, Lombard begins with sacred Scripture and then draws on reason to defend faith. He writes, "As Augustine teaching in *On the Trinity*, book 1: 'First, we must demonstrate in accordance with the authorities of the holy Scriptures whether the faith holds as we say. Then, we must proceed against verbose rationalizers, who are more proud than able,' in order to defend and assert our faith by Catholic reasons and suitable analogies."[45] Lombard finds a stronger image of the Trinity available to human reason than does Thomas. Although they agree "sufficient

---

43. *Scriptum super Sententiis* q.1 a.3 qc 2 sc 1.
44. Peter Lombard, *The Sentences: Book 1: The Mystery of the Trinity*, trans. Giulio Silano (Toronto: Pontifical Institute of Mediaeval Studies, 2007), 11.
45. Ibid., 13.

knowledge" of the Trinity is only possible through revelation, Lombard finds in Rom. 1:20 a basis for an analogy from creatures to Trinity more so than Thomas.[46] Lombard does not ask the question whether a "science" beyond philosophy is necessary for knowledge of God; he simply assumes it. Thomas asks the question and in turn has a more limited but also more precise role for what philosophy can and cannot accomplish.

Has Thomas carefully read the *De Trinitate*, or is he citing what he learned of Augustine in Lombard or some other collection of Augustinian texts? His first use of Augustine would suggest the latter, his second more the former. In his discussion of theology as a science in book 14 Augustine refers to a previous argument in book 12. Aquinas follows Augustine in his second reference to him at *ST* I 1.6, drawing on book 12 of *De Trinitate* for his response to the question whether sacred doctrine constitutes wisdom. Both Augustine and Thomas are clear that the wisdom under consideration is human wisdom, and they agree that the highest human wisdom is of divine things. Thomas's second use of Augustine comes at the conclusion of several biblical passages affirming sacred doctrine as the highest wisdom, 1 Cor. 3:10 and Prov. 10:23. The latter affirms the centrality of prudence or practical wisdom. The former attests God's practical wisdom as a "wise architect." From these passages Aquinas concludes, "Hence wisdom is said to be 'the cognition of divine things' as is clear from Augustine in *De Trinitate* 12" (*sapientia dicitur esse divinorum cognitio*) (*ST* I 1.6 resp.). This statement reproduces faithfully Augustine's claim in book 12, chapter 15: "wisdom belongs to the intellectual cognition of eternal things."[47]

How is wisdom the cognition of divine things? Aquinas's development of Augustine's affirmation sets the stage for much of

---

46. "And so it has been shown how the image of the Trinity in some measure is revealed in creatures. But a sufficient knowledge of the Trinity cannot and could not be had by a contemplation of creatures, without the revelation of doctrine or inner inspiration. So it was that those ancient philosophers saw the truth as if through a shadow, and from a distance, lacking in insight into the Trinity, as was the case with Pharaoh's magicians in the third plague. And yet we are aided in our faith in invisible things through those things which were made"; Lombard, *Sentences*, 21.

47. Augustine, *De Trinitate*, trans. McKenna, bk. 12.15, p. 367.

what follows in the *de Deo*, and it understands Augustine well. Wisdom is a participation in sacred doctrine. He writes,

> Now it is sacred doctrine that most properly makes determinations about God insofar as He is the highest cause. For it does so not only with respect to that which is knowable through creatures—this the philosophers have discovered, as it says in Romans 1:19 ("That which is known of God is manifest to them")—but also with respect to that which He alone knows about Himself and which has been communicated to others by revelation. Hence, sacred doctrine is called wisdom in the highest sense. (*ST* I 1.6 resp.)

The wisdom Augustine acknowledges is, as it is with Lombard and Aquinas, not knowledge discovered through creatures alone; it is a participation in God's self-communication as a wise architect. Augustine is less positive in his interpretation of Rom. 1:19–20 than both Lombard and Aquinas. For him "the distinguished philosophers of the Gentiles, who were able to perceive that the invisible things of God are understood by those things that are made, yet held back the truth in wickedness, as it was said of them, because they philosophized without the Mediator, that is, without the man Christ."[48] The result established idols. Thomas interprets Rom. 1:19–20 more positively. It provides knowledge of God mixed with error, but it is not dismissed as idolatrous. Lombard, as noted above, interpreted it even more positively. The ancient philosophers saw the truth of the Trinity but "in a shadow." Nonetheless, all agree that the true knowledge of God comes from God's self-communication.[49]

This brief discussion of Thomas's first two quotations from Augustine manifests how difficult it is to determine what Thomas knew of Augustine and from where it came. Thomistic and Augustinian scholarship is by no means in agreement on how well Thomas knew

---

48. Ibid., bk. 13.19, p. 406.
49. Note that Thomas also cites Augustine as an objection to the argument that the divine persons cannot be known by "natural reason" from a quote in the *Confessions* (*ST* I 32.1 obj. 1 and obj. 2). He uses a quote from Augustine to suggest it is possible to know the persons from natural reason and then has this very Augustinian response that fits his own position in his reply to objection 2: "Again, the similarity with our intellect does not sufficiently prove anything about God, since the intellect is not found univocally in God and in us. And this is why in *Super Ioannem* Augustine says that it is through faith that one comes to knowledge, and not vice versa."

and interpreted Augustine. Chenu argues Thomas's work could not be "conceived" without Augustine.[50] Likewise, Merriell finds that Thomas "stands out among the disciples of Augustine, for he appears to have been the first of the scholastic masters to grasp the true intention, structure, and development of Augustine's search for the image of the Trinity."[51] Like Chenu, Merriell is convinced that Thomas made a careful study of Augustine's *De Trinitate.*[52] He challenges de Beaurecueil's interpretation that finds Thomas moving away from Augustine and more toward Aristotle and Dionysius. Bruce Marshall, however, doubts whether Thomas did the careful reading of Augustine's *De Trinitate* that Merriell assumes, and he critiques Merriell for not asking whether Thomas's references to Augustine are from Lombard or the *Glossa ordinaria.*[53]

Not only do differences arise among scholars as to whether or not Thomas had direct access to Augustine's works, they also differ over how able an interpreter of Augustine Thomas was. Lewis Ayres finds Thomas's "scholastic culture and tradition" generating "a very different style of work from what we see in Augustine."[54] He is leery in general of the scholastic use of Augustine: "Scholastic Trinitarian theologies draw frequently on Augustine, but often under misapprehensions: Augustine becomes a source for discussions and terminological distinctions in ways that he would not have envisaged." Thomas's first use of Augustine noted above demonstrates Ayres's concern. Thomas uses Aristotelian distinctions to interpret Lombard's Augustine.

Ayres finds Thomas misapprehending Augustine specifically in his terminology for the Trinity. "Thomas's preference for the use of person

---

50. "Thomas Aquinas inherits from Augustine a theological and philosophical patrimony, says Chenu, 'outside of which it is impossible to conceive a Saint Thomas.' During the thirteenth century, he notes, 'the works of Augustine were being more assiduously read in the original form' and Augustine's major writings formed the basis of the new university libraries"; Marie-Dominique Chenu, *Toward Understanding Saint Thomas* (Chicago: H. Regnery Co. 1964, 310n10), cited in Dauphinais, David, and Levering, *Aquinas the Augustinian*, xi.
51. Merriell, *To the Image of the Trinity*, 4.
52. Ibid., 116, 192.
53. Dauphinais, David, and Levering, *Aquinas the Augustinian*, 50n19. I am unfamiliar with any work that tracks down Aquinas's citations of Augustine to their original sources.
54. Ayres, *Augustine and the Trinity*, 270.

and nature terminology found in such Latins as Hilary and Ambrose reflects the fact that he stands in a tradition stretching from Boethius and through Alcuin and Anselm which was far more willing than Augustine to invest with deep significance the structure of the Trinity a complex metaphysical terminology."[55] However, Ayres does find a "deep consonance" between Thomas and Augustine on the constitution of the Triune persons.[56]

Timothy L. Smith finds more consonance between Augustine and Aquinas on the Trinity. He attributes the metaphysics of subsisting relations first to Augustine.[57] Thomas develops it more fully because he has a better account of person, one that was not available to Augustine. He acknowledges, "Thomas does not imitate Augustine's *De Trinitate*." Thomas has a different "sequence of topics," and is "most concerned with the issue of relations, or more specifically with the use of 'person' for identifying what those relations constitute" than Augustine. Moreover, Thomas does not use "divine image" as the "basis for the bulk of his work." Yet Smith finds considerable gains in Thomas's fuller development of Augustine's insight. Augustine was incapable of developing "person" because of its use in theater and politics.[58]

As important as these debates are, they return us to the question of sources Mark Jordan cautioned against in interpreting Thomas. Does it make any sense to affirm Thomas as an Augustinian? Perhaps even more importantly, does it make any sense to affirm Thomas was not an Augustinian? Denys Turner "in principle" and based on "scholarly evidence" appears to say yes to the latter question. He challenges the "'revisionist' Thomism" that finds him Augustinian and Platonist,

---

55. Ibid.

56. "Nevertheless, despite these differences, there is a deep consonance between Augustine's account of persons as constituted by their eternal intra-divine acts, which are in turn identical with their eternally being generated and spirated, and Thomas's account of subsisting relations" (ibid., 271).

57. Ayres disagrees. He writes, "I argue that the tradition of reading *De trinitate* 5–7 as an account of 'subsistent relations' (albeit an inchoate one that awaits Thomas for its full actualization) misses Augustine's focus on questions of predication, and overly concretizes Augustine's inchoate hints about the substantial and immutable quality of relations between the divine three. In this respect these books of the *De trinitate* offer far less of a developed Trinitarian ontology than is frequently assumed" (ibid., 199).

58. Timothy L. Smith, *Thomas Aquinas's Trinitarian Theology: A Study in Theological Method* (Washington, DC: Catholic University of America Press, 2003), 68–70.

and adheres to the "Thomas of rational proof" because this Thomism allows for a debate to be adjudicated by reason qua reason among atheists, nontheists, and theists of all sorts.[59] Although we might debate the character of Thomas's Augustinianism, the evidence marshaled above makes it difficult to sustain Turner's distinction. It may make little sense to call Thomas an "Augustinian," but it makes less to divide him from his most important authority in his teaching on the perfectly simple Triune God. Perhaps the best interpretation of the relationship between the two comes from Levering, Dauphinais, and David in their *Aquinas the Augustinian*. They state, "We might say rather that Aquinas is an 'Augustinian' in the sense that, like all of Augustine's greatest interpreters, he engages with and elaborates upon Augustine's insights in a manner that challenges us to think afresh about the realities known and loved by Augustine."[60] We do not need to make Aquinas Augustine nor Augustine a preamble to Aquinas to recognize that despite their differences on the details of how we arrive at the answer as to who God is, and the differences in Trinitarian terminology, the two provided, as we shall also see with Dionysius, the same form to the answer. Simplicity was at the heart of that form. Augustine, Lombard, and Aquinas share this common theme. Divine simplicity, recognized by many philosophers, renders intelligible the revealed teaching on the Trinity, a teaching no philosopher qua philosopher recognized. The perfectly simple Triune God bound them together in a common venture even when the specifics of the language and presentation of that God differed.

Divine Simplicity

Aquinas makes seven references to Augustine in his first question on sacred doctrine. He then makes an eighth reference to Augustine's *Enchiridion* in order to argue that evil is not a competing infinite to God; God's infinite goodness only permits evil because God can absorb it

---

59. Denys Turner, *Faith, Reason and the Existence of God* (Cambridge: Cambridge University Press, 2004), xi.
60. Dauphinais, David, and Levering, *Aquinas the Augustinian*, xxiv.

into good. Goodness, not evil, is ontologically basic. His ninth reference comes once again in a *sed contra*; it is the second time that Aquinas cites Augustine in a *sed contra* in the *Summa*, and it comes in the question whether God is altogether simple (*ST* I 3.7). As we know, Thomas argues affirmatively. Article 7 of question 3 is the culmination of the previous six articles; they argued God is not a body, nor is God distinguished between form and matter, essence and nature, or essence and *esse*. God is not in a genus and has no accidents. Only after these denials can Thomas ask the question that matters most, "Is God altogether simple?" The answer is yes, and Augustine provides the authoritative support for his answer. He begins by stating objections to God's simplicity. Composite beings come from God and are made in God's image; for us composite beings are higher than simple ones. He counters these objections with the authority of Augustine: "But contrary to this: According to Augustine in *De Trinitate* 7, God is truly and supremely simple."

Of course nearly every previous or contemporary Christian theologian to Aquinas would have provided the same answer, as would Jewish and Islamic philosophers. Thomas could have cited Plato, Aristotle, or Proclus to defend simplicity. Why Augustine? A possible answer is found in Lewis Ayres's interpretation of Augustine's teaching on simplicity. He writes,

> Thus, the idea that Augustine drew his notion of simplicity from non-Christian Platonist sources and then uses it to articulate his developing Trinitarian theology may be too simple a story. Augustine certainly does develop a notion of simplicity in the context of his non-Christian readings, but the manner in which he uses that doctrine in Trinitarian contexts may be dependent on later reading in Christian authors.[61]

What matters to Augustine matters to Thomas. It is not *that* God is simple, but *how*. None of the ancient philosophers imagined a perfectly simple *Triune* God. For Proclus, for example, simplicity had twofold significance. It is both the most and the least perfect being. Proclus states, "Whatever is simple in its being may be either superior to

---

61. Ayres, *Augustine and the Trinity*, 211.

composite things or inferior to them."[62] Although his triad, μονή-πρόοδος-επιστροφή ("abiding-procession-return"), can be found in patristic and Scholastic thought, this movement has a decisive difference in Aquinas. The first being for Proclus is "perfectly simple," but as it processes other composite and simple beings, the perfection diminishes until perfection no longer corresponds with simplicity at all. The last being is also simple, but it is a simplicity that lacks the perfection of the first being. As Proclus states, "For the last being is, like the first, perfectly simple, for the reason that it proceeds from the first alone; but the one is simple as being above all composition, the other as being beneath it."[63] Wayne Hankey argues Thomas is influenced by Proclus, and there is no reason to doubt Proclus is a "source."[64] His influence, of course, gets significantly altered when the perfectly simple first being is understood as the perfectly simple Triune God. Aquinas did not make that alteration; Augustine, Basil of Caesarea, and Gregory of Nyssa had already "transformed" divine simplicity.[65] Augustine did so because he found support for divine simplicity in Nicene Christianity's "Light from Light" and "true God from true God." Ayres states, "In the context of the divine simplicity, therefore, it becomes possible to imagine the generation of another without division, a generation which results in two who are non-identical even as they must also be one. Thus the Father is not wise because his Wisdom is with him; he is wise because he is Wisdom itself."[66] Seven centuries later Anselm parallels Augustine. Peter Lombard makes a similar argument.[67] Aquinas is not unique when he

---

62. Proclus, *The Elements of Theology*, trans. E. R. Dodds (London: Oxford University Press, 1933), proposition 59, p. 57.
63. Ibid., p. 59.
64. Hankey finds Proclus's "invention" of a system in his *Elements of Theology* as the basis for the medieval *summae*. They "recreate" it. Nonetheless, he states, "All of this is not to deny that much stands between Proclus' *Elements of Theology* and Thomas's *Summa Theologiae*." See Hankey, *God in Himself*, 8–9.
65. See Radde-Gallwitz, *Basil of Caesarea, Gregory of Nyssa*.
66. Ayres, *Augustine on the Trinity*, 226.
67. Lombard cites Augustine to argue the Trinity has no "parts," and thus God's essence cannot be considered as a genus and the persons a species. Without simplicity, the teaching on the Trinity makes no sense. See Lombard, *Sentences*, distinction XIX, 108–11.

sets forth divine simplicity as necessary to speak well of Triune processions and agency.

Divine Perfection

Thomas also draws on Augustine to affirm God's perfection and goodness (*ST* I 2.6 rep. obj. 1; I 5.4 rep. obj. 3; I 6.2, sc). Question 6, article 2, on God's goodness, once again cites Augustine in a *sed contra*. Before making his response to the question whether God is the "greatest good," Thomas states, "In *De Trinitate* 1 Augustine says, 'The Trinity of divine persons is the greatest good and is seen by the most purified minds.'" Thomas then affirms in his response that God is the *greatest* good not because God must be compared to other creatures to establish God's goodness but because God is the "first cause" of all "desired perfections." God is the first cause, however, as a "non-univocal cause." A univocal cause would require comparison, for the effect would be on a continuum with the cause. A nonunivocal cause contains the cause "in the most excellent way." What is that most excellent way? Thomas does not yet tell us, although the *sed contra* in question 6 already pointed to the Trinity as "the greatest good." Thomas returns to a similar argument in question 34, article 2 and correlates perfection once again to the Trinity. Once again, Augustine leads the way. The Triune procession of the Son and the diverse names used for him express divine perfection. Thomas writes,

> The name "Word" implies the same property implied by the name "Son," and this is why Augustine says, "'Word' says the same thing as 'Son.'" For the begottenness of the Son, which is His personal property, is signified by different names that are attributed to the Son in order to express the diverse aspects of His perfection. For the fact that He is connatural with the Father is expressed by the name "Son"; the fact that He is coeternal with the Father is expressed by the name "Splendor"; the fact that He is altogether similar to the Father is expressed by the name "Image"; and the fact that He is begotten in an immaterial mode is expressed by the name "Word." And it was impossible to find any one name to designate all of these aspects. (*ST* I 34.2 rep. obj. 3)

The simple perfection of the Son generates a multiplicity of names.

Predications and the Perfectly Simple Triune God

Thomas, like Lombard, finds his way through the thicket of predicating statements about the perfectly simple Triune God by following Augustine.[68] The difficulty with predication is that nothing in creation "perfectly represents" the processions. Thomas explains the difficulty by pitting Arius against Augustine. Arius laid out "twelve modes of generation." Each of them lacks something required for a perfectly simple Triune God. The first, the generation of a line from a point, lacks simplicity. Thomas then explains what each of the other modes lacks and concludes, "in every mode in which one thing comes from another, there is either no equality of nature or no equality of duration" (*ST* I 42.2 obj. 1). Thomas does not deny the truth of what he ascribes to Arius. He agrees that every understanding we have of generation assumes something in the mode of generation that would be inappropriate in its attribution to God. Where he disagrees is how divine predication works. He makes his point by citing Augustine, "As Augustine says in *De Verbis Domini*, there is no mode of procession among creatures that perfectly represents the divine generation, and so it is necessary to gather likenesses from many modes in order that what is lacking in one might in some way be supplied by another" (*ST* I 42.2 rep. obj. 1). As we saw with the multiplicity of divine names for the Son in question 34.2, so now we see that no single, univocal statement or definition expresses well what must be said about the perfectly simple Triune God. Simplicity cannot be reduced to a singular proposition of identity; it must be interpreted via the divine names.

Thomas draws on Augustine to explain predication in a perfectly simple Triune God. His first reference to Augustine in the treatise on divine perfections concerns how predication occurs in the divine essence and the relations. Because different terms are predicated of them, Augustine's predications could suggest the essence is not the same as the relation. He draws on two statements in the *De Trinitate*

---

68. Lombard discusses predication and Trinity at distinctions XXII–XXIV. Many of the questions Thomas answers, such as whether we can call the Father God alone, are questions he inherits from Lombard.

as objections that suggest contrary predications.[69] Thomas's response is of central importance. He has just discussed at length the divine essence. He has predicated many terms for it. Now he discusses the divine processions, and the obvious question is whether he predicates terms for the essence that cannot be predicated for the relations—does this not require an essence that differs from the relations? If this were the case, then Thomas would posit the divine essence as a subject "behind" the relations, and the two treatises on the essence and processions would not be unified. He knows divine predication cannot work this way, even though the terms used for the persons must affirm their distinction while at the same time affirming the unity of the essence. Much as he let Augustine, via Lombard,[70] set the problem up, so he looks to Augustine to resolve it. Aquinas does so by reaffirming "God's utter simplicity." He states,

> This passage from Augustine does not mean that the Paternity or any other relation that exists in God is not in its *esse* the same as God's essence. Rather, it means that the relation is not predicated in the manner of a substance, i.e., as existing in the thing of which it is predicated, but is instead predicated as being connected to another. It is for this reason that only two categories are said to exist in God. For the categories other [than substance and relation] imply a connection to that of which they are predicated, both (a) with respect to their *esse* and (b) with respect to the concept of their proper genus. But nothing that exists in God can have a connection other than the relation of identity to that in which it exists or to that of which it is predicated—and this because of God's utter simplicity. (*ST* I 28.2 rep. obj. 1)

This difficult passage requires careful exegesis, for it sets the context for how Aquinas will predicate terms for God and how he unites the treatises on God's essence and processions. The first thing that must be

---

69. Thomas first objection states: "In *De Trinitate* 5 Augustine says, 'Not everything that is predicated of God is predicated as substance. For some things, e.g., "the Father" with respect to the Son, are predicated as relations, and these are not predicated as substance.' Therefore, a relation is not the divine essence." He follows it with a second: "In *De Trinitate* 7 Augustine says, 'Everything that receives a relational predication is an entity independently of that relation (*est etiam aliquid excepto relativo*); for instance, it is a man who is a master and a man who is a servant.' Therefore, if there are relations in God, there must be something in God over and beyond the relations. But this can be nothing other than the essence. Therefore, the essence is distinct from the relations" (*ST* I 28.2).
70. See Lombard, *Sentences*, distinctions XXII and XXIII for a similar discussion.

noted is that Aquinas denies the adequacy of the category "substance" alone for the Trinity. Instead, substance and relation have been equated. Aristotle's ontology has been upended; a metaphysical transformation has taken place. It is, however, a transformation that took place at Nicea.

In this passage, Aquinas first makes a negative claim—that Augustine predicates different terms for processions such as *paternity* does not mean that its *esse* differs from God's essence. If it were otherwise, he would contradict a central claim in the question on God's simplicity that the *esse* is the essence (*ST* I 3.4). But this restatement of divine simplicity raises the question why we need a treatise on the processions at all. If the procession is the essence, why would it entail different predication for the persons and the essence? Aquinas, following Augustine, develops a second, positive claim as to why we must now predicate relations of God in a way that addresses the need for a second kind of predication. The predication of the relation is not the predication of the substance; relation predicates something as not in itself but in its relation to an other. Let us predicate that "God is F" (Father) and "God is E" (essence). The first predication is not the same as the second because the first assumes a relation F–S (Father to Son) and F,S–HS (Father and Son to Holy Spirit) that the predication "God is E" does not. "God is E" does not require the relations F–S or F,S–HS in order to make sense of it. That we have these different predications does not then logically entail either that the essence differs from the relation or that the relations are species in a genus. "God is E" does not contradict "God is F, S, and HS." Only these two categories, substance and relation, are said of God, Thomas then states, because all other categories (and he must have in mind Aristotle's other eight categories) require a difference of predication between "their *esse*" and "their genus."

This statement harks back to Thomas's discussion of simplicity, question 3, article 5, when he denied this distinction is applicable to God. The result is that even though "God is E" differs in predication from "God is–F,S, and HS," the essence is the relation, and the relation is the essence, so what is predicated of "God is E" can also be predicated of each of the persons while at the same time the persons have their own predications—the Son is not the Father is not the Holy Spirit. Simplicity safeguards these predications, while perfection safeguards that the equality of essence and person does not allow in any sense the diminishment of the essence when the Father generates (the essence does not generate) the Son, and the Father and Son process the Spirit. Only if God is perfectly simple can this Triune predication work.[71] Thomas has developed the complex tradition of the divine names.

Thomas is not Augustine. They differ in their use of terms, their method, their logical analysis, the use of Aristotle, and the role of the *imago Dei* (although the differences can be exaggerated when the *imago* is mistakenly made the controlling factor in Augustine, something Thomas did not do). These differences do not result in a revised doctrine of God for Thomas. He did not approach theology in such a truncated way. What mattered was to express as clearly and briefly what Augustine, Dionysius, John of Damascus, Anselm, Lombard, and others had already expressed—the perfectly simple Triune God. The *how* shifts and changes, but not the *what*. To put it in Thomas's language, the *modus significandi* differs. But Thomas surely thought the *res significatum* was the same. He sees this same *res* in what he learns and receives from Dionysius.

Dionysius

Who is Dionysius, and how is he related to Thomas? Is he a successful forger who hid his identity for fear that his real sources, Proclus and Porphyry, would surface and his Christian theology be called into question?[72] Thomas's use of him as an authority, then, would be

71. A similar argument is found in question 29, article 4: "Does the name 'person' signify a relation in God?" Once again Thomas draws on Augustine's *De Trinitate*, this time to argue that "person" is "the same as the essence." He states, "For in God *that which is* does not differ from *that by which it is*."

72. Sarah Wear and John Dillon interpret Dionysius as a forger. They write, "In the course of Letter 7, written to a certain Bishop Polycarp, Dionysius presents us with a scenario which sheds an ironic light on what must have been a concern to him in real life, the possible unmasking of the extent of his borrowings from the Greeks.... The passage is of interest, as betraying in Dionysius's mind a certain degree of concern as to whether his great enterprise would succeed in evading detection

something of a duping, a successful forgery that makes him unwittingly smuggle into Christian theology alien Greek metaphysical elements not easily assimilated into Christian theology. Or did he provide, as Fran O'Rourke suggests, an "autonomous role to philosophical reflection" based on causality, a trajectory that Thomas Aquinas "unified more profoundly" in his "theory of God as subsistent and absolute Being" by supplementing Dionysius's metaphysics with Aristotle's act and potency?[73] Or is he a thoroughly Christian monk, bringing together Christology, ecclesiology, and the cosmos into a hierarchical ordering based on the Christian liturgy, a liturgy radically distinct from Greek theurgy? As Alexander Golitzen has argued, "Dionysius does not believe in the autonomous human intellect. The latter is neither capable of, nor free to approach, the Godhead on its own. It requires the liturgy, the community of the Church, to form it and render it *capax dei*."[74] Golitzen fears that the Dionysius available to Thomas was a "fractured" one that was "assimilated with magisterial elegance into . . . an already well-established and secure theological *Gestalt*."[75] If O'Rourke is correct about Thomas's use of Dionysius, and Golitzen is correct about Dionysius, then Thomas's use of him could only be considered "fractured."

Andrew Louth makes a similar judgment to Golitzen's that the Dionysius available to Western medieval theology was a fractured one. He writes,

in the event, he need not have worried. He went on to become, in his assumed persona, one of the pillars of the Eastern Orthodox, and to some degree also of the Western mediaeval Church"; Sarah Wear and John Dillon, *Dionysius the Areopagite and the Neoplatonist Tradition* (Aldershot, UK: Ashgate, 2007), 131.

73. Fran O'Rourke, *Pseudo-Dionysius and the Metaphysics of Aquinas* (Leiden: Brill, 1992), xv, 204.

74. Alexander Golitzen, *Mystagogy: A Monastic Reading of Dionysius Areopagita*, ed. Bodgan G. Bucur (Collegeville, MN: Liturgical Press, 2013), 14, 18. Golitzen states, "The Dionysian κοσμος νοητος ('intelligible world') is not the realm of Platonic ideas, nor the Νους of Plotinus, nor the hypostatized categories of Proclus. At the (secondary) level of created being it is instead a cosmos or world of creatures wholly sanctified and altogether transparent to the Creator, a body or organism deriving its being from, and radiating the being of, its single head or 'cause,' the 'divinity of Jesus'" (256). Contrast this statement with that of Fran O'Rourke, "There is in Dionysius, therefore, the assumption of an autonomous activity of natural reason concerning God, although this is itself the object of divine revelation and operates moreover within the horizon of divinely established truth"; O'Rourke, *Pseudo-Dionysius and the Metaphysics of Aquinas*, 6.

75. Golitzen, *Mystagogy*, xiv.

That the heart of Denys's theology was the praise of God continued to be understood in the East. In the West, the influence of Denys was different mainly because by the time his influence was at all deeply felt—in the twelfth century—Western theology had begun to develop its own characteristic emphases (though many of them can be traced back to St. Augustine: the appreciation of inwardness for example) and the Dionysian corpus is pillaged for themes and imagery which are then used in an entirely different context, and often with a meaning quite foreign to anything Denys might have intended.[76]

But Louth, unlike Golitzen, makes Thomas the exception in Western theology: "[Thomas] read Denys with great care and attention: and whole areas of theology—the doctrine of the divine attributes, angelology, to name but two—are deeply in debt to him."[77]

Which Dionysius did Thomas find—a forger, a philosopher, a distorted version, or one fitting to the enigmatic figure Dionysius is? Thomas made a careful study of Dionysius's *Divine Names*, studying the text under Albert, recopying his course notes on that text, and writing a commentary on it sometime between 1261 and 1268.[78] Dionysius's influence on Thomas's teaching on God is significant; as we will see below, Thomas's affirmation of the perfectly simple Triune God was as much indebted to Dionysius as it was Augustine. He makes sixty-seven explicit references to Dionysius in his first forty-three questions. Nearly half of those references come in his objections (thirty). Six appear in a *sed contra*, thirteen in Thomas's responses, and eighteen in replies to the objections. As I previously noted, too much should not be made of such statistics. For even when Dionysius is cited in an objection, it is usually a misunderstanding of his position that Thomas then ameliorates. Much as we saw with Augustine, what matters most in Thomas's development of Dionysius's theology is that God is simple and perfect and that the perfectly simple God helps us understand Triune agency and vice versa.

Following Golitzen's historical ordering of the texts, Dionysius's work begins with the *Celestial Hierarchy*.[79] For Golitzen, it initiates a

76. Andrew Louth, *Denys the Areopagite* (London: Continuum, 1989), 126.
77. Ibid.
78. Torrell, *Saint Thomas Aquinas*, 1:127.

"deliberately progressive 'mystagogy'" that takes us into the "one and unique mystery, Christ." The first note Dionysius sounds in his work is divine simplicity. What is intriguing about his initial use of simplicity is its Trinitarian resonance. He states,

> "Every good endowment and every perfect gift is from above, coming down from the Father of lights." But there is something more, inspired by the Father, each procession of the Light spreads itself generally toward us, and in its power to unify, it stirs us up by lifting us up. It returns us back to the oneness and deifying simplicity of the Father who gathers us in. For as the sacred Word says, "from him and to him are all things."[80]

Romans 11:36 justifies divine simplicity. Dionysius then draws on the image of the Son as light from light to "enlighten" those who make the mystagogical journey. Ayres notes that "light from light" provided a source for Augustine's teaching on simplicity; it does the same for Dionysius. For Dionysius, divine simplicity does not identify an essence, but the "oneness . . . of the Father," and this oneness, which of course the Son shares, is what deifies.

The above passage from Dionysius draws on the Neoplatonic triad of μονή-πρόοδος-ἐπιστροφή ("abiding-procession-return"), but it does so with a decisive twist. The abiding is not a one beyond being but the Trinity. The perfectly simple Triune God is the source of the procession and the return. If divine simplicity is understood as Trinitarian, as I have argued above, then Thomas's use of Dionysius as a whole comports well with his mystagogy, for, as can be seen in chapter 1 of *The Celestial Hierarchy*, Thomas and Dionysius bring together divine perfection, simplicity, and the Triune processions as a way to resituate the Neoplatonist triad of abiding, procession, and return.

Thomas's first reference to Dionysius does not draw on divine simplicity or Trinity. It is from the *Divine Names* and affirms wisdom as

79. Golitzen suggests that the proper ordering of Dionysius's texts should be *Celestial Hierarchy, Ecclesiastical Hierarchy, Divine Names,* and *Mystical Theology,* and then the ten epistles. Golitzen bases his argument on how the ancient manuscripts come down to us as well as the sense of unity this ordering provides for the Dionysian corpus. Its unity is found in a "deliberately progressive 'mystagogy,' that is, as at once the explication of and the entry into the one and unique mystery, Christ." See Golitzen, *Mystagogy,* xxxvi.

80. *The Celestial Hierarchy,* in Pseudo-Dionysius, *The Complete Works,* trans. Colm Luibheid (New York: Paulist Press, 1987), 145.

a gift of the Holy Spirit (*ST* I 1.6 rep. obj. 3). As both Paul and Dionysius teach, wisdom is a gift, and this gift is the "first way" sacred doctrine constitutes wisdom, the other being "study." His second reference is from the *Celestial Hierarchy*, chapter 1, in which Dionysius correlates simplicity and Trinity. Thomas, however, uses this chapter to address the question whether sacred Scripture should use metaphors. He answers yes, "For God provides for all things in a way that is suitable to their nature." The authority for this affirmation is Dionysius. Thomas states, "Hence, it is appropriate for Sacred Scripture to teach us spiritual things by way of metaphors drawn from corporeal things. Dionysius makes this point in *De Caelesti Hierarchia*, chap. 1: 'It is impossible for the divine ray to illumine us unless it is enshrouded by a variety of sacred veils'" (*ST* I 1.9 resp.). For Dionysius, this "divine ray" refers to Jesus, who comes to us through the sacred veils of "beautiful odors," "material lights," "sacred discipleship," "order and rank," and the "most divine Eucharist."[81] The sacred veils are liturgical realities. Thomas neither denies nor affirms the christological and liturgical realities of the "sacred veils." He uses Dionysius's words in order to make a more general point about what is "natural" for the human person. Because "all our cognition takes its origin from the senses," to learn "divine and spiritual things" requires beginning with the senses and moving from them to the divine. This point does not contradict Dionysius, but Thomas does not reference the liturgical significance of Dionysius's appeal to the "sacred veils." Thomas makes a general epistemological point that would find as much support, perhaps more, in Aristotle than Dionysius; Dionysius makes a much more specific christological and ecclesial one. The two are not opposed, but Thomas overlooks the specific beauty of Dionysius's starting point in Christology and ecclesiology and does appear to "fracture" Dionysius's starting point—at least on a first reading that would read no further than question 1, article 9.

---

81. Ibid., 146.

Divine Simplicity and Holy Scripture

After Thomas's initial reference to Dionysius on the question of wisdom, his next four references are concerned with sacred Scripture. More specifically, they all draw on the divine presence in the sacred veils of "metaphor," "sensible figures," "figures of speech," and the "figure" of the old law. Although these references may not fit well with Dionysius's liturgical use of the terms, Thomas connects his use of Dionysius on Scripture with the importance of divine simplicity. Once Thomas draws on Dionysius's authority to argue it is appropriate for the divine to be conveyed by means of these sacred veils, his next three references to Dionysius all concern divine simplicity (ST I 3.1 rep. obj. 1; I 3.8 obj. 1; ST I 3.8 sc). In his first question on simplicity, Thomas notes the obvious objection, "Sacred Scripture attributes three dimensions to God" (ST I 3.1 obj. 1). His *sed contra* counters biblical affirmations of God's dimensionality with the Johannine claim "God is a Spirit." He then explains how reading Scripture properly and affirming divine simplicity fit together. Dionysius provides the basic contours of a mystical reading of God's "dimensionality" in Scripture. Thomas states,

> As was explained above (q. 1, a. 9), Sacred Scripture teaches about spiritual and divine things by means of likenesses drawn from corporeal things. Hence, when it attributes three dimensions to God by a likeness drawn from corporeal quantity, it is signifying the quantitative extent of His power—so that by depth it signifies His power to know what is hidden; by height it signifies the preeminence of His power over all things; by length it signifies the duration of His being; and by width it signifies the affection of His love toward all things. Or, alternatively, as Dionysius says in *De Divinis Nominibus*, chap. 9, by God's depth is meant the incomprehensibility of His essence; by His length is meant the outpouring of His power, which penetrates all things; and by His breadth is meant His reaching out to all things, viz., insofar as all things are taken up under His protection. (ST I 3.1 rep. obj. 1)

Dionysius provides Thomas a way to read Scripture that does not turn God into a mythological creature with dimensions but takes passages that could easily be misread as such and situates them within a doctrine of God fitting with the commandment not to make God into a graven image. It helps us read Scripture well so that we understand the truth is presented under "sacred veils." In fact, Dionysius makes this exact claim in his second chapter of *Celestial Hierarchy*, "I must describe the sacred forms given to these heavenly ranks by scripture, for one has to be lifted up through such shapes to the utter simplicity of what is there."[82] As author of Scripture, God is found not in the obvious visibility of what is there, but as the invisible, simple being who is its source. Thomas's use of Dionysius's sacred veils fits well the latter's correlation between simplicity and the "shapes" Scripture presents. As we shall see, this use has a profound bearing on how he speaks of God in the treatise on the persons.

A second strikingly similar claim between Dionysius and Thomas is found in Thomas's *proemium* to the question on simplicity. In chapter two of *Celestial Hierarchy* Dionysius explains how Scripture praises God through two forms of speech. The first is characterized by terms like *Word*, *Mind*, and *Being*. This first way "shows thereby that rationality and wisdom are, necessarily, attributes of God, that he is also to be deemed a true subsistence and the true cause of the subsistence of every being, and that he may also be represented as light and hailed as life."[83] The first way is more positive; it affirms God's "attributes." Dionysius does not reject this first way but finds a second way "more appropriate." It presents God's praises "in utterly dissimilar revelations." Rather than affirmation, this second way works by negation: "He is described as invisible, infinite, ungraspable, and other things which show not what he is but what in fact he is not."[84] Dionysius refers to this way as a "scriptural device." As demonstrated above, Thomas makes a similar point in his first article in question 3 on simplicity by correlating Scripture and simplicity. Scripture is a "sacred veil" through which one ascends to God's simplicity. Thomas prefaces that argument by reminding us that because we do not have a definition of God's essence, we cannot know "in what manner God

82. Ibid., 147.
83. Ibid., 149.
84. Ibid., 150.

is but rather in what manner God is not (*de Deo quomodo sit sed potius quomodo non sit*)." Although he does not cite Dionysius in this preface, his references to Dionysius's use of Scripture in the very first article after this *proemium* at least suggest that Dionysius is as much behind his claim as any philosopher, and that the warrant for it is Holy Scripture. It is, as Dionysius puts it, a "scriptural device."

Thomas returns to both *Celestial Hierarchy* and *The Divine Names* in article 8 of question 3, "Does God enter into composition with other things?" This article could be understood as his critique of an inappropriate use of Neoplatonist emanation. If *esse* emanates into beings, then it could be construed as entering into composition with them. His first objection states as much: "In *De Caelesti Hierarchia*, chap. 4, Dionysius says, 'The *esse* of all things is that which lies beyond *esse,* the divine nature.' But the *esse* of all things enters into composition with everything. Therefore, God enters into composition with other things" (*ST* I 3.7 obj. 1). Of course Thomas knows the objection is neither Dionysius nor Proclus. *The Divine Names* and *Liber de Causis* are the authorities for the *sed contra.* Both reject any "mixing" of the "first cause" with the things it causes and rules. Thomas connects this argument for simplicity with his teaching on perfection; he will use the exact same quotation in his *sed contra* when he asks whether the perfections of all things are in God.

After setting forth God's simplicity, Thomas adds perfection. Not only is God perfect but the perfection of all things is "in" God. Correlating the two is not easy. He begins with an objection. If God is simple, the perfections of things cannot be in God, because the perfections of things are diverse. This seemingly obvious objection makes good sense. The perfection of a rational creature cannot be identical to that of a nonrational one. Diversities among rational creatures would likewise entail diversities of perfection. If God is the perfection of all things, then God would require diversity in God's self, or the perfections of all things would not be in God. Perfection and simplicity stand in contradiction. Thomas begins his argument against what seems to be the compelling logic of this objection by citing the exact quotation from Dionysius and *Liber de Causis* that he previously cited in favor of divine simplicity: "But contrary to this: In *De Divinis Nominibus*, chap. 2, Dionysius says, 'Neither does anything touch Him (i.e., God) nor is there any other sort of union with Him through a mixing of parts.' Furthermore, in the *Liber de Causis* it says, 'The first cause rules all things without being mixed in with them.'" The beginning of the argument for the perfection of all things existing in God is the same as the argument for God's simplicity. What justifies simplicity justifies perfection.

Thomas then argues that the only way to make perfection consistent with simplicity is by thinking of these perfections as other than "univocal causes" (*ST* I 4.2 resp.). The perfections "preexist" in God, but because God is simple, they do not preexist as potentialities or as matter to be actualized. They exist "in a more eminent mode." What could this mean? He tells us what it does not mean by once again citing Dionysius. "Dionysius touches on this line of reasoning in *De Divinis Nominibus*, chap. 5, when he says of God, 'It is not that He is this thing and not that thing; rather, He is all things as the cause of all'" (*ST* I 4.2 resp.). God cannot be known as a being, or known by God's difference from any being. These kinds of knowledge require univocal causation; a thing standing outside a series initiates a series either as the first cause in an immanent series of causes or as a contrastive transcendent cause originating things caused but then bearing no relation to them. God as simple and the perfection of all things in a more eminent mode cannot be conceived of in terms of either of these two options. If God is *ipsum esse per se subsistens*, then we at least know that neither kind of causation grants access to knowledge of God. Perfection added to simplicity rules out both possibilities; its first function is negative. Whatever we mean by God's perfection and the perfection of all things in God, we cannot mean what we mean by the perfection of a thing itself. What, then, is divine perfection?

We know this much: simplicity and perfection, as difficult as they may be to bring together into coherent speech, must both be said of God if we agree God is "subsistent *esse*" and not a being among beings.

Language may fail to do this well, but an analogy helps point in the direction of how God is perfect and simple. In replying to the objection that they are opposed, Thomas uses an analogy we have already seen in Dionysius—the analogy of light.

> As Dionysius puts it in *De Divinis Nominibus*, chap. 5, "Just as the sun, while itself existing as a unity and shining uniformly, has within itself in a uniform way many different sensible substances and qualities, so too, *a fortiori*, all things must preexist by a sort of natural union in the cause of all things." And so things that in themselves are diverse and opposite preexist as one in God without any detriment to His simplicity.

Light comes from light without detracting or adding to it. Whatever it means to say positively that perfection and simplicity exist together, it entails at least something like that.

Language nearly fails us here. We are clearer on what we cannot say than on what we can. Here is what we cannot say: The perfections of all things in God are potentialities internal to God that God must actualize, and then those actualized potentialities enter into composition with God. Perfections are this for us, so in God they must be something more. Simplicity assists us in saying what that something more is. First, it tells us what God is not, but then it helps us ascend to the deifying simplicity God is. It does not lay hands on God through univocal causation but challenges our familiar categories. All perfection in God is God, for God is simple and eternal. The pure act God is permits diverse participations in God that are other than God, and therefore those other beings will be composites of potency and act; the latter are creatures and therefore not God. Dionysius provides Thomas with the grammar to say this as well as it can be said. Thomas explicitly uses both of Dionysius's forms of speech to affirm God is perfectly simple, and in the process neither says too much nor too little.

Thomas had raised a third objection to the claim that the perfection of all things exists in God. It too depends on divine simplicity. Having already established that God's essence is simply to be (*esse*), Thomas then suggests a hierarchy of terms that finds *esse* at the bottom.

"Living" is more perfect than "being," and "being wise" is more perfect than merely living. So we have this hierarchy:

1. being wise
2. living
3. being

Because God's essence is God's *esse*, the perfections of "living" and "being wise" would not seem to be in God. God merely is. This affirmation was at the heart of the treatise on God's essence in questions 2 and 3, so now Thomas makes a correction against a possible misunderstanding of the affirmation that God *is*. Building on the correlation between simplicity and perfection he has already made, Thomas draws once again on Dionysius's *Divine Names* chapter 5 and makes a twofold argument. When the above three terms are used in distinction from one another—*being* or *life* or *wisdom*—being is more perfect. Wisdom or life without being would be defective; they would not be. When each term would be considered in comparison to the unity of the three, a wise, living being would be more perfect than one that merely is. Because God contains all perfections, and not by way of participating in them, for that would make them greater than God, God must be perfect as a living, wise being (*ST* I 4.2 rep. obj. 3). Nonetheless it would be fitting to make *being* central if the terms are distinguished from another. That God is not only being, but a living wise being, signifies God's dynamic agency.

The Perfectly Simple *Triune God*

The correlation between perfection and simplicity moves in the direction of the Triune God. Thomas does not yet explicitly state as much, but when we see how perfection and simplicity unfold in his treatise on the Triune persons, it becomes clearer. Thomas's correlation between simplicity and perfection sets forth God as a perfection so intense that nothing can be taken away or added to God. The closest analogy is the light from the sun.[85] Not only does God contain all perfections of being within God's essence without violating simplicity, God is in God's own being a giving and receiving so intense it occurs without addition or subtraction. We previously saw how question 27, on the Triune processions, uses the terms found in questions 2–11 in order to elevate those terms to a new and more profound understanding. Whereas it might seem as though simplicity and perfection would prohibit the movement characterized by divine "procession," they actually make it more intelligible and in so doing become something more than they would have been otherwise.

Dionysius is not as prominent in Thomas's treatise on the divine persons as he was in the earlier treatise on the divine essence. Only seven out of sixty-seven explicit citations appear in the second treatise, and they all come from Dionysius's *Divine Names*. Nor is Dionysius as present in the second treatise as is Augustine. Readers should not be surprised that Dionysius appears, much as he did in the first treatise, at those places where Thomas makes reference to the language we use for God. Dionysius presents Thomas with the opportunity to address an overarching question about the language used for traditional Christian teaching on the Trinity. Should language like *person* and *notion* be employed at all, given that neither is found in Scripture? Thomas's first two uses of Dionysius make identical objections to the use of such terms. First is the objection to the use of person in question 29.

> At the beginning of *De Divinis Nominibus* Dionysius says, "In general one should not dare to say or think anything about the super-substantial and hidden divinity beyond those things which have been divinely expressed to us by the sacred declarations." But the name "person" is not expressed to us in the Sacred Scripture of either the Old Testament or the New

---

85. Another example Dionysius uses that Thomas draws on is love. He begins with an objection from Dionysius that love is ecstatic, transporting one outside oneself. God then could not be said to love because God as simple, infinite, and perfect cannot go "outside" God's self. Thomas replies to this objection, stating, "A lover is transported outside of himself into the thing that is loved in the sense that he wills the good for the thing loved and by his providence cares for that thing as for himself. Hence, in *De Divinis Nominibus*, chap. 4, Dionysius says, 'One should dare to say—and take as the truth—that even He who is the cause of all things, through the abundance of His loving goodness, goes outside of Himself in exercising His providence over all the things that exist'" (*ST* I 20.2 rep. obj. 1). Love here functions similarly to perfection and Triune processions. Its intensity is so abundant that it makes possible what is not God without taking away from God or adding to God, for one cannot add something to a perfect, infinite simplicity.

Testament. Therefore, the name "person" should not be used in the case of God. (*ST* I 29.3 obj. 1)

Then he makes an identical objection in question 32 on the use of *notion*. "In *De Divinis Nominibus*, chap. 1, Dionysius says, 'No one should dare to say anything about God beyond those things that are expressed to us in the sacred writings.' But there is no mention of the notions in the writings of Sacred Scripture. Therefore, notions should not be posited in God" (*ST* I 32.1 obj. 1).[86] Thomas's responses to these objections are nearly identical to his use of Dionysius in the question on perfection (*ST* I 4.2 resp.). For Thomas, "person" is "that which is most perfect in all of nature, viz., that which subsists in a rational nature" (*ST* I 29.3 resp.). Being, living, and wisdom are brought together into person. It is capable of self-movement and has "dominion" over its acts, but in God it is so "in a more eminent way." Thomas then responds to the first objection in question 29 by bringing together perfection and simplicity. He states, "Even though the name 'person' is not said of God in the Scriptures of either the Old Testament or the New Testament, nonetheless, what the name signifies—viz., that God is maximally a *per se* being and utterly perfect in His understanding—is asserted of God in many places in Sacred Scripture" (*ST* I 29.3 rep. obj. 1). That God is "maximally a *per se* being" is another way of saying God is simple. Here it is correlated with perfection to argue that even though the term itself is not explicitly used, what it "signifies" is. God is not mere being but a living, wise, perfect being more so than any other, who acts from who he is and not in reaction to what he is not.

The potential objection from Dionysius that only scriptural terms should be used in setting forth the Triune persons reappears in Thomas on four other occasions so that five of the seven citations to Dionysius in the treatise on the divine persons make a similar point.[87] In each

---

86. A similar use of Dionysius can be found in *ST* I 32.1 with respect to the question whether the divine persons can be known by natural reason.
87. It is found in *ST* I 32.1 resp., on whether the persons can be known by reason alone; in *ST* I 36.2 obj. 1, on whether the Spirit proceeds from the Son; and in *ST* I 39.2, on whether we should say that the three persons are "of one essence."

case, Thomas replies to these objections in a Dionysian manner; one that he established earlier when he agreed with Dionysius that Scripture should use metaphors, or what Dionysius referred to as "sacred veils" (*ST* I 1.9). Of the other four occasions, each is also found as an objection to some nonbiblical term, except for question 32, article 1, where Thomas uses it as his "response." This use is significant because it addresses not a specific term—*person, notion, procession, essence*—but the larger issue as to whether the persons can be known by natural reason. Here Thomas repeats an argument about the role of philosophy that he established in question 1, article 8 as to whether sacred doctrine uses arguments. A comparison between Thomas's response to this question with his positive use of Dionysius in question 32, article 1 illumines the place of philosophy in Thomas's theology. First his response in question 1:

> Therefore, since sacred doctrine has no science higher than itself, it disputes with someone who denies its first principles—and this by employing arguments—as long as that adversary concedes some of the things that are had by divine revelation. For example, with heretics we dispute by appealing to passages from Sacred Scripture, and against those who deny one article of the Faith we argue by appealing to another article. However, if our adversary believes nothing that has been divinely revealed, then there is no further way to prove the articles of the Faith by arguments—though there is room for answering his objections to the Faith if he offers any. For since the Faith is based on infallible truth, and since it is impossible to demonstrate the contrary of a truth, it is obvious that proofs brought against the Faith do not constitute demonstrations, but are instead answerable arguments. (*ST* I 18. resp.)

Now compare this early statement by Thomas on the role of argument to his response in question 32 on whether the persons can be known by natural reason:

> Therefore, one should attempt to prove matters of faith only through the authoritative writings and only to those who accept the authoritative writings. As for the others, it is enough to show them that what the faith teaches is not impossible. Thus, in *De Divinis Nominibus*, chap. 2, Dionysius says, "If there is someone who completely resists the writings, then he is far from our philosophy; but if he accepts the writings [*read*: the

sacred writings] as the truth, then we likewise make use of the canonical writings." (ST I 39.2 resp.)

Dionysius may not have provided as much of the content for Thomas's teaching on the divine processions as Augustine, but he has provided the basic form for how one approaches the doctrine of God. One cannot begin with philosophy and either prove or disprove what faith teaches—that the one, perfectly simple God is Triune. One can begin with what the faith teaches and use philosophy to manifest it and counter arguments that will be incapable of being demonstrations because what is certain is what is revealed in faith.

Conclusion

My presentation of Thomas's theological authorities above could easily mislead. I divided into sections what Thomas did not distinguish in his questions—his key theological authorities for the doctrine of God—Scripture, Augustine, and Dionysius. They provide the language for the perfectly simple Triune God, illuminating how we can speak of divine agency given that this is God. If for the sake of clarity my presentation misleads readers, it works against what Mark Jordan suggested is central to Thomas's de Deo. His multiple languages are so intertwined they cannot be easily untangled, nor should they be if our concern is to understand from where the language for Thomas's perfectly simple Triune God arose. He did not identify "sources" as we might. Humanism did not yet arise; there is no call ad fontes. Critical editions are not present that would have allowed him to divide up his sources and use them for a constructive theology that seeks relevance to what he assumes is the best philosophy of his day. That may be the approach of much contemporary systematic theology, but it was not Thomas's. He did not "create" a language for God or make the modern assumption that everything we have received may be outmoded and irrelevant for our unique historical moment(s), and so it must be subject to revision, if not incessant revolution. He thinks with his authorities even when he places them within his scholastic method.

The perfectly simple Triune God is not invented. It is the answer to the question "Who is God?" forged from Scripture and thinking with the ablest Christian thinkers in both the West and the East. It does not draw on something called a "metaphysics of substance" or underwrite a static God incapable of movement, love, or life. Quite the contrary, it expresses God as the perfection of movement, love, and life so that God has nothing static in God's being; there is no potency in God waiting to be activated. God's perfect simplicity entails God is the supreme actor who is an internal "movement" of the Triune persons that exceeds all the static conceptuality that creaturely movement inevitably entails. Because of this excessive activity of life and love "internal" to God, God also acts "externally" through creation and redemption. God's external operations are "personal" even while they are eternal. God is *semper eis esse dando* ("always giving being to creatures"). The *semper* demands we speak of God in terms of *infinity* and *eternity*, as Thomas noted.

The perfectly simple Triune God is a grammar to speak well of God when we know that language never univocally obtains divinity. It cannot. To assume otherwise is to make God an object in the world that could be indicated. That it is a grammar, however, does not lessen its truth, for neither is it equivocal, as if any language would do because we are primarily saying what cannot be said rather than what can. The grammar is complicated and liable to misunderstanding and misuse, but when it is understood as taking us on a "way," a journey into the always elusive subject matter of that, what, and how God is, then it will require the exercise of patience and humility. What must be said about the that, what, and how God is cannot be said in a single proposition or stipulated with a definition. If we say God is simple, then we must acknowledge how what we have said is liable to errors and difficulties, which is why it will need to be followed up with perfection. The task of speaking well of God cannot culminate in a list of attributes or properties, as if they are accidents predicated to a subject. Thomas's way directly opposes such a theological method. His method will be developed and challenged in the next few centuries. Some of those who developed it may have lost the pilgrim way that it was and forced it into a different framework. Humanism reacted against certain versions of Scholasticism, although that history is complicated.[88] Even more complex and contested is the Reformation's relationship to Scholasticism and humanism. None of these is monolithic or easily characterized. Overlap exists among them, much like Wittgenstein's city noted above. The next chapter examines how the "perfectly simple Triune God," set forth by Thomas Aquinas but forged from the church's wisdom by interpreting Scripture with the tradition, was received among Protestants. It will argue that although the locus and the content *de Cognitione Dei* shifted from Thomas to the Reformation, the content *de Deo* did not, and that matters.

---

88. For a good historical account of this complexity see Erika Rummel, *The Humanist-Scholastic Debate in the Renaissance and Reformation* (Cambridge, MA: Harvard University Press, 1995).

PART II

The Ecumenical Consensus on the Perfectly Simple Triune God

The language for the perfectly simple Triune God is a mystery to be received and lived, not a puzzle to be solved (to paraphrase Balthasar). It has been the common language of the Christian church for some time and can be found as the authorized teaching in every church that has authorized teachings. As Roger Olson and Christopher Hall note, the Fourth Lateran Council in 1215 "affirmed as dogma that the one divine substance or essence is absolutely simple (unified in every way) and never changing (unaffected by history) and that the three persons of Father, Son, and Holy Spirit are nothing more than distinct relations within the divine substance distinguished only by their differing relations of origin with regard to one another."[1] The language of "nothing more" is reductive of what the church teaches, but on the whole they are correct. It was also affirmed at the Council of Rheims in 1148.[2] It has been normative in the Roman Catholic Church since and

---

1. Roger E. Olson and Christopher A. Hall, *The Trinity* (Grand Rapids: Eerdmans, 2002), 63.
2. The teaching on simplicity was affirmed at the Council of Rheims in 1148 against a distinction Gilbert de la Porée supposedly made between God and the divine essence. Emery notes,

is present in the Roman Catholic Catechism, where it is associated with the "revelation of the ineffable name 'I AM WHO I AM.'" The divine name reveals that "God is the fullness of Being and of every perfection, without origin and end." It distinguishes God from creatures based on divine simplicity. "All creatures receive all that they are and have from him; but he alone is his very being, and he is of himself everything that he is."[3] As we saw with Thomas Aquinas, Exod. 3:14 is a central authority for God's perfect simplicity. The Reformers never questioned this foundational interpretation. It found its way into nearly every Protestant Confession. This section focuses on Protestant receptions of the perfectly simple Triune God. It also shows how the question it answers subtly shifts from "How we speak well of the mystery of the Trinity" to "How does God predestine all things to God's own glory?" Not all Protestant theologians shifted the question.

"Henceforth, the divine simplicity is imperative for all scholastic theologians: absolute identity of God and the divine essence, identity of the person and the essence; identity of the person (the Father) and the relational property of this person Fatherhood"; Gilles Emery, *Trinity in Aquinas* (Ypsilanti, MI: Sapientia Press of Ave Maria College, 2003), 11.

3. Roman Catholic Catechism, no. 213. "The revelation of the ineffable name 'I AM WHO AM' contains then the truth that God alone IS. The Greek Septuagint translation of the Hebrew Scriptures, and following it the Church's Tradition, understood the divine name in this sense: God is the fullness of Being and of every perfection, without origin and without end. All creatures receive all that they are and have from him; but he alone is his very being, and he is of himself everything that he is." Notice that in the Roman Catholic Catechism, this traditional knowledge of God is not placed in what can be known of God by certainty. For Catholicism, such knowledge is only that God is. Knowledge that God's essence is God's existence comes from the revelation of the divine name in Exod. 3:14.

3

Aquinas's Legacy among the Reformers

This chapter makes two arguments. First, the Reformers never questioned or revised the perfectly simple Triune God. The Reformers affirmed the traditional answer that Thomas inherited from his authorities. Some were and others were not directly drawing on Thomas for this answer. If they did not inherit the answer directly from him, they inherited it from similar authorities, especially Augustine. The second argument traces a shift in the use of the answer from the late Middle Ages through the Reformation and into early modernity. The shift occurs because of debates among and within Catholics and Protestants about divine power and predestination. Simplicity now functions first to explain God's relation to creation rather than first referring to God's essence in a speculative theology. Rather than rendering intelligible the Triune persons, divine simplicity now primarily defines God's relation to creation through an eternal decree. This shift makes God's "external" operation of power too essential to God's being, rendering it as the foundation for God's relation to creatures rather than that foundation emanating from the divine processions. Once power and will become identified as God's essence, then the logic of predestination appears impeccable. If God is simple,

God's acts of will are identical to his essence. The eternal decree to create and redeem is an act of will and is thus eternal, simple, and immutable. The result for Reformed theologian John Owen is God eternally decrees the salvation of the elect and the damnation of the reprobate. Any other conclusion, he stridently insists, cannot express the perfectly simple God. The concluding section of this chapter will assess whether this conclusion is necessary from Thomas's answer. Before arriving at that discussion, however, a discussion of the reception of Thomas's answer among the Reformers is necessary. That discussion consists of two parts:

1. What did the Reformers know of Thomas?
2. How did their answers to the question "Who is God?" correlate to Thomas?

The Perfectly Simple Triune God among the Reformers

To speak of "the Reformers" will raise historians' suspicions. Speaking of "the Reformers" is akin to speaking of "the Scholastics" or "the humanists." While such terms are on occasion necessary locutions, they can only be inadequate generalizations. Differences among German, French, Italian, English, and Dutch Reformers were as significant as differences among Protestants, humanists, and Scholastics. Easy lines of demarcation cannot be drawn among the latter because of the differences present in the former. Reformers in Italy drew on different authorities from those in France or Germany.[1] The Italian Augustinians, Vermigli and Zanchi, like the later British Thomas Barlow and John Owen, as well as the Dutch Jacob Arminius, were familiar with the work of Thomas Aquinas in a way Calvin was not.

Not only does the term *Reformer* carry geographical differences, but

---

1. As Asselt and Dekker have noted, "The pioneers of Reformed scholasticism, the former Augustinian monks Petrus Martyr Vermigli (1500–1562) and Girolamo Zanchi (1516–1590), came from this North-Italian tradition—which was more scholastic than the humanist French Reformed theology"; Willem J. van Asselt and Eef Dekker, eds., *Reformation and Scholasticism: An Ecumenical Enterprise* (Grand Rapids: Baker Academic, 2001), 22.

it also has chronological ones. The early Reformers bore similarities and differences with the later development of Protestant orthodoxy. Richard Muller has set forth a periodization of its development that has gained acceptance among Reformed historians. After the early generation of Reformers, he suggests we should think in terms of three eras. The first is "early orthodoxy" (1565–1640). This era includes the death of second-generation "codifiers" of the Reformation and the "promulgation of the great national confessions of the Reformed churches" (1559–66) to the closing of the Thirty Years' war and the death of major figures who "formulated" the confessions. Muller refers to this time as "the era of the confessional solidification of Protestantism."[2] The second era is that of "high orthodoxy" (1640–1725); it is more polemical and more intentionally dependent on the medieval era.[3] "High orthodoxy" is followed by "late orthodoxy," the post-1725 period when Reformed theologians began "searching for different philosophical models" and became less bound to the confessions. "Internecine polemics" and "deconfessionalization" characterize this third stage.[4]

What Did the Reformers Know of Thomas?

Given the geographical and chronological differences among Reformed theologians, asking the question how the "Reformers" received Thomas's answer will be something of an artificial inquiry. No single category called the "Reformers" can be identified, so no single answer to that question is possible. Some Reformers were acquainted with Aquinas's texts, and others were not. Luther claimed to know his work and offered harsh critiques of aspects of it. Calvin rarely cited Thomas. Philipp Melanchthon (1497–1560) lumped Thomas in with "the Scholastics." He criticized Scholasticism for producing "men like Thomas, Scotus, Durandus, the Seraphic and the Cherubic doctors, and all the rest—a progeny more numerous than the Cadmean brood."[5]

2. Richard Muller, *Post-Reformation Reformed Dogmatics*, vol. 1, *Prolegomena to Theology*, 2nd ed. (Grand Rapids: Baker Academic, 2003), 31.
3. Ibid.
4. Ibid., 32.

Melanchthon did not single Thomas out as the problem, but he did place him as a member of "the scholastic system," for him a problematic genus.

Melanchthon's one reference to Thomas in the *Loci* refers to him as a Pelagian. He states,

> In Hieronymus [St. Jerome] we find two passages which are often quoted and which sound as if they contradict one another. They are old rules which were given in different councils. This first one is: "Cursed be all who teach that God's law can be kept without grace." This is quite right and was directed no doubt against Pelagius and similar Pharisaical teachers, such as the monks and papal teachers like Thomas, Scotus, and many others who have spoken in the same heathenish way, saying that we can entirely keep God's law in our hearts and in external works, without the aid of the Holy Spirit. In other words, they are saying that man can merit forgiveness of sins with such works. These lies and blasphemies should be known, condemned and execrated.[6]

Thomas would, of course, be quite surprised to discover he taught such a thing; Melanchthon cites no source.

A key difference between Thomas and Melanchthon is their respective approaches to "heathenish" knowledge. For Melanchthon, the "heathen," that is to say pagan philosophers, possess, as do all humans, a "natural light" that allows them to know many things about God and morality. The heathens, Melanchthon states, "know a great deal—that God is an omnipotent, wise, and just Lord who created everything—but not where he may be found, nor if he will hear our cries." Such an acknowledgment is not decisively different from Thomas's affirmation that they know God in part, after a long time, and with many errors, but Melanchthon is more suspicious about the usefulness of "heathenish" knowledge. He fears that it, along with Islamic knowledge, could violate the first commandment. Melanchthon unites knowledge and proper worship. If knowledge of God does not entail proper worship, then it is not knowledge of God.

---

5. Cited in Erika Rummel, *The Humanist-Scholastic Debate in the Renaissance and Reformation* (Cambridge, MA: Harvard University Press, 1995), 141.
6. Philipp Melanchthon, *On Christian Doctrine, Loci Communes 1555*, trans. and ed. Clyde L. Manschreck (New York: Oxford University Press, 1965), 66.

This correlation is found in his lengthiest article in the *Loci*, "On Divine Law," in which he offers commentary on each of the Ten Commandments. The first commandment unites knowledge and worship. Melanchthon writes, "The first and highest command is the most necessary, for God created angels and men to have knowledge of the true God, to be like him, to acknowledge, invoke, praise and love him, and to know that he truly gives us life, wisdom, righteousness, nourishment and all good things."[7] If Melanchthon has less of a place for philosophical knowledge of God than Thomas in his theology, it is because he associates knowledge of the true God with keeping the commandments; neither can be done by nature. Revelation and grace are necessary.

Calvin (1509–1564) could also decry the "Scholastics," but as Arvin Vos and Richard Muller point out, his critique was localized to the nominalist Scholastics found at the Sorbonne.[8] His attack on them, states Muller, is "a rather pointed and precise attack *not* on the older scholastic tradition but on a strain of contemporary scholastic theology viewed by Calvin as especially problematic in view of its extreme nominalism."[9] The problematic view, found among the nominalism of the Sorbonne Scholastics, was a sharp distinction between God's *potentia absoluta* and *potentia ordinate*.[10] While this distinction is found in Thomas, it was not distinguished as sharply as it was among the Sorbonne Scholastics. Thomas was not Calvin's "scholastic" foil. Vos notes that Calvin would have known Aquinas "best as the author of a commentary on *The Sentences*—one among many—rather than as a major theologian in his own right."[11] He finds only two explicit references to Aquinas in Calvin's *Institutes*. Neither concerns metaphysics or the doctrine of God; Calvin challenges Aquinas in his "definition of free will" (*Institutes* 2.2.4) and "meriting glory" (*Institutes* 3.12.9).

---

7. Melanchthon, *On Christian Doctrine, Loci Communes 1555*, 89.
8. Arvin Vos, *Aquinas, Calvin and Contemporary Protestant Thought: A Critique of Protestant Views on the Thought of Thomas Aquinas* (Washington, DC: Christian University Press, 1985), 38–39.
9. Richard Muller, *The Unaccommodated Calvin* (New York: Oxford University Press, 2000), 52.
10. Ibid., 47.
11. Vos, *Aquinas, Calvin and Contemporary Protestant Thought*, 39.

Martin Luther had harsh words for Thomas that could easily influence readers into thinking he rejected Thomas's theology outright. His rejection of Thomas, however, arose because he associated Thomas with Aristotle, and he rejected the strict Aristotelianism among some sixteenth-century Thomists. In his *A Prelude to the Babylonian Captivity of the Church* Luther referred to Aristotle as the "Church of Thomas."[12] Luther thought the Scholastics misunderstood Aristotle and the implications of his philosophy for theology. In his letter "To the Christian Nobility" in 1520 he advises the nobility not to use Aristotle's *Physics, Metaphysics, On the Soul,* or *Ethics* in their curriculum. Both the *Ethics* and *On the Soul* he described as "evil." Luther writes, "The book of *Ethics* is the same [as *On the Soul*]; worse than any other book, it goes straight against the grace of God and the Christian virtues."[13] In his own day and since, Luther was accused of not understanding Aristotle or Aquinas well. He countered such an impression, stating, "Nobody can say that I talk too much, or accuse me of knowing nothing. Dear friend, I know well what I say; I know Aristotle as well as you and your sort, I have lectured and heard lectures on him with more understanding than St. Thomas or Scotus."[14]

Luther did not reject Aristotle outright. He wrote, "I would gladly see Aristotle's books of logic, rhetoric, and poetics retained."[15] He rejected Aristotle's understanding of creation. Graham White makes the important observation that Luther rejected Aristotle's works dealing with the world of things but not those dealing with language.[16] For Luther, Aristotle could not understand the soul or creation because he lacked an adequate understanding of God; he could, however, provide an adequate account of language. Luther's semantic theory drew on those who drew on Aristotle. His objections to Thomas then were often objections to Thomistic theologians' use of Aristotle. These objections did not result in any significant variations on Thomas's answer to the

12. Luther, "Pagan Servitude of the Church," in John Dillenberger, ed., *Martin Luther: Selections from His Writings* (Garden City, NY: Doubleday, 1961), 265.

13. Cited in Graham White, *Luther as Nominalist* (Helsinki: Luther-Agricola-Society, 1994), 320.

14. Ibid.

15. Luther, "Letter to Christian Nobility," cited in White, *Luther as Nominalist*, 321.

16. White, *Luther as Nominalist*, 322.

question "Who is God?" Otto Hermann Pesch notes that Luther, unlike Aquinas, did not provide a specific treatise on God. Nonetheless, he suggests, all the elements of Thomas's doctrine of God are present in Luther, and he rightly states, "Luther even took a positive position on the question whether God can be known by the intellect."[17] Luther, Melanchthon, and Calvin were explicit that the doctrine of God was not at issue in their concerns. Nowhere do they offer a criticism of the perfectly simple Triune God, and when they set forth the doctrine of God, their work assumes the scholastic teaching on it.

Luther made explicit references to Thomas and claimed to understand his work; Calvin made fewer references and made no apology that he understood him. As was noted above, Calvin most likely knew Thomas primarily as a commentator on Lombard's *Sentences*. Richard Muller argues that the early Calvin seemed unaware not only of Thomas but of much of medieval theology. "At an early stage in his development Calvin evidences no knowledge of major scholastic theologians like Aquinas, Scotus, Occam, Gregory of Rimini, or Pierre d'Ailly, and, indeed, no knowledge of the thought of John Major."[18] Calvin would evidence such knowledge later in his theological vocation, but Scotus and Gregory of Rimini would be more influential on him than Thomas.[19] Nonetheless, comparisons between Calvin's theology and Aquinas's have been made and strong similarities affirmed. While acknowledging that Thomas was not a major influence on Calvin's theology, Arvin Vos shows how Calvin's theological differences with Thomas are more terminological than substantive.[20]

---

17. Otto Hermann Pesch, OP, *The God Question in Thomas Aquinas and Martin Luther*, trans. Gottfried G. Krodel (Philadelphia: Fortress Press, 1972), 16.
18. Muller, *Unaccommodated Calvin*, 44.
19. Contra Bowsma, Muller argues that Calvin is better compared to Gregory of Rimini or Duns Scotus than Aquinas; Muller, *Unaccommodated Calvin*, 80.
20. In a very thorough and careful analysis of the relation between Calvin and Aquinas that questions the Reformed analytical school's interpretation of a strong difference between them, Arvin Vos states that Calvin's "disagreement with Aquinas is more a matter of terminology than of substance"; Vos, *Aquinas, Calvin and Contemporary Protestant Thought*, 2. His analysis does not focus on the doctrine of God but on the relationship between faith and knowledge. Vos writes, "Without doubt, the most important disagreement between the two concerns faith and knowledge: Is faith a knowledge of God or is it not? Calvin says it is; Aquinas denies it. I would like to suggest, however, that the disagreement is a matter not of substance but of terminology—specifically, that they have in mind different meanings when they use the verb *to know*" (3).

If first-generation Protestant theologians such as Luther, Melanchthon, and Calvin were not indebted to Thomas for their doctrine of God, other Reformers were. Peter Martyr Vermigli and Girolamo Zanchi were well aware of his work and incorporated it into their theology. Their use of Thomas predates the Arminian and Socinian debates within Protestantism. After those debates, second-generation Reformed theologians such as Barlow and Owen could look to Thomas's work as a significant source to challenge what they saw as movements worse than Catholicism, Arminianism.[21] Owen was a devout Trinitarian, opposing the Socinians in his *Vindiciae Evangelicae.*

Barlow and Owen explicitly drew on Thomas's work against other Protestants. Ironically, some of these Protestants, such as Arminius, also knew well and built on Thomas's theology in presenting the very positions Barlow and Owen rejected. Nonetheless, Reformers, humanists, and Scholastics had varied familiarity with his specific texts, and for good reason. Aquinas was not yet the authority in the early part of the sixteenth century that he would become later. Thomas was canonized in 1323, but he was not declared doctor of the church until 1567 at the Council of Trent.[22] The sixteenth century witnessed a renaissance of Thomas's work, and Protestant theologians were not only influenced by that renaissance; they contributed to it.[23] But this

---

21. Carl Trueman acknowledges how influential Thomas was on Owen, especially in his metaphysics, natural theology, theological epistemology, doctrines of providence, and election. He states, "What is clear in all of this is that the thought of Aquinas, particularly as articulated in the First Part of the *Summa Theologiae* and developed by the later Dominican and Thomist tradition, is extremely useful to Owen from the earliest time of his career as a source of argumentation for defending Reformed understandings of God and his sovereignty against Jesuit and Arminian attacks"; Carl R. Trueman, *John Owen: Reformed Catholic, Renaissance Man* (Aldershot, UK: Ashgate, 2007), 23.

22. Charles Anderson states that Thomas was declared doctor only when Trent "affirmed as normative that part of ancient and medieval Christianity which could be read in the light of the teachings of Thomas Aquinas"; introduction to Pesch, *God Question in Thomas Aquinas and Martin Luther*, v.

23. Thus Richard Muller states, "Rather than view Protestant scholasticism as a borrowed theological style—as a style of exposition taken over from Catholic thinkers of the Middle Ages and sixteenth century—we should, perhaps, be ready to recognize the continuity of scholasticism, Protestant and Catholic, and to recognize Calvinist Thomists like Vermigli and Zanchi as Protestant participants in the sixteenth-century revival of Thomism and Aristotelian scholasticism that is usually credited, almost exclusively, to their Catholic contemporaries, Cajetan, Bañez, de Sylvestris, and de Victoria"; Richard Muller, *God, Creation, and Providence in the Thought of Jacobus Arminius* (Grand Rapids: Baker Book House, 1991), 276.

renaissance was at its beginning in the sixteenth century; it was not yet as foundational as it would be for Catholicism after Leo XIII's *Aeterni Patris* in 1879, which made Thomas the philosophical antidote to modern errors.

As influential as Aquinas was on Protestant orthodoxy, he was more so on the Anglican tradition. There were many Caroline divines who knew and drew on Thomas's work.[24] Arthur McGrade acknowledges that Richard Hooker (1554–1600) "sympathized with the sixteenth-century Thomistic revival."[25] Thomas's theology influenced his understanding of the eternal law as the rational basis for all law.[26] Hooker's doctrine of God assumed the traditional answer.[27]

John Norris (1657–1712) wrote a treatise, *Reason and Revelation*, that takes Thomas's question 15 from the *prima pars* as its basis. He begins that work, as did Aquinas his, with the claim that God is the "most intelligible as the most intelligent being in the world." But this poses problems for us. In a sense, God is too knowable, for God is the brightness of light that blinds. "God is too intelligible to be here clearly understood by an imbody'd understanding; and too great a light hinders vision as much as darkness."[28] Revelation will be necessary.

Although little evidence is present that John Wesley ever did an in-depth study of Aquinas, he urged Methodist preachers to study Thomas. He also drew on Aristotelian moral philosophy primarily through his teaching of Gerald Langbaine's *Philosophiae Moralis Compendium, Juventutis Academicae Studiis.*[29] Wesley admonished the clergy to study Aquinas and metaphysics in his 1756 "Address to the Clergy."[30] He admonished the clergy to ask themselves:

24. See H. R. McAdoo, *The Structure of Caroline Moral Theology* (London: Longmans, Green, 1949).
25. Arthur Stephen McGrade, introduction to Richard Hooker, *Of the Laws of Ecclesiastical Polity*, ed. Arthur Stephen McGrade (Cambridge: Cambridge University Press, 1989), xxi.
26. Richard Hooker, *Of the Laws of Ecclesiastical Polity*, in *The Works of that Learned and Judicious Divine Mr. Richard Hooker*, arranged by John Keble (Oxford: Clarendon Press, 1887), 58–59.
27. Hooker, *Of the Laws of Ecclesiastical Polity*, bk V, li, 2, 3.
28. John Norris, *Reason and Religion; or, The Grounds and Measures of Devotion Considered from the Nature of God and the Nature of Man in Several Contemplations*, 2nd ed. (London: Samuel Manship, 1693), 5.
29. See D. Stephen Long, *John Wesley's Moral Theology: The Quest for God and Goodness* (Nashville: Kingswood Books, 2005), 46–52.
30. The best, and most thorough, account of the relationship between Wesley and Aquinas can be found in Edgardo A. Colón-Emeric, *Wesley, Aquinas & Christian Perfection: An Ecumenical Dialogue* (Waco, TX: Baylor University Press, 2009).

> Do I understand metaphysics; if not the depths of the Schoolmen, the subtleties of Scotus or Aquinas, yet the first rudiments, the general principles, of that useful science? Have I conquered so much of it, as to clear my apprehension and range my ideas upon proper heads; so much as enables me to read with ease and pleasure, as well as profit, Dr. Henry More's Works, Malebranche's "Search after Truth," and Dr. Clarke's "Demonstration of the Being and Attributes of God?" Do I understand natural philosophy?[31]

Wesley's familiarity with Thomas was at best indirect. He studied more carefully Henry More, Nicolas Malebranche, and Samuel Clarke. When Wesley does set forth God's attributes, however, he does so in terms very similar to Thomas's. He too affirmed without question the traditional answer.

The above discussion of major Protestant theologians' reception of Aquinas is not intended as an exhaustive review of the influence of Thomas's work on Protestantism. It does suggest that the earliest Protestant thinkers, especially Melanchthon and Luther, tended to be the most suspicious of Aquinas. Calvin was rather indifferent, but later generations affirmed, modified, and adopted many aspects of Thomas's teaching. An examination of the content of their teaching demonstrates its similarities.

How Did Their Answers to the Question Who Is God Correlate to Thomas?

What is most striking among all the Protestant theologians under examination is how closely they follow, intentionally or unintentionally, the basic structure of Thomas's teaching on God when they present such a teaching. The first generation of Reformers did not produce anything as thorough or beautiful as the doctrine of God in Thomas's first forty-three questions in the *Summa*. They did not develop treatises on "God and his attributes" and correlate them to the Triune persons, as did later Protestant theologians such as Franciscus Junius, Lambertus Danaeus, Girolamo Zanchi, and Jacob Arminius. This

---

31. Wesley, "Address to the Clergy," in *Works of John Wesley*, ed. Thomas Jackson (New York: Carlton & Porter, 1872), 10:483.

lack of a well-developed treatise indicates neither that they were uninterested in the doctrine of God nor that they did not offer such a doctrine when it was important to do so, but the first generation of Reformers explicitly stated that this teaching was not a cause for offense. Revising the doctrine of God was never part of the Reformation, and central to my argument in this work is that it should not be now. As Richard Muller has argued, "It is worth recognizing from the outset that the Reformation altered comparatively few of the major *loci* of theology: the doctrines of justification, the sacraments, and the church received the greatest emphasis, while the doctrines of God, the trinity, creation, providence, predestination and the last things were taken over by the magisterial Reformation virtually without alteration."[32]

Between 1536 and 1538 Martin Luther wrote the Schmalkald Articles to set forth what mattered most in his dispute with the pope in response to Pope Paul III's call for what became the Council of Trent. The Schmalkald Articles are Luther's "theological testament" set forth in articles under three parts: "the lofty articles of the divine majesty," "the articles that pertain to the office and work of Jesus Christ, to our redemption," and then an assortment of articles that could be discussed, according to Luther, with "learned" and "reasonable" people of conscience, but not with the "pope and his kingdom."[33] The second and third parts lay out how Luther and the signatories to the Schmalkald Articles believe that the "pope and his kingdom" have diverged from the one, true, holy, and catholic church into a kingdom in which "money, honor and power are everything."[34] The first part, on the "lofty articles of the divine majesty," is the shortest. It contains four articles on the Holy Trinity. Luther presents them in traditional form and concludes, "These articles are not matters of dispute or conflict, for both sides confess them. Therefore, it is not necessary to deal with them at greater length."[35] The Schmalkald Articles were

---

32. Muller, *Unaccommodated Calvin*, 39.
33. The term "theological testament" comes from William R. Russell. See Martin Luther, *The Schmalkald Articles*, trans. William R. Russell (Minneapolis: Fortress Press, 1995), viii.
34. Ibid., 16.

included in the basic confessions of the Lutheran Church, *The Book of Concord*, along with the three ecumenical creeds (Apostles', Nicene, and Athanasian), the Augsburg Confession, Luther's Small and Large Catechism, and other treatises. The teaching on the perfectly simple Triune God was never contested in any of these treatises. At a similar time in October 1536, John Calvin engaged in his Lausanne Disputation. Bernard Cottret refers to it as Calvin's "entry into public life."[36] Calvin defended some Reformers against the charge by Pierre Caroli that they rejected the Trinity. Calvin likewise affirmed the traditional teaching on God. He wrote, "We recognize, in the essence of God, eternal, spiritual infinite ... the Father and the Word without confounding the Father with the Word or the Word with the Spirit."[37] The reason that neither Luther nor Calvin developed as extensive a treatise on God as did Aquinas is quite simple: they did not think it was necessary to do so. They did not find fault with the traditional answer as to who God is.

The structure of the major Protestant confessions demonstrates the similarity between Thomas's teaching on God in the *Summa* and Protestant teaching. The only exception to this structure can be found among the seventeenth-century Socinians' Racovian Catechism and Biddle's Twofold Catechism. These teachings are outliers within Protestant theology. They did seek to revise the traditional answer, and only in them do we find an explicit rejection of divine simplicity. The major confessions did no such thing. The Augsburg Confession, the Anglican (and Methodist) Articles of Religion (1571), and the Westminster Confession (1646) all follow Thomas's basic pattern, first setting forth the divine essence, identifying it with perfect simplicity, and then discussing the persons and relations. The first article of the Anglican Thirty-Nine Articles states, "There is but one living and true God, everlasting, without body, parts, or passions; of infinite power, wisdom, and goodness; the Maker, and Preserver of all things both visible and invisible." To confess God "without body, parts, or

---

35. Ibid., 5.
36. Bernard Cottret, *Calvin: A Biography*, trans. M. Wallace McDonald (Edinburgh: T&T Clark, 2000), 123.
37. Ibid., 124.

passions" is to affirm simplicity. To confess God's infinite goodness is to affirm perfection. Once establishing God's essence and operations, it then affirms, "And in unity of this Godhead there be three Persons, of one substance, power, and eternity; the Father, the Son, and the Holy Ghost."[38]

The Westminster Confession follows a similar pattern. Following the pattern by Thomas more closely than the Anglican Thirty-Nine Articles, it first lays out the need for Holy Scripture (chapter 1) and then sets forth the divine essence and processions. It begins, "There is but one only, living, and true God, who is infinite in being and perfection, a most pure spirit, invisible, without body, parts, or passions; immutable, immense, eternal, incomprehensible, almighty, most wise, most holy, most free, most absolute," and concludes, "In the unity of the Godhead there be three persons, of one substance, power, and eternity: God the Father, God the Son, and God the Holy Ghost: the Father is of none, neither begotten, nor proceeding; the Son is eternally begotten of the Father; the Holy Ghost eternally proceeding from the Father and the Son."[39] The Augsburg Confession draws on the Council of Nicea explicitly to set forth a similar teaching:

> Our Churches, with common consent, do teach that the decree of the Council of Nicaea concerning the Unity of the Divine Essence and concerning the Three Persons, is true and to be believed without any doubting; that is to say, there is one Divine Essence which is called and which is God: eternal, without body, without parts, of infinite power, wisdom, and goodness, the Maker and Preserver of all things, visible and invisible.

It too then follows this statement on the divine essence with one about the processions, "yet there are three Persons, of the same essence and power, who also are coeternal, the Father, the Son, and the Holy Ghost. And the term 'person' they use as the Fathers have used it, to signify, not a part or quality in another, but that which subsists of itself."

---

38. John Wesley amended the first article by removing *passions* from "without body, parts or passions." Why he did so remains obscure, but having left "without body or parts" in Methodism's twenty-five articles he ensured that they too affirm simplicity.

39. Orthodox Presbyterian Church, "Confession of Faith," www.opc.org/wcf.html#Chapter_02.

The Belgic Confession (1618) also begins by affirming God's essence as perfectly simple. Its first article states, "We all believe with the heart and confess with the mouth that there is one only simple and spiritual Being, which we call God; and that He is eternal, incomprehensible, invisible, immutable, infinite, almighty, perfectly wise, just, good, and the overflowing fountain of all good." Unlike the above-mentioned confessions, which then move straight to the Triune persons, however, the Belgic Confession interposes six articles on theological epistemology, beginning with "By what means God is known to us (article 2)," before confessing the three persons in article 8. The Second Helvetic Confession (1566) does not explicitly mention simplicity, although it is implied in the affirmation of its third chapter that "God is one in essence or nature, subsisting in himself, all sufficient in himself, invisible, incorporeal, immense, eternal."

Why did these confessions not only affirm the content found in Thomas's answer but also the form in which it was presented? They were not explicitly following him, and yet these confessions follow a very similar pattern: first is the divine essence and then the procession of the persons. One obvious answer is found in the Augsburg Confession. They are all, like Thomas, following the pattern laid out in Scripture and at the Nicene Council. Melanchthon among others makes explicit that the reason for the shape of the confessions is first Holy Scripture, because God reveals God's oneness in the Old Testament and persons in the New, and second the Council of Nicea. The Protestant confessions do not have separate treatises on the *de deo uno* and *de deo trino* based on Counter-Reformation divisions between nature and grace or reason and faith but reflect an older reason for the shape of Thomas's teaching on God, the divine economy in the Old and New Testaments. Zanchi will be explicit about both following Thomas and the reason for it.

The Canons of Dort (1618–19) are an aberration to the common shape of Protestant confessions. They do not cite "simplicity"; they correlate God's nature to the doctrine of election and the eternal decree in the eleventh article: "Just as God is most wise, unchangeable, all-knowing, and almighty, so the election made by him can neither be suspended nor altered, revoked, or annulled; neither can God's chosen ones be cast off, nor their number reduced." These canons are not a confession and should not be considered as setting forth the Reformed doctrine of God. They presume other confessions. The canons intervene in the debate over predestination with the Arminians. However, it is significant that they correlate the nature of God with election and the eternal decree and nowhere make mention of the Triune persons. The relation between God and creation has been mediated by the eternal decree more than the Triune persons. As we have seen, Thomas stated in principle the latter must be done, but his own practice did the former.

The Augsburg Confession, the Westminster Confession, and the Anglican and Methodist Articles of Religion share a common authority in Philipp Melanchthon (1497–1560), who has been called the "first systematic theologian of the Protestant Reformation."[40] Melanchthon begins his 1555 version of the *Loci Communes* much as Thomas began his *Summa*. His first treatise is "Of God," and the second is "Of the Three Persons." He never cites or refers to Thomas in these two articles; nonetheless, Melanchthon's teaching on God's essence is similar to Thomas's. Melanchthon states, "God is not a physical being, as heaven and earth and other elements are; on the contrary, he is a spiritual being, omnipotent and eternal, unmeasurable in wisdom, goodness and righteousness, one who is true, pure, independent and merciful."[41] The authority for his teaching is John 4:4, "God is a spirit." He identifies "spirit" with the *ousia* or "being" of Nicea and states, "being is rightly understood as the Greek word *ousia*, which is used often in the Church; it means something that definitely exists in and of itself, and is not

---

40. See Clyde Manschreck's introduction to the Library of Protestant Thought edition of Philipp Melanchthon, *On Christian Doctrine, Loci Communes 1555* (New York: Oxford University Press, 1965), vii. Manschreck states, "While it is almost impossible specifically to trace ideas in history, Melanchthon's genius in the Augsburg Confession passed over into the Thirty-nine Articles of the Church of England, and thence into the Twenty-five Articles of Methodism, as well as influencing the Synod of Dort, 1618, and the Westminster Confession, 1648" (xx). He notes that Queen Elizabeth I "memorized large portions" of Melanchthon's *Loci Communes*, and Henry VIII "commanded instruction" in them (xx).
41. Melanchthon, *On Christian Doctrine, Loci Communes 1555*, 7.

dependent on some other foundation as a contingent thing is."[42] He then affirms divine simplicity without using the term. He states, "This also should be realized: that in God, power, wisdom, righteousness, and other virtues are not contingent things, but are one with the divine Being." The positive use of this teaching on divine simplicity is that it distinguishes God as Creator from creation. Melanchthon argues, like Thomas, that God differs from creation because creaturely attributes are not identical to a creature's essence as God's attributes are identical "with the divine Being." He finds divine simplicity in Genesis 1 and states, "*Because* God created all things, he is *not created*." He also has a negative use for divine simplicity. It counters Valentinians and others of their ilk (whom he does not name) who separate God's "virtues" from God's being, turning God into a composite.[43]

Melanchthon then moves from God's "unified" essence to the divine processions. Although he clearly draws on what amounts to simplicity to set forth the divine essence, he does not use it to explain the processions. Instead, he cites Ps. 115:3 as the consequence of simplicity, "Our God does whatever he pleases," and then states, "*i.e.* he is independent, self-subsistent and unconstrained; he is not bound to creatures."[44] Thomas would agree that God is not bound to creatures and that this is an implication of simplicity. However, there is a shift in emphases on two points. First, Melanchthon has already begun to address the relationship between God and creatures in terms of the divine essence alone, something Thomas avoided. Second, Melanchthon primarily uses simplicity to account for divine sovereignty rather than Trinity. However, Melanchthon has offered a speculative theology that has no bearing to creation. The so-called Melanchthonian epistemology in which we only know God as God is "for us" is not present in his speculative teaching.

Despite subtle differences, who God is for Melanchthon is nearly identical to who God is for Thomas. Why is their teaching so similar when there is no direct causation? Common authorities provide an

42. Ibid., 8.
43. Ibid.
44. Ibid., 9.

answer. Melanchthon explicitly appeals to Scripture and the Nicene Creed as the basis for the order and content of his teaching. In his dedication to the *Loci* he states,

> And such true teachers do not invent new or peculiar doctrines about God; instead they stay close to the unadulterated [*einigen*] meaning, which God himself has revealed through the words which are found in the writings of the prophets and apostles and in the creeds. The entire office of preaching, which God has ordained for public assemblies, is to present to the people these and no other writings, except the writings of the prophets and apostles, and the creeds, and thus unfold, as in a grammar, the true meaning of the words, what God is called, what created things are, and what such terms as body, spirit, person, law, sin, gospel, promise, faith, grace, justification, and worship mean.[45]

The similarities emerge from the "grammar" found in Scripture and the creeds. In his foreword he states, "God himself has given us the most fitting order in the writings of the prophets and apostles. He puts his doctrine in the form of a story."[46] Melanchthon's point is that the "order" of God's unified essence followed by the Triune persons follows the narrative order of Scripture; it is founded on the relation between the Old and New Testaments. He finds the same order in the Nicene Creed. Like Aquinas, Melanchthon also draws his teaching from Augustine. Their authorities are similar, although the influence of Dionysius is not present in Melanchthon's work as it is in Zanchi.

Luther is often credited (or faulted) for revising the traditional answer. His Christology, it has been argued, required revisions to the doctrine of God, particularly with respect to God's essence. The Lutheran *communicatio idiomatum* draws the human and divine natures into such a unity that divine impassibility, immutability, and by implication simplicity are called into question. Because of this new Christology, Protestant theologians are tempted to reject or revise the traditional answer and reconceive the doctrine of God. David Luy addresses this putative "divergence" from the tradition for which Luther is credited.[47] He acknowledges that if the christological

---

45. Ibid., xliii.
46. Ibid., xlvi.

divergence were correct, then it would entail "a massive reconceptualization of the doctrine of God."[48] Luy, however, questions the extent to which Luther's "modern interpreters" read into Luther their own rejection of "classical accounts of the doctrine of God" because they assume they are more dependent on "Greek specification of divine attributes" than the biblical narrative.[49] Luy takes us through the disputations in which Luther supposedly rejects the traditional answer and demonstrates how Luther continues much that is present in the medieval tradition.

Luther's work, like that of his forebears, assumes a complicated Christology of supposition. The acting subject in Christ is the person. The person always acts secundum quid, that is to say, according to the manner unique to each nature. Although all other persons act in a single nature, the person Christ always acts in both natures. As Luy notes, "when Luther speaks in terms of human properties being ascribed to 'divinity,' he is expressing the point that the person of Christ, who is truly divine, is the attributive object to which all predicates are rightly assigned; and that, in this sense, one may rightly say that God descended, receives gifts, suffers, is crucified, dies, and so forth."[50] What matters here, of course, is the qualification "in this sense." Luther is not arguing the divine nature suffers, changes, or is composed; he is arguing the single, acting subject Jesus suffers, changes, and is composed but always secundum quid. There is little that is divergent from, or revisionary to, the medieval theological tradition in his argument. Luther also affirms the traditional answer.

Luther introduced new emphases in theology. He emphasized the role of the Holy Spirit in providing knowledge of the Trinity. He cited as a central text for the Trinity the transfiguration, when the Father says, "This is my Son . . . listen to him" (Matt. 17:5).[51] The new language

47. David Luy, *Dominus Mortis: Martin Luther on the Incorruptibility of God in Christ* (Minneapolis: Fortress Press, 2014).
48. Ibid., 3.
49. Ibid., 47.
50. Ibid., 138.
51. See the *Promotionsdisputation* of Georg Major and Johannes Faber (Dec. 12, 1544). "1. So the Father wished to put to rest all disputations over articles of faith when He said concerning God His own Son: 'Listen to this one!' [Matt. 17:5]" (198).

of the Holy Spirit provided knowledge of the Trinity.[52] Luther also disagreed with Lombard's teaching that the divine essence does not generate. Thomas agreed with Lombard, but the difference here could be one of semantics. Luther thought that the biblical, Nicene, and Augustinian teaching of "God from God" and "Light from Light" meant that the essence did generate, but it did so on a theory of predication that distinguished absolute from relative terms. The essence as essence does not generate; that would entail a fourth person behind the three in the Trinity, something Lombard sought to avoid and the reason simplicity was given dogmatic status. The essence as essence does nothing because the essence as essence is not the acting subject. Because each Person is the essence, however, the essence generates relatively. So, *in this sense*, Luther argued the essence generates. His argument is nuanced.

Luther's teaching on God is scattered throughout his corpus. Late in life he focused on the doctrine of the Trinity; that focus not only posed no challenge to the traditional answer that God is the perfectly simple Triune God, but it also developed it with logical thoroughness. His teaching can be found among his late disputations between 1543 and 1545, the *Promotionsdisputation* of Erasmus Alberus (Aug. 24, 1543), of Georg Major and Johannes Faber (Dec. 12, 1544), and of Petrus Hegemon (July 3, 1545).[53] In the Alberus disputation Luther begins with a clear, explicit affirmation of divine simplicity: "1. Sacred Scripture teaches that God is most simply one and, as they say, most truly three

---

52. As Helmer notes, Luther's emphasis on the "new" can easily cause readers to miss how medieval his theology is. "Although Luther seems to maximize a novel insight regarding the pneumatological source of theological language, his focus reflects what his theological predecessors had already acknowledged. For Aquinas, Scotus, Ockham and Biel, the Trinity is not accessible by natural reason. It is the subject matter of revelation"; Christine Helmer, *The Trinity and Martin Luther: A Study on the Relationship between Genre, Language and the Trinity in Luther's Works (1523-1546)* (Mainz: Verlag Philip von Zabern, 1999), 268.

53. See Helmer, *Trinity and Martin Luther*. Helmer's work demonstrates how important the Trinity was in Luther's theology. She distanced Luther studies from the "neo-Kantian paradigm" that had identified it by making epistemology its central concern. She writes, "For Luther scholars working within the neo-Kantian paradigm, the reduction of Luther's understanding of God to Christology is a function of privileging the cross as the epistemically accessible location of the divine self-disclosure" (17). Helmer shows the inadequacy of this epistemological paradigm. Luther's teaching on the Trinity can be found at the following places in his collected works (among others): WA 26, 500, 27; WA 50, 197, 2–3; WA 46, 436, 7–12; WA 41, 270, 3.6; WA 36, 184, 17–18; WA 17/I 278 6.7.

distinct persons."[54] As with Aquinas, Zanchi, and Arminius, Luther draws on divine simplicity in order to predicate divine persons without introducing composition in God. Having affirmed divine simplicity and unity, his next two statements refer to the Triune persons: "2. Each of these persons is the whole God, beyond which there is no other God. 3. Nevertheless, one cannot say that any one person alone is God."[55] Divine simplicity establishes the rules for how we must speak of the relations between each person and "the whole God," even though the logic for such speech is counterintuitive. How can God be "most simply one" and "most truly three"? Having established what must be said, Luther uses different qualifiers to explain how it can be said. "*Each*" person is God but "*any one person alone*" is not God. The language matters. Luther explains, "6. It is a different thing to say, 'one person is all of God' and 'one person alone is the one God.'"[56] Luther's approach to the Trinity carefully spells out how divine simplicity and Trinity are logically reconciled.

Luther continues this line of thinking in the *Promotionsdisputation* of Georg Major. Once again he begins with divine simplicity and unity. "7. This unity of the Trinity (as we say it) is a greater oneness than that of any creature, or even of mathematical unity." Here Luther could have cited Aquinas to make his point. In the *tertia pars*, Thomas wrote that the union of divine persons "surpasses numerical unity" because it is self-subsisting and not by participation. Because the unity of divine and human nature in the incarnation is in the Second Person of the Trinity, it too "transcends numerical unity" by reason of the person, but not the human nature.[57] Luther's position is identical to that of Aquinas. Having affirmed divine unity, Luther then moves to the Triune persons in his next two affirmations: "8. Nevertheless at the same time this unity is a trinity, or a divine threeness of distinct persons. 9. So that whichever of these persons you please is itself

---

54. *Promotionsdisputation* of Alberus in Dennis Bielfeldt, Mickey L. Mattox, and Paul R. Hinlicky, *The Substance of the Faith: Luther's Doctrinal Theology for Today* (Minneapolis: Fortress Press, 2008), 192.
55. Ibid., 192, 193.
56. Ibid., 193.
57. *ST* III. 2.9 rep. obj. 1.

the whole divinity, even if no other one is there." Here again the qualifiers *whole* and *alone* explain how the affirmations are not a logical contradiction.[58]

Luther makes an affirmation that Thomas might not be able to affirm. Luther writes, "11. This distinction of persons is so strong that only the person of the Son assumed human being."[59] Thomas would not object to this statement as it stands. It is true and most fitting, Thomas states, that only the person of the Son assumed human nature. But Thomas asks a speculative question Luther did not. Could the Father or Holy Spirit have assumed human nature? His answer is complex and ranges over the eight articles in the third question of the *tertia pars*. He begins by asking whether it is fitting for a divine person to assume human nature. It would seem unfitting because nothing could be added to the simple unity of the divine nature, but to assume something is being added to the divine nature with the incarnation, Thomas argues, misunderstands divine infinity. It is not a quantity to which anything can be added or subtracted. Each person is infinite, and thus the assumption of a human nature by a divine person adds nothing to the person.[60]

Thomas makes a distinction early on that is essential for his argument; this distinction assumes the teaching on divine simplicity and its relationship to Trinity for its viability. The assumption of human nature only occurs through a person. Only a person properly acts, but the power (the operation) by which the person acts is the divine nature. So the *principium actus* is the divine nature or essence by which the person acts to assume that which is not the nature, but its *terminus* is the person. This means that the unity of the two natures in Jesus is the full divine essence and the human nature. However, the divine nature qua nature does not assume humanity; the person does. Thomas states that normally a nature is not a *principium quo agens agit* ("a principle by which an agent acts"), but in God because the person is

---

58. "10. And nevertheless it is true, no person alone is the divinity, as if the others were not"; *Promotionsdiputation* of Georg Major in Bielfeldt, Mattox, and Hinlicky, *Substance of the Faith*, 199.
59. Ibid., 200.
60. *ST* III 3.1 rep. obj. 1.

the essence the *quod est* ("the divine essence") and *quo est* ("the person who acts") is the same.[61] For this reason the *actum assumentis* proceeds from the divine power and is common to all three persons, but the *terminum assumptionis* only belongs to a person. This distinction leads Thomas to affirm the possibility that the Father or Spirit could assume human nature because they are also each the divine essence, and here is where he may differ from Luther.

This argument is an example of the *potentia absoluta* in Thomas's work. Given his speculative theology, he is willing to make claims about what God could have done even if it is not what God has done. For Thomas, the two are not opposed. As the previous argument demonstrates, it is only from what God has done that the basis for speculating what God could have done is known. Nonetheless, he concludes this discussion by asking whether it is more fitting that the Son of God be incarnate than the Father or Spirit, and he must say yes, for that is how the divine economy has in fact worked. Thomas then explains that the incarnation of the Son as the "Eternal Word" is more fitting because the Son is the "exemplar of creation," fulfills the predestination of creatures as "sons" [and daughters] of God, and counteracts the first sin of desiring knowledge of God that is false (see Gen. 3:6) with true knowledge of God.[62] Thomas would seem to agree with Luther that only the Son assumed human nature, but he raises and answers a question Luther did not ask: because God is perfectly simple in three persons, is it possible that the Father or Spirit, both of whom are the divine essence, could have assumed human nature? He answers that it is possible, although what God does is most fitting. Aquinas and Luther do not disagree, but Aquinas is more open to speculative questions than Luther on this point. We will see in later chapters that this difference holds great significance for modern theologians. To assume that any of the persons could have been incarnate becomes a sign of the failure of the traditional answer and a reason for revision.

While Luther, like many Protestant theologians, disagreed with

---

61. *ST* III 3.2 obj. 3 and rep. obj. 3.
62. *ST* III 2.8. resp.

Thomas on speculative theology, he agreed with him on natural theology. Based on Rom. 1:19, Luther assumed that all people have some knowledge of God.[63] Like Aquinas, however, he acknowledges this knowledge is limited.[64] What can be known of God via natural theology will always be partial and need correction and perfection by revealed knowledge.[65] God is simple, but as with Aquinas, simplicity alone does not do much until it is drawn on to set forth how it helps us understand the Triune relations.

Calvin likewise taught a twofold knowledge of God; we know God from creation and from Scripture, but like every Christian theologian he finds the latter more certain. He states, "We have taught that the knowledge of God, otherwise clearly set forth in the system of the universe and in all creatures is nonetheless more intimately and also more vividly revealed in his Word."[66] Calvin asks whether what we know from creatures is consistent with Scripture and concludes that it is, but the more "intimate" and "vivid" knowledge is found in the revelation of God's name. He cites Exod. 34:6–7, when God passes before Moses and proclaims God's name: "Jehovah, Jehovah a merciful and gracious God, patient and of much compassion, and true, who keepest mercy for thousands, who takest away iniquity and transgression" (Vulgate). He then comments on the text, finding in it some key traditional attributes: "Here let us observe that his eternity and his self-existence are announced by that wonderful name twice repeated. Thereupon his powers are mentioned, by which he is shown to us not as he is in himself, but as he is toward us: so that this recognition of him consists more in living experience than in vain and

---

63. *Promotionsdisputation* of Alberus, "28. His own past always is, his own future always has been, his own present always has been and will be, that is, eternal." "35. St. Paul says rightly in Romans I: 'The knowledge of God is manifest to all people, that is, his eternal power and divinity'" (196).

64. *Promotionsdisputation* of Alberus, "36. But this knowledge is obscure and partial (although the knowledge of faith is also in its own way partial), as a line touches the whole sphere but at a point, and thus does not comprehend the whole thing" (197).

65. As Helmer notes, "Although Luther seems to maximize a novel insight regarding the pneumatological source of theological language, his focus reflects what his theological predecessors had already acknowledged. For Aquinas, Scotus, Ockham and Biel, the Trinity is not accessible by natural reason. It is the subject matter of revelation"; Helmer, *Trinity and Martin Luther*, 268.

66. Calvin, *Institutes of the Christian Religion*, vol. 1, ed. John T. McNeill, trans. Ford Lewis Battles (Philadelphia: Westminster, 1960), 97.

high-flown speculation."[67] The powers are "kindness, goodness, mercy, justice, judgment and truth."[68]

A significant difference from Thomas in Calvin's work, as we also saw above in Luther, is his eschewal of the speculative theological task. This eschewal is often more in theory than in practice, for Calvin finds speculative results from what he claims is a practical affirmation. Take for instance his affirmation above that the divine name provides knowledge of God's eternity and self-existence. For this reason Richard Muller notes:

> Thus, the absence of any extended treatment of such topics as natural theology or the divine essence and attributes from the *Institutes*, together with Calvin's frequent attacks on excessive speculation, ought not to be interpreted as implicit denials on Calvin's part of the legitimacy of those topics. In certain cases, this kind of interpretation of the *Institutes* has been thrust back upon the commentaries to the loss of the larger content of Calvin's thought.[69]

Muller points to Calvin's commentary on Exodus for the legitimacy of the traditional teaching.[70] In his *Harmony of the Last Four Books of Moses*, Calvin exegetes the divine name, "I am who I am" or "I will be who I will be." Unlike Aquinas, Calvin takes care to examine the tense of the verbs and finds the future tense to signify not only eternity but also "the perpetual continuance of duration." He does not explicitly use the term *simplicity* in his exegesis of the divine name, but he uses the traditional terms. God is "from himself" (*sit a seipso*) and thus eternal. He gives *esse* or *subsistere* to all creatures, but nothing "common to others" is predicated of him. Calvin acknowledges that the philosophers, and especially Plato, affirmed divine eternity. He does not find fault with their philosophical presentation of it. They "magnificently discussed" (*magnifice disserunt*) God as τὸ ὄν. They did

---

67. Ibid., I.X.1, 97.
68. Ibid., I.X.1, 98.
69. Muller, *Unaccommodated Calvin*, 115.
70. Ibid., 54: "First, Calvin's reading of Exodus 3:14, both in the *Institutes* and in his commentary on the text, falls precisely into the traditional, 'essentialist' reading of the text and indicates Calvin's continuity with both the patristic and the medieval past: God's 'eternity and self-existence are announced by that wonderful name,' declares Calvin in the *Institutes*."

not, however, "apply its use" (*suum usum accomodant*). Here again we see Calvin's emphasis on the practical theological task. What the name provides Moses is the assurance that God's power and rule will allow him to be victorious.[71]

Muller recognizes Calvin is more reticent to engage in metaphysical speculation than a theologian like Aquinas. He writes, "To be sure, Calvin does evidence caution about metaphysical speculation concerning the tetragrammaton that was not always present, in either the earlier or the later exegetical tradition."[72] Calvin cautions that too much should not be made of the divine essence, but rather exegetes should focus on God's works. "I do not approve of the subtle speculations of those who think the name of God means nothing else but God himself. It ought rather to be referred to the works and properties by which he is known than to his essence."[73] This statement appears to conflict with what he wrote in his *Harmony of the Last Four Books of Moses*, in which he spoke about God's essence, but the two works are connected in that Calvin focuses on what we can know of God by what God has done for us. Consistent with his opposition to the Sorbonne Scholastics and their strong distinction between God's *potentia absoluta* and *potentia ordinate*, Calvin eschews speculation on an absolute divine power separate from the divine economy. Calvin does not eschew discussing God's power. As cited above, Calvin interprets the benefits of the divine name revealed to Moses as the assurance of God's power and rule to make Moses victor over Pharaoh and the Egyptians.

Shifting the Question the Traditional Answer Answers

Calvin is logically consistent in affirming divine simplicity. It

---

71. *Futurum verbi tempus legitur Hebraice, Ero qui ero: sed quod praefenti aequipollet, nisi quod designat perpetuum durationis tenorem. Hoc quidem satis liquet, Deum sibi uni asserere divinitatis gloriam, quia sit à seipso, ideoque aeternus: & ita omnibus creaturis det esse, vel subsistere in Calvin*, "Harmony of the Last Four Books of Moses," in Commentarii in quatuor reliquos libros Mosis, in formam harmoniae digestos Amstelodami: Apud viduam Ioannis Iacobi Schipperi, 1671. In *The Digital Library of Classical Protestant Texts*, Alexander Street, at alexanderstreet.com, 261–62.
72. Muller, *Unaccommodated Calvin*, 153.
73. Ibid., 154.

challenges the nominalist distinction between God's absolute and ordained power and strongly correlates what God has done with how we can know who God is. This leads, as it did with Aquinas, to a doctrine of predestination, but Calvin places more emphasis on it than did Thomas. Salvation and reprobation are both the direct result of God's will. This new emphasis (not a new teaching) will be taken up by Peter Vermigli and John Owen. The emphasis on predestination subtly shifts how simplicity functions. It now figures less in helping to render intelligible the mystery of the Trinity and more to assert the consistency between the divine will and the outcome of salvation. It has been relocated to explain the relationship between God and creation. The importance of distinguishing between the divine relations and the God-creation relation becomes diminished.

Peter Martyr Vermigli (1499–1562) was an Italian Augustinian prior to becoming a central figure in the Reformation, especially in England. He was well trained in Thomism, as was his student Girolamo Zanchi.[74] John Donnelly finds Vermigli representing "the transition from the charismatic early Reformers to the 'scholastic' development of their doctrine in the next century."[75] Unlike Zanchi, Vermigli does not offer an extensive treatise on God and the divine attributes. Like Luther and Calvin, he assumes it is not a disputed theological locus.

Vermigli's doctrine of God contains nothing unusual; it is the traditional answer. He uses it for the purposes of theological epistemology, natural theology, and the doctrine of predestination. Although he never denies its usefulness for the Trinity, he makes no explicit connection between simplicity and the divine relations.

Vermigli, like many Reformed theologians, emphasizes theological epistemology, and simplicity is put to use for that purpose.[76] In his

---

74. John Donnelly suggests that "Dominicans and Thomists" were primarily responsible for Vermigli's training during his time in Padua. He was not attracted to Scotus. See John Patrick Donnelly, SJ, *Calvinism and Scholasticism in Vermigli's Doctrine of Man and Grace* (Leiden: Brill, 1976), 18, 24.

75. John Donnelly, SJ, *The Peter Martyr Reader* (Kirksville, MO: Truman State University Press, 1999), 2.

76. Donnelly notes, "As philosopher and theologian, Martyr gave theology of knowledge (epistemology) precedence over speculation on being (ontology)" (ibid., 107).

Commentary on Judges he affirms simplicity for the sake of denying "sensible knowledge" of God. He writes,

> I hold that the nature, substance, and essence of God cannot be grasped by the senses. In fact whatever is perceived by the senses has not affinity with God but is far removed from him. In order to be named, qualities that belong to a certain genus and are regarded as accidents arouse sensible knowledge. Since God is completely uncompounded [*simplicissimus*] he is not subject to such qualities and, therefore, cannot be known by the senses.[77]

Such an apophatic use of simplicity places him solidly in the tradition. He also acknowledges simplicity was taught by the "pagan philosophers."[78] Vermigli had a robust natural theology.

Like Melanchthon, Vermigli's theology was presented in terms of loci, although in his case it was done posthumously. His 1576 *Loci Communes* consists of four "classes," each containing between fifteen and twenty loci. The first class is on the knowledge of God the Creator, the second on God the redeemer. Vermigli's *Loci* does not discuss at length who God is but focus on our knowledge of God and what God has done for us. His first locus under the first class, our knowledge of God the Creator, is on the "end of good and evil" for Christians. What matters first for Vermigli is the *telos* that characterizes creatureliness. This focus in his first locus exhibits a strong Aristotelian influence. He follows the locus on humanity's *telos* with a second locus, "On the natural knowledge of God from created things," in which he defends a natural knowledge of God. He begins, as do almost all Reformed accounts of natural theology, by referring to Paul in Rom. 1:20. Vermigli then affirms, "every truth is from God. For it does not arise from us. But what is from God is a twofold judgment" (*omne verum a Deo esse. Non enim ex nobis nascitur. Sed quomodo sit a Deo, duplex est sententia*). The twofold judgment that gives us knowledge of God is from creatures and from Scripture. The knowledge from creatures is available to non-Christian philosophers such as Aristotle and Plato, whom Vermigli

---

77. Ibid., 109.
78. "Even the pagan philosophers discovered that all composition is against the nature of God" (ibid., 110).

calls God's "organs and instruments" although not "authorities." The natural knowledge of God, he suggests, is "proleptically" placed in creation and refined through time. The Greeks and the Jews offer anticipations and representations of God, but such knowledge for Vermigli is knowledge that comes "through the law" rather than through God himself. In an argument similar to Thomas's proof from the efficient cause, Vermigli argues that Plato and Aristotle are able to observe "a series of causes and their connections with their effects" and conclude from this that there cannot be an infinite regress. The series extends to some first cause, and that must be God. He says this knowledge of God is most beautifully taught by Plato, Aristotle, and Galen.[79] For Vermigli, pagan philosophers know that God is and that God is simple. In the next century, when the Socinians will challenge divine simplicity, John Owen will use a similar argument against them—even the "pagans" know God is simple. Unlike Vermigli, Owen will make this argument in a polemical context, for the seventeenth century finds Christian theologians for the first time rejecting simplicity based on an overly literal interpretation of Scripture. Vermigli, however, does not argue against anyone in his natural law argument for simplicity. It is not affirmed in a polemical context in which it has been called into question.

He also puts the traditional answer to work to defend his doctrine of predestination. In the second article of his treatise on predestination, he addresses the question whether predestination has a "cause." The cause could be something in the creature to merit election or even the work of Jesus in the economy. Vermigli denies both as the cause of predestination and states it has no cause at all other than the divine will.[80] The tacit reason behind his argument is simplicity. He writes,

Just as predestination is the purpose or will of God, and the same will of

---

79. Vermigli, *Loci Communes*, Londini: Excudebat Thomas Vautrollerius typographus, 1583. 4–5 in *Digital Library of Classical Protestant Texts*, Alexander Street at alexanderstreet.com.

80. "Christ and his death is the principal and chief effect of predestination"—"Therefore, we deny that Christ is the cause of predestination in terms of his humanity or death, although he is the beginning and cause of all good things, which come to us from the purpose of God"; Peter Martyr Vermigli, *Predestination and Justification*, trans. and ed. Frank A. James III (Kirksville, MO: Truman State University Press, 2003), 39.

God is the first cause of all things and is one and the same with the essence of God; therefore, it is impossible that it should have a cause. We do not deny that sometimes some reason for God's will may be evident. Although such may be called reasons, they should not be called causes, especially efficient causes.[81]

Predestination is a work of the divine will prior to creation. Because God has no composition, God's will and God's essence are one. Nothing outside that causes predestination and reprobation. They both result from an eternal decree.

He makes a similar argument in his *Commentary on Samuel*, once again using simplicity to buttress predestination:

God is completely single-minded [*simplicissimus*]; yet for the sake of our capacity we say that there are two faculties in him, Understanding and Willing. God understands and sees everything; not only that, but he also wills everything. At this point I bring no needless discussion whether the will of God precedes the understanding, or the understanding the will. Any who wish to know such things I send to Scotus and Thomas. This power and faculty of which I speak refers to quality [Aristotle, *Meta* V.14.1020a33], since it is a natural power. The difference is that by this power God directs all things that are or will be. Even more, he also leads them to their ends. To which end? Whatever is appropriate [*ad congruous*]. They are appropriate which his purpose determines. The cause is the power or faculty; the effect is that things are brought to their proper ends. Here we include all kinds of causes that can be assigned in this matter.[82]

If, as Muller suggests, the doctrine of predestination did not divide the Reformed Scholastics from their medieval predecessors, Vermigli's own assessment of the relation between the two is at best mixed. He agrees with "the Scholastics" that reprobation is not predestination. He writes, "I said before that I was of the same mind with the Scholastics, that is to say, the reprobate are not predestined." But he disagrees as to the reason that they give for their common teaching. The Scholastics teach that God cannot will sin. Vermigli's reasons are more nuanced. He writes, "This is their reason, that predestination directs not only to the end, but also to the means which lead to the end.

---

81. Ibid., 25.
82. Donnelly, *Peter Martyr Reader*, 195.

Since sins are the means by which men are damned, they argue that God cannot be the cause of sins."[83] He agrees, speaking "correctly and properly"; God is not the cause of sins. But then he continues,

> Certainly, if we speak correctly and properly, God cannot be said to be the cause of sins, yet we cannot utterly exclude him from the government and ordering of sins, for he is the cause of those actions which to us are sins; although since they are from God, they are simple justice, for God punishes sins by sins. Therefore, sins as punishments are laid upon men by God, as by a just judge.[84]

God is not the cause of sin per se, but God does use sin as a means to punish sinners for their sins, and in that sense Vermigli is willing to go so far as to state that God wills sin.[85]

In a similar discussion on predestination in his *Commentary on the Book of Judges*, Vermigli follows Thomas's argument in question 23, article 5 of the *prima pars*.[86] He uses similar examples to Thomas's and then cites him explicitly. He states,

> But we have absolutely no explanation which we are able to bring for individual election. Thomas Aquinas has a wonderful analogy. When a builder builds a house, he has in front of him bricks of exactly the same shape and quality, and will be able to give a general reason as to why he places some of then on the highest part, but others on the lowest part. Because when he builds a house he must lay a foundation, then put on the gable and roof. But if you were to ask him, "Why do you put that stone on the foundation but another on the top?" He would doubtless be able to give you no other answer than that it was according to the judgment of his will, since in theory all were viewed in the same way.[87]

---

83. Vermigli, *Predestination and Justification*, 23.
84. Ibid.
85. Taking up the accusation that his teaching makes God will sin, he writes, "To solve this dilemma, they should first recall that it cannot be denied that God in a sense wills or (as some others say) permits sin." He argues something similar later in this work reflecting on the sin of Adam. "Thus it is evident that in a sense God willed that sin and was in a way its author, even though it was not the punishment for a previous sin" (ibid., 45, 53).
86. Frank A. James III states, "Aquinas was a more rigorous predestinarian than many admit, but the differences between his predestinarian vision and that of Vermigli suggest that Aquinas, although an intellectual contributor, is unlikely to have been a primary source. Gregory of Rimini, however, drew out the full implications of Augustine's doctrine of predestination and concluded with the most rigorous doctrine of double predestination in the later Middle Ages"; introduction to Vermigli, *Predestination and Justification*, xxx.
87. Donnelly, *Peter Martyr Reader*, 178.

Vermigli recognizes Thomas as an explicit source for his teaching.[88] He concludes,

> Thus, as to why this person and that person should be chosen individually by the Lord but another should be forsaken into depravity and cursing, no sort of explanation can be given other than the free purpose of God.[89]

He acknowledges humans are not bricks but suggests Paul's image of "earthen vessels" is similar to Thomas's reasoning. Like Thomas and Calvin, he prohibits too much speculation as to the reasons for election and reprobation. "At this point you will say that not enough allowance is being made for human reason, and we confess this openly. Furthermore, we add that it is impossible that the purposes of God should be perceived or approved by human reason, since the human spirit does not perceive the things of God. Indeed, they rather seem to him to be the greatest foolishness and futility."[90]

Vermigli taught the traditional answer to the question "Who is God?" God is the perfectly simple Triune God.[91] He put the teaching on divine simplicity and perfection to uses we also saw in Thomas Aquinas— theological epistemology and the doctrine of predestination. However, a shift in emphasis has occurred. The latter has become the primary question for the traditional answer. Thomas presents a question on predestination; Vermigli presents a treatise. He has made arguments Thomas did not make. God has decreed from eternity not to have mercy on some of God's creatures, the ones God hates.[92] The answer remains the same, but the question has changed. It now

---

88. Vermigli and Zanchi also explicitly affirmed, and claimed to defend, Calvin on predestination. Vermigli and Zanchi followed Calvin on predestination. In May 1554, Vermigli wrote to Calvin, "I want you to know that this sadly grieves me, along with others, that they [the Lutherans] spread very foul and false reports concerning the eternal election of God against the truth and against your name. . . . We here, especially Zanchi and I, defend your part and the truth as far as we can"; Vermigli, *Predestination and Justification*, xxiv.

89. Donnelly, *Peter Martyr Reader*, 178.

90. Ibid., 179.

91. Donnelly notes how this teaching emerged from Aristotle in Vermigli's teaching. "The Aristotelian concept of accidents plays an important part in Martyr's philosophy and theology. God's immutability and impassibilty can be deduced from his simplicity, that is from the fact that God, being simple, has no accidents"; Donnelly, *Calvinism and Scholasticism*, 73.

92. "God delivers some out of this misery; those he is said to love. Others he passes over, and these he is said to hate, since he has not had mercy on them, so that by their just condemnation he might declare his anger against sins and also his justice"; Vermigli, *Predestination and Justification*, 25.

responds to the question of God's eternal will, an act of power, that decrees even before the divine economy who will be saved and who damned. Vermigli does not explicitly use simplicity to set forth the mystery of the Trinity, although he nowhere denies this use. He emphasizes the connection between simplicity and predestination to such an extent that he paves the way for the Synod of Dort. His student Girolamo Zanchi (1516–1590) also emphasizes the relationship between simplicity and predestination, further contributing to a Reformed theology that leads to Dort. But Zanchi still has the older use of simplicity present in his treatise on God and the divine attributes. He makes the connection between simplicity and Trinity explicit.[93]

Zanchi was converted to Protestantism under the ministry of Vermigli "in the Lucchese monastery at S. Frediano" and "notes that he heard Vermigli lecture on Romans in Lucca."[94] While Calvin, Luther, and Vermigli did not develop full-length treatises on the doctrine of God, Zanchi offered one of the more thorough treatises on God and God's "nature" in either the Protestant or Catholic tradition. He followed Calvin and Aquinas in teaching a doctrine of predestination, but Zanchi was better equipped than Calvin to address the specific locus of the doctrine of God. He was not as averse to speculative theology. In the second book of his *De Natura Dei*—"*De Natura Dei in Genere*," he explicitly makes Thomas's argument that divine simplicity helps make sense of the Triune relations because it allows theologians to speak of real relations without implying composition.

Zanchi cites Thomas in forty-one passages in his *De Natura Dei*. One of those citations sets forth the relationship among divine perfection, simplicity, and the divine relations that shows Zanchi to be a faithful interpreter of Thomas, perhaps better than the Counter-Reformation tradition that divides his work between a *de deo uno* known by philosophy and a *de deo trino* known by revelation. Zanchi recognizes that the pattern in Thomas's teaching is that of Nicea: the one essence

---

93. Donnelly writes, "There is, therefore, a line running from Martyr through Ursinus and Zanchi to the Synod of Dort in 1619 which made the extreme interpretation of predestination normative for Reformed orthodoxy"; Donnelly, *Calvinism and Scholasticism*, 191.
94. James, introduction to Vermigli, *Predestination and Justification*, xx.

is the persons, and each person is the essence. Simplicity ensures that this mysterious teaching does not imply composition. Zanchi states this clearly and cites Thomas as an authority. He writes,

> This is the use of the doctrine of the perfection of God: Of course because he is most perfect, he is necessary being, as he is in himself and in his unique simple essence, and the relations by which the persons are distinguished; which relations, however, establish no composition in God. The reason for this is, of course, that the relations in God are not accidents. For accidents are not able to apply to God, because he is most perfect. And yet they [the relations] are not nothing; for they are real relations because the persons are really distinguished. What therefore are they? As Thomas said, they really are the essence itself, but differ from it by a certain reason, by which reason it would be that one person is not the other; yet without any composition in God.[95]

With Zanchi we see that the traditional answer finds a home within an established Protestant thinker. He too will follow Calvin and Vermigli in their doctrine of predestination, but he sees more clearly than they that the "use of the doctrine of perfection" and simplicity is in a speculative theology. Before it can be used to address the relationship between God and creation, it answers who God is. This insight into Thomas's teaching was not always preserved in either Roman Catholic or Protestant theology. The polemical context between and within both traditions obscured the use of the doctrine. For instance, John Owen (1616–1683), one of the more faithful representatives of the traditional teaching, makes for an interesting contrast to Zanchi in the use of simplicity. His faithfulness to the perfectly simple Triune God is unsurprising. Owen studied Aquinas with his tutor at Queen's College, Oxford, Thomas Barlow, who emphasized Thomas's work and the commentary tradition on it in his "basic theological reading list."[96]

---

95. *Et hic est usus doctrinae de perfectione Dei: nempe, quia perfectissimus est, necessum esse, ut in eo sit & unica simplex essentia: & relationes, quibus distinguantur personae: quae tamen relationes, nullam in Deo statuunt compositionem. Ratio est, propterea quòd, relationes in Deo, non sunt accidentia. Accidens enim in Deum cadere nequit: quia perfectissimus est. Neque sunt nihil. Sunt enim relationes reales: quia personae realiter distinguuntur. Quid igitur sunt? secundum rem, ut loquitur Thomas, idem sunt cum ipsa essentia: sed ratione quadam, ab ea differentes: qua ratione fit, ut una persona non sit alia: sine ulla tamen in Deo compositione.* In *De Natura Dei*—"De Natura Dei in Genere" (Neustadt an der Weinstrasse: Typis Matthaei Harnisii, 1590). First edition 1577, 137 in *Digital Library of Classical Protestant Texts*, Alexander Street, at alexanderstreet.com.

But unlike in Zanchi, its use is not found in the contemplation of God's being for its own sake but in the polemical context in which he takes on the Socinians and Arminians.

John Owen faced a new dilemma in Protestant theology. The traditional answer to the question "Who is God?" had come under attack by members in the Polish Reformed Church, led by Faustus Socinus. In 1654 John Biddle (1615–1662), who received his master's degree from Oxford, published two small catechisms consistent with the Racovian Catechism published by the Socinians in Poland in 1605. John Owen was called on to respond to Biddle's catechism, and he did so in his 1655 *Vindiciae Evangelicae*. Prior to Owen's work, the British Parliament passed a law making the denial of God's being and perfections as well as the deity of the Son and Spirit a capital offense. Biddle, who was jailed for his teaching, could have been executed for it, but the law was never acted on.[97]

Owen's *Vindiciae Evangelicae* is a long, studious polemic against Biddle. Rather than in Roman Catholicism, Owen finds his enemies within the Reformed tradition, or at least in its radical wings. Biddle shares Owen's commitment to *sola scriptura* but develops a doctrine of God from it that Owen finds detestable. Biddle's doctrine of God is based on a literal interpretation of Scripture that accuses the traditional teaching of being composed by human traditions in councils based on a "mystical" or "figurative" reading. For Biddle, if such an interpretation is granted without the "express warrant of Scripture itself, we shall have no settled belief, but be liable continually to be turned aside by any one that can invent a new mystical meaning of the Scripture, there being no certain rule to judge of such meaning,

---

96. Christopher Cleveland, *Thomism in John Owen* (Burlington, VT: Ashgate, 2013), 4; Trueman, *John Owen*, 9. Cleveland identifies "three major areas of Thomistic influence upon Owen's theology." They are "the concept of God as pure act of being," "the concept of infused habits of grace," and the "understanding of the hypostatic union." Cleveland writes, "Owen here presents the Thomistic doctrine of divine simplicity in order to demonstrate that the will of God is God Himself. If the will of God is God Himself, then it cannot be resisted or frustrated." If my previous interpretation of Thomas's first forty-three questions is correct, then such a use of divine simplicity is not what Thomas primarily demonstrates; Cleveland, *Thomism in John Owen*, 4.

97. William Goold, "Prefatory Note," in John Owen, *Vindiciae Evangelicae*, in *The Works of John Owen*, ed. William H. Goold, vol. XII (Carlisle, PA: Banner of Truth Trust, 1976).

as there is of the literal ones."[98] Biddle argues the tradition goes wrong after Constantine convened the Nicene Council. He writes, "for after Constantine the Great, together with the council of Nice[sic], had once deviated from the language of the Scripture in the business touching the Son of God, calling him 'coessential with the Father,' this opened a gap for others afterward, under a pretence of guarding the truth from heretics, to devise new terms at pleasure."[99]

Biddle draws on themes in Reformed theology—an emphasis on theological epistemology, the central role of Scripture in that epistemology, and a willingness to critique tradition if it does not fit a literal interpretation of Scripture. Biddle finds the Scripture infallible, and with the literal rule of Scripture in hand, he radically revises the traditional answer. God is located in heaven, has figure or shape, and thus is composite, has passions, is not Triune, and has limited knowledge of the future. Biddle understands himself as "continuing the Reformation."[100]

Owen challenges every aspect of Biddle's theology. He takes the reader through Biddle's catechism chapter by chapter and refutes it using Scripture and philosophy. Unlike Zanchi and Aquinas, Owen's treatise is not a contemplative development of God's nature and attributes as they relate to Trinity, but Owen nonetheless provides in his lengthy treatise a substantive teaching on God's nature. It is most clearly represented not in his second chapter, titled "Of the nature of God," but in his "examination" of Biddle's preface to his catechism.

Owen finds the pagan philosophers preferable to Biddle's theology. He writes, "never any of the Platonical philosophers spoke so unworthily of God or vented such gross, carnal conceptions of him as Mr. B. hath done."[101] Because Biddle finds the doctrine of Christ's two natures and of the Trinity "repugnant" to reason, Owen argues that philosophical reason is capable of knowledge of the "things of God."

---

98. John Biddle, *A Twofold Catechism: The One Simply called A Scripture Catechism; The Other A brief Scripture-Catechism for Children* (London: printed by J. Cottrel, 1654), 6–7.
99. Quoted by Owen in *Vindiciae Evangelicae*, 58.
100. Ibid., 57.
101. Ibid., 66.

"Nor do we here plead that reason is blind and corrupted, and that the natural man cannot discern the things of God, and so require that men do prove themselves regenerate before we admit them to judge of the truth of the propositions under debate."[102] For Owen, *sola scriptura* did not entail a rejection of philosophical knowledge of God.

Biddle explicitly rejects simplicity in the preface to his catechism. It contains three pages of errors that arise from "Platonists," "wise and learned men," and "mystical interpretation" that goes beyond the plain interpretation of Scripture. Here are a few of the "expressions" that he states cannot be found in Scripture: "of God's being infinite and incomprehensible, of his being a simple Act, of his subsisting in three persons, or after a threefold manner, of a Divine Circumincession, of an Eternal Generation, of an Eternal Procession, of an Incarnation, of an Hypostatical Union, of a Communication of Properties, of the Mother of God."[103] Owen goes through each of the attributes Biddle denies, first examining his opposition to the terms "infinite and incomprehensible" and then to simplicity.

Owen has one of the more in-depth accounts of simplicity found among Reformed theologians. He begins, as did Aquinas and most Reformed theologians, by correlating simplicity with the divine name given in Exod. 3:14, defending it against Biddle.

> That God is a *simple act* is the next thing excepted against and decried, name and thing; in the room whereof, that he is compounded of matter and form, or the like, must be asserted. Those who affirm God to be a simple act do only deny him to be compounded of divers principles, and assert him to be always actually in being, existence, and intent operation. God says of himself that his name is *Ehejeh*, and he is I AM,—that is, a simple being, existing in and of itself; and this is that which is intended by the simplicity of the nature of God, and this being is a simple act. The Scripture tells us he is eternal, I AM, always the same, and so never what he was not ever. This is decried, and in opposition to it his being compounded, and so obnoxious to dissolution, and his being *in potential*, in a disposition and passive capacity to be when he is not, is asserted; for it is only to deny these things that the term "simple" is used, which he condemns and rejects.[104]

---

102. Ibid., 209.
103. Biddle, *Two Catechisms*, 22.

To be fair to Biddle, although he denied God as "simple act" he did not explicitly state God was "compounded of matter and form." However, Owen is correct in his understanding of simplicity. If it is rejected, what must then follow but composition? Biddle's affirmation of God's "figure" or "shape," "location," and "passions" suggests as much.

Owen then explains what simplicity is. He cites Suarez and Cajetan, arguing it is "pure negation." This negation, or *remotio*, is not, however, the last word. The negation serves the purpose of God's "eminent perfection." Owen writes, "And though this only it immediately denotes, yet there is a most eminent perfection of the nature of God thereby signified to us: which is negatively proposed, because it is in the use of things that are proper to us, in which case we can only conceive what is not to be ascribed to God."[105] Owen brings simplicity and perfection together. He then makes four points about simplicity. First, it signifies God's "absolute independence and firstness in being and operation." Second, it signifies "God is absolutely and perfectly *one and the same*." Third, it means that the "essence" and "attributes" of God "*are all of them essentially the same with one another*, and every one the same with the essence of God." Finally, the only option to divine simplicity is to posit "potentiality" in God.[106] After challenging Biddle's rejection of simplicity, Owen then takes up his rejection of Trinity and subsistent being. He makes an argument for subsistent relations in God that would seem to depend on simplicity. He states, "If that person be God, God subsists in that person." Owen's argument for the Trinity is theologically and metaphysically sophisticated. However, in the ensuing discussion on the Trinity, he does not, unlike Zanchi, explicitly link simplicity to the Triune relations.

What work does divine simplicity do in Owen? An early work also devoted to theological polemics, *A Display of Arminianism*, shows its use. For Owen, divine simplicity ensures God's eternal decree to save some and damn others, against the Arminians, whom Owen argues lose the importance of simplicity and sovereignty. He writes,

104. Owen, *Vindiciae Evangelicae*, 71.
105. Ibid.
106. Ibid., 71–72.

the decrees of God being conformable to his nature, and essence, does require eternitie, and immutabilitie, as their unseparable properties: God, and he only, never was, nor ever can be, what now he is not; passive possibilitie to any thing, which is the fountaine of all change, can have no place in him who is *actus simplex*, and purely free from all composition. . . . the eternall acts of his will, not really differing from his unchangeable essence, must needs be immutable.[107]

God decrees by his immutable and eternal will who is damned and who elect. To suggest otherwise is to lose simplicity, for it divides God's will and act. If God willed the salvation of all, all would be saved. All are not saved. Therefore, because God is "simple act," God must have willed the salvation only of the elect and the reprobation of the damned.[108] To argue otherwise imports composition and temporality into God, for what God wills is then not necessarily how the world is. For Owen, divine simplicity rules out that possible distinction.

Owen used the concept of God's perfect simplicity against his opponents, the Socinians and Arminians. By challenging the doctrine of predestination, including reprobation, the Arminians, he argues, challenge God's eternity, immutability, omniscience, and especially divine omnipotence. Owen makes his argument against the Arminians by drawing on the Scholastics:

> *Divinum velle est eius esse*, say the Schoolemen. *The will of God is nothing but God willing*, not differing from his essence, *secundum rem*, in the thing its self, but only *secundum rationem*, in that it importeth a relation to the thing willed: the essence of God then, being a most absolute pure simple act or substance: his will consequently can be but simply one, whereof we ought not to make neither division, nor distinction: if that whereby it is signified, were taken always properly and strictly for the eternall will of God: the differences hereof, that are usually given, are rather distinctions of the signification of the word, than of the thing.[109]

Here we see, however, a Scholastic position transforming into a

---

107. John Owen, *A Display of Arminianism* (London: Printed by I. L. for Phil Stephens, 1643), 11, accessed at early English books online.
108. He writes, "they denie the irresistibilitie and uncontrollable power of God's will affirming, that oftentimes he seriously willeth, and intendeth what he cannot accomplish, and so is deceived of his ayme" because they falsely assume God wills the salvation of all (ibid., 10).
109. Ibid., 40–44.

modern one, one that Katherine Sonderegger finds in Friedrich Schleiermacher and Charles Hodge. God's will has become identified not only with God's nature but also with God's causal power.[110] The perfectly simple God becomes detached from a speculative theology, rendering intelligible Triune relations, and instead identifies the relation between God and creation. The result is a troubled understanding of divine power.

Owen finds support for this position in Aquinas, whom he cites to make his point. Commands are "signs" of the will that demonstrate its essence. He writes, "for in as much, as our commands are the figures of our wills, the same is said of the precepts of God."[111] The commands demonstrate God's will, which demonstrates God's essence. The Arminians cannot sustain this teaching on simplicity because they divide God's essence and God's will. "And here me thinks they place God in a most unhappy condition, by affirming that they are often damned, whom he would have to be saved, though he desire their salvation with a most vehement desire and natural affection."[112] The causal efficacy of God's will demonstrates God's essence. All will not be saved, therefore God did not will their salvation. A minor note in Thomas's teaching has become a major chord in Owen's.

Restoring the Question: Advancing the Answer

One of Owen's targets for his modified Thomism was as influenced by Thomas as was Owen, if not more so.[113] Jacob Arminius (1560–1609) is best characterized as a Reformed theologian, although the characterization is contested. His mother and siblings were killed in the Battle of Oudewater when Spanish mercenaries sought to regain Catholic control of Holland. Arminius left for Marburg and then went to Leiden, where he studied and later became professor. During his studies he traveled with his friend Junius to Padua and Rome.[114] Junius

---

110. See Katherine Sonderegger, *Systematic Theology*, vol. 1, *God* (Minneapolis: Fortress Press, 2015), 176–88, for an excellent analysis of the problem of divine power and its relationship to causality.
111. Owen, *Display of Arminianism*, 41.
112. Ibid., 47.
113. Muller, *God, Creation, and Providence*, 27.

was influenced by Thomas, and his *De vera theologia*, along with two other Reformed texts, Zanchi's *De natura Dei* and Danaeus's *Christiana Isagoges*, were important sources for Arminius's theology. Arminius was so influenced by Thomism that some Reformed theologians accused him of becoming Catholic. One of his students at Leiden, Casper Sibelius, charged him with moving students away from Reformed theology and toward "Socinus . . . Thomas Aquinas, Molina, Suárez and other enemies of grace."[115] Sibelius does not seem to have differentiated among them.

Arminius's reading of Thomas is consistent with and yet differs from Owen's. Both affirm the traditional answer that God is simple, perfect, and Triune. But they do so for diverging purposes. While Owen emphasizes the Augustinian teaching on predestination mediated through Aquinas, Arminius shows evidence of the Dionysian influence of God's self-diffusive goodness on Thomas.[116] Richard Muller notes that "Arminius clearly goes farther along the line of Thomistic logic than did the Reformed and he does so, significantly, in relation to his equally Thomistic view of the priority of the divine intellect and the self-diffusive character of the divine goodness. On neither of these points were the Reformed willing to follow out the Thomist logic without modification."[117] Because God is self-diffusive goodness, God could not directly will reprobation for God's creation. Although marked by the Reformation, Arminius did not see how the trajectory that led to Franciscus Gomarus from Zanchi with its extreme predestination failed to make God the author of evil, all protestations notwithstanding. The focus on this important difference with other Reformed theologians, and its association with the appellation *Arminian*, has led theologians to neglect Arminius's substantive doctrine of God.[118]

---

114. See Rustin E. Brian, *Jakob Arminius: The Man from Oudewater* (Eugene, OR: Cascade, 2015), 10–18, 29.

115. Muller, *God, Creation, and Providence*, 27.

116. The distinction here is not an either-or. Augustine also held to God's self-diffusive goodness. It is a matter of emphasis.

117. Muller, *God, Creation, and Providence*, 195. Arminius states, "Goodness in God is an affection of communicating his own good. (Rev. 4.11; Gen. 1.31)"; Arminius, *Works*, trans. James Nichols and William Bagnall (Grand Rapids: Baker, 1977), I:335.

118. An important exception is Muller's *God, Creation, and Providence in the Thought of Jacobus Arminius.*

Arminius emphasizes God's goodness, perfection, and holiness. Of course, none of the Reformed nor the Catholic theologians denied these attributes. The debate between Arminius and his Reformed interlocutors centered on the implications of their doctrines of God and its relation to creation. Arminius found Gomarus and other Reformed theologians calling into question divine goodness and perfection by making God the source for evil. They denied the implication. Gomarus and others found Arminius denying God's omnipotence and making the human will the source of salvation. Arminius denied the implication. This unfortunate debate deters us from Arminius's important contribution to Protestant theology. It is less his insistence on the freedom of the will (no Protestant theologian ever denied the will's freedom) and more his inheritance of the perfectly simple Triune God. His teaching on God can be found in his fourth public disputation, discussed between 1603 and 1609.[119] These disputations were still the method of teaching and were intended for classroom discussion.

Arminius begins his fourth disputation affirming that "a nature is correctly ascribed to God." He cites Gal. 4:8; 2 Pet. 1:4; Aristotle, Plato, and Cicero for support.[120] After affirming God's nature, he immediately affirms simplicity in order to problematize our knowledge of that nature. Like Aquinas, God's nature or essence is self-evident, but only to God. Arminius writes, "It is adequately known only by God, and God by it; because God is the same as it is."[121] We know God either through the beatific vision reserved for the "blessed in heaven" or "mediately through analogical images and signs" in creation and above all in Christ. This latter knowledge is always "through a glass in an enigma" and is for all who are "travelers and pilgrims."[122] Arminius then states there are two ways we have this latter knowledge of God, and here he explicitly cites Thomas. "The First is that of Affirmation,

---

119. Arminius's works can be found at http://wesley.nnu.edu/arminianism/the-works-of-james-arminius and at http://www.ccel.org/ccel/arminius.
120. Arminius, *Works*, I:320.
121. Ibid.
122. Ibid.

(which is also styled by Thomas Aquinas, 'the mode of Causality and by the habitude of the principle,') according to which the simple perfections which are in the creatures, as being the productions of God, are attributed analogically to God according to some similitude." The second is "negation" or "remotion," in which the imperfections of creatures are removed from God. He raises the question whether any analogy between God's essence and life and creaturely essence and life exists, and affirms that there is, yet whatever signs are found in creaturely reality that point toward God are more excellent in God's nature. The way of preeminence allows Arminius to speak of God in creaturely terms, always cognizant that such terms must be negated and perfected. He refers to God as "essence" and "life" and then states, "But in God both these are to be considered in the mode of Pre-eminence, that is, in excellence far surpassing the Essence and Life of all the creatures."[123]

Arminius then presents a profound statement on God's essence, developing all the traditional names from the fact that God is not understood in terms of causality, either external or internal. From this fact arises simplicity and infinity, and from them all the other attributes. It can be found in this important, lengthy quotation:

> Because the Essence of God is devoid of all cause, from this circumstance arise, in the first place, Simplicity and Infinity of Being in the Essence of God. Simplicity is a preeminent mode of the Essence of God, by which he is void of all composition, and of component parts whether they belong to the senses or to the understanding. He is without composition, because without external cause; and He is without component parts, because without internal cause. (Romans 11:35, 36; Hebrews 2:10; Isaiah 40:12, 22.). The Essence of God, therefore, neither consists of material, integral and quantitative parts, of matter and form, of kind and difference, of subject and accident, nor of form and the thing formed, (for it is to itself a form, existing by itself and its own individuality,) neither hypothetically and through nature, through capability and actuality, nor through essence and being. Hence God is his own Essence and his own Being, and is the same in that which is, and that by which it is. He is all eye, ear, hand and foot, because he entirely sees, hears, works, and is in every place. (Psalm 139:8–12.) THEREFORE, Whatever is absolutely predicated about God, it is

123. Ibid., I:321.

understood essentially and not accidentally; and those things (whether many or diverse,) which are predicated concerning God, are, in God, not many but one: (James 1.17). It is only in our mode of considering them, which is a compound mode, that they are distinguished as being many and diverse; though this may, not inappropriately, be said, because they are likewise distinguished by a formal reason.[124]

Infinity, states Arminius, emerges from simplicity, because without distinction of parts, God is without limits. Arminius generates all the other divine attributes from simplicity and infinity. He writes, "From the Simplicity and Infinity of the Divine sense, arise Infinity with regard to time, which is called 'Eternity;' and with regard to place, which is called 'Immensity:' Impassability, Immutability and Incorruptibility."[125] The generation of eternity and immensity from simplicity and infinity is important for his teaching on the Trinity in his fifth disputation.

Arminius, like Owen, is a Trinitarian theologian. The deductions of these attributes are essential for his Trinitarian teaching. In the fourth disputation he begins with the divine essence as uncaused and first deduces simplicity and infinity. From them he deduces immensity and eternity. He begins with these attributes in his fifth disputation to argue for the coessentiality of the Father and Son. In the eleventh section of his fifth disputation he argues for the coessentiality of the Father and Son from "immensity" and "eternity." From immensity and eternity, he then affirms immutability, omniscience, omnipotence, and majesty and glory. Scripture, he states, demonstrates the Son bears these "essential attributes":

> (1.) Immensity: "My Father and I will come unto him, and make our abode with him." (John 14:23.) "That Christ may dwell in your hearts by faith." (Ephesians 3:17.) "I am with you always, even unto the end of the world." (Matthew 28:20.)

> (2.) Eternity: "In the beginning was the Word." (John 1:1.) "I am Alpha and Omega, the first and the last." (Revelation 1:11; 2:8.)

124. Ibid., I:322.
125. Ibid., I:323.

Much like Aquinas and Zanchi, Arminius has used simplicity for the purposes of setting forth the Triune persons as really distinct from one another and yet coessential. Once the Father and Son are understood as coessential in terms of immensity and eternity, he then argues that all the other attributes are communicable between the Father and Son. The essential attributes of God function to demonstrate that the Father, Son, and Spirit each is the essence of God, and the essence is not other than the Father, Son, and Spirit.

After Arminius develops the essential attributes and their application to the Triune persons, he then discusses the relation between God and creation as a communication of divine goodness. Arminius affirms all the "attributes" Aquinas did. Like Aquinas, he begins with simplicity, but Arminius follows it with infinity rather than, as Thomas did, with perfection and goodness. There may be a reason for this. For Arminius, the essential attributes are incommunicable.[126] Goodness is not placed as an essential attribute because it is communicable. He states this explicitly: "The Goodness of the Essence of God is that according to which it is, essentially in itself, the Supreme and very Good; from a participation in which all other things have an existence and are good; and to which all other things are to be referred as to their supreme end: for this reason it is called communicable."[127] God communicates God's goodness to creatures, and this communication is central to Arminius's teaching on God's omnipotence and will. The latter can only be rightly understood if Arminius's Thomistic understanding of divine operations and his teaching on simplicity as an incommunicable divine attribute are taken into account.

Arminius follows Thomas in identifying three divine operations:

---

126. In his fourth disputation, section nineteen, Arminius emphasizes this to argue against the Lutheran teaching on Christ's bodily ubiquity after the resurrection: "19. These modes of the Essence of God belong so peculiarly to Him, as to render them incapable of being communicated to any other thing; and of whatever kind these modes may be, they are, according to themselves, as proper to God as His Essence itself, without which they cannot be communicated, unless we wish to destroy it after despoiling it of its peculiar modes of being; and according to analogy, they are more peculiar to Him than his Essence, because they are pre-eminent, for nothing can be analogous to them. THEREFORE, Christ, according to his humanity, is not in every place."

127. Ibid., I:325.

understanding, will, and power. He also follows Thomas in teaching that the divine understanding and will are primarily internal operations, but power is only external.[128] Like Thomas, he correlates the operations of divine understanding and will with the Father's generation of the Son and the Spirit.[129] There is no correlation between a personal relation and power because God does not exercise power internal to God's self. To make power an internal operation would entail a real relation between God and that which is external to God, creation. Power is an act that is only possible toward creation. For that reason, Arminius formally differentiates God's will and power. God's will and understanding are the basis for God's power.[130] God could

128. "But the life of God is active in three faculties, in the understanding, the will, and the power or capability properly so called. In the Understanding, inwardly considering its object of what kind soever, whether it be one [with it] or united to it in the act of understanding. In the Will, inwardly willing its first, chief, and proper object; and extrinsically willing the rest. In the Power, or capability operating only extrinsically, which may be the cause of its being called by the particular name of capability, as being that which is capable of operating on all its objects, before it actually operates" (ibid., I:326).

129. Arminius notes: "For it is in reference to his life, that God the Father produces out of his own essence his Word and his Spirit; and in reference to his life, God understands, wills, is able to do, and does, all those things which He understands, wills, is able to do, and actually does" (ibid., I:326).

130. Arminius first presents the divine understanding. It is "certain and infallible, yet it does not impose any necessity on things, nay, it rather establishes in them a contingency. For since it is an understanding not only of the thing itself, but likewise of its mode, it must know the thing and its mode such as they both are; and therefore if the mode of the thing be contingent, it will know it to be contingent; which cannot be done, if this mode of the thing be changed into a necessary one, even solely by reason of the Divine understanding. (Acts 27.22-25, 31; 23.11, in connection with verses 17, 18, etc., with 25.10, 12; and with 26.32; Rom. 11.33; Psalm 147.5)"; Arminius, *Works*, I:329. He accepts the scholastic distinction between a "knowledge of vision"—"that by which God knows himself and all other beings, which are, will be, or have been," and a "knowledge of simple intelligence"—"that by which He knows things possible" (ibid., I:329). He also acknowledges that the "schoolmen" divide God's knowledge among the "natural and necessary," the "free" and "middle knowledge." However, because of divine simplicity he does not find these distinctions that helpful. He writes, "But, in strictness of speech, every kind of God's knowledge is necessary"—it is the knowledge "by which God understands himself and all things possible." God's knowledge is not causal for Arminius, and although it is necessary to God, it does not impose necessity on things. Secondary causes are free and do actual work in the world (ibid.). After presenting the divine understanding, Arminius then characterizes the divine will by five themes. First, "God wills his own Essence and Goodness." Second, God "wills all those things which, by the extreme judgment of his wisdom, He hath determined to be made out of infinite beings possible to himself." Third, God wills "those things which God judges it to be right that they should be done by creatures endowed with understanding and free-will," and that includes "prohibitions." Fourth, God wills "divine permission, by which God permits a rational creature to do what He forbade." Finally, God wills "those things which, according to his own infinite wisdom, God judges to be one from the acts of rational creatures." As with Thomas, Arminius also affirms an antecedent and consequent will. Arminius says the former should be called "velleity" rather than will (ibid., I:331–33).

be God without power, because God is free.[131] God could not be God without will and understanding. The divine understanding and will are prior to, and more basic than, any external operation of divine power.[132]

For Arminius both the divine understanding and will are "simple." Simplicity here, however, does not relate to creation; it is an incommunicable attribute of God. The divine will wills first the perfection/goodness that God is in God's being. Then divine power exercises the simple will, externally making possible beings other than God.[133] God wills and knows creatures solely in the goodness and truth of God's own essence. This goodness and truth comes first. Then creatures arise from God's power as participants in that goodness.[134] The power God then operates on creatures arises from what is communicable of God's goodness and knowledge.

For Arminius, this communication to creatures does not require any diminishment of God's omnipotence or omniscience. God is in no sense limited. God "moves" toward creatures only as the simple, infinite, eternal, immutable, and holy God. This movement or power toward creatures is holy "because God advances towards his object only on

131. Arminius states that divine power "resembles a principle which executes what the will commands under the direction of knowledge." It is both free and dependent on God's nature. These are not in opposition. "For whatsoever God can will freely, He can likewise do it; and whatsoever it is possible for Him to do, He can freely will it; and whatever it is impossible for Him to will, He cannot do it; and that which He cannot do, He also cannot will." What God can do, however, is because of God's goodness. "God is deservedly said to be capable of doing all things that are possible. For how can there be an entity, a truth, or a good, which is contrary to His Essence and Natural Will, and incomprehensible to his Understanding?" (ibid., I:337, 338).
132. Arminius affirms the distinction between an absolute and ordained power, but he locates it in the will rather than in power. "The distinction of Power into absolute, and ordinary or actual, has not reference to God's Power so much as to his Will, which uses his Power to do some things when it wills to use it, and which does not use it when it does not will; though it would be possible for it to use the Power if it would; and it if did use it, the Divine Will would, through it, do far more things than it does" (ibid., I:338–39).
133. Arminius states, "so the Will of God, by a single and simple act, wills its own goodness and all things in its goodness. Therefore, the multitude of things willed is not repugnant to the simplicity of the Divine Will" (ibid., I:331).
134. Ibid, I:326. Because of simplicity, Arminius has a very high understanding of divine omniscience. He writes, "The act of understanding in God is his own being and essence" (ibid., I:327). Because of this God's knowledge is defined by simplicity and eternity. "The mode by which God understands, is not that which is successive, and which is either through composition and division, or through deductive argumentation; but it is simple, and through infinite intuition" (ibid., I:327). Divine knowledge has no temporal mode. God "certainly and infallibly sees even future contingencies" (ibid., I:328).

account of its being good, not on account of any other thing which is added to it; and only because his Understanding accounts it good, not because feeling inclines [him] towards it without right reason."[135] God's goodness and truth (right reason) are the basis for creation and redemption. Arminius's complicated Thomistic metaphysics avoids any hint that God's will is irrational or that God decrees something other than God's goodness and perfection for his creatures.

Arminius concludes his discussion on God's nature by examining divine perfection, blessedness, and glory. They are related. Blessedness, he states, "is an act of the life of God, by which he enjoys his own perfection, that is fully known by his Understanding and supremely loved by his Will; and by which He complacently reposes in this Perfection with satisfaction."[136] God does not need creation for God's sake. Creation is a diffusion of God's perfection externally by God's power.

Arminius may be the most Thomist of the Reformers we have considered. He taught something akin to what became known as the *analogia entis*.[137] He rejects a sharp Scotist division between theology and metaphysics without affirming either theology without metaphysics or metaphysics without theology.[138] He does not begin with an eternal decree God executes toward creatures but with the Trinitarian operations of will and knowledge. His teaching found a home within the Wesleyan tradition.

Wesley was a Reformed and Arminian theologian who affirmed the perfectly simple Triune God and all the attributes that teaching entailed.[139] Wesley thought Arminius's good name was unfortunately

---

135. Ibid., I:331.

136. Ibid., I:339.

137. Muller states, "By pointing toward this theme of the intelligibility of being on the basis of an analogy between the Being of God and the being of the finite order (the *analogia entis*) Arminius has, from the very beginning of his system, pointed towards a more Thomistic orientation than indicated in Junius' prolegomena"; Muller, *God, Creation, and Providence*, 60.

138. "Arminius appears here to set aside the cautions of Scotism concerning the separation of theology from metaphysics and to advocate the use of the concept and language of Being in theology at the fundamental level of the identification of the object of the discipline"; Muller, *God, Creation, and Providence*, 59.

139. Wesley admonished his hearers not to set Arminians and Calvinists against each other by using these names as invectives. The significant difference among them, he argued, was that the former taught conditional rather than absolute predestination, universal rather than limited atonement,

disparaged by "some zealous men with the Prince of Orange at their head" who

> furiously assaulted all that held what were called his opinions; and having procured them to be solemnly condemned, in the famous Synod of Dort, (not so numerous or learned, but full as impartial, as the Council or Synod of Trent,) some were put to death, some banished, some imprisoned for life, all turned out of their employments, and made incapable of holding any office, either in Church or State.[140]

Wesley viewed the Synod of Dort akin to Trent.

As with many other Protestant theologians, he did not exert great effort on the doctrine of God because it was not a matter of dispute. He never presented a profound treatise on the nature of God, but all the elements of the traditional answer can be found in his sermons and treatises.[141] He was nonetheless on to something significant when he listed these attributes in his sermon "Catholic Spirit." The traditional answer is a basis for true catholicity. This sermon should not be misunderstood; it was not a rapprochement with Roman Catholicism. Wesley affirms a "catholic spirit" against what he finds to be the constriction of conscience in Roman Catholicism. His sermon is a means of affirming what is "Catholic" among competing Protestant communions. Drawing on 2 Kgs. 10:15, Wesley asks the question, "is thine heart right as with mine heart?" If it is, then the appropriate conclusion is "give me thine hand." In this sermon Wesley sets forth seven conditions by which one determines catholicity, or whether one's heart is right with another's. The first is intriguing:

> The first thing implied is this: Is thy heart right with God? Dost thou believe his being, and his perfections? His eternity, immensity, wisdom, power; his justice, mercy, and truth? Dost thou believe that he now "upholdeth all things by the word of his power"? And that he governs

---

and grace's resistibility. See his "What Is an Arminian?" (1872), www.umcmission.org/Find-Resources/John-Wesley-Sermons/The-Wesleys-and-Their-Times/What-Is-an-Arminian.

140. Ibid.

141. His sermon "On the Trinity" is one of his most disappointing. It is unusually anti-intellectual, admonishing his hearers to affirm it as a mystery by arguing they affirm other things they cannot understand.

even the most minute, even the most noxious, to his own glory, and the good of them that love him?[142]

Only if his hearers could say yes to this question could he give them his hand. The divine being and perfections were essential for any true catholic spirit. Wesley did not list the Trinity among his seven conditions, although it is implied. Nor did he relate simplicity to it. He emphasized "God's being and perfections" without attending to their Trinitarian context.

Conclusion: Uses and Meanings of the Perfectly Simple Triune God

Thomas taught predestination. Vermigli, Zanchi, and Owen taught both predestination and reprobation. Arminius and Wesley did not. They taught conditional predestination that refused to consider the possibility that God made some of God's creatures expressly for the purpose of damning them. Yet all these theologians affirmed the perfectly simple Triune God and would correlate their understanding of God's relation to creation with the traditional answer. How might we account for this difference?

The above analysis suggests that divine simplicity was put to diverse uses. Four were identified. First, it is used for a theological epistemology. Then its purpose is apophatic. Because God's essence and existence are the same, and ours are not, only God knows who God is. We can have at most analogical understanding of God based on remotion and the way of eminence. What we see as pilgrims in this life we only see dimly. Simplicity helps us not to say too much nor to say too little. Second, simplicity is evidence of the use of natural theology. It is a consequence of it. Neither Catholics nor Protestants were troubled that "pagan" philosophers argued to simplicity. Their understanding of it could not be affirmed without reservations, but it showed a shared rationality among them. The rejection of any natural

---

142. John Wesley, "Catholic Spirit," in *The Works of John Wesley*, vol. II, ed. Albert Outler (Nashville: Abingdon, 1985), 87.

theology by Biddle led to an incoherent teaching of God. Scripture could not be used as Biddle attempted without disaster. Owen affirmed pagan wisdom against a supposed Reforming theologian who sought to continue the Reformation by radically revising the perfectly simple Triune God. Third, simplicity provided a logical grammar for the divine essence that had to be sustained once the daring and risky attribution of real relations in the divine essence was affirmed. Simplicity without real relations remains at the level of a natural theology that is inadequate for Christian revelation. Real relations without simplicity loses the divine economy, the manifestation of the one essence of God that appears in time prior to the explicit manifestation of the persons. An articulation of the unified divine essence is as essential to the Christian understanding of God as is that of the persons. In fact, it comes first if we are not to be misled into imagining divine composition.

Simplicity as a logical grammar does not exclude the fact that it makes positive affirmations of God. Although it is a grammar related to the first use seeking to "remove" creaturely realities inappropriate for deity, it is not mere negation. Here Owen offers wise counsel. Recall that simplicity for him is a remotion, and through it "is a most eminent perfection of the nature of God thereby signified to us." What is removed allows an "eminent perfection" better to come into focus. Arminius is likewise significant in helping us understand this point. Because God communicates God's goodness with creaturely existence, it bears signs of that goodness.

Remotion and abstraction allow for a speculative theology. Most of the Reformed theologians were suspicious of this theology such that the theological semantics of "abstraction" and "speculation" shifted. They no longer meant following a way from creatures to God by removing inappropriate characteristics, abstracting from them and through the way of eminence and perfection daring to make affirmations about God in himself based also on the names revealed in Scripture. Now they meant something different, unjustified knowledge or invectives. What can be known of God can primarily, if not solely, be known through God's relation to creation. Divine causality becomes decisive for knowledge of God, and this causality loses its analogical shape. The result is a fourth use of simplicity; it is used to express God's power over creation. If God is a unified essence, and no distinction between an absolute and ordained power was to be accepted, as many of the Reformed theologians argued, then God's will and power are identical. The logical conclusion is an eternal decree that becomes the foundation for creation whereby God elects and damns in God's eternal, simple immutability. Yet this fourth use of simplicity does not necessarily follow from the first three. In fact, the third use, simplicity as the logical grammar for Triune relations, calls this fourth use into question, as Arminius and Wesley demonstrate. If the foundation for creation is the perfectly simple Triune God whose perfection is goodness, then the evil of reprobation (and it can only be evil, as Vermigli acknowledged) has no foothold in that foundation. It is because of the third and most basic use of simplicity that the fourth use must be rejected. It stands in such tension and conflict with it that both cannot be affirmed.

Rejecting the fourth use of simplicity will create problems for divine reprobation. It would seem to lead to universal salvation. An obvious response is, why is this a problem? If the options are universal salvation or an eternal decree in which God wills the reprobation of part of God's creation, then the preferable Christian response must be universal salvation. Better that the perfectly simple Triune God leads to the conclusion that all creation will be saved than that God creates in order to damn. The doctrine of divine reprobation should not be more basic than the doctrine of the Trinity, nor should anyone find comfort or joy in damnation (despite what many church fathers taught). This understanding of simplicity does mean that God's simple perfection cannot but communicate its goodness even to those who irrationally refuse. If God must communicate God's goodness, it would seem to diminish God's freedom. But this misunderstands freedom. Such communication is not a rejection of divine freedom; it constitutes it, for divine freedom is not a liberty of indifference that selects among various options—these creatures will be condemned and these elect. Divine freedom is the ability to will the good without deliberation.

Such an understanding of divine simplicity does not mean that any theologian can unequivocally affirm that no one will refuse to live in God's presence. Hell is not rendered impossible. As Aquinas and Arminius explicitly argued, God cannot directly know evil. It is not something that can be known, for it has no being, no substance, no reason. God only acknowledges it under the aspect of the good. Hell, then, does not exist. That is to say, there is no place outside God in which God's goodness does not communicate and make being possible. Rather than a place, hell would be that state of limited existence in which redemption has occurred, for God wills the salvation of all God's creation, but creatures exercise a secondary causality that refuses to acknowledge what already is. Salvation is a new creation in which exclusion, hatred, violence, vengeance, and all the vices that work against the communication of perfection have no place. To seek to give them place in God's presence is impossible; it would be a hellish state, an unbearable lightness of being.

PART III

Challenges to the Perfectly Simple Triune God

Since the eighteenth century, many theologians have become suspicious of the traditional answer and called for its revision or rejection. It has been subjected to, as John Sanders has noted, a "remarkable reexamination."[1] Or, as Michael Lodahl puts it,

> There is . . . a relatively recent suspicion afoot among some thinkers that the omni doctrines [omnipotence, omniscience, omnipresence] owe their existence more to abstract analysis and deductive logic about what God "must be in order to be God," and less to the way in which God is encountered and described in the biblical story. The omni-God is metaphysically unimpeachable, but is this deity a philosophical construction, the idealistic invention of human minds, rather than the living God of Abraham and Sarah, Isaac and Rebekah, Jacob and Leah and Rachel?[2]

The calls for revision almost always identify the teaching of Thomas Aquinas as faulty. Many of the revisions arise from a perceived inability of a perfectly simple God to answer some significant questions. How can we solve the theoretical problem of evil and still have a God worthy

1. John Sanders, *The God Who Risks* (Downers Grove, IL: InterVarsity, 2007), 160.
2. Michael Lodahl, *The Story of God* (Kansas City, MO: Beacon Hill, 2008), 55–56.

of worship (the theodicy question)? How can we affirm our and God's freedom if God possesses the attributes the traditional answer posits (the question of divine and human freedom)? Others find the traditional answer needs revision through a more rigorous logical analysis of deity, drawing on the tools of analytical philosophy (the logical question). Yet another question is based on the political and cultural significance of the traditional answer. It is viewed as a product of Western culture. If so, why should the inheritance of one culture have normative significance in theology? How might we incorporate non-Eurocentric voices into theology and hear their concerns about the traditional teaching, which is sometimes accused of perpetuating racism and male, Eurocentric power? The language functions to authorize an all-powerful Sovereign, who then shares "his" sovereignty with other select male candidates either in the church or the secular realm. Theologians criticize the traditional language to challenge this hegemony (the political and cultural question). Almost all the above questions assume the traditional answer was based on a faulty "substance metaphysics" inherited from the Greeks, especially Aristotle. We no longer assume Aristotle's physics or cosmology, so why should we assume his metaphysics? Others ask whether metaphysics is necessary at all after Kant's criticisms. Major theologians such as Karl Rahner and Karl Barth, or the schools they established, find the metaphysics of the traditional answer incapable of adequately incorporating salvation history. They ask whether that metaphysics can be salvaged (the metaphysical question). I will discuss each of these questions in turn, recognizing that not every theological movement, or theologian, discussed shares the same reason for revising the traditional answer or revises it the same way.

The questions noted above are not easily distinguished. Most of them share in common the fifth concern, that the traditional answer draws on a faulty "substance metaphysics." G. W. F. Hegel and Alfred North Whitehead coined that term. Process theology draws on Whitehead's philosophy, arguing that substance metaphysics is unable to address the question of evil, but the concern is shared widely among those who call for revision; even nonprocess theologians invoke it as something that needs to be overcome. In fact, almost all the critics, including those who raise the cultural and political questions, and some Barthian and Lutheran critics of divine simplicity, accept the analysis that "substance metaphysics" misled Aquinas and others who set forth the traditional answer.

Although I am dividing the concerns into the five questions noted above, the concerns raised cannot be isolated from one another. Most calls for revision range across the categories, and the analyses will need to take that into account, just as they must take into account the diversity among and within the theological movements calling for revision. For instance, Michael Lodahl's process theology calls for far less radical revision than Catherine Keller's. Some revisions are so thorough that they go beyond revision to a doctrine of God that intentionally lacks continuity with previous Christian teaching. What we will discover is that, despite the different reasons for revision, the result among these calls is strikingly similar.

4

The Theodicy Question: Process Theism

Process theology calls for a rejection of the traditional answer and the most thoroughgoing revisions to the doctrine of God. Feminist process theologian Catherine Keller finds insuperable problems with it. She does not, however, place all the blame on Thomas. He attempted to move beyond the impassible God to one who could love, but he was hampered by his inherited language. She writes, "when God can be defined only as *actus purus*, pure act, with no receptivity, a classical fantasy of power has surely trumped the vision of love."[1] The ancient creeds also fail us because of their reliance on substance metaphysics:

> Faith here means a set of metaphysical *beliefs* about one God in three persons, "without either confusing the persons or dividing the substance." Such conciliar statements often waxed uninhibited in their threats and curses or "anathemas" follow. For instance, "If anyone will not confess that the Father, Son and Holy Spirit have one nature or substance . . . let him be anathema." A whole series of anathemas follow, all demanding "confession" of a theology processed with Hellenistic substance metaphysics. Institutional unity was achieved at the cost of massive divisions and expulsions, with repercussions to this day.[2]

---

1. Catherine Keller, *On the Mystery: Discerning Divinity in Process* (Minneapolis: Fortress Press, 2008), 127.

Substance Metaphysics

Keller does not state explicitly that "substance metaphysics" causes these "massive divisions and expulsions," but she does suggest it contributes to them. The problem is the relationship between substance and truth. She writes, "The claim of absolute truth is the greatest single obstruction to theological *honesty*."[3] As with Whitehead, the problem with substance metaphysics is its putative desire to fix being and therefore truth in stable entities. Keller's "*tehomic* theology" offers an alternative. God does not create *ex nihilo*; God is not the foundation for creation; that teaching leads to dangerous "foundationalisms" that "mobilize crusades, holy wars, market reforms and other mobile extensions of their uncompromising truths."[4] For Keller, the traditional answer is not only wrong but dangerous and immoral. We need radical surgery, a cut in the simply perfect God that would acknowledge God is a "leaky" God.[5] God creates by engaging the *chaos* that eternally exists with (leaks from?) God. The patriarchal desire for the harmonious order of the perfectly simple God comes undone with the chaos that always eludes any such order. There is no God before creation, no solitary, absolute Sovereign. There is a "leaky God," a deity of "becoming" who works on preexisting chaos. None of the traditional answer remains.

David Ray Griffin and John Cobb share Keller's generic concern about Greek philosophy and substance metaphysics, but they specify Thomas Aquinas's teaching on God as pernicious. Griffin identifies Thomas's theology as the epitome of the problem that must be remedied if theism has a future. The problem is simplicity; it is the wormwood in the beams that topples the edifice of traditional theism. He states,

---

2. Ibid., 7–8. She cites the Athanasian Creed and the Second Council of Constantinople as evidence for her claim. Keller is correct that the early and medieval church, until Vatican II, often coupled orthodox teaching with anathemas. (Vatican II was unique in not anathematizing those who disagreed.) As we saw above, Protestants were no better. Seventeenth-century England passed a law that was mercifully never enforced making it a capital offense to deny God's being and perfections. However, that there were "massive divisions and expulsions" in the fourth century needs to be explained.

3. Ibid., 8.

4. Catherine Keller, *Faces of the Deep: A Theology of Becoming* (London: Routledge, 2003), 10.

5. Ibid., 90.

"This notion [simplicity] is, paradoxically, the most complex, and really provides the clearest insight into the core of Thomistic realism." He summarizes it in "three verbally different formulations," which are that God's essence equals God's existence, that there is no distinction between God's essence and attributes, and that every attribute is "identical with every other one."[6] Herein lies the problem. If God is simple, then no distinction between God's primordial and consequent will, or God's knowing and willing, should be permitted. Simplicity requires that they are identical. What God knows is what God wills. If God knows all events that will happen in history, then that knowledge is causal, because it is also what God wills. Griffin associates God's will with causation. Because God is all-knowing and omnipotent, God's simplicity makes God directly responsible for evil. Griffin writes, "I take Thomas simply to have stated more clearly than others what is involved in the traditional synthesis of Hebrew and Greek ideas of deity. In particular, Thomas stated with utmost clarity (even though he sometimes tried to avoid its implications) the doctrine of divine simplicity which is required by the assumption that deity must be totally devoid of process."[7] Griffin acknowledges that Thomas distinguished divine knowing and willing, but he finds this to be a capitulation to process and a tacit denial of simplicity.

In another foundational text for process theology, *Process Theology: An Introductory Exposition*, both Griffin and John Cobb identify the problem as Thomism: "Much of the modern argument is about the existence of the God of classical theism, especially the God of Thomism."[8] They affirm that God is "perfect," but correlating perfection to a futureless, eternal, impassible God cannot sustain the "basic character" of divinity—love. An impassible God cannot love, because love requires sympathy and response. They write, "We are told by psychologists, and we know from our own experience, that love in the fullest sense involves a sympathetic response to the loved one.

6. David Ray Griffin, *God, Power and Evil: A Process Theodicy* (Philadelphia: Westminster, 1976), 75.
7. Ibid., 94.
8. John Cobb and David Ray Griffin, *Process Theology: An Introductory Exposition* (Philadelphia: Westminster, 1976), 42.

Sympathy means feeling the feelings of the other, hurting with the pains of the other, grieving with the grief, rejoicing with the joys."[9] They then univocally compare what love is among human creatures to what love must be for God; God too must have sympathy, and this "traditional theism" denied. "Nevertheless, traditional theism said that God is completely impassive, that there was no element of sympathy in the divine love for the creatures."[10] Traditional theism made this error because of its indebtedness to Greek substance metaphysics, in which an entity is supposedly an isolated, unchanging, static substance to which accidents are attributed. This metaphysics is in such profound tension with the biblical teaching that God is love that even Anselm and Aquinas had to acknowledge and resolve the tension. They cite Anselm's statement—"When thou beholdest us in our wretchedness, we experience the effect of compassion, but thou dost not experience the feeling"—and Aquinas's—"God loves without passion"—as evidence they could not sustain impassibility.[11] They do not pause to ask why impassibility and love are not found to be contradictory in Anselm and Aquinas, or whether their understanding of simplicity is the same as Thomas's; they have stipulated that love entails passions in the same sense that humans have passions and thus we must choose, either God is love, or God is impassible. If God is to love, God must suffer and be complex.

Having identified the problem as "classical theism" or "substance metaphysics," and associating it with the teaching of Thomas Aquinas, process theology then reacts against this teaching in order to solve the theoretical problem of evil.[12] It does so by replacing the perceived

---

9. Ibid., 44.

10. Ibid.

11. Ibid.

12. Process theology may have invented the term "classical theism." I have not used that term prior to this because it is laden with evaluative connotations. To invoke it is almost always already to have opposed it; it functions as a term of derision. David Burrell considers the term to be "concocted" as a "foil" for philosophers and theologians who seek "to develop an alternative set of metaphysical categories to handle certain issues in natural theology." In other words, "classical theism" is a term used to caricature a position for the purpose of reacting against it in order to establish a different metaphysics than that found in traditional Christian reflection. Classical theism did not exist prior to its invention as this foil. I have not defended "classical theism" in this work, nor do I intend to do so. See David Burrell, *Aquinas: God & Action* (London: Routledge & Kegan Paul, 1979), 177n3. See also Katherine Sonderegger, who suggests, "Process theologians seem to

"substance metaphysics" in the traditional answer with Alfred North Whitehead's process metaphysics. To understand and evaluate its call for rejection of the traditional answer requires first examining how it claims to have solved the theoretical problem of evil, second the new metaphysics it used to do so, and third the consequences for the traditional answer.

Solving the Theoretical Problem of Evil

Process theologians universally claim to have solved the theoretical problem of evil, a problem the traditional answer supposedly generates. Catherine Keller puts the problem succinctly, "If God is *good* in any moral sense of the word; and if God is literally all-controlling; and there is real evil in the world; it follows that this God doesn't exist."[13] David Ray Griffin sets forth the formal statement of the problem in eight logical steps:

1. God is a perfect reality. (Definition)
2. A perfect reality is an omnipotent being. (By definition)
3. An omnipotent being could unilaterally bring about an actual world without any genuine evil. (By definition)
4. A perfect reality is a morally perfect being. (By definition)
5. A morally perfect being would want to bring about an actual world without any genuine evil. (By definition)
6. If there is genuine evil in the world, then there is no God. (Logical conclusion from 1 through 5)
7. There is genuine evil in the world. (Factual statement)
8. Therefore there is no God. (Logical conclusion from 6 and 7)[14]

Griffin's first statement, "God is a perfect reality," places him within the traditional language for God in which perfection followed immediately on simplicity. Griffin never challenges God's perfection; however, simplicity must be abandoned, for it contributes to his steps

---

have coined the category *classical theism*, now so widely used as to seem self-evident." She goes on to suggest it does not exist; Katherine Sonderegger, *Systematic Theology*, vol. 1, *God* (Minneapolis: Fortress Press, 2015), 165 and n. 11.

13. Keller, *On the Mystery*, 83.

14. Griffin, *God, Power and Evil*, 19. Michael Lodahl has a similar setup of the problem of evil in his *The Story of God* (Kansas City, MO: Beacon Hill, 2008), 56, but his calls for revision are not nearly as thoroughgoing as Griffin's.

2 and 3 that make God an omnipotent being who could have prevented evil but does not do so. If God's knowledge and will are simple and eternal, then what God knows of the possibility of evil in creating must also be what God wills. He fears that without attending to the metaphysical and theological problems in those steps, intelligent persons will inevitably conclude, "there is no God." He affirms steps 1, 4, and 5, but does not want such an affirmation to lead to the conclusion in step 8. His purpose is to block successful arguments for atheism by answering the question of evil. Many of the movements we will examine assume, with process theology, that the revisions are necessary in order to make an apology for theism against atheism.

How are theologians to affirm God's perfection and avoid the logical conclusion in step 8—there is no God? Griffin acknowledges how thoroughgoing the revision must be to the traditional answer in order to avoid atheism. The only way forward is "by completely reconceiving the idea of a perfect reality."[15] Reconceiving a perfect reality entails rejecting steps 2 and 3: "A perfect reality is an omnipotent being" and "An omnipotent being could unilaterally bring about an actual world without any genuine evil."[16] Thus Griffin rejects every term other than *perfection* used to describe God in the traditional answer. We will see how he does so after examining the Whiteheadian metaphysics his project depends on.

Michael Lodahl offers a more nuanced process theology, but he too finds it necessary because of the problem of evil. Like Griffin, Lodahl acknowledges that "one of the primary reasons" for suspicion toward the traditional answer is "a concern for theodicy." He sets forth the "problem of evil" as well:

- An omnipresent God would certainly be aware of the presence of evil.
- An omniscient God would certainly know how to overcome that evil.
- An omnipotent God would certainly be able to enforce victory over that evil.
- A God of love presumably would desire to be rid of evil.

15. Griffin, *God, Power and Evil*, 95.
16. Ibid., 23.

- Yet evil continues to plague us all.[17]

Lodahl then draws on narrative theology to set forth a doctrine of God that is an interesting mix of the traditional answer with process metaphysics in order to address the problem of evil. His *The Story of God* begins by taking a form similar to that of Thomas's *Summa Theologiae*; he starts with Scripture and moves into a discussion of the demonstration of God's existence, drawing on Thomas's five ways. He sets forth the traditional answer but then raises the suspicion noted above about the "metaphysically unimpeachable omni-God" by asking whether this God is the same as the biblical God who takes risks. He answers negatively and revises the traditional answer. God is passible, God lacks foreknowledge, and divine power is limited.[18]

Lodahl is less indebted to Whitehead's metaphysics in his call for revisions than Griffin. He interprets his revised divine attributes through Christ's suffering on the cross. He writes, "The very fact that Christ, the Word become flesh, was nailed to a cross by other men reveals a vulnerability of God's part, a willingness to suffer our abuses of freedom."[19] However, Whitehead's metaphysics is still the horizon in which divine vulnerability is intelligible. Lodahl connects the two by stating,

> When the Christian tradition pays heed to the cross of Jesus, it lays to rest any notion of an impassive, omnipotent deity on a distant heavenly throne, untouched and unaffected by the pains of creation. The God revealed in Jesus' suffering with and for us is a God who is vulnerable, who shares in the pain. The philosopher Alfred North Whitehead reflected this appreciation for the Christian vision when he called God, "the fellow-sufferer who understands."[20]

Does this term adequately capture the oddness of the God of Holy Scripture? We will evaluate that claim below. Suffice it for now to

---

17. Lodahl, *Story of God*, 56.
18. See ibid., 62. He also writes, "In so creating us, God apparently does place limitations upon divine power and knowledge in the very act of extending to every human being the real possibility of choosing" (88).
19. Ibid., 62.
20. Ibid., 63.

see the positive reasons Lodahl calls for revision. First, he seeks to be faithful to the dramatic character of the God of Holy Scripture. Second, he attempts to address the problem of evil; it is a problem he, like Griffin, finds leading people into atheism. The traditional answer does not provide the resources to attend to these two concerns as much as his process appropriation of biblical narratives does.

Thomas Oord also claims to have resolved a "theoretical aspect" of the problem of evil. He finds it insufficient (as did Calvin) to distinguish God's directly willing evil and merely permitting it. He writes, "It is not enough to say that God does not cause but merely allows genuine evil to occur. The God who allows genuine evil despite possessing the capacity to stop it remains culpable for failing to prevent the occurrence of genuine evil."[21] How do we speak about God so that God is not culpable for evil? Oord answers, "The hypothesis I offer ... claims that God necessarily relates to and loves all creatures. God has necessarily related to and loves whatever God creates, and God everlastingly creates, relates and loves."[22] Oord distinguishes the "necessity" by which God relates to creatures from the necessity of God's Trinitarian relations. One necessity does not entail the other. In the traditional answer, only the Triune relations would be necessary; it is why they were termed "real relations." Oord has posited a second kind of necessary relation, the relation between God and creation. He does not explain how its necessity differs from that of the Triune relations. As will be seen, he does speak of this necessity as "deriving" from "God's essence." A necessary relation between God and creation that derives from God's essence would seem to differ little from God's Trinitarian relations. If no distinction is present in these relations, then creation is tacitly made a fourth divine hypostasis.

Oord draws on the necessary relation between God and creation to resolve a theoretical aspect of the problem of evil. It has been solved because God must "essentially" relate to creatures. He writes,

21. Thomas Jay Oord, *Defining Love: A Philosophical, Scientific, and Theological Engagement* (Grand Rapids: Brazos, 2010), 205.
22. Ibid., 207.

The key to solving the problem of evil is my claim that God's prevenient provision of the power for freedom to every creature is a provision that derives from God's essence. This means that prevenient grace is a necessary, not wholly voluntary or arbitrary, aspect of deity. Because God necessarily provides freedom to all individuals as God essentially relates to them, it makes no sense to suggest that God could fail to provide freedom and power. God's essential relatedness to and omnipresence in creation entails that God cannot withdraw, fail to offer, or override the freedom that God necessarily gives creatures each moment. God's loving gift of freedom derives from God's very nature.[23]

God's essence is love that seeks the flourishing of the creature. Such flourishing requires the gift of freedom.

Oord is an incompatibilist (as will be discussed below), so God's freedom to act cannot override the creature's without calling the creature's freedom into question. The existence of evil is not because of divine permission. God does not give the creature permission to do what God otherwise would not will for the creature; God cannot do otherwise, for God's essence is to communicate this freedom to the creature. God and creation are essentially related because God's essence is freedom. God is a causal force who, once freedom is given to the creature, loses control of it in a sense.

Like all process theologians who solve the theoretical problem of evil, Oord does so by drawing on Whitehead's metaphysics. Central to his revisionism is this claim, a claim found among all process theologians, and one that makes their work highly contested as bearing continuity with the Christian tradition: "A key insight in Whitehead's enterprise is his insight that 'God is not to be treated as an exception to all metaphysical principles, invoked to save their collapse. He is their chief exemplification.' This insight is important because theologians often attribute to God categories of being that make God different from creatures in *all* ways."[24] As we have seen from the discussion in the first two chapters, Oord is only partially correct in his reading of nonprocess theologians. The purpose of the language of divine perfection and simplicity is that similarities between God and

23. Ibid., 209.
24. Ibid., 118.

creatures exist, but not because the distinction between God and creation is nullified. God and creatures cannot be brought together under a single category of being that allows for a univocal application of methodological principles, but this univocity is precisely what allows for Oord's relational theology. Here is a decisive commonality among nearly all calls for revision, the rejection of analogy and advocacy of univocity. Oord writes, "If we consider God an agent metaphysically similar to other agents, what we say about love—for example, love involves responsive relations to others—can apply both to God and to creatures."[25] Unlike Thomas, Owen, or Arminius, Oord has not followed the attribution, remotion, and the way of eminence in using language about God. He gains direct access to God based on a univocal causality. He writes, "I consider God an actual, causal, agent to whose inspiration or 'call,' creatures respond appropriately when expressing love. I will claim that this causal influence does not violate the dominant methods of science which rely primarily on observation through sense perception."[26] The metaphysical assumptions that warrant this claim take us into a discussion of Whitehead's philosophy.

God as an Actual Entity on the Same Level as All Entities

Process theology leans heavily on the work of mathematician and metaphysician Alfred North Whitehead, who was one of the first philosophers to identify and challenge "substance metaphysics." He found it no longer acceptable to modern philosophy because of advances in science, and he offered an alternative that he called a "philosophy of organism." For Whitehead, Aristotle's "primary substances" mislead us. They tempt us to assume that the "'subject-predicate' form of proposition embodies the finally adequate mode

25. Ibid., 182. I find it confusing and a contradiction that Oord can later state, "Versions of process theology that suppose an external metaphysical constraint or the imposition of outside conditions on God's power ought to be rejected" (206). I take his point to be this. The "limitation" on God's power by God's necessary relation to creatures through the communication of freedom is not an external constraint because that necessary relation is God's essence. If this is his point, it only makes distinguishing the necessary God-creation relation from the Triune relations all the more difficult.

26. Ibid., 21.

of statement about the actual world."[27] Substance is what perdures beneath the changing accidents. Whitehead found the philosophical and theological tradition captured by the image of changeless substances. Modern science held no place for them or the *demonstratio propter quid* based on such stable essences. The question *quid est* no longer makes sense. We do not look for stable quiddities, not even in God.

In opposition to Aristotle's misleading use of language, Whitehead specified what is required for any "actual entity." He writes, "It is fundamental to the metaphysical doctrine of the philosophy of organism, that the notion of an actual entity as the unchanging subject of change is completely abandoned. An actual entity is at once the subject experiencing and the superject of its experiences."[28] For Whitehead, everything that is is an "actual entity," including God; so he states, "God is an actual entity and so is the most trivial puff of existence in far-off empty space. But, though there are gradations of importance and diversities of function, yet in the principles which actuality exemplifies all are on the same level."[29] That final statement, "all are on the same level," is foundational for process theology. Process theology would not work without this basic metaphysical assumption, as we saw in the previous section. God is an actual entity who can be known like other actual entities, for they are related in a process that exists "on the same level." If process theologians are not this explicit about the univocity within which they work, they must still assume a greater metaphysical entity—process—in which God and creation can then be really related. It is the reason Oord can invoke "the dominant method of science" based on "causal influence" and relying "primarily on observation through sense perception" as appropriate for both knowing fruit flies and God.[30] The ironic

---

27. Alfred North Whitehead, *Process and Reality* (New York: Free Press, 1978), 30. As we shall see below, St. Augustine echoed this concern about Aristotle in his *Confessions*.
28. Ibid., 29.
29. Ibid., 18.
30. Oord, *Defining Love*, 21.

consequence of this revision, however, is that God is understood more in terms of a causal power than God ever was in Thomas Aquinas.

Whitehead is rigorously consistent in his application of this foundational principle of actuality. He denies God a past, but God still has the "same threefold character" as all other actual entities: a "primordial nature," a "consequent nature" that includes the "physical prehension by God of the actualities of the evolving universe," and a "superjective nature," which is the "pragmatic value of his specific satisfaction qualifying the transcendent creativity in the various temporal instances."[31] God, then, is the "outcome of creativity."[32] God is a future event that happens. God is also the "primordial, non-temporal, accident" of creativity.[33]

To call God an accident of creativity is confusing. It can only mean that we have indeed thought something greater than God to which God is potentially ordered, that something greater is "creativity" or "process," and this makes it difficult if not impossible for process theology to uphold God's "perfection" in either Anselm's or Aquinas's sense. God has a future in which God's being is affected by creation such that who God is remains open.

The majority of theologians and theological projects that raise the metaphysical question agree to some degree with Whitehead's diagnosis. The problem in the traditional teaching on God is "substance metaphysics," because it posits "substance" as an unchanging source and then identifies it with God. Substance metaphysics then gives rise to a static, lifeless deity who cannot be made to cohere with the biblical God. God becomes impassible and consequently aloof, distant, and unloving. God is a God of power who causes all things to be but refuses to use his power to prevent evil.

---

31. Whitehead, *Process and Reality*, 87.
32. Whitehead states, "This is the conception of God, according to which he is considered as the outcome of creativity, as the foundation of order, and as the good towards novelty" (88).
33. "In the philosophy of organism this ultimate is termed 'creativity'; and God is its primordial, non-temporal accident. In monistic philosophies, Spinoza's or absolute idealism, this ultimate is God, who is also equivalently termed 'The Absolute'" (ibid., 7).

Revisions to the Traditional Answer

Griffin's remedy to the inference to atheism is to reject divine simplicity. God's knowledge and will must be distinguished, and thus God must be composite, constituted as an actual entity by the process in which God operates. God wills a future but does not have secure knowledge of it nor the power to ensure its outcome. The most God can do is "lure" us toward it, and the process in which God and creatures share cannot but affect God. Once divinity is shorn of simplicity, other terms, like *eternity*, must also be jettisoned. Griffin writes, "But, while for me religious faith involves believing in a greatest conceivable being, and this means one who is perfect in knowledge and power, I deny that it follows that this being can know or determine the details of the future."[34] God only lures us into that future. In order to do so, impassibility and immutability must be abandoned. God is affected by creatures' actions and responds accordingly. That God must be so affected is a metaphysical principle "to which God must conform."[35] God must conform to it because each being who exercises power is an "actual entity." No actual entity can act for another, and the presence of more than one entails that they are linked by a process within which one actual entity's exercise of power sets conditions on that of another. God is no exception to this metaphysical principle but must work within it. Evil, then, is not willed by God but is a byproduct of the metaphysical principles within which every actual entity, including God, works.

If the traditional language fails to express the central divine reality that God is love, then of course it must be abandoned. But no theologian who offered the traditional answer ever suggested God is not love. Thomas presented "Love" as one of God's Names. He did not, however, univocally move from what love is among creatures to what it must be for God. Here we see the effects of the rejection of remotion, abstraction, and analogy among process theologians. As an

---

34. Griffin, *God, Power and Evil*, 142.
35. Ibid., 297.

actual entity based on the same level as all other entities, language applied to God now functions identically to language applied to creatures. This option was not available to Aquinas because he was a metaphysician who affirmed that God is "the measure that cannot be measured" (to quote Aristotle) and a biblical interpreter who recognized God cannot be spoken of in such a way that God is turned into a creature, a clear violation of the First Commandment. He did not reject the good of the human body and its necessary affectivity, but he could not univocally apply such a condition to God. God cannot have passions because God has no body. Such passion is possible for Cobb and Griffin because, following Whitehead closely, God is an actual entity among other entities. Thus they give this definition of God: "In sum, God is that factor in the universe which establishes what-is-not as relevant to what-is, and lures the world toward new forms of realization."[36] Notice God's location—"a factor in the universe."

One of the theological difficulties in process metaphysics is the use of the indefinite article in speaking of God. As Griffin puts it, God is "an individual actual being."[37] By this he means more than the traditional language that God is one; he means that God, like all actual beings, can only work within a reality always already defined by metaphysical principles that God neither creates nor controls. The "metaphysical principle of reality" is called "creativity," and it "is not a contingent feature of reality. It is beyond all volition, even God's."[38]

Creativity becomes a metaphysical principle that does significant dogmatic work for Cobb and Griffin. It defines how they can understand incarnation and Trinity. They state, "God as creative love, the Primordial Nature of God, is what is incarnate in Jesus. This is not a creature of God or a derivative and subordinate aspect of deity. It is distinguishable from other aspects of deity, but it is coequal with them and participates equally with them in deity itself."[39] Although this affirmation of the incarnation of God's "primordial nature" incarnate

---

36. Cobb and Griffin, *Process Theology*.
37. Griffin, *God, Power and Evil*, 268.
38. Ibid., 279.
39. Cobb and Griffin, *Process Theology*, 109.

in Jesus is supposed to be Athanasian, their revision to the doctrine of the Trinity does not support their claim. They deny the Spirit is a "person" in the traditional sense. God's processions are to be understood in terms of the metaphysics of creativity. Thus persons in God are only "God as creative love" and "God as responsive love," both of which have a transcendent and immanent aspect, and so they assert that it would be more fitting to speak of a "quaternity" than a Trinity. The most they can affirm of the Trinity is the following: "If instead we add to the thought of the two persons the unity in which they are held together in the one God, then we have a trinity, but the unity is not another person in the same sense that the other two are persons."[40] Any reasonable, arm's-length analysis of this claim could only conclude it is at best binitarian.

Lodahl also finds revisions necessary because the traditional answer misses "the central biblical affirmation that God is a God of relation."[41] My exposition of Thomas in chapter 1 sought to show how this criticism is a caricature. For Thomas, God's "substance," "essence," or "nature" is in itself "relation." There is no static, abstract "being" behind the relations; that is the main point for the presentation of the perfectly simple God in questions 2–11 of the *Summa*. The criticism of "substance metaphysics" seldom if ever takes this into account. It repeats Whitehead's criticism without attention to how "substance" works in Christian, Jewish, or Islamic theologians and philosophers. It assumes a caricatured Aristotelianism was taken up into the Christian tradition without transformation. It does not address the common understanding, as we shall see, that the tradition already transformed divine simplicity by making substance and relation primary ontological categories.

Lodahl, however, is not raising the question whether God is relation in God's substance, but whether the traditional answer adequately affirms God's covenanting relation with creation. If God were the static, abstract deity of a putative "substance metaphysics," then God would

---

40. Ibid. They also state, "The doctrine of the Trinity is the heart of Christian faith, a source of distortion, and an artificial game that has brought theology into justifiable disrepute" (109).
41. Lodahl, *Story of God*, 91.

not seem to be able to enter into relation with creation. Here an odd twist accompanies Lodahl and many other calls for revision. God has the ability to be this absolute, abstract deity that they find objectionable, but God chooses not to remain as such. Take, for instance, this claim: "God the Sole Power, the omnipotent Creator, empties himself of the prerogatives of Absolute Being in order to enter into relation with beings of his own making."[42] God is what process theologians fear God could be—a God of absolute Power—but by creating others God chooses not to be what God otherwise would have been. Creation assists God in "emptying" God's being of those "prerogatives" so that God can now enter into "relation with beings of his own making."

Conclusion

The suspicion and reexamination that leads to a call to revise the traditional answer has diverse roots, some laudable, others not so much. Two reasons for it can be dismissed immediately—sentimentality and the inevitability of "progress." Some calls for rejection or revision arise from a sentimental view of love in which God must be conceptualized as capable of suffering, feeling pain, or being affected by what affects us if God is to be loving. We need God to be "one of us." Rather than the disturbing God of "holy fire" found in Scripture, we need God to be the fellow sufferer who understands.[43] A second reason is the desire to make progress in theology. Rejecting and revising is what moderns do—we reject what is past as obsolete in order to make way for the "new and improved" that is always on the way, even if it never quite arrives. This cultural default position is known as "progress." We find it in fashion, automobiles, entertainment, and philosophy. We should not be surprised it is also found in modern theology. Sentimentality and progress are poor

---

42. Ibid., 92.
43. Katherine Sonderegger has a beautiful account of God as "Holy Fire." See Sonderegger, *Systematic Theology*, 1:489.

reasons for the call for rejection and revision. They do not deserve consideration.

Process theology can be guilty of sentimentality. Whitehead's "the fellow-sufferer who understands" is certainly riddled with it, but process theology also raises some important concerns about God and power, the problem of evil, and the problem divine simplicity coupled with causality raises for theology. The three concerns are related. If God is all-powerful, as the traditional answer affirms, and God is simple such that God's knowledge is God's will, then how can everything that exists not be directly caused by God, including evil? The perfectly simple Triune God cannot pass the test of the theoretical problem of evil. The radical revision is to replace divine simplicity and all its correlates with a processual deity who is an actual entity in relation with other entities. This move, however, still takes God to be causal power, but now that power has been curtailed. As a causal power, God will inevitably be implicated in the causal nexus of creation. This modern emphasis on deity had roots deep in Western theology, even in Thomism. It is a problem that must be dealt with below. Suffice it for now to raise it in terms David Hart has set forth:

> This donation of being [by God to creatures] is so utterly beyond any species of causality we can conceive that the very word "cause" has only the most remotely analogous value in regard to it. And, whatever warrant Thomists might find in speaking of God, as the first efficient cause of creation (which I believe to be in principle wrong), such language is misleading unless the analogical scope of the concept of efficiency has been extended almost to the point of apophasis.[44]

Ironically, process theology poses no challenge to a Western tradition that depicts God primarily in terms of cause; it accentuates that tradition. It colludes with such a deity and asks how we can limit his power.

Process theologians claim to have solved the theoretical problem of evil. God is neither the cause of evil nor the one culpable for it.

---

44. David Hart, "Providence and Causality: On Divine Innocence," in Francesca Murphy and Philip Ziegler, *Providence of God: Deus Habet Consilium* (London: T&T Clark, 2009), 40.

Oord puts it succinctly: "this God is not culpable for failing to prevent the evils caused by free or indeterminate creatures."[45] If he is correct, it might not be good news. The results are sobering. The apologetic desire to liberate God from culpability for evil drives process theology. Without this desire it has no persuasive lure. But is there not an important distinction between making God the cause of evil, which Christian theology must reject, and making God in some sense "culpable" for it? I do not mean to suggest that God wills evil or even permits it for some greater good, but I do mean to suggest that whatever evil is, for what it is will remain an insoluble mystery, Jews and Christians have looked to God to redeem it; otherwise they could not pray the Psalms:

Why, O Lord, do you stand far off?
Why do you hide yourself in times of trouble?
In arrogance the wicked persecute the poor—
let them be caught in the schemes they have devised. (Ps. 10:1–2)
My God, my God, why have you forsaken me?
Why are you so far from helping me, from the words of my groaning?
O my God, I cry by day, but you do not answer,
and by night, but find no rest. (Ps. 22:1–2)

God is not the cause of evil. God is not a "cause" at all in the sense process theology sets forth, turning God into an actual entity among other entities, entangling God in a Greek cosmology of an eternal creation. But God is culpable for evil and thus can be called on to remedy it. God can be argued with; Moses can stand in the breach. Process theology has a God whose primary response to these real situations of distress is that God is doing the best that can be done given the metaphysical structure of creativity within which God must work. It is no wonder that in the end, God makes little difference. As Keller baldly states, "It is not up to God to right our moral wrongs, to fix our injustices and correct our oppressions. That doesn't happen. To depend on God to intervene, to justify 'himself,' to operate as the just patriarch is to abdicate our own moral responsibility for the earth."[46]

45. Oord, *Defining Love*, 167.
46. Keller, *Face of the Deep*, 140.

Given the depth of the injustices and oppression that have littered human history, this ethical conclusion to process theology holds little comfort. Process theology does not resolve the problem of evil; it makes evil irresolvable even by God. It generates a metaphysics that gets God off the hook for evil, but evil remains—perhaps for eternity. Process theologians have no guarantee that evil will not have the last word. Would not atheism be preferable? It too resolves the theoretical problem of evil.

Process theology depends on a Greek metaphysics of chaos. Whitehead states this explicitly, referencing the *Timaeus* and acknowledging it was the source for his "philosophy of organism." He writes, "In the *Timaeus* the origin of the present cosmic epoch is traced back to an aboriginal disorder, chaotic according to our ideals. This is the evolutionary doctrine of the philosophy of organism. Plato's notion has puzzled critics who are obsessed with the Semitic theory of a wholly transcendent God creating out of nothing an accidental universe."[47] It should come as no surprise, then, that process theologians find deep difficulties with *creatio ex nihilo* and opt for Plato's *Timaeus* instead. Oord overlooks the Platonic origins of his own metaphysics when he states that *creatio ex nihilo* "fit well with the Neoplatonic doctrine of God that was gaining influence in early Christianity. Neoplatonism taught that God is eternal, self-sufficient, simple, impassible, omnipotent, immutable and commands the world through the divine will."[48] After wrongly stating that *creatio ex nihilo* was the product of Greek thought, he then says, "The idea that God could have created the universe from something rather than nothing did not disappear altogether, however. Thomas Aquinas, for instance, affirmed that creation from something was a logical possibility."[49] He fails to note that it was only a logical possibility because Aristotle taught it and for Thomas reason qua reason could not reject it. It was his reading of Holy Scripture that made him reject it. *Creatio ex nihilo* emerges not from Plato and Aristotle, as Whitehead rightly

47. Whitehead, *Process and Reality*, 95.
48. Oord, *Defining Love*, 158.
49. Ibid., 159.

acknowledged, but from Jewish and Christian reflection on the origin of creation. It does not emerge from a contest between God, who must contain, control, or lure a chaos that always escapes its form—the *khora*. It emerges out of love and gift. Here the importance of Thomas's statement on the reason for the divine processions must be emphasized again. They help us understand creation. Because God is already relation, God does not need creation to enter into relation. Creation then is entirely gift; it is not necessary. That does not make it arbitrary; it does make it contingent. To make the God-creation relation necessary is not to revise Christianity; it is to replace it with something else, something more like an unbaptized Aristotle or Plato.

Process theology caricatures previous theological answers, concocting a strange creature called "classical theism" that is static, aloof, and unloving, asserting this creature was what earlier generations called God. Process theology then reacts against it, countering it with an unbaptized Greek metaphysics of becoming, filtered through Whitehead, that modifies every aspect of Christian theology, including the doctrine of creation. It conceives God primarily as causal power and has little to no place for the doctrine of the Trinity; it does no work in process theology. The only relation that matters is the relation between God and creation, and despite all protests to the contrary, that relation is indistinguishable from the Triune relations. It makes God an actual being among beings who can be known through common metaphysical, or even worse empirical, scientific, principles. It claims to know too much about God while critiquing others for claiming too much truth about God. In fact, the traditional answer is much more reserved than process theology in what it claims to know. William Desmond offers the proper verdict: "Whiteheadians insist that God cannot be an exception to the system of metaphysical principles. But if God is God and nothing but God is God, we are dealing with the *absolute exception*. To insist on metaphysical homogeneity to uphold integral intelligibility would have something unintelligible, if not obtuse about it. If it is God they are talking about, we do not know what they are talking about. For it if is God they are talking about, then they are not talking about God."[50]

50. William Desmond, *God and the Between* (Oxford: Blackwell, 2008), 245.

5

The Question of Divine and Human
Freedom: Open Theism

If process theology is motivated by addressing the theoretical problem of evil, open theism, and its call for revision, is motivated more by the question of the relationship between human and divine freedom. This problem, as we shall see, is one that drives a great deal of modern ethics and politics. It was the driving force behind Immanuel Kant's important philosophical work and its metaphysical revisions. The problem can be stated in different forms, but its basic form is this: If a perfectly simple, omnipotent, and omniscient being exists who creates the world, then how can human creatures be free? Linda Zagzebski poses the problem as one of divine foreknowledge and human freedom. The difficulty is in affirming two central Christian beliefs without contradiction: "first, that God has infallibly true beliefs about everything that will happen in the future, and second, that human beings have free will in a sense of 'free' that is incompatible with determinism."[1] Zagzebski will later challenge this formulation by rightly challenging whether God has "beliefs" altogether. She recognizes that the Thomist teaching on God does not allow "beliefs" to be attributed to God; they are ruled out by eternity. As we shall see, eternity is one of the attributes open theists challenge.

In setting forth the problem, Zagzebski uses the term *incompatible*. The terms *compatibilism* and *incompatibilism* have diverse meanings in philosophy and theology, but a basic meaning behind them is this: *Compatibilism* assumes that something being willed or determined by God (or nature) does not rule out human freedom. There could be a God who providentially orders the world in its details, and that does not entail that humans are determined and unfree. If these terms are applicable to Thomas, and that is contested since he never drew on such a term or concept, he would be found in the compatibilist camp. *Incompatibilism* finds compatibilism illogical. If divine providence meticulously knows everything that has, is, or will happen, and if that knowledge is the same as divine will, then human agency is determined and unfree. Process theologians, analytic theologians, open theists, and liberation theologians all raise the question of freedom; many of them are incompatibilists. This chapter will focus on open theists, for the question of freedom has a motivating power for them as the problem of evil does for process theology, but the question arises as much for analytic theologians and philosophers as it does for open theists. This similarity is unsurprising. Open theists and analytic theologians share an analytic method for conceiving the doctrine of God.

The analytic method finds real difficulties with Thomas Aquinas's resolution to the problem of divine knowledge and will. William Lane Craig finds Thomas unpersuasive and falling into determinism. He concludes an analysis of Thomas's position by stating,

> Therefore, it seems to me that having sought to escape the clutches of theological fatalism, Aquinas flees into the arms of divine determinism. In maintaining that God's knowledge is the cause of everything God knows, Thomas transforms the universe into a nexus which, though freely chosen by God, is causally determined from above, thus eliminating human freedom.[2]

---

1. Linda Trinkaus Zagzebski, *The Dilemma of Freedom and Foreknowledge* (New York: Oxford University Press, 1991), 3.

Many open theists draw on an analytic method and come to a similar conclusion as, for instance, John Sanders, when he asks in response to my defense of Thomas:

> Are God's desires ever thwarted in the least detail? If not, then I fail to see how Long's view escapes theological determinism. His response may be that these questions embody the wrong way to speak about God. But as I have already stated, this is the language of the Bible and has been the language of billions of Christians so I prefer to stick with this traditional language rather than jettison it in favor of language drawn from a metaphysical system.[3]

Sanders, like Craig, will claim biblical warrant for his rejection of the perfectly simple Triune God and his revisions to it.

What Is Open Theism?

Open theism is a call for revision to the traditional answer by primarily evangelical theologians. It generated a great deal of controversy; theologians lost academic positions for teaching it. Like process theology, open theists position their view of "theism" against the "classical theism" of Thomas Aquinas. Unlike process theology, open theism grounds its position not in a revised metaphysics but in Scripture. Gregory Boyd draws on 2 Kgs. 20:1–6 to show the difficulties with the traditional answer.[4] God speaks to King Hezekiah through the prophet Isaiah and tells him he will die from his current illness so it is time for him to "set his house in order." King Hezekiah prays consistent with the lament of the psalms noted in the previous section: "Remember now, O Lord, I implore you, how I have walked before you in faithfulness with a whole heart and have done what is good in your sight." An open theist like Boyd acknowledges what Oord and Keller deny. Boyd writes, "In a general sense, the Creator must be responsible for everything that transpires in his creation."[5] Boyd's theology does

2. William Lane Craig, *The Problem of Divine Foreknowledge and Future Contingents from Aristotle to Suarez* (Leiden: Brill, 1988), 126.
3. "John Sanders's Response," in D. Stephen Long and George Kalantzis, eds., *The Sovereignty of God Debate* (Eugene, OR: Cascade Books, 2009), 163.
4. Gregory Boyd, *God of the Possible* (Grand Rapids: Baker Books, 2000), 7.

not make God inculpable for evil such that God can do nothing about it. We are to lament, to bring our frustrations, anger, fears, and tears to God. God hears Hezekiah's prayers, sees his tears, and decides to give him fifteen more years to live. Boyd asks how the perfectly simple God who is without change or passion fits with the God who changes his plan for Hezekiah. Open theism emerges from attention to Scripture.

John Sanders is one of the most articulate open theists. He presents it as a subset of freewill theism. Sanders contrasts freewill theism to classical theism; Thomas Aquinas is his exemplar for the latter. Freewill theism has nine points, most of which challenge the traditional answer to some degree. He lists the following points as characterizing freewill theism:

1. God is either atemporal (eternal) or temporal (everlasting).
2. Rejects pure actuality, for God does receive our prayers and worship. Rejects divine simplicity.
3. Weakly immutable. The *character* of God does not change, but God can have changing plans, thoughts, and emotions.
4. Weakly impassible. God is affected by and responds to our prayers and actions.
5. General sovereignty. God ordains the structures of creation (our boundaries) and allows for human free will (libertarian freedom). Sometimes God acts to ensure that specific things happen.
6. God does not have a meticulous blueprint for everything that happens.
7. God does not exercise meticulous providence. The divine will can be frustrated for some things as God takes risks.
8. God is omniscient (knows all that is knowable).
9. God has either simple foreknowledge or dynamic omniscience.[6]

Open theism differs from freewill theism in that it rejects the conjunctions in numbers 1 and 9, opting for God's temporal everlastingness rather than eternity, and dynamic omniscience rather than simple foreknowledge.[7]

Like process theology, open theism affirms God's perfection but does

---

5. Ibid., 135.
6. John Sanders, *The God Who Risks* (Downers Grove, IL: InterVarsity, 2007), 197.
7. For a more elaborate chart setting forth the similarities and differences between traditional freewill theism and open theism, see John Sanders, "Divine Suffering in an Openness of God Perspective," in Long and Kalantzis, *Sovereignty of God Debate*, 137–38.

so by cordoning it off from divine simplicity and timeless eternity. It affirms a weak version of immutability and impassibility. Because open theism rejects simplicity, it attributes different parts to God, such as plans, thoughts, and emotions that are other than God's character. God's "character" does not change, but God's "plans, thoughts and emotions" do. God is weakly impassible in that God is not necessarily affected by creation, but God can will to be so affected. God can voluntarily choose to be so affected at some moment, and, it would seem, God can also voluntarily choose not to be so affected, for this is necessary for divine freedom. This voluntary decision by God to be affected by creation is a variation on a similar position we saw in Lodahl's process theology. God could be impassible, but God chooses not to be in God's freedom.

Open Theism's Similarities and Dissimilarities to Process Theology

Although open theists seek to distance their position from process theism for good theological reasons, open theism is a theology that bears some family resemblance to process theology. It shares a common diagnosis as to what ails modern theology. First and foremost, open theism finds substance metaphysics to be a problem that modern theology must address and remedy. Like most of the calls for revision, it identifies the problem with "Hellenistic philosophy" in general and Thomas Aquinas in specific. Greg Boyd states, "My fundamental thesis is that the classical theological tradition became misguided when, under the influence of Hellenistic philosophy, it defined God's perfection in static, timeless terms."[8] Sanders sees Thomas's "classical theism" and "freewill theism" as two legitimate traditional options. He refers to Thomas as "a brilliant thinker and devout believer" who "greatly advanced the development of classical theism in Medieval Christianity. Classical theism will become an extremely influential theological model, taking its place alongside freewill theism as the

---

8. Boyd, *God of the Possible*, 17.

other main explanation of the divine-human relationship."[9] As noted above, open theists find classical and freewill theism to be incompatible, especially because of Thomas's Boethian teaching on eternity and his affirmation of simplicity. If God is "perfect" in this timeless sense, then God cannot be the dramatic agent Scripture portrays.

Once substance metaphysics is found wanting, other shared assumptions with process theology follow. They share at least these assumptions: (1) Substance metaphysics or classical theism is no longer viable, Thomas Aquinas being their most visible proponent. (2) Because of number 1, divine attributes such as simplicity, impassibility, eternity, and immutability must be rejected or revised. (3) The traditional answer cannot handle the problem of evil as well as the called-for revisions can. (4) Freedom, both divine and human, is libertarian. Agents are free only when they can choose to act or not act in a given situation. (5) Affirming God's primary causality as a meticulous providential ordering of creaturely life is incompatible with affirming a free human secondary causality. Although open theism is not a modern apologetic to address the problem of evil based on the normative method of science, it shares a worry that the God of absolute power leads to horrendous conclusions that exacerbate the problem of evil. As William Hasker states, "If we accentuate God's absolute control over everything that happens, we are forced to attribute to him the same control over evil events and actions as over good."[10] However, the driving force behind open theism is not the theoretical problem of evil, and open theists do not claim to have solved it. John Sanders notes, "There is no *single* problem of evil. Different models of God and different views of providence generate different problems of evil."[11] Open theists like Sanders acknowledge the persistent difficulty evil poses for every doctrine of God. Rather than the theoretical problem of evil, the problem of freedom motivates

9. Sanders, *God Who Risks*, 154.
10. William Hasker, *God, Time, and Knowledge* (Ithaca, NY, and London: Cornell University Press, 1989), 199.
11. Sanders, *God Who Risks*, 261.

open theists. Here is a significant difference, as shall be shown below. Process theology and open theists share an assumption of incompatibilism, but process theology resolves it by following Whitehead's metaphysics and interpreting God as an actual being among other actual beings. Open theism disavows this resolution. They claim to reject setting God within an overarching metaphysical structure that limits God's freedom and instead seek to be consistent with the divine agency narrated in Holy Scripture.

Libertarian Freedom and the Call for Revision

Open theists argue that the traditional answer loses human freedom for a similar reason that process theologians reject the doctrine of simplicity. God's knowledge and will supposedly cannot, or should not, be divided in classical theism. If God knows the future, God wills it. Like process theology, open theism rejects the Thomistic affirmation of secondary causality. For Thomas, God can will the future, even future contingents, and humans remain free agents exercising a genuine secondary causality. God's meticulous providential will and human freedom are compatible. Process theology, open theism, and much of analytic theology find secondary causality logically absurd. If God elects human creatures through a meticulous providence, then creatures are not free. God and creatures are free only if they possess a libertarian freedom.

Hasker explains what is required for libertarian freedom: "A situation in which an agent makes a libertarian free choice with respect to doing or not doing something is a situation in which the agent *might* do that thing but also might refrain from doing it."[12] Freedom entails God and creatures have a power of acting or not acting in every temporal succession. Anything less is not freedom. Hasker goes so far as to argue that if the redeemed in heaven cannot sin, then "acts of this sort are *not* free in the very strict sense required by libertarianism."[13] This libertarian understanding of freedom is present

---

12. Hasker, *God, Time, and Knowledge*, 28.
13. Ibid., 24n9.

among process theologians as well. Thomas Oord argues that a scientific definition of love entails that to love is "to act intentionally." Then he states, "To say it another way: love is meaningless if individuals are not free to choose one action rather than others. In philosophical circles, this understanding of self-determination fits best in the libertarian or incompatibilist traditions."[14] This particular account of freedom is then applied to God, with significant consequences. God will need to deliberate about available options in order to be loving. If God deliberates, some kind of successiveness must be attributed; God will then have "beliefs" that are, of course, other than knowledge. In other words, God might believe that if God does x, a human agent will do y. But until God does x, God does not know whether the human agent will do y. Both God and the human agent must be free to do other than x or y. On this understanding of freedom, the traditional answer is a priori ruled out because God's eternity excludes deliberation, and God's simple perfection entails that God's will is free only to love what is good and perfect. Freedom is not choice but to know and will the good. God's knowledge is the knowledge of God's own essence; it is a simultaneous, perfect possession of God's self and all the ways creatures can participate in God's gift of being.

Despite their similar conceptions of freedom, open theism's emphasis on libertarian freedom reveals a significant difference from process theologians. The latter condition God's freedom through an overarching metaphysical framework known as creativity or process. God is not free to act beyond that framework, even though, as we saw with Oord, the divine nature gets redefined in terms of that framework. Open theists deny any such framework. If God's future is not open and free, then, Sanders suggests, God would be captive to his own metaphysical nature. "God is not captive to an *arche* (exterior ruler); but if libertarian freedom is not predicated of God, then God is 'captive' to his own nature in that God is not free to do otherwise than what

---

14. Thomas Jay Oord, *Defining Love: A Philosophical, Scientific, and Theological Engagement* (Grand Rapids: Brazos, 2010), 17. Oord does reject freedom as "unfettered personal autonomy."

he does. The divine freedom and contingency of the creatures are thus rendered suspect."[15] Whatever God has done, is doing, or will do must have the possibility of being otherwise if God is free. Whether this understanding of freedom is itself a metaphysical framework within which open theism conceives God will be discussed below.

Divine libertarianism requires a rejection of classical theism, which Sanders finds to be a later development in Christian tradition beginning with Augustine, and a (re)affirmation of at least freewill theism, which he finds in the Cappadocians.[16] We will see below that other theologians who call for revision make a similar distinction between Augustine and the Cappadocians. While there are differences between them, however, divine simplicity was not one of them. For Sanders, simplicity must be rejected, and once it is rejected the other names in the traditional answer fall away. He states this position forthrightly: "The great classical theists ... understood the inter-connectedness between simplicity, immutability, impassibility, absolute unconditionedness and meticulous providence. These theologians understood that these doctrines are a package deal and you cannot, without being *logically inconsistent*, pick-and-choose among them as some do today."[17] But if we hold to meticulous providence, then not only must we make God the author of evil, we also lose human and divine freedom. If God knows everything that will happen in the future, and God's knowledge is infallible, then those events will take place regardless of human agency; Hezekiah's prayers would be useless. If human beings are to be free, self-determining agents, then God cannot have exhaustive foreknowledge of everything that will happen.

Boyd notes that the controversy over "open theism" is not about God's knowledge. He states, "The issue is not about God's knowledge at all. Everyone agrees he knows reality perfectly. The issue is the *content* of the reality God perfectly knows."[18] God knows all future possibilities,

---

15. Sanders, *God Who Risks*, 185.
16. Ibid., 148.
17. Ibid., 196.
18. Boyd, *God of the Possible*, 125.

but God knows them as possibilities because they do not yet exist. The open theism debate is less about God's knowledge and more about God's will. If God's knowledge determined actualities, then God would have less power than human creatures, because we would have abilities denied to God, especially the power of novelty. Boyd writes, "We can enjoy novelty—new songs, fresh poems, original paintings, unanticipated twists in stories, spontaneous play, creative dances, and so on. We can wonder, experience adventure and enjoy surprises when encountering the unexpected. Though the Bible is explicit in ascribing many of these experiences to God, the classical view rules them out. Is this not limiting God?"[19] John Sanders puts similar questions to the traditional answer. He asks, "Does God take risks of any sort? Is the world, in every respect, exactly the way God wants it to be? Does God ever respond to our prayers? Are any of God's decisions contingent upon what creatures decide? Are God's desires ever thwarted in the least detail?"[20] Boyd and Sanders's questions are important. They are grounded in Scripture and affirm its dramatic import.

A Metaphysics of Freedom?

The questions also assume a libertarian conception of freedom, and that raises the question whether this conception is most appropriate to express divine freedom. For open theism, freedom for both God and creatures entails the possibility of novelty. There could be no surprise, no risk, no drama if God does not have a freedom to choose among alternatives. Boyd writes, "The bottom line is that *life is all about possibilities*. We are thinking, feeling, willing, personal beings only because we, like God, are beings who can reflect on and choose between possibilities."[21] Boyd goes as far as to suggest that if God cannot choose among possibilities, then God cannot love. "As a triangle must have three sides and all bachelors must be unmarried, so love must be chosen."[22] John Sanders holds a similar position and

19. Ibid., 129.
20. "John Sanders's Response," in Long and Kalantzis, Sovereignty of God Debate, 163.
21. Boyd, God of the Possible, 94.
22. Ibid., 135.

acknowledges similarities between open theism's understanding of freedom and that found among analytic theologians. He approves of Nicholas Wolterstorff's statement, "Yet, *ontologically*, God cannot be a redeeming God without there being changeful variation among his states."[23] If God is to love, to redeem, then God must have the freedom to change God's mind, to engage with humans who are free to thwart God's will and revise God's plans. If God cannot change and decide among options, then God cannot bring them back from their misuse of freedom. Scripture would appear to be on their side, and they claim it, setting it against metaphysical intrusions, but this either-or, either Scripture or metaphysics, might not be as clear as it appears.

Sanders and Boyd cite many biblical narratives that support their view, but one important question that needs to be asked is whether they bring a philosophical presupposition to their reading of Scripture that results in their call for revising the traditional answer. In other words, is the necessity of libertarian freedom for God and creatures something they have found in Holy Scripture or brought to it? It is a philosophical position that is contested.[24] How we read Scripture depends on how we conceive its Author. If the Author is already defined by libertarian freedom, then the Author's actions will also be defined as such. That triangles have three sides and bachelors are unmarried should be noncontroversial; that love must be chosen among possibilities in order to be love is not. The problem of freedom that motivates them may be less biblical than modern; it may be one problem among others, and the question is which one should be addressed.

Various problems of freedom antedate the Christian theological tradition. Ancient philosophers such as Aristotle, Cicero, Plato, and Plotinus addressed it, as did many church fathers and theologians, including Origen, Augustine, Boethius, Thomas, Ockham, Scotus, and Suarez, among others.[25] Although it is an ancient philosophical and theological problem, it is also the quintessential problem for modern

---

23. Sanders, *God Who Risks*, 205.
24. For one such challenge see Zagzebski, *Dilemma of Freedom and Foreknowledge*, 154–62.
25. See Aristotle, *De interpretatione*, chap. 9; and Cicero's *De fato*. For a historical discussion of the

accounts of political sovereignty. Those accounts assume an autonomous exercise of freedom, and reason must be at the origin of a legitimate sovereignty. Beginning with this particular construal of freedom, God then becomes a problem. God could be the condition that makes that exercise possible, or God could be a barrier that poses limits to its exercise. If human beings are created by God, and God is the active agent who makes their being and agency possible, then how can they be free and sovereign over their actions? If political sovereignty is grounded in the autonomous exercise of the human will, then this problem must be resolved. The ethical and political dimensions of the problem of freedom are at the core of one of the most important modern philosophers—Immanuel Kant.

Open theists are not directly influenced by Kant. However, their motivating problem was also his. As Christopher Insole notes, "Kant struggles with a problem that is irreducibly theological: how can it be said that human beings are free, given that they are created by God?"[26] The problem is divine simplicity insofar as it assumes that what God creates must be one thing rather than another, and yet freedom requires that I can make of myself one thing rather than another. Kant originally affirmed divine simplicity, although the depth of his understanding of the doctrine is suspect. He never correlated it to the Trinity nor found the Trinity either useful or true in his many reflections on Christianity. Nonetheless, the God he assumed was the perfectly simple God, and this God posed problems for the freedom intrinsic to his philosophy. Kant insisted that human freedom should be self-determining, grounded in an autonomous will that chooses what is good not from incentive or self-interest but only because it is good. The good is what human reason "formulates a priori" by positing universal laws everyone can observe.[27] It has a political correlate in the

problem see Craig, *Problem of Divine Foreknowledge and Future Contingents*; and Zagzebski, *Dilemma of Freedom and Foreknowledge*.

26. Christopher J. Insole, *Kant and the Creation of Freedom: A Theological Problem* (Oxford: Oxford University Press, 2013), 1.

27. Immanuel Kant, *Foundations of the Metaphysics of Morals*, trans. Lewis White Beck (New York: Macmillan, 1987), 25.

development of nation-states that are governed by constitutional laws that they make for themselves.

Kant was originally a compatibilist who argued divine agency could be causal with respect to creatures and creatures could still be free. Christopher Insole traces the history of his transition from compatibilism to incompatibilism and finds it occurring in the 1760s, after Kant read Rousseau. Rousseau did not write on religion to the same extend Kant did, but in *Emile* he tells the story of "The Savoyard Vicar," a priest who has lost his faith in the church but still found a way to hold on to faith in God. His restored faith arises when he consults the "simplicity of his heart."[28] The vicar's faith is not based on reason or revelation but "sentiment," "subjective feelings" that are concerned with "well being." His faith has three main tenets. Rousseau puts them in the vicar's mouth in narrative form. First, the vicar tells Emile, "I believe therefore that a will moves the universe and animates nature. This is my first article of faith."[29] Second, "If moved matter shows me a will, matter moved according to certain laws shows me an intelligence. This is my second article of faith."[30] Third, "Man is therefore free in his actions and as such is animated by an immaterial substance. This is my third article of faith."[31] Rousseau offers a version of compatibilism, but one that begins with human freedom and reconceives divinity based on its needs. Mark Lilla argues that Kant developed a similar relationship between divine and human agency by systematizing three fundamental thoughts from Rousseau that then "completely reorient western philosophy." First, "man's faculties are limited." Second, "he yearns for answers that outstrip those limits." Third, "he can have answers of a sort so long as he formulates them with reference to his moral certainty."[32] That moral certainty can only be had with the presumption of a libertarian freedom. The previous Christian

---

28. Jean-Jacques Rousseau, *Emile or On Education*, trans. Allan Bloom (New York: Basic Books, 1979), 266–68.
29. Ibid., 273.
30. Ibid., 275.
31. Ibid., 281.
32. Mark Lilla, *The Stillborn God: Religion, Politics and the Modern West* (New York: Vintage Books, 2008), 120.

theological tradition asked the question, Given what we know of the perfectly simple Triune God, how can we conceive human freedom? Kant reversed the poles and asked, Given what we know of human freedom, how can we conceive, if we can, the divine nature?

Kant, however, was dissatisfied with grounding these fundamental tenets in sentiment. He sought a more rational foundation. In doing so, Insole finds him shifting from compatibilism to incompatibilism as he adopts two conditions necessary for freedom. First is the "alternative-possibility condition." For an agent to be free, the agent must be able to act otherwise than he or she acted. Second is the "ultimate responsibility condition." Freedom entails that an agent is "ultimately responsible" for his actions.[33] When both conditions are satisfied, the result is "transcendental freedom."[34] No external cause can determine the agent if transcendental freedom is to obtain. Here is where the specifically modern problem of God and freedom originates. Once Kant stipulates these conditions for transcendental freedom, and God is understood in terms of external causal power, then the freedom necessary for moral certainty will push against any speculative theology. Given the starting point in moral certainty and its basis in libertarian freedom, God can either not be known in speculative terms, or God can be hypothesized, but only consistent with transcendental freedom and a practical theology. Both the form and content of speculative theology will be called into question.

Kant also dismisses divine concurrence as a theological option. It moves beyond the compatibilism/incompatibilism distinction, for that distinction assumes God is an external cause that either acts on the creature remotely consistent with the creature's actions (compatibilism) or in opposition to the creature's actions (incompatibilism). The doctrine of concurrence, based on a metaphysics of participation, assumes that given God's nature as simple, infinite being, God is not an external cause at all. There is, after all, no "outside" to infinity on which God acts. God's actions are

33. Insole, *Kant and the Creation of Freedom*, 58.
34. Ibid.

donative, sustaining the creature in being and freedom as other than God so that divine and human action are never competitive. Kant's transcendental freedom had no place for divine concursus.[35] Insole finds this rejection of concurrence mistaken, for if concurrence is properly understood, it would have helped Kant reconcile divine and human freedom, a reconciliation he finally abandoned:

> Where concurrence is properly understood and assented to, God would be conceived of as an autonomous rather than a heteronomous influence on the creature, part of the creature's own movement, rather than "vying" with the creature. . . . If we consider that the law is grounded by rationality, which is itself grounded by, and constitutive of, the divine understanding, then my action of giving myself the law, in which God acts, becomes also a form of participation in the divine nature. God would act in the action by which I move closer to the divine nature.[36]

Kant's inability to affirm divine concursus, suggests Insole, is related to his "neglect of core doctrines such as the Trinity and divine simplicity."[37] They have the potential to move beyond the compatibilist versus incompatibilist construal of divine and human agency to a different model altogether. God is not an external cause who determines the will's action but a source more intimate to the agent than the agent is to her- or himself. God does not displace the human agent's freedom in order to work through it, but the two concur in a free act. Eleonore Stump finds something similar in Thomas's work. She writes,

> However, it is perhaps safe to say that, since Aquinas emphatically denies that any volition caused by something extrinsic to the agent can be free, his account of freedom of will is not a version of compatibilism. The only apparent exception has to do with God's acting on a human will. Aquinas holds that among extrinsic forces, God alone can act directly

35. Ibid., 171, 222, 232.

36. Ibid., 242.

37. "Theologians who have misgivings about Kant might find some illumination as to why they can feel uneasy in his company; where these misgivings are already well articulated, the denial of concurrence might be added to a list, which could include Kant's neglect of core doctrines such as the Trinity and divine simplicity, or his brisk translation (into terms useful to practical reason) of the bodily resurrection . . . and the hypostatic union of God and man in Jesus" (ibid., 232).

on some other's will without violating the will's nature, that is, without undermining its freedom.[38]

Thomas is an incompatibilist in that something external to the agent cannot determine the agent's action and that action still be free. He is a compatibilist in that God's actions are not "external" in the sense that they violate the will's nature and question its freedom. God is a different kind of force altogether. Thus the two terms do not fit well how divine and human agency work. If we understand human agency as freely participating in a divine agency that is not a causal force but a donating source of being, then we have a freedom that is not bound to libertarianism.[39] Freedom is not choice among competing options, but to will the good because it is desirable and one's will has been freed for it. No fatalism follows from this account of divine and human agency. God's gift to us is what makes us free, just as God's willing God's self makes God what God is, perfectly simple. God cannot be other.

This account of agency resists the libertarian assumption that freedom always requires the condition of novelty. G. K. Chesterton challenged such a view of freedom, finding it consistent with the "towering materialism which dominates the modern mind." It rests, he suggests, "upon one assumption, a false assumption." Chesterton explains,

> It is supposed that if a thing goes on repeating itself it is probably dead; a piece of clockwork. People feel that if the universe was personal it would vary; if the sun were alive it would dance. This is a fallacy even in relation to known fact. For the variation in human affairs is generally brought into them, not by life, but by death; by the dying down or breaking off of their strength or desire. . . . His routine might be due not to lifelessness, but to a rush of life. The thing I mean can be seen, for instance, in children, when they find some game or joke they specially enjoy. A child kicks his legs rhythmically through excess, not absence of life. Because children have abounding vitality, because they are spirit fierce and free, therefore they want things repeated and unchanged. They always say, "Do it again"; and the grown-up person does it again until he is nearly dead. For grown-up people are not strong enough to exult in monotony. But perhaps God is

---

38. Eleonore Stump, *Aquinas* (London: Routledge, 2003), 22–23.
39. The importance of this point will be more fully explained in the final chapter.

strong enough to exult in monotony. It is possible that God says every morning, "Do it again" to the sun; and every evening, "Do it again" to the moon. . . . It may be that He has the eternal appetite of infancy; for we have sinned and grown old, and our Father is younger than we. The repetition in Nature may not be a mere recurrence; it may be a theatrical ENCORE.[40]

Open theists are not Kantians, but they seem to be answering a problem of freedom with Kantian resonances. The emphases on novelty, spontaneity, and choice suggest that they have made philosophical judgments in which they then read Scripture. Like most biblical interpretation, who the Author is conceived to be determines a great deal of the narrative. Coupled with the shared assumption with process theology that "substance metaphysics" depicts a stable, static, abstract deity who is incapable of drama, the result is massive revisions in the doctrine of God and an overly literal reliance on biblical narrative. Chesterton's response is the best defense of "substance metaphysics." God's perfect simplicity is not a cage that destroys freedom, deadens passion, and dulls life; God is an excess of life, *actus purus*, possessing it in a repeatable eternity at the same time God donates and communicates it to creatures. That excess does not need the change and variation death brings for the sake of freedom; it is a freedom that always says "let's do it again."

Scripture Revisited

Still, Sanders and Boyd have raised an important question. How is the perfectly simple Triune God consistent with Holy Scripture? Suggesting that they are not innocent of incorporating metaphysical assumptions into their reading of Scripture is only to offer a negative argument. Something more positive needs to be set forth as well. Is the perfectly simple Triune God found in Scripture? I demonstrated in the first two chapters how the authorities for it thought they were drawing on Scripture, but more still needs to be done. Of course, individual texts could be cited for each of the divine attributes, just as individual texts could be cited against them, but such a procedure should have

40. G. K. Chesteron, *Orthodoxy* (Charleston, SC: Bibliobazar, 2007), 59–60.

little success in discerning whether or not to heed the call for doctrinal revisions. We could debate how to read Gen. 3:8, when Adam and Eve "heard the sound of the Lord God walking in the garden at the time of the evening breeze," and Gen. 7:16, where God "shut Noah in" the ark. We could also address the odd stories in which God tells Moses and others that they cannot see God's face and live, yet God does show Moses God's backside so that he gains a glimpse of divine glory (Exod. 33:17–23). How can we square that story with the odd narrative a few chapters earlier when we were told that Moses, Aaron, Nadab, Abihu, and seventy elders went up the mountain and "saw the God of Israel"? In fact, "they beheld God, and they ate and drank" (Exod. 24:9–11). How do we make sense of God speaking, walking, shutting doors, and appearing in bodily form? We could compare those passages in which few would suggest that God has legs, hands, vocal cords, mouth, or a finite form with passages that are less material but also challenge the traditional answer in which God repents, changes plans, suggests various options with consequences depending on human actions, and is affected by prayer. No one reads all these narratives literally. No one reads all of them allegorically.

What image of God does Holy Scripture present? The Christian God has agency; God acts in time without being constrained by it. But to make God a character in a story is to misread Scripture. It is, again, to use the indefinite article to speak of God that cannot but make God an actual entity among entities. A sign that theology has gone wrong is when the language "a being" is used for God. A better way forward is to speak and think of God not as a character in a story but as its Author. The theophanies by which God manifests his presence, especially the theophanies of the burning bush in Exodus 3, the glory of God presented to Moses, the overshadowing of the tabernacle by that glory, and the transfiguration, help us see God not as a biblical character but as the Bible's Author.

When God speaks, God does so through a manifestation that allows the hearers to know that they are being addressed in an unusual and odd way. A blazing light appears that overshadows—a strange juxtaposition of an all-consuming light that brings invisibility more than it brings visibility. The oddness of God's manifestation provokes fear. When Moses is addressed by God from the burning bush we are told that he "hid his face, for he was afraid to look at God" (Exod. 3:6). When Peter, James, and John heard the voice of God at the transfiguration "they fell to the ground and were overcome by fear" (Matt. 17:6). These divine manifestations attest to the unusual characteristics of divine communication. It does not fit within regularities of space and time necessary for basic human communication, for seldom is human communication bathed in light. A common theme is that the divine presence "overshadows." We see this term used in key passages of Scripture from Exodus through the Gospels. For instance, in the Transfiguration, we are told that while Peter was still speaking, "a bright cloud overshadowed them" (νεφέλη φωτεινὴ ἐπεσκίασεν αὐτούς) (Matt. 17:5). The image is intriguing; it is a "bright" cloud, but the effect of its brightness is to "overshadow." The image appears in all three Gospel accounts of the transfiguration; the same verb ἐπισκιάζω is used in Mark and Luke.[41] It is also present in Luke 1:35, when the angel announces to Mary that she will bear Jesus, "the power of the Most High will overshadow you" (δύναμις ὑψίστου ἐπισκιάσει σοι). The "overshadowing" used in these passages harks back to what occurs when the glory of God descends upon the tabernacle in Exodus 40. The word for tabernacle, σκηνή, is also used in Matthew, Mark, and Luke's account of the transfiguration.

Prior to the "overshadowing" in the transfiguration, Peter suggested to Jesus that they build three "dwellings" (τρεῖς σκηνάς) (Mark 9:5; Matt. 17:4; Luke 9:33). John also uses a verb form of dwelling to announce that "the word became flesh and dwelt among us" (ἐσκήνωσεν). These two words, "overshadow" (ἐπισκιάζω) and "dwelling" (σκηνή) are related, not etymologically but by way of theophany. I am not arguing all these texts have a similar historical source, but I think it reasonable to conclude they are all drawing on a common biblical image to express

---

41. Each Gospel uses a different version of it. Mark has ἐπισκιάζουσα, the present participle; Luke uses ἐπεσκίαζεν, the imperfect with a continuing aspect; while Matthew used the aorist indicative with a completed aspect. I am grateful to Michael Cover for conversation about these verbs.

divine agency. The association of these terms brings together a blazing light that descends upon something—a bush, a mountain, the skin of Moses' face, and the tabernacle, and finally manifested through Jesus—that is a condition for divine communication. These words are associated in the Septuagint version of Exod. 40:34–35, verses that are the culmination of the construction of the tabernacle (σκηνή) and all that is necessary for God to dwell with Israel and Israel to worship God. When everything was finished, we are told according to the Septuagint, "Then the cloud covered the tent of meeting (τὴν σκηνὴν τοῦ μαρτυρίου) and the glory of the Lord filled the tabernacle (ἡ σκηνή). Moses was not able to enter the tent of meeting because the cloud settled upon it (ὅτι ἐπεσκίαζεν ἐπ' αὐτὴν ἡ νεφέλη), and the glory of the Lord filled the tabernacle" (Exod. 40:34–35). The cloud that overshadows the tabernacle stands above the glory that fills the tabernacle. This glory, uncreated Light, is manifest in Jesus at his transfiguration. The divine communication occurs not only in terms of a narrative sequence but also through the glory that overshadows, a blazing fire that communicates through the bush without destroying it (Exod. 3:2), descends upon Mount Sinai (Exod. 24:17),[42] shines through Moses' face so that he veils it (Exod. 34:29, 33–34),[43] overshadows the tabernacle (Exod. 40:34–35), comes upon Mary (Luke 1:35), and dwells in Jesus (John 1:14) and shines through his entire being (Mark 9:7; Matt. 17:5; Luke 9:34). The oddness of these manifestations transcends the finite material through which they are presented, just as the Author of the biblical narrative uses the "sacred veils" to convey who he is.

These theophanous images of Light do not settle the debate as to whether we should think of God in terms of a temporal narrative sequence or in terms of a simple, eternal perfection, but they do demonstrate that the latter has as much biblical warrant as the former for the following reasons. First, they remind us why the creed refers

---

42. "Now the appearance of the Lord was like a devouring fire on the top of the mountain in the sight of the people of Israel" (Exod. 24:17).

43. "Moses came down from Mount Sinai. As he came down from the mountain with the two tablets of the covenant in his hand, Moses did not know that the skin of his face shone because he had been talking with God."

to Christ as "Light from Light." Whether or not the image also has Platonic resonances is inconsequential; the image comes from Holy Scripture, especially those places in which light is used as the way in which God communicates to creatures. Any curt dismissal of divine illumination, or "Light from Light," or a metaphysics of participation associated with light as a corrupt Platonic metaphysics overlooks how central light is to divine communication in both testaments. If Platonists also found "light" helpful to explain divinity, then this similarity should be considered a "serendipitous congruence" (as Robert Wilken has noted about other similarities to Christianity with Greek thought).[44] Second, the expression "Light from Light" was evidence for Augustine of divine simplicity. Light, unlike language, cannot be divided into bits and set forth in terms of temporal beginning, middle, and end.[45] It removes God from the narrative as much as it places God within it; it troubles the narrative sequence. Third, this Light is as much unlike creaturely light as it is like it. It causes fear, overshadows, and creates confusion. The Light cannot be absorbed by the temporality of the narrative. Finally, the Light brings these temporal moments together, allowing us to identify that the God who spoke to Moses, descended upon Mount Sinai and the tabernacle, is also the same God manifest through Jesus.

Open theism seeks to be faithful to God revealed in Holy Scripture. However, it brings to Scripture the assumption that its Author must have libertarian freedom and the possibility of novelty. It too easily reads off a doctrine of God from the temporality of Scripture, succumbing to a temptation of overly literal readings of God culled from narrative sequences without the necessary mystical disposition to contemplate sacred veils well. It overlooks divine invisibility manifest in the blazing fire of theophany, or what Anselm referred to as "light inaccessible." Open theism assumes that God can know everything of the future that can be known, but having rejected simplicity and eternity, what can be known of the future is more

---

44. Robert Wilken, *The Spirit of Early Christian Thought* (New Haven, CT: Yale University Press, 2003), 273.
45. At least not without a spectrometer, but we are discussing uncreated Light.

limited than the traditional answer suggested. The future is open to God, as it is for us. Such a move places God in a univocal category of being that refuses to acknowledge the analogical differences present in God's relation to creatures and creatures' relations to God. The analytic method the open theists draw on often assumes such univocity; not everyone who uses that method, however, makes that assumption. Linda Zagzebski does not fit seamlessly in the analytic philosophical camp, but she certainly avails herself of it in her philosophical theology. She too seeks an answer to the foreknowledge dilemma open theism addresses, but she finds their conclusion less preferable to others. She writes,

> Just how far a divine being can make a mistake about the future and still be worthy of the absolute trust Christians place in him may, of course, be debated, but at least the initial tendency of most such believers is to say that it is not very far. And even if God's knowledge of future contingents is not religiously mandatory, it certainly seems to be religiously preferable. So if a solution to the foreknowledge dilemma can be given that does not involve limiting God's knowledge of the future, so much the better.[46]

Most analytic theologians would agree with Zagzebski; open theism would be an outlier among its practitioners. Analytic theologians tend to defend strong versions of divine omniscience and omnipotence. However, many agree with the process and open theists that simplicity, eternity, and immutability should be discarded. What is striking is that despite the disagreements among them, nearly all those who call for revisions conclude with a God who has composition of some sort, temporal differentiation, and passibility.

46. Zagzebski, *Dilemma of Freedom and Foreknowledge*, 34.

6

The Logical Question: Analytic Theology

Open theism is a species of analytic philosophy or theology.[1] They share a common method or approach to resolving dilemmas that advocates precision and rigor in the use of concepts in order to solve theological and philosophical dilemmas such as the problems of freedom and evil, but they use this method to different conclusions. Most analytic theologians disagree with open theists that future contingents either cannot be known or that God's knowledge of the future is open. However, many of the major figures in analytic theology do agree with open theists that Thomas's teaching on simplicity, eternity, and immutability is unsustainable. They too call for significant revisions to the traditional answer.

What Is Analytic Philosophy/Theology?

The analytic method arose in England during the twentieth century and was associated with philosophers such as Bertrand Russell, G. E.

------

1. Most of the early work in this discipline was in the "philosophy of religion." Recently a number of persons working in this area refer to their work as "analytic theology." I will use the terms "analytic philosophy" and "analytic theology" interchangeably because it is the method that unites them more than a specific academic discipline.

Moore, the early Wittgenstein, Gilbert Ryle, Rudolf Carnap, and A. J. Ayer, among others. The analysis of concepts was nothing new; it was present in Greek philosophy from the pre-Socratics on, as well as in the Catholic and Protestant Scholastics. Yet in the twentieth century in England proponents of the analytic method set it apart from other philosophical approaches. As Morris Weitz explains it, "Although analysis of concepts or complexes are present in philosophy from the pre-Socratics on, it is only in philosophy of recent years that the contrast between analysis and other methods is sharply drawn and the precise nature and role of philosophical analysis are clearly stated."[2] Once analytic philosophy became a distinct method, its proponents then distinguished it from "continental" philosophy. The usefulness of this distinction has been challenged. Simon Critchley notes that it sets a method, "analysis," against a geography, "continental," which would seem to be a distinction lacking precision for careful analysis.[3] Critchley, citing Stanley Rosen's humorous account, notes the stereotypes present in this distinction: "precision, conceptual clarity and systematic rigour are the property of analytic philosophy, whilst the continentals indulge in speculative metaphysics or cultural hermeneutics, or, alternatively, depending on one's sympathies, in wool-gathering and bathos."[4] Sharp distinctions between these two approaches to philosophy are seldom persuasively established. Do continental philosophers reject precision, rigor, and clarification? Can analytic philosophers ignore hermeneutics, culture, or speculative metaphysics? Nonetheless, the styles of the two philosophies are distinct.

The distinct styles of analytic and continental philosophy have entered into theology, especially among its English-speaking practitioners, calling for sides to be taken. William Lane Craig, a confident defender of the analytic approach, encourages Christian

---

2. Morris Weitz, "Philosophical Analysis," in *The Encyclopedia of Philosophy* (London: Collier Macmillan, 1967), 1:97.
3. For a good comparison between continental and analytic philosophy see Simon Critchley, *Continental Philosophy: A Very Short Introduction* (Oxford: Oxford University Press, 2001), 32–53.
4. Ibid., 34.

apologists to study it rather than contemporary continental philosophy or theology:

> Analytic philosophy is the kind of philosophy that predominates in the Anglophone world. This style of philosophizing contrasts sharply with that of Continental philosophy. Whereas Continental philosophy tends to be obscure, imprecise, and emotive, analytic philosophy lays great worth and emphasis on clarity of definitions, careful delineation of premises, and logical rigor of argumentation. Unfortunately, theology has for a long time learned to follow the lead of Continental philosophy, which tends to result in darkness being piled upon darkness.[5]

His claims have a direct bearing on the argument present in this volume because Craig finds analytic philosophy more fitting for setting forth divine attributes than theology, and its use requires rejection and revision of the traditional answer. For Craig, analytic Christian philosophers explain divine omniscience and eternity better than theologians. He writes, "Some readers of my study of divine omniscience, *The Only Wise God*, expressed surprise at my remark that someone desiring to learn more about God's attribute of omniscience would be better advised to read the works of Christian philosophers than of Christian theologians. Not only was that remark true, but the same holds for divine eternity."[6] The remark is surprising given the depth of the revisions that Craig's analytic approach calls for.

Nicholas Wolterstorff makes similar claims for what analytic philosophy has accomplished. He writes, "Never since the late Middle Ages has philosophical theology so flourished as it has during the past thirty years. . . . This flourishing has occurred within the analytic tradition of philosophy; thus far there has been no counterpart flourishing within the continental tradition."[7] Not all those who adopt

---

5. William Lane Craig, "Apologetics Training: Advice to Christian Apologists," *Reasonable Faith with William Lane Craig* (website), accessed March 5, 2016, www.reasonablefaith.org/apologetics-training-advice-to-christian-apologists#ixzz3luZ4DEXB.

6. William Lane Craig, *Time and Eternity: Exploring God's Relationship to Time* (Wheaton, IL: Crossway, 2001), 11.

7. One wonders how a sweeping statement like this could be defended on analytic grounds. How, for instance, could we compare the flourishing of analytic philosophy of religion to the work of French phenomenologists or William Desmond's Platonic Metaxology and decide which has flourished more or which has resulted in substantive theological gains? To state that the "continental tradition" has not had any such flourishing without attending to the theological

the analytic approach find it as successful as do Craig and Wolterstorff. Eleonore Stump questions its viability if it becomes the exclusive approach to theology. She writes, "But left to itself, because it values intricate, technically expert argument, the analytic approach has a tendency to focus more and more on less and less; and so, at its worst, it can become plodding, pedestrian, sterile, and inadequate to its task."[8] She suggests that its "shortcoming" might be addressed by "marrying it to the study of narrative."[9]

Orthodox theologian David Hart has less confidence in the usefulness of analytic philosophy for theology and more in continental philosophy. The latter bears strong affinities with Christian theology, but the analytic method has yet to demonstrate its affinity. He states:

> Modern continental philosophy is very much the misbegotten child of theology, indeed a kind of secularized theology; even at present its governing themes everywhere declare its filiation—ontology is concerned with the being of beings, phenomenology with truth as manifestation and the unity of knowledge and being, hermeneutics with interpretation and the transmission of texts; the questions of transcendence and immanence, the moral law, the transcendentals, the meaning of being, substance and event, time and eternity, freedom and fate, and the logic of history remain the essential matters of Continental thought.[10]

This affinity is a reason for theological engagement; continental philosophy needs theology in order to overcome its "internal struggle against itself." He is less confident analytic theology has something to offer theology. "There are theologians who believe theology has something to learn from and contribute to the analytic tradition of philosophy (here I reserve judgment), but even if this is so the encounter would be a purely apologetic enterprise; there is no natural kinship."[11]

---

turn in parts of it seems too inexact to be taken seriously. See Nicholas Wolterstorff, "How Philosophical Theology Became Possible within the Analytic Tradition of Philosophy," in Oliver D. Crisp and Michael C. Rea, eds., *Analytic Theology: New Essays in the Philosophy of Theology* (Oxford: Oxford University Press, 2009), 155.

8. Eleonore Stump, "The Problem of Evil: Analytic Philosophy and Narrative," in Crisp and Rea, *Analytic Theology*, 253.

9. Ibid., 254.

10. David Hart, *The Beauty of the Infinite: The Aesthetics of Christian Truth* (Grand Rapids: Eerdmans, 2004), 30.

Given the claims some analytic philosophers and theologians make for the analytic method, readers should expect its use of precision and rigor would lead to results that provide consensus for a doctrine of God. As we shall see, those expectations will be disappointed. The more confident analytic theologians appear to find consensus in the use of their method only at one point: the traditional answer found in Thomas is incoherent or illogical and cannot be sustained. They call for revisions as thorough as process theology or open theism. William Alston, Alvin Plantinga, and Craig reject divine simplicity.[12] Richard Swinburne and Craig reject eternity.[13] Marilyn McCord Adams, along with Swinburne, Plantinga, and Craig, rejects or revises immutability and impassibility.[14] However, not all philosophers or theologians who adopt the analytic approach call for the revisions of its more confident practitioners. Eleonore Stump, Linda Zagzebski, Thomas McCall, Brian Leftow, Alexander Pruss, and Jeffrey Brower use it to defend a doctrine of God more akin to the traditional answer.

Analytic theology is difficult to define with clarity. It is more of an approach, style, or procedure than a well-developed method, but perhaps it is best to refer to it as a method. Michael Rea acknowledges that it is somewhat vague. He writes, "Roughly (and I think that 'rough' is the best that we can do here), it refers to an approach to philosophical problems that is characterized by a particular rhetorical style, some common ambitions, an evolving technical vocabulary, and a tendency to pursue projects in dialogue with a certain evolving body of literature."[15] Its ambitions are "to identify the scope and limits of our powers to obtain knowledge of the world" and "to provide such true explanatory theories as we can in areas of inquiry (metaphysics, morals, and the like) that fall outside the scope of the natural sciences."[16] Analytic theology assumes the following points. Theology

11. Ibid.
12. See Alvin Plantinga, *Does God Have a Nature?* (Milwaukee: Marquette University Press, 1980), 37–61.
13. Richard Swinburne, *Coherence of Theism* (Oxford: Clarendon Press, 1977), 222.
14. Marilyn McCord Adams, *Horrendous Evils and the Goodness of God* (Ithaca, NY, and London: Cornell University Press, 1999), 85; Marilyn McCord Adams, *Christ and Horrors* (Cambridge: Cambridge University Press, 2006), 142.
15. Michael C. Rea, "Introduction," in Crisp and Rea, *Analytic Theology*, 3.
16. Ibid., 4.

should: (1) be "formulated in sentences that can be formalized and logically manipulated"; (2) "prioritize precision, clarity and logical coherence"; (3) "avoid substantive (non-decorative) use of metaphor and other tropes whose semantic content outstrips their propositional content"; (4) "work as much as possible with well-understood primitive concepts, and concepts that can be analyzed in terms of those"; and (5) "treat conceptual analysis (insofar as it is possible) as a source of evidence."[17]

Richard Swinburne clarifies the analytic method further by distinguishing between two types of statement. All "coherent statements" are either analytic or synthetic. Synthetic statements are "factual." Analytic statements are "logically necessary." The distinction, he acknowledges, begins with Kant, but Kant's use needed refinement; it is found in logical positivist A. J. Ayer. Swinburne states, "a proposition is analytic if and only if any sentence which expresses it expresses a true proposition and does so solely because the words in the sentences mean what they do, that is, is by itself sufficient to guarantee that the statement which the sentence expresses is true."[18] The building blocks of analytic theology then are sentences that express propositions whose symbols or words bear a univocal meaning to what is expressed inasmuch as that is possible. The use of metaphor or analogy will be necessary, but it must be limited, because the more metaphor or analogy is used the less guarantee there is that words bear the univocal meaning necessary for truth.[19] Primitive concepts are the bedrock for analytic theology; they are concepts that refuse further analysis and thus provide the basis for logical extension for other nonprimitive concepts.

Why Should the Traditional Answer Be Rejected?

The following section assesses the work done by analytic theologians

---

17. Ibid., 5.
18. Richard Swinburne, *Coherence of Theism*, 14–17.
19. Swinburne refers to analogy as "a perfectly proper card to play but it must not be played too often. It is a joker which it would be self-defeating to play more than two or three times in a game"; Swinburne, *Coherence of Theism*, 272.

only on the doctrine of God. The conclusion will be, to this point so far, it has not proven itself in clarifying the doctrine. Its calls for revisions should be treated with caution. Analytic theology has primarily been invested in epistemology, examining in particular whether theistic belief can be justified. Alvin Plantinga is well known for his work on epistemology. He finds "warrant" turns belief into knowledge; much of the work in analytic theology follows his lead. His work has put the question of theism back into philosophy departments, where that question had been neglected.[20] Along with the epistemological question is also the question of God's existence. Analytic theology examines the strengths and weaknesses of arguments for God. Their primary interest has not been the specifics of the dogmatic Christian tradition but rather theism—the nature and existence of God known by warranted belief. However, they have suggested incoherencies are present in the Christian doctrine of God that could be remedied through careful attention to the analytic method. They are not of one mind on what the incoherencies are, nor why they arise. Analytic philosophers and theologians can be found who call for revisions in response to (1) the problem of evil and the foreknowledge dilemma, (2) a mistaken Platonism that holds sway over theology, (3) a more precise use of language that minimizes metaphor and analogy, and (4) the incoherence and obscurity of divine simplicity. This fourth reason for revising the perfectly simple God of Christian tradition bears most directly on the argument at hand. This section is primarily devoted to explaining why analytic theologians find simplicity misleading us. The other three reasons for revision—an inability to handle dilemmas, the dominance of Platonism, and a lack of linguistic precision—have the affirmation of simplicity at their base.

These four reasons find no unanimous support as the reason the traditional answer needs revision. Unlike process theology, which addresses a primary concern (the theoretical problem of evil), and open theism, which does likewise (the divine foreknowledge dilemma),

---

20. See Sennett's introduction to *The Analytic Theist: An Alvin Plantinga Reader* for evidence that Plantinga changed the shape of the philosophical discussion; James F. Sennett, ed., *The Analytic Theist: An Alvin Plantinga Reader* (Grand Rapids: Eerdmans, 1998).

analytic theologians are not addressing a single concern or dilemma. They differ among themselves as to which dilemmas require theological revisions. Some find that a revised teaching on God better addresses the dilemma of divine foreknowledge and freedom and the problem of evil; others are less convinced. For instance, on the one hand, Alvin Plantinga does not seek to revise the traditional teaching because of the problem of evil. He challenges the problem. On the other hand, Marilyn McCord Adams revises the traditional answer, revising immutability and impassibility, in order to make better sense of horrendous evils. Likewise, the foreknowledge dilemma elicits contradictory responses. Linda Zagzebski finds Boethian eternity defensible, but William Craig does not.[21] Many key analytic theologians find Platonism to be a philosophical albatross around the neck of Christian theology and seek to purify the doctrine of God from it by means of the analytic method. Swinburne, like many analytic thinkers, affirms philosophical nominalism against Platonism and finds nominalism to be a better fit with the analytic method.[22] The majority of analytic theologians would affirm nominalism, but not all. Another issue for some analytic theologians is the meaning of words. Although almost everyone recognizes analogy and metaphor are unavoidable, they should be used as minimally as possible. Univocal meaning between ordinary language and our language about God ensures that sentences and/or the propositions they express will be defensible as truth claims. On the one hand, Swinburne finds analogy unavoidable but problematic. "Some claims" theists make about God, he states, require that words are used in "a different sense from the normal sense," and that means they are used analogically. However, the more the meaning of words is analogically extended, the less informative the words are. Care should be exercised not to appeal too often to analogy. "For words used in analogical senses have wide applications and woolly boundaries. ... If theology uses too many words in analogical senses it will convey virtually nothing by what it says."[23] On the other hand,

---

21. The what and why of these revisions will be discussed more below.
22. See Richard Swinburne, *The Existence of God* (Cambridge: Cambridge University Press, 2004), 105.
23. Swinburne, *Coherence of Theism*, 70.

Alexander Pruss affirms the importance of analogical predication. His defense of divine simplicity "requires a robust theory of analogical predication."[24]

Swinburne's concern about the use of analogy does not cause him to reject Thomas's teaching, but this is because Swinburne does not see significant difference between Thomas's use of "analogy" and Scotus's univocity. He writes, "At any rate Aquinas does not seem to be denying that in our sense of 'univocally' predicates attributed to God and man are being used univocally. His position ultimately boils down to that of Scotus."[25] Thomas's use of analogy poses no problem for Swinburne, but his affirmation of eternity and immutability does.

Divine simplicity, in particular, is held up as unsustainable by the most ardent analytic theologians. If any commonality can be found as to why many of them seek to revise the traditional answer, problems they find with divine simplicity would have to be primary. The influence of Scotus on analytic theology is significant at this point. Richard Cross notes that Scotus found Thomists, Henry of Ghent in particular, incapable of avoiding modalism through differentiating the Triune persons only by relations. He sought to differentiate them by adding to the relations distinct personal properties. The result is a "weakening of the classical restraints on divine simplicity."[26] This weakening is a basis for the social trinitarianism we will see below in Swinburne, something Cross affirms. Most analytic theologians do not call for a weakening of divine simplicity; it is to be rejected outright. Once it goes, the doctrine of God will be thoroughly reimagined.

Craig is as dismissive of Thomas's teaching on divine simplicity as the process theologians and more so than the open theists. He finds the perfectly simple God illogical. He offers this commentary on divine simplicity:

This medieval doctrine is not popular among theologians today, and even

---

24. Alexander R. Pruss, "On Two Problems of Divine Simplicity," in Jonathan Kvanvig, ed., *Oxford Studies in Philosophy of Religion* (Oxford: Oxford University Press, 2008), 1:166.
25. Swinburne, *Coherence of Theism*, 79.
26. Richard Cross, "Medieval Trinitarianism and Modern Theology," in Robert J. Wozniak and Giulio Maspero, eds., *Rethinking Trinitarian Theology* (London: T&T Clark International, 2012), 36–37.

when Christians do lip service to it, they usually do not appreciate how truly radical the doctrine is. It implies not merely that God does not have parts, but that He does not possess even distinct attributes. In some mysterious way His omnipotence is His goodness, for example. He stands in no relations whatsoever. Thus, He does not literally love, know or cause His creatures. He is not really composed of three distinct persons, a claim notoriously difficult to reconcile with the doctrine of the Trinity.[27]

Craig does not mention which theologians fail to find the doctrine "popular," or why that would matter in a philosophical or theological doctrine of God. If the interpretation of Thomas in the first chapter was correct, then Craig's understanding of divine simplicity is of something other than what Thomas taught. As was shown, it did not rule out "distinct attributes" but ruled them out as real distinctions *in divinis*. It did not entail God has no "relations" but that the relations God has must be differentiated so that creation could be properly understood. For Thomas there are, first, real relations founded on real distinctions within divinity that account for the Persons; second, logical relations between God and creatures that signify creation is no fourth hypostasis based on a real distinction within divinity; and, third, a second kind of real relation between creatures and God that signifies God can exist without creatures, but creatures cannot exist without God. Creatures depend on God for existence, but God does not depend on creatures.

To suggest that the Cappadocians, Augustine, Dionysius, Anselm, Aquinas, the Reformers, and Protestant Scholastics, all of whom taught divine simplicity, would have suggested God does not "literally love, know or cause His creatures" either misunderstands their teaching or suggests they did not know the implications of what they taught. Craig seems inclined to the latter and thus calls for this ancient tradition's thorough rejection. He writes, "Philosophically, there seem to be no good reasons to embrace these radical doctrines, and weighty objections have been lodged against them." But his footnote explaining these objections reveals an underlying problem with his method. He states, "Omnipotence is not the same property as goodness, for a being may have one and not the other."[28] In other words, we begin by

27. Craig, *Time and Eternity*, 30.

dividing up the attributes of omnipotence and goodness, attributing them to a being, and placing them in sentences capable of being formalized and logically manipulated. He then asks whether there might be an example of "a being" who has omnipotence and not goodness in some possible world. (I hope there is no world in which such a being exists.) He has moved from discussing the traditional answer to a discussion of "a being" who might have omnipotence without goodness. Once again we find the indefinite article.

Alvin Plantinga also rejects divine simplicity. His controversial Aquinas lecture, "Does God Have a Nature?," challenged Thomas's teaching on simplicity. He set forth the problem of simplicity as the problem of relating "abstract objects" to God. Abstract objects are objects such as Plato's ideas, and Plantinga finds the source of the problem in Augustine. Augustine "felt obliged to transform Plato's theory of ideas in such a way that these abstract objects become, obscurely, *part* of God—perhaps identical with his intellect."[29] Augustine's attempt to make abstract objects "*part* of God" is an unfortunate expression, because simplicity is precisely the attempt to do the opposite, to insist God does not have abstract objects as "parts." This unfortunate expression could be a lapse in precision, or it could be a sign Plantinga is not yet discussing divine simplicity as it was set forth in the Christian tradition. When he begins to assess Thomas's use of simplicity, the suspicion that it is the latter increases. He states, "When Thomas Aquinas embarks on the task of characterizing God's attributes, simplicity is the first item on his list."[30] That initial sentence, as should be clear from chapter 1, begins with two, perhaps three mistakes in interpretation. First and most important, simplicity is not the "first item" on Thomas's "list"; it is existence. That God *is* is a fundamental affirmation from Holy Scripture from which Thomas then derives simplicity. Second, the six "attributes" Thomas discusses

28. Ibid., 31n3.
29. Alvin Plantinga, "Does God Have a Nature?," in Sennett, *Analytic Theist*, 226. I am working from two versions of this important essay. One is from the original publication as the Marquette lecture, and the second its reprint in Sennett. Unless otherwise specified, the version will be from the Marquette University Press publication.
30. Plantinga, "Does God Have a Nature?," in Sennett, *Analytic Theist*, 229.

are not "items" on a "list." Like the use of *part* to discuss Augustine's use of simplicity, Plantinga forces Thomas's discussion into an analytic procedure that does not fit Thomas's use of these terms well. He makes Thomas's account a "property account." Third, the use of *attributes* is questionable. As Soskice has noted, these terms are much more extensions of the Dionysian tradition of the divine names than they are properties as predicables attributed to a subject called "God." The term *attribute* could be neutral, if what is meant by it is nothing more than a name or term *attributed* to God, but if we begin with the assumption that simplicity seeks to take abstract objects, turn them into predicable properties, and assign them to divinity, then the analysis has not yet begun with what the Cappadocians, Augustine, Dionysius, Aquinas, or the Reformers were doing with divine simplicity.

Having begun with this hermeneutical claim as to what the tradition was doing with simplicity (making Platonic abstract objects part of God by listing them as properties), it is no surprise that Plantinga then argues God has a nature that is "not identical with him."[31] This nature contains analyzable properties that allow for the analytic approach to be used to address the divine attributes. If God has no analyzable properties, Plantinga's approach would not work. Thus it must challenge simplicity.

Plantinga acknowledges simplicity is in the ancient and Reformation creeds; he nonetheless rejects it for two reasons.[32] "In the first place, it is exceedingly hard to grasp or construe this doctrine, to see just what divine simplicity *is*. Secondly, insofar as we do have a grasp of this doctrine, it is difficult to see why anyone would be inclined to accept it; the motivation for this doctrine seems shrouded in obscurity."[33] The purpose of the analytic method is to clarify theological propositions, but that a Christian doctrine is difficult to grasp and "shrouded in obscurity" are odd reasons to reject it. Could not the same be said of the doctrine of the Trinity or the incarnation? Surely something more than this must be the reason to reject a doctrine with such

31. Ibid., 10.
32. Ibid., 27.
33. Ibid., 28.

an ancient and creedal pedigree? I think there is something more occurring and it is twofold: First, Plantinga's primary interest in this essay is to ensure divine sovereignty. Second, the doctrine of simplicity resists the analytic approach because it disallows positing a distinction between God's essence and existence that permits the analysis of conceptual properties necessary for Plantinga's use of this method.

Plantinga sets up the problem as one of divine aseity and sovereignty. If abstract objects become "part of" God, then they inevitably limit divine power. Here Plantinga's analysis is also based on a faulty historical interpretation of Thomas. He writes,

> [Thomas] is quite clear, furthermore, as to his reasons for holding this doctrine; the fundamental reason is to accommodate God's aseity and sovereignty. Aquinas believes that if God had a nature and properties distinct from him, then there would be beings distinct from him to which he is subsequent and on which he depends; this would compromise his aseity and ill befits the status of the First Being.[34]

But it is not at all clear that this reason is "fundamental" for Thomas's treatment of simplicity. Simplicity is a concern of Thomas's speculative theology. It is not yet concerned with sovereignty or power because in speculative theology Thomas presents who God is, not who God is in relation to us. God is not a sovereign power over God. Nor is Thomas concerned that anyone is compromising God's aseity in his question on divine simplicity. It never arises as an objection.

Once Plantinga sets up the problem as one of divine aseity, then he asks whether Thomas is correct that dividing God and God's nature assumes the problems Thomas thinks it does. He writes, "Now I think the intuition—call it the sovereignty-aseity intuition—underlying the doctrine of divine simplicity must be taken with a real seriousness. Suppose God has essentially the property of being omnipotent and suppose that property is an object distinct from him, is uncreated by him and exists necessarily. Then in some sense he does depend on that property."[35] It is telling that Plantinga immediately moves to the

34. Ibid., 229.
35. Ibid., 231.

property of omnipotence, for, as we have repeatedly noted, it is not one of the "attributes" discussed by Thomas in his first eleven questions. What motivates Thomas in this discussion is not what motivates Plantinga. Power is for Thomas an external operation, not a divine name.

The problem is, Plantinga assumes, Platonic. Not only God's properties but "the rest of the Platonic menagerie" impinge on divine sovereignty. He finds this Platonic infringement to be one solid reason for nominalism.[36] He knows this conclusion is not Thomas's, but he does not think Thomas has solved the problem of divine sovereignty. "God is identical with his properties and with his essence. The latter, furthermore, is in some obscure way identical with the Divine Ideas, among which are to be found properties, kinds and exemplars."[37] So the problem is that the obscurity does not finally preserve divine aseity and sovereignty.[38] Here is where the analytic method is employed to gain clarity, but the question is, at what expense?

The more that is going on can also be found in Plantinga's statement that a nonessential property God has is "being such that Adam sinned." Here he challenges Thomas's denial of a distinction between God's substance and accidents. Once creation exists, then God does have analyzable nonessential properties like accidents. He states, "one property God has is *being such that Adam sinned*, and surely this property is not essential either to Adam or to God."[39] He admits that it seems odd to make this a property of God but defends it because God created Adam knowing that Adam would sin.[40] Because these properties are nonessential, God's nature cannot be identical with God's essence. As we will see below, Plantinga assumes analytic philosophy's logical necessitation where for something to be essential it must be necessitated in all possible worlds.

Plantinga's second reason for rejecting simplicity is that the

36. Ibid.
37. Ibid., 232.
38. Plantinga does not find the simplicity doctrine getting us out of the "dilemma whose horns were: either God has no nature or else God isn't genuinely sovereign" (ibid., 236).
39. Plantinga, *Does God Have a Nature?*, 40.
40. Ibid., 42.

"motivation" for it is "shrouded in obscurity." I tried to show the motivation for it in the first chapter. It is to render intelligible, as much as can be rendered intelligible, the revealed teaching on the Trinity, without dispensing with its mysterious character. Simplicity makes sense of the Christian teaching that God is one in three and three in one without those three becoming "parts" such as individuals with centers of consciousness. Plantinga thinks primarily in terms of God's nature as related to creation, what Aquinas referred to as "practical theology." Simplicity prevents us from conceptualizing and analyzing God's real relation to creation. Of course, that only restates why Thomas affirmed it. It was intended to block such a real relation. Simplicity's motivation is found in Thomas's speculative theology in support of the doctrine of the Trinity. As we saw, for Thomas, the Trinity must first be affirmed before we can speak well of the God-creation relation. Plantinga, like much modern theology, begins with practical theology (the God-creation relation), and consistent with many analytic theologians then revises the doctrine of God based on a real relation between God and creation.

Swinburne does not reject simplicity, but his revision of it lacks continuity with the previous tradition. He too thinks of God's attributes as analyzable properties, but he does not divide God's nature from God's essence. He first defines God's nature as "pure, limitless intentional power" and argues that all the divine attributes arise from it.[41] This single property unifies the other divine properties. He writes, "The unity of the divine properties follow from their being included in a simple property, which I have called having pure, limitless, intentional power."[42] Although he claims this as similar to Aquinas, it is not. Power could not unify the divine nature, for God does not exercise power on himself.

Swinburne thinks of divine attributes as "properties," as something God has, and then finds their unity in divine intentional power. From it he affirms an attenuated teaching on simplicity. Its attenuation can

---

41. Richard Swinburne, *The Christian God* (Oxford: Oxford University Press, 1994), 150–51.
42. Ibid., 162.

be seen in his critique of Aquinas on simplicity and his endorsement of nominalism. He makes an argument similar to Plantinga's.

> What moved Aquinas, who saw this, to talk of instances of the divine properties as being identical with each other was, I think, a residual Platonism which so hypostatized abstract entities such as properties that it had to say that unless they were part of God, they would be entities independent of God—which would be a view which did not fit well with theism. And since God cannot have distinct parts, they must be identical with each other. All of this becomes quite unnecessary once we abandon Platonism and acknowledge that abstract entities are not constituents of the universe but mere convenient fictions.[43]

Swinburne's interpretation of Aquinas is odd. Thomas never speaks of God's properties, and he did not appear to be working with a "Platonic" problematic that hypostasized them. Such a problem never appears in the first eleven questions of the *Summa*.[44] Swinburne's claims do not make sense of how Thomas uses simplicity but arise from a priori philosophical commitments that side with nominalism against Platonism and then seek to purify the Christian tradition of the latter.

Swinburne's affirmation of simplicity correlates to the criterion of simplicity that features prominently in his work. In defending simplicity, he states,

> It is because God's essential properties all follow from the very simple property of having pure, limitless, intentional power, that I claim that God is an individual of a very simple kind; certainly the simplest kind of person there can be. The divine essence, as defined so far, of necessarily having pure, limitless, intentional power, makes God the kind of being he is in virtue of his power, of what he can do, of his control over things.[45]

God as "an individual" who is "the kind of being he is in virtue of his power" has an apologetic function in Swinburne's philosophy. His *Coherence of Theism*, the first of his trilogy, began with a similar definition of "God."[46]

---

43. Ibid.
44. It does appear in question 15, after the divine attributes have been presented, but without any indication that it was the reason for the first eleven questions.
45. Swinburne, *Christian God*, 154.
46. "By a theist I understand a man who believes that there is a God. By a 'God' he understands

The second work of his trilogy, *The Existence of God*, draws on this definition and argues that theism is more probable than its opposite because it gives the simplest explanation for creation.[47] As a simple being defined by power, God is the simplest scientific explanation for the cause of the universe.[48] "To posit [via scientific explanation] many or extended such substances [as cause of the universe] (an always existing universe; or an extended volume of matter-energy from which uncaused by God, all began) is to postulate more entities than theism." It would not "possess the simplicity of infinity."[49] Simplicity then is affirmed, but a very different version and for very different reasons.

The reason Swinburne affirms simplicity is that God as an individual of pure, intentional power provides the most probable explanation for creation on scientific grounds. One might assume this will cause difficulties for the doctrine of the Trinity. Swinburne thinks not. He writes,

> My claim is that the data which suggest that there is a God suggest that the most probable kind of God is such that inevitably he becomes tripersonal. It is for this reason that the doctrine of the Trinity is not a more complicated hypothesis than the hypothesis of a sole individual; the simplest sort of God to whom arguments lead inevitably tripersonalizes, to coin a word. If some simple hypothesis put forward by a scientist to explain complex data entails some further complex consequences, that

something like a 'person' without a body (i.e. a spirit) who is eternal, free, able to do anything, knows everything, is perfectly good, is the proper object of human worship and obedience, the creator and sustainer of the universe"; Swinburne, *Coherence of Theism*, 1. By *person*, Swinburne does not mean a Triune person. "I am using this word in the modern sense. Some theists of course also wish to maintain that God is 'three persons in one substance.' But in claiming this they are using 'person' in a special and rather different sense, as a translation (and I suspect a rather unsatisfactory one) of the Latin *persona* and the Greek ὑπόστασις." He argues in his second volume that this person is the Father, and in his *Christian God*, he lays out the metaphysics of a person and shows how God fits it.

47. Swinburne, *Existence of God*, 96–109. He also draws on a version of divine simplicity for this argument. "Theism postulates God as a person with intentions, beliefs, and basic powers, but ones of a very simple kind, so simple that it postulates the simplest kind of person that there could be" (97).

48. Swinburne consistently adopts the scientific criterion of simplicity for his philosophy of religion and encourages others to do so as well. In his second volume in his trilogy he writes, "All I have been concerned to show here is the crucial influence of the criteria of simplicity within science. If we are to adopt in our investigations into religion the criteria of rational inquiry that are used in science and ordinary life, we must use this criterion there" (*Existence of God*, 59).

49. Ibid., 106.

makes it no less simple—especially if there can be other evidence for those consequences.[50]

The move to divine "tripersonalizing" from the simple God of pure, intentional power means that Swinburne finds the Trinity more amenable to reason than Aquinas did.[51] But Swinburne's argument for the coherence of moving from God as an individual characterized by the property of power to the Trinity does seem strained. John Haldane suggests the move was more a matter of "convenience."[52]

Two central thinkers working within analytic philosophy of religion reject simplicity, and another defends an attenuated version of it. These examples could be multiplied. Whatever its status should be, Craig's claim that it is "not popular among theologians today" may very well be true. Perhaps it is even less popular among philosophers. However, a number of analytic philosophers have pushed back against the claim that simplicity is incoherent. Oppy Graham, Michael Bergmann, Jeffrey Brower, Pruss, and Stump defend it.[53] All but Stump defend it based on a "truthmaker" theory. A truthmaker theory assumes that if x is true, then something makes x true. Once we have identified what it is that makes x true, then we arrive at a primitive concept that explains the truth of x. So, for instance, if the proposition is "the Cubs won the World Series in 2017," then the truthmaker for that proposition would be that state of affairs that exists in which the Cubs won the World Series in 2017. This might seem trivial, but the point is that truth cannot be merely asserted; something makes it true. For the analytic defenders of divine simplicity noted above, it works

---

50. Swinburne, *Christian God*, 191.
51. See ibid. He finds Aquinas overestimating reason's role in arguments for the existence of God and underestimating it with respect to Trinity.
52. "Swinburne may be thought guilty of a different kind of excess in his attempt to offer *a priori* arguments in favour of trinitarianism. The discussion is absorbing and merits serious attention but it has the look of convenience about it and it is difficult to resist the thought that had the Creeds affirmed a four-personhood Godhead, Swinburne would have been arguing *a priori* for this"; John Haldane, Review of *The Christian God*, *Religious Studies* 32 (1996): 283.
53. See M. Bergmann and J. Brower, "A Theistic Argument against Platonism and in Support of Truthmakers and Divine Simplicity," *Oxford Studies in Metaphysics* 2 (2006): 357–86; Jeffrey E. Brower, "Simplicity and Aseity," in Thomas P. Flint and Michael Rea, eds., *The Oxford Handbook of Philosophical Theology* (Oxford: Oxford University Press, 2011); Oppy Graham, "The Devilish Complexities of Divine Simplicity," *Philo* 6 (2003): 10–22; Pruss, "On Two Problems of Divine Simplicity."

because it is a truthmaker that clarifies what we are saying when we say God is wise, just, merciful, etc.

Alexander Pruss defends divine simplicity against two of the common charges against it. First, that ordinary language cannot render intelligible the claim that multiple attributes such as wisdom, justice, mercy, etc. are really the same. We saw a version of this argument in Craig's dismissal of simplicity. Second, that God has intrinsic accidental properties that would differ in different worlds.[54] We saw a version of this in Plantinga. Pruss defends simplicity against the multiple-attributes critique through an analogy to a science-fiction alien whose hearing and feeling are the same event. If such an entity is conceivable, then it undercuts the argument that multiple attributes in God are incoherent. The second critique of divine simplicity assumes that if God has differing accidental properties in different worlds, then God's nature would not be the same in all those possible worlds. Analytic philosophers often use "different worlds" arguments that assume history could have been otherwise than it is and ask, if it were, how would that affect propositions? For instance, if God is free to create the world, it is possible for God not to create. In the "world" that God did not create, would God be the same God? This argument is a modal one, examining possibility and necessity. If a property of God would be the same in all possible worlds, then that property would be necessary. Because it is an essential property, divine simplicity requires necessity. God is who God is independently of the possible worlds within which God exists. The problem of intrinsic accidental properties is that if God has them, and they differ in different worlds, then God would not be identical in all those worlds, and divine simplicity would be incoherent. Pruss argues the critique fails. Such accidental properties are extrinsic, not intrinsic, and they can be avoided if we understand simplicity as a truthmaker, but a problem still exists.

The remaining difficulty for Pruss is the "entailment principle"—"if T is truthmaker for p then that T exists entails p." So if God is the

54. Pruss, "On Two Problems of Divine Simplicity," 150–51.

truthmaker for "God creates the world," then if God is simple, creation would be entailed in all possible worlds, and it would appear God is not free to create. Pruss's response is to assert that the truthmaker is not just God but God and something that is "contingent and distinct from God."[55] God is the truthmaker for propositions about him, but God and the contingent reality is the truthmaker for God in other possible worlds. So the truthmaker for God's wisdom is divine simplicity, but the truthmaker for God who creates in one world and God who does not create in another is God and creation or not-creation. The latter—God plus creation or God plus noncreation—would be "accidental extrinsic properties." Pruss concludes,

> If we understand divine simplicity as the claim that the minimal truthmaker of any claim solely about God and his parts is God himself, then it appears we can make coherent sense of the idea that divine attributes all collapse without endangering language. They collapse not in the language-endangering sense that one is saying the same thing by claiming that God is merciful as by claiming that God is just, but in the sense that the very same thing makes both claims true. Understanding how this works in practice almost surely requires a robust theory of analogical predication.[56]

The conclusion is intriguing, but the language used for it is odd. How can divine simplicity be about "God and his parts," even if the "minimal truthmaker" for it is God himself, when the point of simplicity is that God has no parts? The language is misleading. Has Pruss reduced simplicity to mere functionality? Is it nothing more than how we express propositions through statements? His turn toward analogical predication is persuasive, especially as he uses it to counter the multiple-attributes problem, but how simplicity is a "minimal truthmaker for God and his parts" remains obscure. We have not yet gained much clarity.

Jeffrey Brower also affirms simplicity is a truthmaker, but he does not adopt Pruss's solution to the problem of divine accidental, intrinsic properties by making God *and some contingent reality* the truthmaker

---

55. Ibid., 158.
56. Ibid., 166.

for them. Brower begins his argument with Plantinga's critique of simplicity. If God is "identical with each of his intrinsic properties," then "God must himself be a property," and that would be absurd, for God is a person.[57] Brower identifies the difficulty in Plantinga's critique in terms of two statements. The first expresses divine simplicity, and the second is the "property account" of simplicity that is often assumed but is unnecessary. (1) "(DS) If an intrinsic predication of the form 'God is F' is true, then *God's F-ness* exists and is identical with God."[58] What Brower adds to the conversation is to question what is F. Must it be a property? Too often, he suggests, the proposition noted above about divine simplicity (DS) is coupled with the following "property account" of F. (2) "(PA) If an intrinsic predication of the form '*a* is F' is true, then *a's F-ness* exists, where this entity is understood as a property."[59] Brower refers to the property account as the "standard interpretation" of simplicity. It assumes a subject to whom properties are predicated, but an "alternative interpretation" is plausible that understands F not as a property but in terms of truthmakers. Brower refers to his alternative interpretation as TA, the truthmaker account. So now we get: (3) "(TA) If an intrinsic predication of the form '*a* is F' is true, then *a's F-ness* exists, where this entity is to be understood as the truthmaker for '*a* is F.'"[60] This approach does not require any specific take on what F is; it could be a Platonic idea or a linguistic convention. What it does is suggest the following: "if God is divine, he is identical with that which makes him divine; if he is good, he is identical with that which makes him good; and so on in every other such case. On this interpretation, therefore, divine simplicity just amounts to the claim that God is the truthmaker for each of his true intrinsic predications."[61] Much as we saw with Pruss's discussion of "God and God's parts," so too with Brower we find a theologically inartful expression—God is identical with whatever "makes God." I take "makes" here, however,

57. Brower, "Simplicity and Aseity," 108.
58. Ibid.
59. Ibid., 109.
60. Ibid., 112.
61. Ibid.

to be a logical or conceptual claim, not an ontological one. God is not made up of Fs, whatever they may be. This restates Brower's point.

Brower acknowledges that the problem of contingency still exists. This problem is the one Pruss addressed above in his discussion of accidental, intrinsic properties. Brower puts the problem in terms of two statements, G6 and G7.

(G6) God freely chooses to create the universe.
(G7) God knows that p, where p is a contingent truth.[62]

Brower rejects that these predications are intrinsic, and if they are not intrinsic then "truthmaker interpretation fits well with the assumption that God is capable of contingent volition and knowledge."[63] In other words, God is free to create and know not only the world he does make but also all other possible worlds.

Brower, like Plantinga, Pruss, and Dolezal, understand the primary context for divine simplicity to be aseity. The difficulty for the doctrine then becomes how it makes sense of God's relationship to creation—how can we account for divine cognition and volition if God must be the same across all God's relations to possible worlds? If we cannot account for God's free acts, then the world as it is must be. Two troubling consequences would emerge. First, evil is necessary for creation. Second, everything is determined; neither God nor creatures are free. No reputable theologian or philosopher finds such consequences satisfactory. If divine simplicity leads to them, then it should be jettisoned. Pruss and Brower show how simplicity need not lead to these unsatisfactory consequences.

Neither Brower's nor Pruss's position requires that God has a real relation with creation, so they avoid the theological mistake present in Craig and Plantinga's rejection of simplicity. But as philosophers they do not have the same theological nuance found in Aquinas. The relation between divine simplicity and creation is not mediated through the Triune persons for them as it is for him. As I hope to show

---

62. Ibid., 118.
63. Ibid.

below, that makes a great difference in what dilemmas can emerge with respect to divine simplicity. Brower and Pruss have, however, advanced our understanding by highlighting the difficulty in the analytic tradition's rejection of simplicity. It too often correlates divine simplicity with a "property account" of attributes that is unnecessary and sets up the wrong dilemma. Eleonore Stump offers a different kind of defense of simplicity, one that also challenges the property account. Her defense offers something missing in previous dismissals of simplicity—a nuanced, historical interpretation of its place in medieval theology. Her analytic approach is supplemented with thoughtful hermeneutics.

Eleonore Stump agrees that divine simplicity is "perhaps the most difficult and controversial piece of medieval philosophy," but she does not reject it for that reason. Instead, she acknowledges it is "also one of the most important." Simplicity is not optional for Thomas's theology. "It is foundational for everything in Aquinas's thought from his metaphysics to his ethics."[64] Simplicity is indispensable. Her work certainly falls in the category of analytic philosophy, but it does not reduce Thomas's complex defense of simplicity to a few propositional claims. Too often, analytic theology reduces simplicity to either a "property-property identity" or a "property-nature identity." Once it is so reduced, then simplicity can be analyzed without the hermeneutical journey Thomas takes us on. Stump is more nuanced.

Stump puts forth Thomas's teaching on divine simplicity in three theses. "(1) It is impossible that God have any spatial or temporal parts that could be distinguished from one another as here rather than there or as now rather than then, and so God cannot be a physical entity."[65] From this first thesis the importance of divine eternity follows. Although every theologian would affirm God has no spatial parts, as we shall see in the discussion of divine eternity below, Craig argues God has something like temporal parts in order for God to be active in the world and know tensed facts.

---

64. Eleonore Stump, *Aquinas* (London: Routledge, 2003), 92.
65. Ibid., 96.

The second thesis is: "(2) It is impossible that God have any accidental properties." Plantinga denies this thesis based on his affirmation of substance and accidents in the divine nature. Stump finds this unnecessary because it confuses intrinsic versus extrinsic properties. Divine simplicity refers to intrinsic properties. Extrinsic properties, such as God created Adam knowing he would sin, still refer to the same simple God. God has not changed who God is in creating Adam, but the *sense* of divine simplicity differs. The sense differs due to the assumption that "the one thing that is God and is atemporally actual has a variety of effects in time."[66] Diverse effects produce different senses of simplicity as it relates to creatures, but the reference to all those diverse effects remains the same.

The second thesis leads to the third: "(3) Whatever can be intrinsically attributed to God must in reality just be the unity that is his essence."[67] Stump's defense of these theses assumes Thomas's teaching that God is not really related to creation. It is similar to what Kathryn Tanner has termed "non-contrastive" transcendence.[68] God and creation are not two entities that compete for space or time on any single continuum, so God's transcendence does not imply that in order for God to work temporally God must first become something other than what God is. God's transcendence and God's ability to relate to creatures would be in opposition only if the relation between God and creation is viewed as contrastive—either God or creaturely agency. The compatibilism/incompatiblism disjunction often assumes contrastive transcendence. If the relation between God and creatures is noncontrastive, then it need not set up the false dilemma that the only way for God to act temporally is for God to be temporal. To posit a real relation between God and creation requires a contrastive transcendence, for then the being of God and the being of creatures gets flattened out onto a similar horizon of being in which one can

---

66. Ibid., 99.
67. Ibid., 97.
68. Kathryn Tanner, *God and Creation in Christian Theology: Tyranny or Empowerment* (Minneapolis: Fortress Press, 2005), 45. The importance of Tanner's work for the perfectly simple Triune God will be more fully discussed in the concluding chapter.

only act by either determining the other or evacuating its freedom. This contrastive transcendence is common among process theologians, open theists, and analytic philosophers of religion. Because of her careful hermeneutical work, Stump does not set the dilemma up in these terms. From a very different set of assumptions, she approaches God's relation to creation similar to Tanner's noncontrastive transcendence.

Stump admits one difficulty continues to haunt divine simplicity. "In my view, the most troublesome problem arises from the distinction between what God can and cannot freely choose."[69] She first addresses an apparent paradox simplicity seems to raise, which she calls the "paradox of essential goodness." If God is perfectly simple, then does this entail that God lacks freedom of choice, for a perfectly simple God does not have the option to choose evil. We saw this dilemma was at the heart of open theism. Her answer is that this false dilemma turns on the adoption of modern notions of the free will and misses how Aquinas understands freedom. She writes,

> one presupposition in the discussion of the apparent incoherence of the notion of essential goodness is that a free will is essentially an independent, neutral activity for choosing among alternatives, but this is certainly not Aquinas's position. On the contrary, Aquinas takes the will to be a natural inclination towards goodness associated with the agent's understanding of goodness.[70]

If Thomas's metaphysics of goodness is accepted, then the dilemma of essential goodness disappears.

Her answer to the dilemma of essential goodness does not, however, answer all the difficulties involved in divine freedom. She poses the ongoing problem this way: "If we can distinguish between necessitated divine acts and divine acts such that it is possible for God to have done otherwise, in what sense is there no distinction within God?"[71] Here we see another version of the problem of contingency addressed by

---

69. Stump, *Aquinas*, 93.
70. Ibid., 103.
71. Ibid., 109.

Plantinga, Pruss, and Brower. For Stump, God's inability to will evil is due to the necessity of his nature, but God's willing creation is not. God does not need to create; if God did, there would be a real relation between God and creation. The fact that there is no such relation means that God was free not to create. To use the common language of analytic philosophy, there are possible worlds in which God did not create, and that ensures divine freedom. But now we have two types of divine action—necessitated and nonnecessitated. How does this distinction support simplicity? Her first response assumes, once again, no real relation between God and creation. That God does not have accidents does not mean that God cannot have diverse effects in creation. Those diverse effects do not entail that they are accidents intrinsic to the divine nature.

Yet a problem of modality still exists. For modern analytic philosophy, necessity requires that something be identical in all possible worlds. If this is what necessity requires, then creation as it is would seem to be necessary for God. If God could have willed that Adam did not sin or that Adam did not exist, then we have possible worlds in which God's nature is not identical. God's nature is then contingent, but divine simplicity does not seem to be able to acknowledge its contingency, especially if God's essence and nature are identical. The distinction between necessitated and nonnecessitated actions, coupled with divine simplicity, appears to come into conflict.

Stump's response shows the limitation of the analytic method and its property account when applied to a medieval such as Thomas. For the medieval, she writes, "an accident is not being thought of simply as a property a thing has in some but not all of the possible worlds in which it exists." Instead, an accident is an "incomplete being."[72] As Thomas put it, accidents do not have "being *per se*, devoid of a subject."[73] An accident is not a property that exists by itself and becomes part of the definition of something's essence. Accidents

---

72. Ibid., 111.
73. Ibid., 112. See also *Thomas Aquinas on Being and Essence*, trans. Armand Mauer (Toronto: Pontifical Institute of Mediaeval Studies, 1983), 67; and *Opusculum de Ente et Essentia*, 3rd ed. (Torino: Marietti, 1957), 19.

require subjects because they do not stand on their own. God plus creation and God without creation are not two different Gods. The modality of necessity among analytic philosophers, then, cannot be used to clarify what Thomas thought was an accident. Stump concludes, "If this is right, then this is the sense in which we should understand that God has no accidents—not that God is exactly the same in all possible worlds in which he exists but that there is nothing at all incomplete or insubstantial about God in any respect, even though God is not the same in all possible worlds."[74] Simplicity identifies the divine essence in all possible worlds as the God who was free to create or not, but as importantly, and inextricably linked, it identifies the simple God as perfect, complete being lacking nothing. God plus creation is not greater than God alone. From Augustine through Anselm into Aquinas, divine simplicity sustains perfection. Lose simplicity, and perfection will follow.

Stump offers a compelling defense of simplicity from within the analytic method, supplementing it with careful historical research. It is a philosophical defense that draws on Thomas's work to defend simplicity against its modern detractors. She points in the direction of God's perfection as rendering simplicity intelligible and vice versa, but as a philosopher she does not connect simplicity with the Triune relations. Early in her work on Aquinas, she notifies the reader that she will "leave unexplored" the persons of the Trinity.[75] She never discusses the relationship between simplicity and the Triune persons, even though she notes the importance of this discussion in the last four books of Thomas's *de Potentia*.[76] Here the current disciplinary divisions between philosophy and theology, which at other places Stump reminds us do not fit Thomas's work, prevent the most important use of simplicity for Thomas and thus one of its central meanings. Nonetheless, her philosophy provides what philosophy should do. It clarifies difficult concepts and points to their theological significance.

This section demonstrates that analytic philosophers of religion,

---

74. Stump, *Aquinas*, 113.
75. Ibid., x.
76. Ibid., 7.

unlike process theologians and open theists, do not have a single dilemma that their method addresses. They differ over what the dilemma should be and whether it has been logically characterized. But simplicity in particular is identified as a central problem by what could be called the first generation of analytic philosophers of religion. If that were the only result of the use of this method in the doctrine of God, David Hart's suspicions about it would be warranted. However, the rethinking of simplicity among second-generation analytic philosophers offers more promise to theologians. As we will see in the next section, the call for revisions largely depends on whether or not simplicity is abandoned. Once it is rejected, other attributes will inevitably be challenged.

What Should Be Revised?

Some analytic philosophers of religion reject simplicity and then call for theologians to revise the traditional answer by revising or rejecting eternity, immutability, impassibility, and by implication divine unity. This section will examine these calls for revision, focusing on eternity, immutability, impassibility, and unity. As will be seen, the revision of one affects the revision of the others.

Eternity

Like Craig, Plantinga makes the God-creation relation a real relation such that it makes possible accidental properties that define God's nature but not God's essence, such as the nonessential property "God–having-created-Adam." He explicitly claims that there is a real relationship between God and Adam. God's creation of Adam, he writes, "characterizes God, and it is something such that its characterizing him makes him different from what he would have been had it not characterized him. It seems plainly mistaken to say that the proposition *God created Adam* characterizes Adam but not God or says something about the former but not the latter."[77] Why is this plainly

---

77. Plantinga, *Does God Have a Nature?*, 42–43.

mistaken? As noted above, not all analytic philosophers find it to be so, let alone theologians. If God is eternal, infinite, and simple, then it would not be mistaken to say that Adam's creation adds nothing to God's nature. Only if we first reject simplicity and posit real relations between God and creation can this appear to be "plainly mistaken." Of course, once simplicity is rejected, immutability and *actus purus* follow. For Plantinga, God is "in potentiality" to some of his properties/ characteristics. Once simplicity, immutability, and *actus purus* are rejected, eternity must be jettisoned as well.[78] A warrant for the latter is that in the Bible, "God acts in time."[79] Notice that for Plantinga, divine eternity creates the difficulty for theology that it somehow prevents God from acting in time. We have already seen how Stump answers this critique. There is no reason to suggest that a single, eternal, simple divine act cannot have diverse, multiple temporal effects. Craig agrees with Stump that eternity does not make God an impersonal actor, but like Plantinga he questions how an eternal God acts in time and knows tensed fact.

Craig acknowledges that if we begin with divine simplicity, eternity necessarily follows. He sets forth the following analysis:

1. God is simple
   (or) 1'. God is immutable.
2. If God is simple or immutable, then He is not temporal.
3. Therefore, God is not temporal.
4. Therefore, God is timeless.[80]

He then asks whether there are reasons to begin with simplicity and answers no for three reasons. First, divine simplicity is more obscure than eternity, so the former provides no clarity for the latter. Second, "the doctrines of divine simplicity and immutability find absolutely no support in Scripture, which at most speaks of God's immutability in terms of His faithfulness and unchanging character (Mal. 3:6, Jas.

---

78. Ibid., 44. "Here I shall say only that I think Aquinas, in company with much of the theistic tradition, is mistaken in taking God to be timeless. God's life is of endless (and beginningless) duration" (ibid., 45).
79. Ibid., 46.
80. Craig, *Time and Eternity*, 29–30.

1:17)." Third, philosophy presents "weighty objections" against both simplicity and immutability.[81] Once the argument for eternity founded on simplicity has been cleared away, Craig then mounts an argument for divine temporality. It begins with philosophy of science and defends a "cosmic time" that exists prior to the big bang, although he acknowledges that there is no literal "prior to" the big bang. Cosmic time is "an empirical measure of God's time," which is an "absolute time." It is a time that does not need to have a beginning.[82] To someone not schooled in analytic philosophy or the debates about special or general theories of relativity, the claims made here do not seem to bring more clarity than what the tradition held with divine simplicity. If cosmic time is the "empirical measure" of God's time, then one would expect we would get some hard data as to how such an empirical measure works, otherwise the term *empirical* is being oddly used. As it stands in the argument, it is difficult to see how this is more than a strained metaphor.

Craig then begins with Duns Scotus to argue for divine temporality. Scotus offers a "temporalist understanding of divine eternity."[83] Craig sides with Scotus, interpreting him as suggesting God is temporal, and then examines three arguments for divine temporality. The three arguments are: (1) "the impossibility of atemporal personhood," (2) "divine relations with the world," and (3) "divine knowledge of tensed facts."[84] He finds the first, "the impossibility of atemporal personhood," unsuccessful. Craig acknowledges that divine eternity can sustain God's "personhood" as well as divine temporality, but he finds the second and third convincing.

Craig accepts the second argument for divine temporality because of God's relation with the world. The argument takes this form:

1. God is creatively active in the temporal world.
2. If God is creatively active in the temporal world, God is really related to the temporal world.

81. Ibid., 31.
82. Ibid., 65–66.
83. Ibid., 77.
84. Ibid., 77–112.

3. If God is really related to the temporal world, God is temporal.
4. Therefore, God is temporal.[85]

The crucial move is his premise 2. Given that he has conceded the possibility of divine atemporal personhood, it is confusing that he finds 2 successful. He defends this argument primarily by "defeating" Thomas with respect to it. Craig finds Thomas's argument that God has no real relations with the world to be "very problematic." Because God's relation to the world "is a causal relation rooted in the active power and intrinsic properties of God as First Cause," it will not do to differentiate creation's relation to God as "real" and God's relation to creation as "logical." For Craig, the relation is real both ways. He seems unaware that this poses any theological problems at all. Nor does he offer a discussion on how he can distinguish the "real relations" in God, the Triune persons, from the real relation God now has to creation. If the first real relation, God to creation, is based on a first cause and its effects, then how could he avoid the implication that the second real relation, creation to God, will also permit creation to be a cause that has effects on God? He offers no argument against this possibility.

Craig also defends divine temporality based on "divine knowledge of tensed facts." The argument runs as follows:

1. A temporal world exists.
2. God is omniscient.
3. If a temporal world exists, then if God is omniscient, God knows tensed facts.
4. If God is timeless, He does not know tensed facts.
5. Therefore, God is not timeless.

Craig argues against Jonathan Kvanvig, Edward Wierenga, and Brian Leftow, who use the analytic method to argue that a timeless God can know tensed facts. He then states that their only recourse is to revise premise 3 by revising divine omniscience. Craig finds that their revision fails and concludes God is timeless for two reasons: God has

---

85. Ibid., 87.

real relations with creatures, and God knows tensed facts. Only a temporal God can know tensed facts.

Craig concludes his argument defending a "dynamic" view of time against a "static" one. His argument for the former draws on what he knows about the divine mind. He must reject space-time realism, in which time is related to space, because he still maintains God's infinity and does not locate God in space even though God is in time. The reason for rejecting space-time realism is based on God's mental processes. Here is the argument:

> I think we have very substantive reasons to reject space-time realism. For inherent to the concept of space-time is the indissoluble unification of space and time into a four-dimensional continuum. But we have seen that time can exist independently of space. For if God, existing alone without creation, were to experience a sequence of mental events in the contents of consciousness, time would exist wholly in the absence of space. I take this consideration to be a knock-down argument against the view that time and space are indissolubly linked in space-time.[86]

How can such an odd theological argument be put forth as a "knock-down argument" against a claim from the science of physics? Few theologians would accept the theological argument, for it is clearly based on a strong doctrine of univocity—if God is to have personhood, then God must have conscious, mental events, and we know they require time. If theologians find this problematic, why would we expect physicists to accept it?

In this argument, Craig moves from what he knows about God to how the world should be. In other arguments, he moves from what he knows about the world to how God should be. For example, he acknowledges that divine temporality requires that he adopt a prior position on the A theory versus B theory of time. The two theories originated with the philosopher J. M. E. McTaggert in a 1908 essay. He suggested that time is either conceived in terms of past, present, or future (A series), or earlier than and later than (B series). The A series assumes truth will be tensed, and the B that truth will be tenseless

86. Ibid., 180.

or atemporal. Craig finds divine eternity to assume the B series, and because he is inclined to the A series he finds it more logical to affirm divine temporality than eternity. He writes, "I am, however, inclined to grant that the A-theory is correct. I therefore regard any theory of divine foreknowledge presupposing the B-theory of time as ontologically impossible."[87] Notice that we went from what he is inclined toward to a conclusion that the latter is "ontologically impossible." Here is an example of Craig moving from what he knows about time to how God must be given that the B series is "ontologically impossible." When, however, he discusses God's beliefs, he moves, like he did with eternity, in a different direction. Beliefs are not usually considered knowledge by philosophers; knowledge is understood as justified belief. If God has beliefs, then the question will be raised, what justifies them? Craig posits beliefs for God, but he does not answer what justifies them. The question, he suggests, is inappropriate given what we know of God. He writes, "objections to divine omniscience which are based on current definitions of knowledge are very tenuous and therefore not very impressive."[88] Craig, then, affirms the traditional answer on divine omniscience but not on simplicity and eternity. But why could we not respond to his revisions to simplicity and eternity with a similar statement by which he defends omniscience? "Objections to divine [eternity and simplicity] which are based on current definitions of [McTaggert's A theory of time] are very tenuous and therefore not very impressive."

Swinburne also calls us to revise divine eternity. Much like Craig, his revision begins with his affirmation that God is a person in the "modern sense" of person. He begins his trilogy with this definition of God: "By a theist I understand a man who believes that there is a God. By a 'God' he understands something like a 'person' without a body (i.e. a spirit) who is eternal, free, able to do anything, knows everything, is perfectly good, is the proper object of human worship and obedience, the creator and sustainer of the universe."[89] He further

---

87. William Lane Craig, *The Only Wise God: The Compatibility of Divine Foreknowledge and Human Freedom* (Eugene, OR: Wipf & Stock, 2000), 120.
88. Ibid., 124.

defines *person* by stating, "I am using this word in the modern sense."[90] This initial definition would seem to affirm eternity, for *eternal* is in the definition. However, in his analysis of divine personhood Swinburne modifies his definition and concludes God is eternal only in the sense of being everlasting.

The key to understanding his call for revision is this claim that God is a person in the modern sense. Swinburne acknowledges that some theologians are reticent to make this claim because it appears to make God an object in the world among other objects, but he is convinced this can be avoided "so long as you bring out the difference between the person which is God and other persons by other devices."[91] The device that brings out the difference is the ascription of M predicates and P predicates. The distinction comes from Strawson as a way to distinguish human persons from other creatures. M predicates are material predicates such as "weighs ten pounds." P predicates are predicates such as "an individual who thought, perhaps talked, made moral judgements, wanted this and not that, knew things, favoured this suppliant and not that, etc., but had no body." If there is such an individual, then we have a spirit who has all the necessary P predicates for a person but has no body.[92]

Swinburne then applies his definition of the divine person to traditional attributes such as eternity in order to address the foreknowledge dilemma. If God knows a future contingent, he suggests, then it necessarily comes to pass, but this knowledge is incompatible with human free will.[93] He resolves the dilemma by first revising divine omniscience. Omniscience is not God's foreknowledge of everything; God only knows everything that has occurred up until a time t, and everything that is "physically necessitated" at t or before. God does not know future contingents that "are not physically necessitated by anything in the past."[94] If God knew them, then God could not be free.

89. Swinburne, *Coherence of Theism*, 1.
90. Ibid., 1n1.
91. Ibid., 100.
92. Ibid., 102.
93. Ibid., 173.
94. Ibid., 175.

"For a perfectly free person could not hold justified beliefs about his future free actions (apart from any for doing which he would have overriding reasons)."[95] It is not "logically possible" for God to be free and have the traditional understanding of omniscience. Although theologians have traditionally claimed more, such claims exceed biblical warrant. They went beyond Scripture. He writes, "It seem to me also that the Bible, or at any rate the Old Testament, contains implicitly the view that God is omniscient only in the attenuated sense."[96] The biblical warrant for this is divine mutability; God changes God's mind concerning "his own future actions, and so his knowledge cannot be unlimited." His biblical references are God's change of heart to destroy Nineveh in the book of Jonah, Abraham's intercession for Sodom (Genesis 18), and Moses' intercessions for Israel (Exodus 32).[97] Swinburne then applies his teaching on God as a person to eternity and immutability, asking the question, what is necessary for theism to be coherent? It does not require divine timelessness, nor immutability, but only that God, as Creator and sustainer of the universe, is "backwardly eternal" and that he "go on existing forever." For Swinburne, these minimal claims are sufficient to refer to God as eternal. "A being who is both backwardly and forwardly eternal we may term an eternal being."[98]

We must keep in mind what Swinburne has done in the first book in his trilogy. He has not argued for the truth of these revised attributes but suggested these revisions are what is necessary for theism to be coherent; his concern is coherence, not truth. It was possible for him to then go on and make stronger claims for divine omniscience, eternity, and immutability consistent with the Christian tradition than he did

---

95. Ibid., 174.
96. Ibid., 177.
97. Ibid. He then revises his definition of God. "The theists' claim then, if it is to be coherent, is, I suggest, a claim that there exists (now) an omnipresent spirit, perfectly free, creator of the universe, omnipotent and omniscient (in the attenuated sense). The God thus postulated brings about all things which exist (or permits them to exist) and in so doing knows what he brings about and what that will lead to, in so far as he has brought about things which physically necessitate certain effects. Yet to maintain his freedom, he limits his knowledge of his own future choice" (ibid., 178).
98. Ibid., 211.

in this work. But his later work calls for these same revisions, and they are concerned with more than coherence. While he modifies and lessens omniscience, immutability, and eternity, he accentuates divine omnipotence.[99]

Swinburne asks theologians to abandon divine timelessness and think of God as everlasting. Both Scripture and the Fathers of the first three centuries, he suggests, viewed God as eternal only in the sense of everlasting. Boethius objected because it made God "time's prisoner."[100] Boethius represents an unfortunate transition in expressing divine attributes, for he introduces the "Neoplatonic" view that God is outside time. Swinburne finds that a proper metaphysics of time renders divine timelessness incoherent. Divine timelessness violates two metaphysical principles. The first is that an "instant" cannot be sufficiently temporal. Any "state of affairs" must be more than an "instant," but divine eternity views every state of affairs as present to God in an "instant." Swinburne states, "A state of affairs must last for a period of time; it cannot occur at an instant. God cannot be omnipotent or omniscient just at an instant."[101]

The second metaphysical principle it violates is that every cause must precede its effects. If God, then, creates, sustains, or "interferes" in creation, "his acting must be prior to the effects which his action causes." Moreover, divine "perception" of "events in the world must be later than those events."[102] Because divine timelessness violates these metaphysical principles, and it asks more of God than Scripture presents, Swinburne calls for revision. Divine temporality can avoid making God a prisoner to time as long as God enters into it voluntarily. He writes,

> So we must revert to the doctrine that God is everlasting, which we must read as claiming that God exists throughout all periods of time. I now

---

99. Ibid., 160. He also suggests, "But the omnipotence of a person at a certain time includes the ability to make himself no longer omnipotent, an ability which he may or may not choose to exercise. A person may remain omnipotent for ever because he never exercises his power to create stones too heavy to lift, forces too strong to resist, or universes too wayward to control" (158).

100. Swinburne, *Christian God*, 138.

101. Ibid.

102. Ibid.

seek to show that that doctrine does not have the consequences that God is time's prisoner, for the reason that although God and time exist together—God is a temporal being—those aspects of time which seem so threatening to his sovereignty only occur through his own voluntary choice. To the extent to which he is time's prisoner, he has chosen to be so. It is God, not time, who calls the shots.[103]

Notice how Swinburne's emphasis on divine omnipotence and modification of divine omniscience and eternity come together in this passage. Because God has the power to do something other than what his nature would seem to permit, to be time's prisoner, God can voluntarily subject himself to time. But this subjection to time is not what it seems if God can choose either to be subject to it or refuse to be so subject.

Craig, Plantinga, and Swinburne employ the analytic method to divine attributes and find the tradition seriously lacking. In order to address its logical incoherence, they call for significant revisions. They do so because of the "foreknowledge dilemma." Linda Zagzebski also addresses the foreknowledge dilemma using the analytic method, but with different results. She sets it up according to the following premises.

(1) God's belief at $t1$ that I will do S at $t3$ is accidentally necessary at $t2$.
(2) If A is accidentally necessary at t and A strictly implies B, then B is accidentally necessary* at t.
(3) God's belief at $t1$ strictly implies my act at $t3$.
(4) So my act at $t3$ is accidentally necessary* at $t2$.
(5) If my act at $t3$ is accidentally necessary* at $t2$, I cannot do otherwise than bring about that act at $t3$.
(6) If when I bring about an act I cannot do otherwise, I do not bring it about freely.
(7) Therefore, I do not bring about my act at $t3$ freely.[104]

This formulation of the dilemma emerges after William of Ockham because of his teaching on "accidental necessity." It is a form of necessity that is neither logical nor causal. It assumes Aristotle's act/

103. Ibid., 140.
104. Linda Trinkaus Zagzebski, *The Dilemma of Freedom and Foreknowledge* (New York: Oxford University Press, 1991), 36.

potency distinction. The future is in potency, and so it has no necessity. I could ride my bike tomorrow or refuse to do so. The past, however, is no longer in potency. I rode my bike yesterday, and I cannot unride today what I rode yesterday. That I rode yesterday had no logical or causal necessity to it, but it is now accidentally necessary because it is past. God believed two days ago that I would ride my bike yesterday. God's knowledge is infallible, so once God believes this it becomes "accidentally necessary" before I actually ride my bike. But if it is accidentally necessary at that time, then I am no longer free to ride my bike at the time I do.

Zagzebski, unlike most analytic approaches to this problem, finds Boethius and Thomas's understanding of eternity defensible, and so she challenges the premises undergirding the dilemma. Her own position is what she calls "Thomistic Ockhamism." As Zagzebski notes, the dilemma begins with the assumption (premise 1) that God has "beliefs," and such an assumption itself is controversial. Boethius and Thomas both reject this assumption because divine beliefs already assume some form of divine temporality, for if God has "beliefs" that something will come about, then God is not understood as eternal but everlasting; beliefs alone are not knowledge but assume that some future state of affairs will occur. Drawing on Thomas's understanding of divine eternity, she argues, "if God's state of knowing has the features described by Aquinas, it is so unlike other past events that even if it is in time, both premises (1) and (3) are false."[105] Stump and Norman Kretzmann made a similar point against this formulation of the foreknowledge dilemma in their well-discussed 1981 essay defending divine eternity. They write, "First, the short answer to the question whether God can foreknow contingent events is no. It is impossible that any event occur later than an eternal entity's present state of awareness, since every temporal event is ET [Eternal-Temporal]-simultaneous with that state, and so an eternal entity cannot foreknow anything."[106] If premise 1 is rejected, then premise

---

105. Ibid., 37.
106. Eleonore Stump and Norman Kretzmann, "Eternity," *The Journal of Philosophy* 78, no. 8 (August 1981): 453. ET simultaneity is a problem in the concept of eternity in which divine eternity implies

3 no longer holds. The difference between Stump, Kretzmann, and Zagzebski with Plantinga, Craig, and Swinburne is what constitutes a logical presentation of the foreknowledge dilemma.

Immutability and Impassibility

We have already seen that Plantinga affirms divine mutability if God is to redeem creatures, and Swinburne affirms it based on divine personhood. Like Sanders, he affirms "weak immutability" instead of "strong immutability." The former affirms that God's character does not change; the latter affirms that God "cannot change *at all*."[107] Scripture requires the former because of God's interaction with his creation:

> the God of the Old Testament, in which Judaism, Islam, and Christianity have their roots, is a God in continual interaction with men, moved by men as they speak to him, his action being often in no way decided in advance. We should note, further, that if God did not change at all, he would not think now of this, now of that. His thoughts would be one thought which lasted for ever.[108]

God could be immutable in that he acts on an intention he held eternally, but then he would not be "a perfectly free person" who is able to interact with others in time. A free person requires choice that is not determined by anything "other than what he had previously intended to do."[109] Strong immutability does not permit perfect freedom. Once again, the culprit for introducing strong immutability

that all of a person's life is present to God simultaneously such that it leads to the contradictory conclusion that God knows someone is and is not alive simultaneously. Stump and Kretzmann's "ET simultaneity" addresses this problem. They state, "What the concept of eternity implies instead is that there is one objective reality that contains two modes of real existence in which two different sorts of duration are measured by two irreducibly different sorts of measure: time and eternity" (444).

107. Swinburne, *Coherence of Theism*, 212.

108. Ibid., 212.

109. He writes, "a perfectly free person could not be immutable in the strong sense, that is *unable* to change. For an agent is perfectly free at a certain time if his action results from his own choice at that time and if his choice is not itself brought about by anything else. Yet a person immutable in the strong sense would be unable to perform any action at a certain time other than what he had previously intended to do. His course of action being fixed by his past choices, he would not be perfectly free. Being perfectly free is incompatible with being immutable in the strong sense" (ibid., 214).

into the Christian tradition is Neoplatonism and those who have "absorbed Thomism fairly thoroughly."[110]

Marilyn McCord Adams also calls for revisions to divine immutability and impassibility. Her call, however, differs markedly from those of Swinburne and Plantinga. The problem of evil demands revisions. Unlike process theology and McCord Adams, Plantinga does not think the problem of evil requires revision. He offers a careful analysis of the problem of evil and notes that the two statements "(1) God is omniscient, omnipotent, and wholly good and (2) There is evil" are neither "explicitly nor *formally* contradictory."[111] He offers a "free will defense" that is less than a "free will theodicy" by stating that there might be reasons why a perfect, omnipotent, omniscient God would permit evil. He revises immutability, but not as a response to the problem of evil. Although McCord Adams agrees with process theism that the problem of evil requires doctrinal revisions, she finds its solution inadequate. She is critical of theologians and philosophers who reject "substance metaphysics" and questions whether they have understood what they are rejecting. In that sense, she affirms the traditional answer—in part. But she does think evil, particularly horrendous evils, raises questions that the traditional answer cannot adequately address. In both her *Horrendous Evils and the Goodness of God* and *Christ and Horrors* McCord Adams addresses questions of "horrendous evil" through a Chalcedonian Christology.

Her first work, *Horrendous Evils and the Goodness of God*, argues that "free fall attempts to shift responsibility for horrors from God to humans fail."[112] These arguments fail for two reasons. First is "the necessary disproportion between human agency and horrendous evils." Second, internal to the free-fall argument is the assumption that human agency can only produce disproportionate evil when placed in an environment that God "produced."[113] The conclusion is that God must not only be "the source and sustainer of being and goodness, but

---

110. Ibid., 215.
111. Alvin Plantinga, "The Free Will Defense," in Sennett, *Analytic Theist*, 24.
112. McCord Adams, *Horrendous Evils*, 38.
113. Ibid., 38.

also the defeater of horrors."[114] God does this by suffering horrendous evils in his divinity but without "jeopardiz[ing] Divine existence or perfection."[115] *Horrendous Evils* points to Chalcedonian Christology in order to defeat horrors.[116] *Christ and Horrors* assumes the work accomplished in that work and develops more thoroughly the positive "coherence of Christology" as a possible "defeater" against moral objections to Christianity because of horrendous evils, but in order for Christology to defeat the problem of evil, divine immutability and impassibility must be revised.

Neither work is easily categorized. On the one hand, her work stands outside the mainstream of Christian tradition, especially on the two points central to the argument in both works. First, McCord Adams finds God responsible for evil. God cannot but create human creatures than through a "metaphysical misfit" between God's own being and creaturely being, and it is this framework, not the fall or human freedom, that makes evil necessary.[117] Therefore God "perpetrates" evil on us. Second, she jettisons traditional doctrines of impassibility and immutability in order to address the question why horrendous evils exist.[118] For the only way God defeats horrendous evils is through "divine participation," which requires more than the traditional doctrine that God participates in the human suffering of Jesus without confusing the divine and human natures. For McCord Adams, more is required in order to "defeat" horrendous evils. God must participate in them such that God suffers and changes in divinity.[119] Both positions come together in her claim that such horrors are defeated and that God's suffering and change occurs "when God participates in the horrors God has perpetrated on us."[120] Note the language is not *permits*

114. Ibid., 80.
115. Ibid., 85.
116. Ibid., 164–67.
117. McCord Adams, *Christ and Horrors*, 36. In *Horrendous Evils* this framework has a twofold character: the "metaphysical gap" between God and creatures and the "metaphysical straddling" of creatures as soul/body, mind/matter, etc. (94).
118. This latter point may no longer stand that far outside the mainstream of Protestant Christian tradition, as there seem to be few left who think impassibility must be affirmed.
119. God's participation in horrendous evils "defeats their prima facie life-ruining powers"; McCord Adams, *Christ and Horrors*, 40.
120. Ibid., 41.

but *perpetrates*. To argue that God "perpetrates" evils on us and then participates in them via divinity certainly stands outside normative Christian tradition.

On the other hand, McCord Adams's work approximates Christian tradition better than other attempts to address the question of evil because she seeks to be so thoroughly Chalcedonian in her response. McCord Adams's work is distinguished from other theological approaches to evil, such as Jürgen Moltmann's theology, open theism, and especially process thought in that it is less revisionistic in adhering to some traditional metaphysical Christian claims. She critiques Moltmann for "dismissing the responsibility to be metaphysically clear" by simply stating that "every German is a Lutheran and Hegelian."[121] Likewise she critiques process theologian Schubert Ogden for "dismissing Greek philosophical categories as 'incredible' while replacing it confidently with process philosophy." She then states,

> At the superficial level this is remarkable. Aristotle's metaphysics of substance and accidents—of things that have some losable and other unlosable features—is virtually a commonsense position, by comparison with the pan-psychism, much less the view that everything is a society of actual occasions, which are mini-minds that receive data and respond with an integration of it, and so do instantaneously![122]

Surely open theism would likewise fall afoul in its simple dismissal of a traditional Christian metaphysics by wrongly interpreting it as well.

McCord Adams offers a persuasive critique of the rejection of metaphysics in much of biblical scholarship and theology and makes three important points for our discussion. First, she issues a call to take metaphysics seriously. Second, she offers a compelling case that moral arguments that correlate Christian doctrine with political evils are not persuasive if all they do is suggest a concomitance between a doctrine and evil without demonstrating causation. Third, she reminds us that Chalcedonian claims are more than negative; they offer us a metaphysics that should guide our theology. These three points are

---

121. Ibid., 106n67.
122. Ibid., 107n68.

related. To reclaim metaphysics against contemporary critiques is to recognize that the conciliar Fathers meant something more than an apophatic theology or merely a logical grammar when setting forth the Chalcedonian definition. She suggests that Harnack's Hellenization thesis produced a mythologizing of the doctrine of the incarnation that is no longer persuasive and thus "a return to metaphysics is required."[123] Her return to metaphysics in the form of skeptical realism challenges the "historicism" of the twentieth century and states, "the truth of metaphysics is independent of current convention."[124] Her recovery of metaphysics contributes to a persuasive argument against the moralism that often dismisses the metaphysics of the incarnation without attention to the truth or logic of it. McCord Adams dismantles an argument present in John Hick by arguing, "It is not enough to point to *concomitance*: one must show that religion is a *salient* cause of the deplored effects. In fact, Christians do not seem *more* disposed to ethnic strife than others."[125] Her argument applies to Catherine Keller's dismissal of "substance metaphysics" and its putative association with "massive divisions and expulsions." Thus she boldly develops the metaphysical logic of the incarnation in order to take on not just the question of evil but of horrendous evils.

Yet it is the development of the metaphysics of the incarnation in order to resolve the dilemma of horrendous evils that confuses. Take, for instance, these three claims. First, because of horrendous evils "Godhead changes" and "is very likely acted upon." Second, although God changes and is acted upon, the "Divine mind" cannot be "blown" by horrendous evils. In other words, unlike us God cannot lose the ability to make meaning because of the paralyzing character of horrendous evils. Third, "As Anselm says, Divine Wisdom doesn't start what it can't finish, and Divine Power always finishes what it starts. Put otherwise, even if Divinity is mutable and passible, the Divine Persons in their Divine nature are not vulnerable to horrors. For God to share the horrors God has to become a kind of thing that can be

---

123. Ibid., 80–81.
124. Ibid., 106.
125. Ibid., 9.

radically vulnerable to horrors."[126] The third claim does not seem to follow from the first; it would require only the traditional doctrine of the incarnation—God becomes flesh in the person of Jesus and suffers in his humanity. But the first and third claim together establish a contradiction in the Trinity between a Godhead that can change and be acted on and the persons who are not vulnerable to such change and passion. The second claim challenges the extent to which God can participate in horrors. On the one hand, to defeat horrors God must participate in them in the same way God perpetrates them on us. On the other hand, God cannot participate in horrors as we do where they have the potential to destroy meaning making. Why then must immutability and impassibility be revised at all?

Having rejected impassibility and immutability, McCord Adams nevertheless affirms divine omnipotence.[127] It is central for her argument that the metaphysics of the incarnation does not produce the logical contradiction that on the surface it would seem to assume. Because Jesus is God and a human being, he is therefore "both finite and infinite, immutable and mutable, omnipotent but limited in power, etc."[128] Why is this not a contradiction? Because "it is metaphysically possible for any created substance nature to be ontologically dependent upon something else as its subject."[129] She draws on Jesus' enhypostatic existence in order to argue, via Chalcedon, that in his singular person we do not have two substances in competition. The metaphysical justification for this position appears to be divine power, which then allows the incarnation to be an instance of a greater metaphysical principle. She states, "Ockham went on explicitly to draw the conclusion that not only Divine persons, but each and every created individual ... has the metaphysical possibility of being an 'alien' supposit for a created individual substance nature of another kind." Thus it is possible that God could make Socrates an "alien

---

126. Ibid., 142.
127. It is qualified by the logic of noncontradiction. She states, following medieval theologians, God can "bring about whatever does not involve a contradiction" (ibid., 76).
128. This argument is clearly laid out in *Christ and Horrors*, 113.
129. Ibid., 134.

supposit of bovine nature."[130] Does this then mean that the incarnation would not be a unique event but a logical explication of what God could do to any substance by divine power?

McCord Adams works with the "technical vocabulary" of the analytic method. She sets up a dilemma and uses the specifics of Christian theology to respond to it. Like Stump, she does not depend on the analytic method alone but sets it within a rich historical, dogmatic, and metaphysical narrative. Should her summons to revise the traditional answer be heeded? It remains unclear why the traditional doctrine that the incarnate one who suffers the sins of the world in his human nature is inadequate to accomplish her purpose, except that she sets up the dilemma in terms of a metaphysical size gap that then requires radical revisions. But if God can only create through a "metaphysical mismatch" in which God is responsible for evil, why would we hope that God could redeem in such a way that this metaphysical mismatch and its "metaphysical straddling" in us could be overcome? In seeking to render evil intelligible, it becomes too real, that is to say, it becomes ontological in such a way that it is doubtful it can be overcome. How can God "establish a new world order" with "enmattered spirits" if this "metaphysical mismatch" is necessary for creation? How is this not a "design flaw" that God simply cannot overcome but we are destined to replay eternally?[131]

McCord Adams revises impassibilty and immutability because the "free fall" defense does not work, and something more than it is necessary to solve the problem of horrendous evils. Plantinga defends a freewill argument; the problem of evil is not a reason to revise immutability and impassibility. More akin to Swinburne, it should be revised due to God's interactions with creatures, but McCord Adams more than other analytic philosophers and theologians does not shy away from developing her response to the dilemma of evil by using specific Christian doctrines. Her work offers something more than "theism." Does the analytic approach, on the whole, have a place for

130. Ibid., 135–36.
131. Ibid., 213, 150.

specific Christian teachings, or is it more a preamble to faith, clearing the way for the rationality of belief and the existence of a god?

Unity

In order to address the previous questions, let us return to Oliver Crisp's example of how the analytic approach assists in making sense of the doctrine of the Trinity. He begins by telling us of the benefits of the analytic approach:

> The benefit of an analytic approach to systematic theology should be obvious. It provides a means by which complex problems can be made sense of with logical rigour within a metaphysical framework of thought for decidedly theological purposes. But it might be objected that an analytic approach to theological problems suggests a kind of "atomism." What if it turns out that certain doctrines are the theological equivalent of uncrackable molecules, the complexity of which makes them unsuited to analysis?[132]

Crisp offers two responses. The first is that analysis may not be able to resolve all problems "because they are mysterious." Second, some problems such as the "threeness-oneness problem" will benefit from analysis in order "to make sense of the whole."[133] He asks whether this method is reductionistic and uses as an example, assembling an Ikea chair.

> Thus, if I am attempting to assemble an Ikea chair but find that I am confused by the instruction manual and end up with something that looks more like a cubist painting than an object I can sit on in comfort, I might think the best way of resolving the problem is to take the chair to pieces and make sure I have all the right parts, before carefully reassembling it. But no one would think me guilty of a reductionistic method of chair assembly if this were to take place.[134]

Crisp then provides an example of how the analytic approach could address the doctrine of the Trinity:

---

132. Crisp and Rea, *Analytic Theology*, 38.
133. Ibid.
134. Ibid., 40.

To take one example, the threeness-oneness problematic associated with the doctrine of the Trinity may be approached by dividing it up into smaller parts: what do we mean by "divine person"; what is meant by "trinitarian perichoresis"; what can be said about "divine substance," and so forth. A resolution of these issues that are elements of the larger threeness-oneness problem, will certainly help the theologian to make sense of the whole (to the extent one can make sense of this doctrine).[135]

His example is only an analogy; too much should not be made of it. Crisp's point does not assume we break God down into parts like an Ikea chair and then put divinity back together; that would be an uncharitable read. He also acknowledges an element of mystery in the doctrine of God that cannot and should not be eliminated. His point is more that we break down our propositions, statements, and concepts into more basic "parts" to gain clarity as to what we mean by *person*, *essence*, and *perichoresis*. Every theologian seeks clarity on these terms; the first chapter of this work sought to provide clarity on how *simplicity* is used in Thomas. The analytic method is not inherently reductionistic for seeking clarity, but is there an impetus in the analytic method to divide into parts such that it accounts for divine unity with difficulty?

Theologians who have addressed the Trinity using the analytic method have, to this point, not been successful in articulating divine unity. Following social Trinitarian trends, analytic theologians tend to speak of the three persons as members or individuals. Take, for instance, the following claim by William P. Alston, "To be sure, we must always remember that terms originally developed for application to creatures cannot, usually, be truly applied to God in exactly the same sense, though that does not prevent a partial univocity such as I believe to hold with respect to 'person' as applied to the members of the Trinity and to human beings."[136] Alston, like McCord Adams, defends "substance metaphysics" against its critics, but he then accepts their critique of simplicity, accepting like Craig, Plantinga, and Swinburne

---

135. Ibid., 38.
136. William P. Alston, "Substance and the Trinity," in Stephen Davis, Daniel Kendall, and Gerald O'Collins, eds., *The Trinity* (Oxford: Oxford University Press, 1999), 187–88.

that the traditional answer cannot account for God's relationship with the world. He writes,

> unless we are able to scrap any significant relations of God to the world, we cannot think of God as pure act, free of any potentiality, and as unaffected in his being by relations to us, and hence not as purely simple as Augustine and Aquinas would have it. But there is absolutely no justification for saddling substance metaphysics as such with these commitments to timelessness, immutability, pure actuality with no potentiality, and being unaffected by relations to other beings.[137]

He then struggles to account for divine unity, suggesting, "It is by virtue of a more intimate interrelationship that the members of the Trinity distinguish themselves from a group of men or other created substances," finding that "more intimate relationship" in "perichoresis."[138] Having jettisoned simplicity, "perichoresis" is invoked as a not-very-clarifying resolution to divine unity. But as Lewis Ayres has pointed out, the Fathers who gave us perichoresis also affirmed simplicity. One cannot be had without the other.[139]

Richard Swinburne also offers an analytic approach to the doctrine of the Trinity. It too is a version of social trinitarianism. Recall that he refers to God as a person in the modern sense. His Trinitarian theology asks whether more than one "divine individual" would be appropriate. He answers yes based on an a priori analysis of what love requires. One divine individual brings forth another, and for the sake of unity of action, they bring forth a third. How then are they one? The unity of action could be had in a variety of ways. He examines how the persons might cooperate:

> One of them could take all the decisions and the others simply execute those decisions. Another way is to have a vote on every issue and for each then to carry out the results of the vote. A third way is to have a division of functions. One individual takes decisions on certain kinds of issues,

---

137. Ibid., 195.
138. Ibid., 192.
139. Ayres states that "Pro-Nicenes reflect on this mystery"—the unity and diversity in the Trinity—"always bearing in mind the absolute distinction between God as the only truly simple reality and creation"; Lewis Ayres, *Nicaea and Its Legacy: An Approach to Fourth-Century Trinitarian Theology* (Oxford: Oxford University Press, 2004), 278.

and the others support him in these. Another individual takes decisions on other issues, and the others support him in those, and so on. Which would be the best way for divine individuals to secure unity of action, to determine a choice between alternatives equally available to a perfectly good individual?[140]

His answer is that each "confine his acts of will to a narrower field of activity."[141] This would "limit the absolute power of each individual, but not the compatibilist power" of God as a "collective source of the being of all other things; the members would be totally mutually dependent and necessarily jointly behind each other's acts. . . . The collective would also be indivisible in its causal action in the sense that each would back totally the causal action of the others."[142] Swinburne's analytic approach to the Trinity resembles too much the part analysis of Crisp's Ikea analysis. However, it has not found favor even among analytic philosophers. Alston and Haldane suspect it of "pushing" toward, if not being, tritheistic.[143]

Like Swinburne, Zagzebski develops a personal understanding of the Trinity. God is, for her, "clearly a person and nothing like the Greek ideal of metaphysical perfection."[144] Unlike Swinburne, she does not then reject Greek metaphysics. She calls for revisions, but they are not as thoroughgoing as Swinburne's. She draws on Boethius's person as "rational nature" and supplements it, arguing that a person has subjectivity, freedom, and relationship with others, and is incommunicable.[145] It is the latter aspect of personhood that requires revision to divine simplicity. The incommunicability of persons entails a distinction between the divine nature and the divine persons. Here she acknowledges she differs from Aquinas, citing his question on simplicity, in which he teaches that "God is identical with his nature

---

140. Swinburne, *Christian God*, 174.
141. Ibid., 176.
142. Ibid., 181.
143. According to John Haldane, "More significant than such enthusiastic rationalism" for Swinburne's a priori argument for tripersonalization, "however, is the suspicion that the account of Trinity is a version of tritheism"; Haldane, Review of *The Christian God*, 283.
144. Linda Trinkaus Zagzebski, *Divine Motivation Theory* (Cambridge: Cambridge University Press, 2004), 190.
145. Ibid., 193–95.

(ST I,q. 3, a. 3)."[146] She does not explicitly reject simplicity or explain how incommunicability of persons challenges it. However, she does make the following claim that would be difficult to square with simplicity: "If a person is in a different ontological category than an instance of nature, then the ontological difference must obtain even when the nature is an individual nature. If that is the case, the work of traditional natural theology on the divine attributes is independent of God's personhood and therefore leaves aside what is valuable about the persons in God *qua* persons."[147] If I understand her argument, it assumes that even in the Trinity the divine nature or essence is in a "different ontological category" from the persons. If that is the meaning, then it could not sustain divine simplicity, and it leads to a real distinction between the divine essence and persons, which simplicity guarded against. Her claim makes perfectly good sense applied to human creatures who are marked by a real distinction. Human nature exists without a particular human being existing, but this distinction cannot be applied to God, or it will lead to the concept of a divine essence that is behind the persons, and each of the persons has an agency that it would seem the others do not share. Once again divine unity will be maintained with difficulty.

Conclusion

Analytic philosophers of religion and theologians have an impressive mastery of logical technique, but to this point the application of their method to the doctrine of God has not brought clarity but confusion. Analytic philosophers of religion find no consensus as to whether divine simplicity, eternity, and immutability should be revised or not; nor have they found a common reason as to why revisions should be made. The method, for all its claims for precision and rigor, does not result in a coherent teaching on God, but the resulting doctrine looks more like a cubist painting. In fact, it leaves everything in a muddle. The difficulty seems to be this. Is God a person or individual

---

146. Ibid., 200.
147. Ibid., 201.

who can be posited as having temporal beliefs similar to other persons, and then analyzed based on a "property account" of attributes? Barry Smith, Craig, Plantinga, Swinburne, and Wolterstorff, despite their differences, share the working assumption that the answer is yes. For Smith, even Leftow's analytic defense of simplicity does not work because it violates the bedrock rules analytic philosophy must assume. In response to Leftow's argument against Plantinga that God can be identified with God's properties as "a concrete object" that "exemplifies" them, and thus as a valid exception to the rules of analytic philosophy, Smith writes, "For him [Plantinga], as for most analytical philosophers, the distinction between a property, an abstract object, and the individual that exemplifies, a concrete object, is presuppositional and absolute; the identification of the two is a category mistake, confusing one type of thing for another."[148] Given these unassailable presuppositions, it comes as no surprise that analytic theologians must reject simplicity. It also comes as no surprise that, protests notwithstanding, God becomes analyzed, similar to what we saw in process theology, as a being fit within a larger metaphysical context of being. As an example, take a common move Wolterstorff makes in his theology. In his analysis of divine discourse he asks, "Could God fit into the texture of moral rights and duties in the way necessary for speaking?"[149] He answers yes. We have a metaphysical setting of a "texture of moral rights," and God fits into it. In his analysis of divine justice, he asks a similar question, whether the "texture of rights" God and creatures share illumines justice. He argues that it

---

148. Barry D. Smith, *The Oneness and Simplicity of God* (Eugene, OR: Pickwick, 2014). Smith rejects traditional arguments for simplicity because they lack "terminological precision" (90). However, to be precise he should say "terminological precision as required by analytic philosophy." Smith himself rejects the terminological precision of the Western metaphysical tradition. His main argument is that when it comes to God a "metaphysical part" need not be inferior, have potentiality, be finite, be imperfect. Of course that just means Smith does not use "metaphysical part" in the same way Aristotle, Plato, Philo, Proclus, Plotinus, the Cappadocians, Augustine, Dionysius, Anselm, Aquinas, the Reformers, and the Protestant Scholastics used it. Here Smith makes a "valid exception" to terminological precision that he does not permit to others, not even for language about God. Smith also rejects Aquinas's position because it "scandalously violates the basic ontological distinction between a nature (or essence) and its suppositum" (101). But this scandalous violation did not occur with Aquinas; it occurred with Nicea and its equation of nature and hypostasis.

149. Nicholas Wolterstorff, *Divine Discourse* (Cambridge: Cambridge University Press, 1995), 95.

does, and much as we saw a real relation between God and creation among some analytic philosophers, now we find a real relation of rights God and creatures hold "toward" and "against" each other:

> Just as we have moral obligations toward God and God has moral rights against us prior to God's issuing of commands, so too God has moral obligations to us and we have moral rights against God prior to God's making promises to us and covenants with us. I am well aware that many members of the Christian tradition, past and present, will find the latter suggestion abhorrent.[150]

The difficulty is not that we have "moral rights" against God per se but that we find ourselves in a situation that we might need them.

Stump, Zagzebski, Kretzmann, and others seem less confident that God can be set within the framework necessary for setting up dilemmas in the same terms as Craig, Plantinga, Swinburne, and Wolterstorff. This distinction is revealing. It suggests that the analytic method is not arguing to divine nature, but it begins with a priori philosophical assumptions and argues from them. Then the question is—whence came those assumptions?

The three theological movements examined so far share certain commitments. First, each sees its task to solve dilemmas. What was once considered a mystery has now become a problem or dilemma to be solved. Whereas Thomas Aquinas found simplicity and perfection to be the best language available for expressing the mystery of the Trinity, the analytic method begins with the different assumption that simplicity and Trinity are contraries. Barry Smith's erudite history and philosophy of divine simplicity shares this assumption with the analytic method. He writes, "The doctrine of the Trinity complicates matters for Christian theologians who hold to the simplicity doctrine. They must deny that the fact that God exists in three persons (*personae*) constitutes a type of composition in God, but at the same time avoiding the pitfall of Sabellianism or modalism."[151] He is correct that simplicity,

---

150. Nicholas Wolterstorff, *Justice* (Princeton, NJ: Princeton University Press, 2010), 283.
151. Smith, *Oneness and Simplicity of God*, 54. Smith acknowledges the role divine simplicity played in the doctrine of the Trinity, but he suggests its function is "question begging" (55).

perfection, and Trinity must avoid any hint of modalism, but this statement already assumes what Thomas denied. It assumes simplicity is somehow an "add-on" to the doctrine of the Trinity that manifests a tension to the teaching that the Western tradition never resolved. Rather than "complicating" matters, simplicity rendered them intelligible without diminishing the mystery. Processions in God are not movements among composite beings, because there is no "outside" to which God moves. The analytic method has not, to this point, been able to relate simplicity and Trinity, but nor has it given a satisfactory account of divine unity.

For analytic theology, dilemmas generate the questions to which theology or philosophy responds. In turn, they are "secular" disciplines. By that I mean that they too often seek to disenchant the world, to render it less mysteriousness and present God as coherent and nonmysterious in terms of the analytical or process tools used to render God understandable. What I have called the "traditional answer" is not generated in order to solve dilemmas but to set forth a mystery in language, recognizing that language for it will always be limited. In fact, as Augustine said, "if you comprehend it, it is not God." The purpose of the "perfectly simple Triune God" is to speak as well as we can about a mystery, not solve a logical puzzle. Analytic theology, process theology, and open theism make stronger claims on what can be known about God than the traditional answer. At times they seem to be describing God; their use of theological language seems to apply directly to God. If our language about God is to be true, then it must name a property formulable in a proposition, and that proposition must then have a truth value consistent with the logic of noncontradiction or the excluded middle. Theology then becomes setting forth these propositions. It only works with a strong doctrine of univocity.[152] Once the purpose of theology is to solve dilemmas and

---

152. Christopher Hughes's criticism of simplicity only works if analogical predication is rejected and univocity adopted. He is unapologetic in the rejection of analogy, writing, "Guilty as charged: I am assuming that 'is good' and 'is wise' are predicated univocally of God and creatures"; Hughes, *On a Complex Theory of a Simple God: An Investigation in Aquinas' Philosophical Theology* (Ithaca, NY: Cornell University Press, 1989), 68. To claim that "God is F" and creatures are F must have the same F (ibid., 70).

describe God, then apophasis, like analogy, is a threat to the theological task. If it is used, much like metaphor, poetry, or a good story, it is a sign of weakness in an argument.

If the purpose of theology is to resolve dilemmas through precision, clarity, and coherence, have these theologies been successful? Any reading of the literature would have to be cautious in saying they have. Philosophers or theologians using these tools have not come to any common consensus on the doctrine of God except for the fact that, on the whole, they find the traditional answer illogical. They do so for reasons different from process and open theism, but the results for a revised doctrine of God are similar.

7

———

The Cultural and Political Questions

If process theology primarily, albeit not exclusively, addresses the theoretical problem of evil; open theism the divine foreknowledge and freedom dilemma; and analytic theology a myriad of logical puzzles about the nature of God, each of them calling for revisions to the perfectly simple Triune God, there remains an influential theological movement oriented toward a more practical question—the liberation of oppressed peoples—that also calls for revisions. Theologians concerned with this practical question may be found among process theologians, open theists, and analytic theologians, but none of those theologies has the same starting point as does the theology that begins with the cultural and political question.

How to describe theologies that raise the cultural and political question is fraught with difficulty. They are sometimes referred to as "contextual" theologies, which is a self-description of many working with this question. Nonetheless, to refer to them as a separate discipline—"contextual" theology—could assume there is another form of theology that is not historically contextual. If the answer to the question "Who is God?" with which I began this work is taken as neutral or universal and applicable to any time or place, then contextual theologies will demand to know where a theologian would stand to offer such a theology. They would ask whether it takes into account the lived experiences of Christians in a diversity of settings. Is there a God's-eye view some noncontextual theology possesses that contextual theologies do not have?

But the term *contextual* alone does not speak to the varieties of theologies posing the cultural and political question. Others working with postcolonial theory are critical of the use of the term *context*. Willie James Jennings finds not only putative, universal European theologies contributing to a diseased theological imagination, but also contextual theologies content with an "adoptionist habit of mind" that "turns peoples toward an isolating theological creativity, imagining the divine among one's own people. Such imagining is not wholly wrong, but it is impoverishing."[1] Rather than the universal and contextual theologies on offer, he urges "the possibilities of a truly cosmopolitan citizenship."[2] The term *contextual theology* does not define everyone working with the political and cultural question, nor does *liberation*, nor *postcolonial*. No single theological school is responsible for the importance of the cultural and political questions examined in this chapter.

Contextual and postcolonial theologies are often understood as theologies of liberation that begin with the premise that any adequate theology will have as its motive, aim, or consequence that it liberates persons from unjust structures of oppression, including unjust theological structures. Although earlier proponents of liberation could be traced back to the abolitionism of Gregory of Nyssa, the anti-imperialism of Bartolomé de Las Casas, the call for emancipation of slaves by Frederick Douglass and others, or even Jesus' sermon in Luke 4, liberation theologies coalesced in the late 1960s in response to situations of injustice. James Cone, Rosemary Radford Ruether, and Gustavo Gutiérrez produced three different liberation theologies in the

---

1. Willie James Jennings, *The Christian Imagination: Theology and the Origins of Race* (New Haven, CT: Yale University Press, 2010), 167.
2. Ibid., 10. See also his concluding chapter, "Those Near Belonging," for how he contributes to the conversation for a cosmopolitan citizenship.

span of a few years: James Cone's 1970 *A Black Theology of Liberation*, Gustavo Gutiérrez's 1971 *A Theology of Liberation*, and Rosemary Radford Ruether's 1972 *Liberation Theology: Human Hope Confronts Christian History and American Power*. These theologies do not have a unified approach to the doctrine of God. Ruether calls for revisions consistent with process theism, but Gutiérrez and Cone do not. However, because many who affirmed the traditional answer were either silent toward or supportive of unjust structures, many theologians who ask the political and cultural question are not beholden to it. They ask whether it contributed to unjust structures. In 1974 R. H. S. Boyd asked this question, "Can the western Church break out of its bondage to Greek philosophy, to the Latin language and to Roman structures?"[3] Unaware of its own historical context, the argument goes, the Western church held its doctrine of God as universal, as if it were not grounded in a historical context. Because it too was historical, it should not have claimed to speak for all other contexts, neither diachronically nor synchronically.

Liberation, contextual, and postcolonial theologies burgeoned after the late 1960s. Colonial rule was being challenged politically and theologically throughout the world. Was the traditional teaching on God implicated in that colonial rule? Feminist, womanist, mujerista, Black, African, Latin American, and Asian liberation theologies challenged the Eurocentric basis of theology. Liberation theologies based on sexual orientation followed suit. Some of these theologies follow Boyd and others questioning the traditional answer in order to open theology up to previously excluded and dispossessed voices. Such theologies produce a rich panoply of persons speaking and writing contemporary theology, contributing to a broadening of theology that examines gender, race, sexual orientation, culture, and politics, and draws on neglected, overlooked, or intentionally rejected resources such as spirituals, blues, tortured victims' testimonies, slave narratives, and everyday practices found among dispossessed peoples. The

---

3. R. H. S. Boyd, *India and the Latin Captivity of the Church* (London: Cambridge University Press, 1974), xiii. Cited by Choan-Seng Song, *Third-Eye Theology* (Eugene, OR: Wipf & Stock, 1974), 10.

beneficial results of this theological expansion have been profound. Cone has brought to our attention the theological significance of how black suffering is normative in the United States and queried why such an obvious reality has been overlooked in mainline Protestant theology. Jon Sobrino introduces us to the martyred in Latin America—both named and unnamed—and shows the holiness of their lives and deaths, asking whether the impassible God can render their witness intelligible. Ada Maria Isasi-Díaz gives voice to poor women who would not otherwise have access to theology, and from whom we would not be able to hear if not for her work. How do we incorporate their daily struggle, *lo cotidiano*, into our understanding of who God is? Can the traditional answer not only accommodate but also encourage and support these questions? Any doctrine of God that cannot address these concerns will be inadequate.

Thomas Aquinas does not accommodate these questions well. Jennings and J. Kameron Carter remind us that colonialism occurred in the context of an Aristotelian-Thomistic framework. Moreover, Thomas was an apologist for a bygone Christendom and sought its defense through means that the great majority of Christians rightly find objectionable today, such as capital punishment against heretics and lapsed sinners. David Bentley Hart, who would not be classified as a liberation or contextual theologian but also raises intriguing political questions, offers a telling objection to Thomas's inability to account for the solidarity of a corporate life that embodies the gospel. He draws a contrast between two episodes during the High Middle Ages in Italy that demonstrate how laypersons could embody the character of the Christian gospel while some of the church's greatest theologians did not. On August 25, 1256, the secular leaders in Bologna emancipated 5,855 serfs, giving as the reason for doing so that God originally gave human creatures "perfect and perpetual freedom" and only sin led to servitude. Since Christ redeemed us, bondage should no longer be practiced. A little over a decade later, Thomas Aquinas made an argument that heretics should be executed because they were a greater threat than forgers. Forgers only threaten "money, which supports temporal life," but heretics "corrupt the faith which quickens the soul."[4] Hart acknowledges the different historical context of Thomas's day from ours. Thomas's thought was not anomalous. Yet Hart notes a serious limitation in Thomas's theology:

> Rather than the new pattern of corporate human life inaugurated in Christ's ministry—the practice of a life redeemed by God, the vital shape of a social order that executes neither heretics nor forgers—the Gospel had now become merely the deposit of sacred doctrine, which must be defended, if necessary, by the power of the sword; for it is occasionally expedient that, for the sake of a Christian nation, one man should die.[5]

Is there any necessary connection between this serious social and political limitation and Thomas's doctrine of God? Should the doctrine of the perfectly simple Triune God be blamed for the church's failures? If it contributed to, or cannot address, the failures of Christian practice, then revisions or development should be heeded. This chapter addresses the theological reasons noted for oppression and injustice, assesses those reasons, and attends to the calls for revision set forth by those who remind us of the cultural and political questions.

Theological Reasons for Oppression and Injustice

Liberation theologies are more like process and open theism than analytic theology in that they address a specific problem. Unlike process and open theism, however, the problem is not theoretical; it is practical. In fact, liberation theologies have little time for speculative theology, so we seldom find among its authors something like Thomas's first forty-three questions. They do, nonetheless, produce theology, relate the doctrine of God to cultural and political practices, and correlate cultural and political practices to doctrines of God. Liberation theologians present diverse causes for oppression and injustice, many of them focused on specific political and economic social configurations.[6] For the sake of the argument in this work,

---

4. See *ST* II.II 11.3 resp.
5. See David Hart, "No Enduring City: The Gospel Both Created and Destroyed Christendom," in *First Things*, August 2013, www.firstthings.com/article/2013/08/no-enduring-city.

causes primarily related to the doctrine of God will be noted. However, because most of these theologians raise cultural and political questions, the doctrine of God cannot finally be separated from those questions. It is the cultural matrices within which, and affirmed by, the doctrine of God to which these theologians direct our attention.

Although the cultural and political question emerges from a common, practical concern, its diverse authors do not identify a single, or even the same, theological reasons for injustice and oppression. Some, especially feminist theologians, find the cause in arguments we have already seen, especially in process theism. They find the cause in Greek or "substance" metaphysics that conceives God as a dispassionate, abstract, static God. Another theological source for injustice is found in the unexamined patriarchal culture that depicted God as male. Mary Daly identifies this cultural assumption with her pithy aphorism, "If God is male, then the male is God." A similar source is the unexamined "whiteness" by which, and in which, God becomes conceived. Associated with these cultural assumptions, and yet distinct from them, is the "diseased social imagination" that Willie James Jennings traces in the Western Christian tradition. It often goes hand in hand with a "scholastic disposition" that allows for a doctrine of God independent from lived reality. J. Kameron Carter finds a source, much like Cone has suggested, in heretical traits present in Western Christianity, particularly a "revitalized Gnosticism" or a "neo-Marcionism" based on a universalism that neglects that God elected the Jews and disclosed himself to them. Others find any distinction between orthodoxy and heresy itself to be the problem. Catholic Latin American liberation theologians identify a source for inattentiveness to the cultural and political question to a sharp nature-supernature distinction that confined God to a supernatural realm and allowed the cultural and political questions to be pursued in a narrow, natural realm. These are a few of the reasons identified either as a theological

---

6. I have addressed these elsewhere, especially in *Divine Economy: Theology and the Market* (London: Routledge, 2000).

source for injustice or at least theological inattention, neglect, or indifference to it. More could be added.

On the one hand, the multiple reasons for injustice make perfectly good sense. There are many factors contributing to it, and no single one could be isolated and identified as the sole cause. Some of them, such as "whiteness," can be misunderstood as putting forth a monocausal answer when they are in fact used for a set of cultural and theological habits that are present but seldom surfaced in traditional theology. On the other hand, some of the theological reasons identified as contributing to the injustice, and the concomitant remedies for them, conflict. This conflict is especially evident when it comes to the doctrine of God. Gary Dorrien notes the difference between black and feminist theology when he states, "Black liberation theology kept faith with the black church emphasis on the omnipotence and moral perfection of God, while feminist theology as developed by Daly, Rosemary Radford Ruether, Carter Heyward, and Beverly Harrison conceived the divine as immanent, not omnipotent, and in process."[7] Much of early feminist theology coupled it with process metaphysics. Take, for instance, the different interpretations of divine transcendence in Gustavo Gutiérrez and Mary Daly.

Mary Daly was one of the first liberation theologians to reject the traditional answer. God as the "Supreme Being" who transcended creation and ruled everything by *his* omnipotence and omniscience contributes to women's oppression. This "inadequate God" then "functions to legitimate the existing social, economic and political status quo, in which women and other victimized groups are subordinate."[8] Rather than affirming divine transcendence, she turns to process metaphysics as a corrective. Gustavo Gutiérrez, however, finds theologians of transcendence, especially Karl Barth and Dietrich

---

7. Gary Dorrien, *Social Ethics in the Making: Interpreting an American Tradition* (Oxford: Wiley-Blackwell, 2011), 390. He also makes this important observation: "Black liberation theology treasured the biblical themes of exodus and liberation, the sovereignty of God, Jesus as redeemer, and the kingdom of God as the sign of Christ's resurrection. Feminist theology, from the beginning of its modern rebirth, was more conflicted about retrieving much of anything from the past" (411).
8. Mary Daly, *Beyond God the Father* (Boston: Beacon, 1972), 19.

Bonhoeffer, more attentive to injustice than theologians who begin with something immanent such as anthropology. He writes,

> The theologian of God's transcendence pays little attention to the hearer of the Word. And yet he is sensitive to the situation of exploitation in which these broad segments of humanity live. . . . The one who starts with heaven is sensitive to those who live in the hell of this earth; whereas the one who begins with earth is blind to the situation of exploitation upon which the earth is built. Many will find this paradoxical but the paradox is only apparent. . . . For an authentic deep sense of God is not only not opposed to a sensitivity to the poor and their social world, but is ultimately lived only in those persons and that world.[9]

The difference between Daly and Gutiérrez is not easy to resolve. Perhaps it is not an either-or. Much as we argued that the traditional answer does not depend on any doctrine of simplicity, but one that does certain work in certain contexts, so divine transcendence and/or immanence will do different work in diverse contexts.

Feminist theology offers less a speculative theological critique and more a practical one that examines the "symbolic associations" doctrines of God produce. Sallie McFague argues theology is metaphor, analogy, and fiction. It is, she states, "mostly fiction."[10] If theology is mostly fiction, then what are the status of its claims? Are they true? McFague finds such questions inappropriate. "The question we must ask is not whether one is true or the other false, but which one is a better portrait of Christian faith *for our day*."[11] Theology consists of constructing better models in order to take into account new information that arises in every generation. She notes seven "assumptions" that "form the context" in our era that require new models of God: more appreciation of nature, less for technology, a recognition that we are always on the brink of nuclear holocaust, an understanding of the "radical interdependence of life at all levels," the rise of religious pluralism, an acknowledgment that all our doctrines of God are bound by their language and thus require "interpretation and

---

9. Gustavo Gutiérrez, *The Power of the Poor in History* (Maryknoll, NY: Orbis, 1983), 203.
10. Sallie McFague, *Models of God* (Minneapolis: Fortress Press, 1987), xi.
11. Ibid., xiii.

construction," and "a sense of the displacement of the white, Western male and the rise of those dispossessed because of gender, race or class."[12] This new cultural matrix requires a theology that treats nature more like theologians treat God. Like Daly, this new model will require a focus on God's immanence rather than transcendence. Liberation is expanded to include the earth threatened by ecological devastation. A new theological model that constructs the earth as God's body is necessary in our day. Although the language is intentionally metaphoric and not metaphysical, it obviously questions divine simplicity as a useful linguistic rule for speaking well of God.

Mary McClintock Fulkerson follows Daly and McFague. The problem with the traditional answer is not its metaphysical or logical truthfulness but its "symbolic associations" that instantiate patriarchy. She writes, "A religion that names the divine 'Father,' attributes the role of savior to a 'son,' and identifies maleness as a key qualification for representational ministry throughout most of its communal life is not only saying something with negative implications for women; it is creating a reality where women *must be fundamentally marginalized*."[13] McClintock Fulkerson understands Daly as offering "parody" and not countering putative realistic truth claims about God with alternative realistic truth claims.[14] Like McFague, she understands theology as bound by culture and language such that it cannot achieve the kind of rational explication sought by analytic theologians. She writes,

> Theological arguments cannot be presented in purely objective language because there is no such thing; moreover, the subject matter, *theos*, is defined by a long tradition of negative theology to mark its ungraspable character. "Divine things" inevitably invite imaginal and highly figurative expressions, and it is difficult to use solely technical, bloodless language to describe such matters.[15]

Sarah Coakley is more open to analytic theology and the reasons it

---

12. Ibid., x.
13. Mary McClintock Fulkerson, *Changing the Subject: Women's Discourses and Feminist Theology* (Minneapolis: Fortress Press, 1994), 42.
14. Ibid., 343–48. She states that feminist theologies "are not the substitute 'correct' ideas for the wrong ones of critical modernist (or traditional orthodox) theologies."
15. Ibid., 330.

offers, although she too has been critical of it, as we shall see. She also lends support to McClintock Fulkerson's concerns about the "symbolic associations" the doctrine of God produces. The counterargument to the feminist critique is that the Christian doctrine of God has consistently affirmed that God is not male. Simplicity teaches that God does not have a body, so God could not be male. While this counterargument is true theoretically, it is sorely lacking when confronted with practical depictions of God. Coakley makes a compelling case that "if one wishes to demonstrate unambiguously the historic capacity of the church to gender inner-trinitarian relations, while yet emphatically denying that it is doing so, it is to the history of Christian art that one must make first appeal."[16] She takes us through this history and concludes with what she calls the "prevailing paradox in classic Christianity." The paradox is that "God qua God, is beyond gender" in the traditional answer, and yet there is also "the equally persistent appearance of gendered visual representations of that God, often in forms which vividly display cultural assumptions about 'normative' gender roles."[17] All protests to the contrary that God the Father is not male, traditional artistic depictions demonstrate otherwise. They reveal the unavoidable cultural assumptions within which they are produced.

Feminist theologians identify a central source of injustice in symbolic associations that make doctrine function in certain ways despite what the speculative theory attempts to be doing. They turn our attention to those practical dimensions. The above critiques are not about metaphysics per se but the culture in which it works. Not every theologian working with this cultural question would assume the "Hellenization" thesis whereby the incorporation of Greek metaphysics into Christian theology represents a deformation. Catherine Keller, however, does. She makes a direct correlation between Greek metaphysics and patriarchal culture and finds a cause

---

16. Sarah Coakley, *God, Sexuality, and the Self* (Cambridge: Cambridge University Press, 2013), 248.
17. Ibid.

for injustice in the Greek metaphysics behind the dogmas of the first two ecumenical councils. She writes,

> Classical orthodoxy, dependent upon Greek metaphysics, in fact systematically denies that God can feel with us. . . . The Christian God had gotten defined very early in terms of Aristotle's "Unmoved Mover." And Christian theology naturally enough absorbed this ideology as part of the hermeneutical process of translating the biblical witness into the language of empire.

An impassible and immutable God was incapable of feeling our pain; such a God is only useful to emperors who intend, like this god, to remain distant and aloof in order to execute punishment without regret. In fact, "classical theism" expunged an older theology of chaos, which had a place for the other in a way that classical theism does not. It destroys the "other," resulting in racism, sexism, militarism, and capitalism.[18] Keller's argument asserts concomitance, but is short on delivering historical connections between "classical theism" and the political travails in western culture. In fact, this source for injustice is not universally found among theologians who raise the cultural and political question.

Gustavo Gutiérrez offers a somewhat different, and more Catholic, analysis of the source of injustice, or, to put it more precisely, the relegation of cultural and political questions to an immanent, natural sphere cordoned off from questions of faith. Political questions in particular, according to Gutiérrez, were not addressed by specifically theological teachings because they were relegated to a realm of pure nature. The source of *theological* indifference to these questions is found in a rigid nature-supernature distinction in Scholastic theology that was based on Cajetan's interpretation of Aquinas's theology. Cajetan (1468–1534) developed the doctrine of pure nature to insist on grace as a free gift that God could never owe to humanity. Thus he created what is called a "double finality." We have a natural end and a supernatural end, and the two are not intrinsically nor necessarily

---

18. See Catherine Keller, *Faces of the Deep: A Theology of Becoming* (London: Routledge, 2003), xvii, xix, 10, 23.

related. Gutiérrez's analysis is consistent with a mid-twentieth-century theology known as *nouvelle théologie*, found first among French Catholics who sought to move Catholic theology away from rigid distinctions in neo-Scholasticism and retrieve both the patristics and a more theologically inflected Thomas Aquinas. Rather than finding the doctrine of God as a source of oppression, it was the cordoning off of it to an apolitical transcendent realm that created deep difficulties in addressing oppression. They were accused of immanentism and (perhaps) denounced in *Humani generis* by Pius XII, Aug. 12, 1950. Henri de Lubac was silenced for a time but then vindicated; his teachings were widely affirmed at Vatican II. It opened up new possibilities for interpreting Thomas through more historical and biblical registers. Gutiérrez draws on these new registers. The result, as he understands it, is that "the frontiers between the life of faith and temporal works, between Church and world, become more fluid."[19]

For Cone, the cause of injustice is whiteness. It is the inability of white people to see the oppression of African Americans and to accept privilege without being attentive to the everyday reality of people of color. Cone writes, "Religiously or philosophically Black Power means an inner sense of freedom from the structures of white society which builds its economy on the labor of poor blacks and whites."[20] Those structures include the theological economy. Thus Cone writes, "The task of black theology is to take Christian tradition that is so white and make it black, by showing that whites do not really know what they are saying when they affirm Jesus as the Christ."[21] Cone charges the white church with heresy. In order to shake people out of their white indifference and complacency, he poses direct challenges. Take these examples from his works.

> The time has come for white America to be silent and listen to black people.
> All white men are responsible for white oppression.

19. Gustavo Gutiérrez, *A Theology of Liberation* (Maryknoll, NY: Orbis, 1988), 45.
20. James Cone, *Black Theology and Black Power* (Maryknoll, NY: Orbis, 1997), 63.
21. James Cone, *A Black Theology of Liberation* (Maryknoll, NY: Orbis, 1993), 9.

Theologically, Malcolm X was not far wrong when he called the white man "the devil."

To love the white man means the black man confronts him as a thou without any intentions of giving ground by becoming an it.

Any advice from whites to blacks on how to deal with white oppression is automatically under suspicion as a clever device to further enslavement.[22]

Cone has also stated:

No two people in America have had more violent and loving encounters than black and white people. We were made brothers and sisters by the blood of the lynching tree, the blood of sexual union, and the blood of the cross of Jesus. No gulf between blacks and whites is too great to overcome, for our beauty is more enduring than our brutality. What God joined together, no one can tear apart.[23]

Although Cone's work offers pointed political and cultural challenges and incorporates silenced or neglected voices into theology, when it comes to the doctrine of God proper, he seldom calls for the kind of revisions found among process theology, open theism, or analytic theology.

Jennings argues that a theologically "diseased social imagination" led to colonialist injustices. The racism endemic to Western societies will not be adequately addressed unless the analyses "reckon deeply with the foundations of racial imaginings in the deployment of an altered theological vision of creation."[24] That altered vision "displaced" the election of Israel and "reconfigured" it in European terms. European conquests were viewed as the elect bringing something to the world. This reconfigured sense of mission "inverted hospitality," expecting those who were invaded to welcome and learn from the colonizers.[25] Carter offers a similar analysis: "My fundamental contention is that modernity's racial imagination has its genesis in the theological problem of Christianity's quest to sever itself from its Jewish roots."[26] Jennings does not locate the problem in terms of the

---

22. Cone, *Black Theology and Black Power*, 20–21, 24, 40, 53.
23. James Cone, *The Cross and the Lynching Tree* (Maryknoll, NY: Orbis, 2011), 166.
24. Jennings, *Christian Imagination*, 6, 63.
25. Ibid., 8, 33.

content of faith per se (*fides quae creditur*) but more in terms of the "faith of the intellectual at work" (*fides qua creditur*).[27] He does not deny that the diseased Christian imagination distorted faith's content, but he is less concerned than contextual theologians with revising dogma and more with asking how it works. To think the former without the latter is to adopt the "scholastic disposition," a term borrowed from Pierre Bourdieu.[28] Carter makes a similar observation. The "scholastic disposition" is a "forgetting" of the link between the "scholastic mode of thought" and the "mode of existence which is the condition of its acquisition and implementation" that "escapes attention." Bourdieu and Carter's point is not about the "Scholastics" per se, be they Thomist, Catholic, or Protestant; it is about the questions that get raised in scholarship and how they relate to everyday life. The problem of evil or suffering gets solved, but without attention to those who are most vulnerable to "the problem." Carter relates this to the forgetting of the Jews.

> It is the forgetting or overcoming of the Jews as those whose very existence points to YHWH as God and Lord. In forgetting them, they are made to be alien internal to the West, the figure through whom all dark people, as aliens external to the Western imaginary, are forgotten. What is it that is forgotten about them? It is the forgetting of the everyday practices of such people in their real worlds of pain, suffering, poverty and death.[29]

Carter offers something more than the oft-repeated argument about Hellenization. He sees racialization in one aspect of Western theology that some contextual theologians either affirm or assume, Immanuel Kant's rational religion. Demonstrating Kant's racial cast to his philosophy, Carter suggests that his putative universalism underwrites a racial aesthetic. "Christianity as rational religion and Christ as the 'personified idea of the good principle' are the guarantee that whiteness, understood not merely and banally as pigment but as a

---

26. J. Kameron Carter, *Race: A Theological Account* (Oxford: Oxford University Press, 2008), 4.
27. Jennings, *Christian Imagination*, 83.
28. Ibid., 7.
29. Carter, *Race: A Theological Account*, 373.

structural-aesthetic order and a sociopolitical arrangement, can and will be instantiated in the people who continue Christ's work, the work of Western civilization."[30] This racial aesthetic leads to a "revitalized Gnosticism" or "neo-Marcionism" that neglects Jesus' Jewish particularity. Jesus does not reveal Yahweh but a "rational principle."[31] There is still suspicion against Greek thought for Carter. He writes, "For Kant, Christ represents the wisdom of Europe at the moment of its Greek birth."[32] This suspicion leads him to question Thomas's theology even when he draws on his metaphysics.

On the one hand, Carter affirms something akin to Thomas's metaphysics. Being is always, he suggests, "being in act. It is always *actus essendi*, explicating its fullness in the history of concretely existent beings (*ens*) who display in their own concrete existence just this unity of wealth and poverty and thus just this fullness of existence." Carter invokes Aquinas's *actus essendi*, but he does so with caution. On the other hand, he expresses grave concerns about the political uses of Thomism. He calls his own use of *actus essendi* as "strategic" and raises this important caveat about any retrieval of Thomism:

> That is, the argument I am developing here specifically and in this book more generally should not be read as simply a species of the current fascination with Aquinas that has gripped significant quarters of the modern theological guild, for I am acutely aware that any reading of Thomas Aquinas must be done in relation to the history of Thomism, especially in relationship to the colonialist and racial side of this history. In this sense, Thomas and Thomism are not easily separated. The modern vision of the human being as the bearer of race as marked with racial identity was made possible by fifteenth-century and sixteenth-century Portuguese and Spanish Thomist-Aristotelian intellectuals. Which is to say, modern colonialism and the world born of it arose within a Thomistic discursive space. This is undeniable, and it therefore raises questions that have been utterly evaded by modern theologians and philosophers who are turning—at least as this matter is concerned, in an uncritical and ahistorical way—back to Aquinas's thought; to wit, what was it about the Thomistic vision that made it susceptible to such racial-colonial usage?[33]

30. Ibid., 89.
31. Ibid., 107.
32. Ibid., 117.

Carter's question is crucial. It is a question animating much of the argument in this work. Do those who call for revisions to the "traditional answer" demonstrate a connection between this particular doctrine and its racial-colonial usage? I have already noted the deleterious results of Thomas's hierarchy of goods that assumed reprobation was necessary for human complexity. Although he, unlike Aristotle, did not make an explicit argument for racial differences based on that hierarchy, it is easy to see how it follows. Juan Ginés de Sepulveda used Aristotle and Thomistic sources to argue for colonialism based on such a hierarchical ordering. Las Casas used similar sources to argue against it. Charles V, who sought an answer to the debate on whether or not the native peoples of the Americas should be able to govern themselves, or were "naturally" fit to be ruled by those "above" them, adopted neither of their positions but those of Francisco de Vitoria, who used similar sources for yet a third position. Is there a direct correlation between doctrines of God and political injustice or liberation? The relationship between theology and politics is seldom that straightforward. Nonetheless, the cultural and political question trains us to ask about that relationship and be attentive to its possibility. It reminds us that the beauty of Thomas's doctrine of God did not prevent him from a defense of executing heretics.

The previous section represents an all-too-brief smattering of influential and important theological voices who have raised what I am calling the cultural and political questions. They ask, among other things, what are the interests that the doctrine of God serves? Some of these voices call for revisions to the traditional answer consistent with process theology, open theism, and analytic theology, albeit for very different reasons. Others will call less for revision and more for attentiveness to what the answer is doing—its paradoxes, dispositions, inattentions, and failings.

Attention to the uses to which the answer is, and has been, put may entail revisions, or it may entail that we recognize the traditional answer does not address all that needs to be addressed for theology in

33. Ibid., 431n100.

our day. We can discern historical usages, both negative and positive, and ask critical questions about the relations between the doctrine and its usages. This historical endeavor is essential for modern theology; it should not be shirked. We cannot return to a naive, objective metaphysics, as if culture and history are merely epiphenomenal on a reality known without them. Nonetheless, this historical endeavor itself has a history that also must have critical questions posed to it. Its reliance on Hegelian antecedents must be noted and queried, even when they are not explicitly affirmed. Lewis Ayres has argued that much of modern theology presumes Hegelian antecedents, and this presumption influences the calls for putative retrievals of the doctrine of God that revise Latin traditions.[34] His argument differs from what follows, but an undeniable common theme among many who ask the cultural and political question is their indebtedness to a left-wing Hegelianism, particularly Ludwig Feuerbach's. This indebtedness is not surprising. Gary Dorrien finds Hegel to have "made the strongest bid that any thinker has ever made to be the Protestant Thomas Aquinas."[35] Contextual theologians draw on many of the continental philosophers or theologians influenced by Hegel.[36] If Thomas cannot be separated from the history of Thomism, then neither can Hegel from Hegelianism. Hegel's retrieval of a Trinitarian theology fits well many of the criticisms found especially in feminist theology; the Trinity discloses a divine immanence and process whereby practical theology 1 and practical theology 2 now constitute speculative theology. Theology is speculative because it is primarily, if not exclusively, either the projection of cultural and political interests or Spirit that works in and through them.

---

34. See Lewis Ayres, "Into the Cloud of Witnesses: Catholic Trinitarian Theology beyond and before Its Modern 'Revivals,'" in Robert J. Wozniak and Giulio Maspero, *Rethinking Trinitarian Theology* (London: T&T Clark International, 2012), 3–26.
35. Gary Dorrien, *Kantian Reason and the Hegelian Spirit* (Oxford: Wiley-Blackwell, 2012), 160.
36. Dorrien writes, "the philosophies of Marx, Kierkegaard, Nietzsche, Freud, Bradley, Troeltsch, Bergson, Whitehead, Heidegger, Sartre, Derrida and Zizek, plus the schools of existentialism, psychoanalysis, absolute idealism, historicism, phenomenology, process, structuralism and deconstruction—are rooted in his [Hegel's] thought" (ibid., 160).

Hegelian Interlude: Theology as Projection

The relationship between Hegel and process thought has been well documented; it need not be argued for here. Hegel and/or Hegelianism has had little direct influence on open theism, although many of the questions and answers raised in it were first raised by Protestant theologians with Hegelian pedigrees. Hegel has no influence on analytic theology; it emerged in opposition to Hegelianism with its grand narratives. The indebtedness to left-wing Hegelianism by contextual theology is explicit.

Mary Daly draws on Nietzsche's analysis (who was indebted to Feuerbach) to view the God found in the traditional answer as a "projection grounded in specifically patriarchal societal structures and sustained as subjectively real by the usual processes of producing plausibility such as preaching, religious indoctrination, and cult."[37] As we shall see, other contextual theologians draw on Feuerbach for a critique of traditional portrayals of God as projection from their cultural contexts. Karl Barth made a similar move, albeit with different consequences, arguing that Feuerbach brought to completion what was tacitly present in Western theology.

Cone has also affirmed a socially mediated knowledge of God with some influence from Feuerbach. He states, "Theology is not universal language about God. Rather, it is human speech informed by historical and theological traditions and written for particular times and places. Theology is contextual language—that is, defined by the human situation that gives birth to it."[38] Previous to this statement, Cone notes the Hegelian antecedents; citing Feuerbach, with important qualifications, he affirms, "theology is anthropology. What theologians mistake for God is nothing but the 'latent nature' of humanity. . . . It is difficult to ignore the cogency of Feuerbach's logic in view of the obvious sociological context of human speech. What people think

---

37. Daly, *Beyond God the Father*, 18.
38. Cone, "Preface to the 1986 Edition," in *Black Theology of Liberation*, i.

about God cannot be divorced from their place and time in a definite history and culture."[39]

McFague argues that "models of God" are never "descriptions" of the divine nature. Here she sides with analogical theologians, but she takes the point further. She writes, "Predicates such as omniscience, infinity, omnipotence, and omnipresence do not properly apply to God either, for the meaning of all such language—knowledge, finitude, power, presence—applies properly only to our existence, not God's."[40] She too explicitly cites Feuerbach. In her *The Body of God* she states that we cannot imagine God except for imaging God in our own image.[41] And thus we are to think our relationships with God, with neighbors, and with nature on a "continuum."[42] She recognizes that this is a break with Christian tradition, but it is necessary if each "earth other" is to be thought only as an "end" and not as a means. Her *Super, Natural Christians* begins with a critique of Feuerbach. Feuerbach rightly notes, "Nature, the world, has no value, no interest for Christians. The Christian thinks only of himself." She argues that this characterized Christianity in the nineteenth century on both the left and the right. Christians think of God in service to their own interests.[43] McFague does not disagree with Feuerbach, but she disagrees that theology should limit itself to a projection from the human creature's interests alone. Feuerbach did not go far enough. He did not recognize that Christianity can think God not only in terms of human being but the being of "nature" of which human being is one small part.[44] Theological language is still projection of our social and historical context; it says

---

39. James Cone, *God of the Oppressed* (Maryknoll, NY: Orbis, 1997), 37.
40. McFague, *Models of God*, 39.
41. Sallie McFague, *The Body of God: An Ecological Theology* (Minneapolis: Fortress Press, 1993), 20. McFague writes, "As we are inspirited bodies—living, loving, thinking bodies—so, imagining God in our image (for how else *can* we model God?), we speak of her as *the* inspirited body of the entire universe, the animating, living spirit that produces, guides and saves us all."
42. Sallie McFague, *Super, Natural Christians* (Minneapolis: Fortress Press, 2000), 1–2. "My suggestion is that we should relate to the entities in nature in the same basic way that we are supposed to relate to God and other people—as ends, not means, as subjects valuable in themselves, for themselves."
43. Ibid., 5.
44. Harvey suggests Feuerbach was aware of her concern already. See Van Harvey, *Feuerbach and the Interpretation of Religion* (Cambridge: Cambridge University Press, 1997), 37.

more about us than it does God, but the projection should be expanded to address all of creation.

McClintock Fulkerson also speaks of "realities of theological reflection as politically *produced*, discursive objects."[45] Likewise, Isasi-Díaz reveals a Hegelianized dialectic in her theology. The central source for her *mujerista* theology is lo cotidiano. It designates the daily struggle Latinas face to survive. It serves as a "challenge to traditional theology." When she explains what lo cotidiano is, Isasi-Díaz writes,

> Lo cotidiano for us is also a way of understanding theology, our attempt to explain how we understand the divine, what we know about the divine. I contrast this to the academic and churchly attempts to see theology as being about God instead of about what humans know about God. Lo cotidiano makes it possible for us to see our theological knowledge as well as all our knowledge as fragmentary, provisional, conjectural and provisional.[46]

Isasi-Díaz then states, "we are very clear about our partisan perspective."[47] Her work is an intriguing, Hegelian blending of subjectivity and objectivity. Its sophisticated Hegelian antecedents can be found when she writes, "What passes as objectivity in reality merely names the subjectivity of those who have the authority and/or power to impose their point of view."[48] The fact that she claims an objective stance for this (it is true "in reality") shows how objectivity and the political subject are brought together dialectically until those who were subjected to a putative political objectivity render it subjective and become themselves a new form of objectivity.

Jacquelyn Grant offers a similar Hegelian analysis, also with qualifications, in her *White Women's Christ and Black Women's Jesus*. She writes,

> It is my claim that there is a direct relationship between our perception of Jesus Christ and our perception of ourselves. (The very point can be made of God). Ludwig Feuerbach sheds some light on this relationship.

45. McClintock Fulkerson, *Changing the Subject*, 324.
46. Ada Maria Isasi-Díaz, *Mujerista Theology* (Maryknoll, NY: Orbis, 1996), 71–72.
47. Ibid., 85n31.
48. Ibid., 75.

He describes the content of this relationship as one of self-objectification: "The object of any subject is nothing else than the subject's own nature taken objectively."[49]

Grant then argues that Feuerbach "unwittingly" made the same argument now made by feminist and womanist theologians: "Since man is limited by his social context and interests, Jesus Christ has been defined within the narrow parameters of the male consciousness. That is to say, the social context of the men who have been theologizing has been the normative criterion upon which theological interpretation have been based."[50]

Jon Sobrino also finds Hegelian moves helpful in illuminating the place of the suffering of the dispossessed in El Salvador for theology. He too draws on Feuerbach to explain how our suffering relates us to God and language about God.

> If God can be known in the presence of the cross, the principal motor of that knowing is not wonder but suffering. Only through suffering can there by a *sumpatia*, a connaturality, with the object one seeks to know. "Suffering precedes thought" (Feuerbach). Subjective inner suffering, in the presence of objective external suffering, is what can enable us to know something of God on the cross; without it nothing of God will be revealed on the cross.[51]

Theology begins by projecting from the context of the suffering of the dispossessed.

These examples suffice to show implicit and explicit connections between Hegelianism and contextual theology.[52] What should be made of it? One response is to dismiss it as speaking nonsense. Analytic philosophy emerged as an alternative to the Hegelianism in British philosophy, especially by G. E. Moore and Bertrand Russell, so it is no surprise that an analytic theologian would find the language of contextual theology unconvincing.[53] Contextual theology assumes our

---

49. Jacqueline Grant, *White Women's Christ and Black Women's Jesus* (Atlanta: Scholars Press, 1989), 63.
50. Ibid., 64.
51. Jon Sobrino, *Jesus the Liberator* (Maryknoll, NY: Orbis, 1993), 249.
52. As previously noted, both Jennings and Carter reject this move. Their theology is not "contextual" in that sense.

language for God is neither scientific nor logically rigorous; it is metaphorical and poetic. Although it makes truth claims about specific situations, it is unconcerned to make truth claims about God. Analytic theology finds such assertions to have abandoned an essential task of theological discourse—to speak the truth about God. Humans-speaking-about God becomes theology's subject matter rather than God. More can be said about God than metaphorical and fictive language emerging from historical situations provides.

Randall Rauser critiques contextual theology by drawing on Harry Frankfurt's well-known essay "On Bullshit," a term used to describe both popular and academic uses of language where the result, intended or not, is not to tell the truth but to get us to do something—usually to buy, or buy into something. Rauser cites as an example Martin Heidegger's statement: "The nothing *noths.*"[54] He then criticizes much modern theology for being little more than "bullshit," taking McFague's theological approach to task:

> McFague is little different from the used car salesperson who cares not about providing me with factual information on that rusty old Ford Cortina, but rather with getting me to buy it. Just as the salesperson's job description ensures that closing the deal trumps truth telling, so on McFague's view of "theo-poetic persuasion," the theologian's final obligation is not to inform but to persuade (even as she makes it *appear* that she informs). Whether or not you agree that this practice of depicting God in a variety of personas to facilitate transforming love is justified does not change the fact that it is intentional bullshit.[55]

Perhaps contextual theology might respond that the preoccupation by analytic theologians on whether or not God knows whether Jones will mow his lawn eighty years from today (Nelson Pike's much-discussed example) is trivial and unimportant when faced with the injustices present throughout the world today. Theology should be concerned with much more than the issues that motivate analytic theology. Can

53. See Paul Redding, *Analytic Philosophy and the Return of Hegelian Thought* (Cambridge: Cambridge University Press, 2007).
54. Randall Rauser, "Theology as a Bull Session," in Oliver D. Crisp and Michael C. Rea, eds., *Analytic Theology: New Essays in the Philosophy of Theology* (Oxford: Oxford University Press, 2009), 70.
55. Ibid., 79.

it speak a liberative word to these unjust situations? If it has not done so, then it has not yet spoken well of God. Moreover, Rauser misses the proper role for theopoetics in theology. McFague is not alone in doing theology as theopoesis; Hans Urs von Balthasar did so as well. But Balthasar did not set theopoesis in opposition to truth. Theology is eidetic. It is truth not as description of an object but as a disclosure. It is why he could draw on the symbols and visions of the book of Revelation, something the analytic method would have difficulty incorporating into their work. The opposition between metaphor and truth in some contextual theology requires carefully considering Rauser's point, and perhaps we can attempt to do so on his own terms.

Let's take Jacquelyn Grant's quotation from Feuerbach as an example: "The object of any subject is nothing else than the subject's own nature taken objectively." We can call this proposition *KP* (knowledge-projection):

KP: the knowledge of any object is nothing but a subject's nature projected onto the object.

Or to simplify:

KP*: the knowledge of any x is SN projected on x.
(where x is any object, S is the subject seeking to know x, and N is the subject's nature)

Once we seek to analyze this statement, it readily becomes clear that KP* is false. It would not be able to account for the diversity or the content of our knowledge of trees, modes of transportation, cell biology, sociological trends, or astrophysics. It does not fit most objects we seek to know, so the "any" is unreasonable. I do not project my nature on mitochondria or aeronautics, and yet I can know them. Such a claim is so illogical that charity demands that we acknowledge Feuerbach could not have meant something that obviously false. His point must be limited not to "any object," but to specific metaphysical objects such as God or being. If we replace x as "any object" with y as God, then the proposition makes more sense:

KP**: the knowledge of God is *SN* projected on God.

It is not "any object" that is the projection of the subject's nature, but the peculiar object known as God that is. How might we resolve the truth of KP**?

We begin with two "objects"—God and the subject thinking/ projecting God. Whether or not "God" exists, we can think of, and speak about, "God." God could be a fictive object we create for the sake of ourselves or an actually existing object. Either way, KP** could be true. If God is created in the image of humanity, or humanity is created in the image of God, then KP** is justifiable—with different consequences. On the first possibility, God would be nothing other than human projection; on the second, human projection (practical theology 2) would be an essential means for knowledge of God. We have no direct, univocal source for our knowledge of God, for humanity is not divinity. As the traditional answer assumes, the knowledge of God is self-evident only to God. Knowledge of God must be indirect, mediated through creaturely means. On the first possibility, however, it is a direct form of knowledge. "God became human" is taken literally. Christianity represents the final disenchantment of the world, divinity's complete secularization. Humanity is God. On the second possibility, "God became human" can only be taken analogically. Having created humanity as other than God, God then enters into humanity without ceasing to be characterized by distinction from it, for every similarity between them there would remain an ever-greater dissimilarity, and our language would have to somehow express that similarity and dissimilarity.

Contextual and liberation theologians are not atheists, not even by implication. Their Hegelianism only makes sense on the second possibility. Like Hegel, they understand *SN*, the subject's nature that is projected not as the human being qua human being, but the human being mediated through *Sittlichkeit*. Hegel is an important antecedent for contextual theology because, unlike Kant, he located subjectivity in sociohistorical contexts. Human agency is found in the intersubjectivity of *Sittlichkeit* ("ethical life"). Hegel set *Sittlichkeit* against Kant's *Moralität*. As Charles Taylor notes, Hegel found Kant's morality empty because it always set morality and freedom against nature. The subject and object were divided from each other. For this reason, Kant's "kingdom" could never be embodied. It could not be found in nature; it lacked a substantive politics. Hegel turned to the historical mediation of customs (*Sitten*) in particular communities. Spirit moves through these mediations, becoming ever more rational, reconciling freedom and nature.[56]

Hegel drew on the Christian doctrine of the Trinity, developing it as a historical movement of Spirit, to overcome the nature/freedom split Kant bequeathed Western philosophy. Hegel maintained more of the content of historical Christianity than did Kant, but like Kant he understood the historical church as transitional. Revealed religion is "picture religion" that must give way to Spirit as Absolute Knowing, which will be found in a rational state.[57] As Charles Taylor persuasively argues, Hegel was no lackey for the Prussian state, nor is he a source for fascism.[58] He does, however, see the outcome of the historical mediation of Spirit(s) as a free and rational state. His project is nationalist, even if it does not entail nationalism in the negative sense. Hegel's development of Protestant theology emphasized historical mediation. Historical mediation defines contextual theology.

Although left-wing Hegelianism is an important antecedent for contextual theology, as the above section demonstrated, contextual theology is not Hegelian without reserve. Historical mediation is essential to it, but absolute knowledge is not. Among contextual theologians, the church is seldom replaced by the rational state. The revisions found in Hegel's theology are, however, consistent with most of the revisions present in contextual theology. Cyril O'Regan notes these revisions: "Hegelian thought requires massive rethinking of received Christian views on revelation, creation, the nature of the Trinity, and an acceptance of a very different relation between faith

---

56. See Charles Taylor, *Hegel* (Cambridge: Cambridge University Press, 1975), 376–78.
57. G. W. F. Hegel, *Phenomenology of Spirit*, trans. A. V. Miller (Oxford: Oxford University Press, 1977), 764.
58. Taylor, *Hegel*, 374–78.

and philosophy than that sanctioned by magisterial thinkers such as Augustine and Aquinas, and for that matter also Luther and Calvin."[59] The core of these revisions is rethinking the divine essence in terms of the economic Trinity, leading to profound shifts from timeless eternity to divine temporality, immutability to mutability, impassibility to passibility, and positing a real relation between God and creation. The relation between faith and philosophy will be "practical" in the sense noted above. It is found in historical mediations and not in any abstraction from history that would lead to speculative theology. "Speculation," in that sense, becomes pejorative. We have seen how these revisions are called for by most of the previous theological movements, whether influenced by Hegel or not.

Speaking of God: Revising the Doctrine of God

When contextual theology calls for revisions, like process theology, the revisions are nearly always identical to Hegel's rethinking of Christianity. Some eschew the task of a doctrine of a speculative doctrine of God altogether. C. S. Song writes, "But God seems exceedingly impatient with theologians who give him no rest with their 'scientific' inquiries about his nature and his ways in the world. God cannot be the object of scientific investigation, nor can he be subjected to minute theological scrutiny."[60] Can God be an object of investigation? A common refrain in theology is that God is not an object in the world that can be indicated; that is to say, one cannot point to it and say "that is God." To do so is to misunderstand who God is. If Song means this by his statement, then of course he is correct. Likewise, Karl Barth's theology is well known for insisting that God is always the unsublatable Subject of theology and never its object. Katherine Sonderegger, however, has asked us to rethink the question whether God can be object. She finds it utterly plausible that God can and does make Godself object for our contemplation and knowledge.

59. Cyril O'Regan, *The Anatomy of Misremembering: Von Balthasar's Response to Philosophical Modernity*, vol. 1, *Hegel* (New York: Herder & Herder, 2014), 51.
60. Song, *Third-Eye Theology*, 174.

There is nothing in the divine nature that would require that this be a contradiction. In fact, it is consistent with the divine nature. She writes, "The utter Mystery of God is that He is Object and Subject, Nature and Person, altogether and at once, as One, Uniquely One."[61] She has provided a speculative theology that is compelling in its attention to divine unity and at the same time avoiding any "scholastic disposition." We will examine it more fully below, but suffice it for now to suggest that those who ask the cultural and political questions are not as unified as the previous movements in revising the doctrine of God. In fact, we find the traditional answer sometimes affirmed here more so than in the previous examined theologies, sometimes but not always.

Mary Daly's early theology couples Thomas Aquinas's understanding of God as "Final Cause" with process philosophy.[62] In so doing, she made the uncontroversial claim, one that fits well the idea of God as pure act, that we should think of God not as "the supreme being" but rather as "Be-ing."[63] *Be-ing* is a verb that draws people to act courageously and strenuously in the face of oppression. Having defined God in terms of an active verb, she then rejects divine timelessness. This reconceived divine nature, she argues, affords opportunities to challenge patriarchy. "If we perceive the good, the final cause, as *not* identical with the static, timeless being of Parmenides, and *not* identical with the intentions of the institutional fathers and their Heavenly Father, but rather with Be-ing in which we participate actively by the qualitative leap of courage in the face of patriarchy, the magic collar that was choking us is shattered."[64]

McFague calls us to revise most of the language traditionally used for God. She rejects simplicity, arguing that God in some sense has a body, in order to avoid any strong God-creation dualism.[65] Like the process theologians, she rejects *creatio ex nihilo*.[66] Because creation is

61. Katherine Sonderegger, *Systematic Theology*, vol. 1, *God* (Minneapolis: Fortress Press, 2015), 441.
62. Daly, *Beyond God the Father*, 188.
63. Ibid., xvii.
64. Ibid., 189.
65. McFague, *Models of God*, 111.
66. Ibid., 109.

God's body, in some sense, its evil is God's evil. God is passible. "The evil occurs in and to God's body: the pain that those parts of creation affected by evil feel God also feels and feels bodily."[67] She affirms God's "real relations" with creation and understands its significance much better than we saw with analytic theologians who also affirmed it. If God has real relations with creation, then God needs it. She cites C. S. Lewis's affirmation that the only real relations are the Triune relations, only to reject it. "As C. S. Lewis says, God is '"at home" in the land of the Trinity,' presumably finding relations with the other 'persons' sufficiently satisfying so that, needing nothing, God 'loves into existence wholly superfluous creatures.'" She finds this traditional answer to be a "sterile and unattractive view of divine love."[68] In its place is a different "model" of God as a Mother who is indistinct from her creation and who knows the creation because it exists in an intimate relation with her through gestation and lactation. The image is powerful and could help us think infinity well, but it would do this better if she did not reject Lewis's traditional answer, react against it, and require us to choose between them. We can have both. Creation adds nothing to the Divine Mother; she loves it for itself because it is not necessary for her. It is no threat to her being but enfolded and loved within her unfathomable excess. Like a child to her mother, creation is intimately present in God. The key term, however, is *like*. McFague's image identifies similarities but is less successful in identifying the dissimilarities.

Daly and McFague are emblematic of much of the earliest feminist theologies. They coupled feminist critique with process theism. That connection is no longer as binding as it once was, and many theologians who share these same feminist concerns now find resources in the traditional answer to do so. Elizabeth Johnson does not draw on process theism for her summons to revise "classical theism."[69] Instead she draws on "divine incomprehensibility" from "classical theology" in order first to relativize the traditional answer and then to

67. Ibid., 75.
68. Ibid., 102.
69. Elizabeth Johnson, *She Who Is* (New York: Crossroad, 1996), 265.

offer an alternative. Her alternative rejects simplicity and impassibility based on the fact that it cannot be "seriously imaginable" among feminists because these terms make God "unaffected" by creatures' suffering.[70] It makes God other than loving. Johnson assumes an axiom we will also find in Moltmann: God can only love if God can suffer like we suffer. Her move to divine passibility based on this univocal understanding of suffering does not fit well with her move to dislodge the traditional answer by divine incomprehensibility. If we cannot comprehend God, which is what the traditional answer affirms, how can we know that God suffers as we suffer? Is it not possible that God is intimately involved with our suffering so that even the distance of "suffering" cannot adequately account for it? Herbert McCabe also affirms divine incomprehensibility, but it leads him to question the either-or—either God suffers our sufferings, or God is "indifferent" to it. Our "capacity" for suffering, he suggests, keeps us at a distance from one another, which is why we use terms for suffering that remind us we are always "outside the person" who is suffering such as "sympathy" and "compassion." God is never "outside" because God as Creator is the "center" of every creature's existence. Far from making God indifferent to our suffering, God is more intimate to it than we are to ourselves.[71] McCabe's position has the advantage of maintaining divine incomprehensibility and the central place of analogy in our language, positions Johnson also affirms, but without importing a univocity into practical theology by assuming God must suffer as we suffer.

Johnson also names and rejects "classical theism" because it is based on a "root metaphor" of motion that cannot render intelligible the root metaphor of love. The metaphor of motion refuses to affirm divine passibility. She acknowledges that the traditional answer viewed God not as static and abstract but as a motion without potentiality: "something already purely in act cannot pass from potency into act,"

---

70. "From a feminist perspective, the idea that God might permit great suffering while at the same time remaining unaffected by the distress of beloved creatures is not seriously imaginable" (ibid., 253).
71. Herbert McCabe, OP, *God Matters* (Springfield, IL: Templegate, 1991), 44.

but then she adds, "nor can something completely in motion be in any way passive or receptive." Here she has missed something essential to the answer, something noted above when Thomas affirmed that because of the divine processions, there is a *receptum esse* in God. Thomas found no contradiction in understanding God as pure act without potentiality and at the same time processions that allow for a receptivity. Johnson affirms something similar. Once "the essence of God" is understood as "the motion of personal relations and the act that is love," she argues, then suffering could be "not necessarily a passive state nor a movement from potentiality to act." She seeks to affirm divine suffering without potentiality, but she does this by attributing voluntariness to divine suffering so that it is something God engages freely rather than something necessarily affecting God. God suffers with creatures by voluntarily "engaging" it. She writes, "The personal analogy makes it possible to interpret divine suffering as Sophia-God's act of love freely overflowing in compassion."[72] It is, in the end, *divine* suffering that must be affirmed for her if God is to love. The existential need for God to suffer as we do requires significant revisions to the traditional answer.[73] But, as will be argued in the next chapter, in the end, no theologian truly believes God suffers as we do. Our suffering always ends in death.

Gutiérrez is less revisionist than either Daly or McFague. He affirms most of the traditional answer and adds something not adequately emphasized in Thomas's first forty-three questions—the importance of divine holiness. He writes,

> The Bible brings home the holiness of God through great and terrifying images provided by certain theophanies (manifestations of God) as well as through images of God's love, mercy and forgiveness. The essential point is that the life of God immeasurably surpasses any human measure or

---

72. Johnson, *She Who Is*, 265.
73. The central source for Johnson's theology, like Ruether's, is women's experience. A central criterion to evaluate theology is whether it liberates women and leads to their human flourishing. As Mary McClintock Fulkerson has argued, one of the difficulties with this criterion and evaluation is that it assumes a universal category no single feminist theologian could logically invoke. How does a theologian determine what about the doctrine of God must be revised based on women's experience in the plural?

anticipation. This is also the experience of every believer: J. Cone puts it well: "God is always more than our experience of him."[74]

Here we see Gutiérrez and Cone breaking with Feuerbach. Although our knowledge of God emerges out of social and historical contexts (practical theology 2), they refuse to allow it to define all of theology. God is still more.

Cone may be in a minority in refusing to reject the traditional teaching on God among contextual and liberation theologians. He acknowledges the power that the problem of evil and suffering raises and states, "The reality of suffering and evil challenges the affirmation that God is liberating the oppressed from human captivity. If God is unlimited both in power and in goodness, as the Christian faith claims, why does God not destroy the powers of evil through the establishment of divine righteousness?"[75] Such unanswerable questions, he suggests, tempt the theologian "to deny either the perfect goodness or the unlimited power of God." But he refuses to go either route. "Black Theology," he affirms, can "weaken" neither. In one respect, then, it sides with the "classic theologies of the Christian tradition." However, it adds something significant to those theologies by taking "the liberation of the oppressed as its starting point."[76] Cone further addresses divine power in *The Cross and the Lynching Tree* by thinking divine omnipotence in terms of the cross. "The cross," he writes, "was God's critique of power—white power—with powerless love, snatching victory out of defeat."[77] For Cone, the problem is not first and foremost theoretical; it has a specific object—black suffering in the United States and throughout the world. Those who have experienced suffering and oppression will be the source for addressing the question "Who is God?" If they are not consulted, then the answer will be mistaken.

J. Kameron Carter takes Cone's doctrine of God further than Cone himself took it. He thematizes Cone's unthematized "Trinitarian presuppositions." Carter puts it this way: "the divine nature, in

---

74. Gustavo Gutiérrez, *The God of Life* (Maryknoll, NY: Orbis, 1996), 27.
75. Cone, *God of the Oppressed*, 150.
76. Ibid.
77. Cone, *Cross and the Lynching Tree*, 2.

eternally actualizing itself, is always already poised to relate itself to creation: that is, to that which is by nature not God, should God elect to create." This relation to creation is God's "positive nothingness" found in the "not" of the Father being "not" the Son and the Son being "not" the Spirit. Carter does not explicitly reject simplicity or affirm divine potentiality, so I would not read this "not" as ascribing lack, need, or potential to God. In fact, we saw earlier that he affirms Being as *actus essendi*; it presumes simplicity. He explains this well in Trinitarian terms: "In the Father's self-surrender to the Son lies the possibility of creation. This is because the Father's self-surrender to the Son is the articulation of himself as Word, indeed, as the Word in whom is contained all other possible words, even the word of creation. Insofar as this is the case, the risky exposure and vulnerability of love lies at the ground of creaturely being."[78]

Carter's Trinitarian theology bears similarities to the variation on the traditional answer found in Balthasar and Barth. He has, of course, moved their theology in a more political direction.

Jennings find Barth's theology helpful in diagnosing the diseased Christian imagination that led to and lives from colonialism. He writes,

> The theologian Karl Barth . . . speaks of God as the One revealed in his act. God is the One whose *being* is revealed in divine action. Such a recognition not only banishes our abstraction regarding the identity of God, but also renders a God who is unconditioned by us. . . . Barth's positive ontology of divine being, of a God revealed in divine act, a being in becoming, casts light on the distorted ontology of being that is found in the colonialist moment.[79]

The relationship between "Barth's positive ontology of divine being" and the traditional answer is a source of controversy. Some find Barth correcting Western metaphysics, especially a Roman Catholic preoccupation with metaphysics, by extending Reformation insights that our knowledge of God comes from God mediated through the divine economy and not from metaphysical abstraction. Others find

---

78. Carter, *Race: A Theological Account*, 165.
79. Jennings, *Christian Imagination*, 61.

more continuity between Barth and the metaphysical tradition, albeit not the one that produced the Roman Catholic modernist oath and the twenty-four theses set forth in 1914 by the Sacred Congregation of Studies as necessary to combat Kantian subjectivism, historicism, and (putative) Protestant fideism with an objective metaphysics.[80] The relation between Barth's ontology of divine being and Thomas Aquinas depends, of course, on how one understands Barth and Thomas. Some set Barth against Thomas and seek to do theology without metaphysics. Others set Thomas against Barth and seek a metaphysical foundation as the operative condition for revelation.[81] The last theological movement we will examine is the one that largely comes from Barth and raises this metaphysical question.

Conclusion

Contextual, liberation, and postcolonial theologies are not as oppositional to the traditional answer as are process, open, and analytic theologies. The latter three explicitly call for revisions to be made to it; the former do so primarily as they are coupled with process theism. There is an indifference to the answer among some who address the cultural and political questions, especially when it is presented as a noncontextual speculative theology that does not attend to the historical realities of oppression and injustice. When he is understood well, Thomas also affirms that our knowledge of God always begins with practical theology 2. There is a moment of projection of *affirmatio* in every theology. Theology is produced by human agents in historical and social contexts. Every theology is contextual. The question is whether theology can be more than that, and whether it is appropriate to use this truism as an instrument *against* other theologies. Contextual theology differs from this starting point in that it is not the historical situation of creaturely being that

80. See Fergus Kerr, "A Different Word: Neoscholasticism and Its Discontents," *International Journal of Systematic Theology* 8 (2006): 128–48.
81. See my *Saving Karl Barth: Hans Urs von Balthasar's Preoccupation* (Minneapolis: Fortress Press, 2014), 154–75, for a fuller discussion of these interpretations.

originates good theology—it is the historical situation of those who suffer injustice. Their voice is privileged in conceiving God.

Offering a criticism of such a laudable theological beginning point could be impious. Yet precisely how the poor and dispossessed should be the source for our knowledge of God still requires careful attention. The poor and dispossessed are not monolithic any more than any other group of people. Few are engaged in producing theology, at least in terms that all the theologians in this chapter and the previous ones have produced. I take it that it is not explicit teachings that the poor and dispossessed might advance as the beginning of theology, but it is their needs, and attending to those needs, that initiates theology. Such a beginning point need not be in opposition to either speculative theology or practical theology 1. Nor has it been at the forefront of the traditional answer. If the traditional answer is to be affirmed in our generation, then it must find a way to incorporate these concerns or it will be nothing but a work generated from a "scholastic disposition." Holding up as exemplars those who have incorporated these questions, such as Nyssa, Las Casas, Frederick Douglass, and Jarena Lee will be an important supplement. Asking critical questions as to how vicious social practices could emerge in some intellectual frameworks will also be necessary—including Thomist and Hegelian ones.

8

The Metaphysical Question

A theme running through the previous chapters is the problem "substance metaphysics" poses for theology. The problem appears so self-evident to many theologians that we are seldom told what it is, or why it is a problem. Teasing out the reasons why it has become a problem for modern theologians when it was not for our forebears is complex. Since the Reformation, a number of analyses converge that motivate theologians to purify the tradition of its metaphysical "ballast." Caution must be exercised here, however, for the motivation for such a purification cannot be found in the Reformation itself. As we saw in chapter 3, neither the first nor the second eras of the Reformation argued anything remotely similar to these calls for revision. It only begins to emerge in the post-1725 period. The called-for revisions emerge less from the Reformation and more from a perceived crisis of metaphysics that characterizes that period. They emerge from retrospective, historical analyses that find implicit errors in the tradition based on one, or more, of the following analyses:

1. Once the Christian tradition adopted the language of hypostasis for person rather than substance, a slow revolution in ontology began in which person and relation became more basic than substance. This

revolution was slow in development and only came into its own, first, when Kant offered his criticisms of Western metaphysics, and, second, Hegel developed Kant's criticisms by providing a dialectic of freedom that advanced Spirit from Substance to Subject. The result is that the old metaphysics has been proven false, and now several options are available. Theology can be done without metaphysics. Theology can be done with a more relational process metaphysics or a relational Hegelian one. Theology can look East for a social trinitarianism. This latter option relates to a second analysis common among theologians who ask the metaphysical question.

2. Augustine and the Western (or Latin) tradition began with the essence or substance of God and then explained the persons. Despite his protests to the contrary, Augustine's order brought a Greek metaphysical substance into the doctrine of the Trinity that is in opposition to the Eastern (or Greek) theological tradition, in which the Father is the primal font for the unity of God. In discussing the divine essence first, the Western tradition did not adopt a Trinitarian ontology as fully as the East. The deep difficulty in the Christian doctrine of God is that the tradition claims to know the essence without reference to the persons or the economy of salvation.

3. A third more radical and revisionary analysis is that the fourth century was altogether mistaken in both Eastern and Western teachings on the doctrine of God. There are several versions of this analysis.

(a) The Constantinian shift in that century brought in pagan ideas of being, unity, and power that either led or contributed to the errors of Christendom. Now that we are after Christendom, it is time to rethink the doctrine of God on a much more biblical, christological, especially crucicentric, foundation. What we know of God can be found not in metaphysics or a theology of glory but in the cross. Luther, then, is given credit for challenging the traditional answer, especially impassibility. Any challenge to impassibility will logically challenge simplicity.

(b) Although the Fathers attempted to free theology from Greek metaphysics, their insistence that the divine essence could not be known, dependence on negative theology, and restrictions on language imposed by analogical predication prohibited expressing divine revelation well.

(c) The Old Testament was displaced by Greek metaphysics early in the tradition.

4. The Western metaphysical tradition and the dogmas that followed on it were misguided from the beginning. The metaphysics of Christian doctrine was distorted by a static Hellenism (Harnack) or it was "ontotheological" (Heidegger), in which God is understood as the *causa sui*—the self-caused cause who is the origin of all being. "Before the causa sui," Heidegger writes, "man can neither fall to his knees in awe nor can he play music and dance before this god."[1] Heidegger's criticism of the Western tradition becomes a theological program of de-Hellenization; it gets identified (rightly or wrongly) with Luther, Pascal, Kierkegaard, and Barth. This program seeks an "end to metaphysics."[2]

Calls for revision by contemporary theologians either draw on, or tacitly assume, versions of these analyses. They lie behind many of the critics we have already examined; they are also present among influential theologians in the twentieth and twenty-first centuries: Reformed theologians Jürgen Moltmann and Colin Gunton; Lutherans Eberhard Jüngel, Wolfhart Pannenberg, Robert Jenson, and Paul Hinlicky; Baptist theologian James W. McClendon; Catholic theologian Catherine LaCugna; and evangelicals Roger Olson and Christopher Hall. Others could be named to this list.

Four themes emerge from the above analyses that prompt theologians to revise the tradition. Those themes are (1) the order of, and basis for, divine knowledge; (2) the problem with Augustine and the emphasis on the divine essence; (3) Luther (or Hegel's) revolution; and (4) overcoming the Constantinian shift and de-Hellenization. As

---

1. Merold Westphal, *Overcoming Ontotheology: Toward a Postmodern Christian Faith* (New York: Fordham University Press, 2001), 2; Martin Heidegger, *Identity and Difference*, trans. Joan Stambaugh (New York: Harper & Row, 1969), 72.

2. Westphal, *Overcoming Ontotheology*, 18.

we shall see, these four themes intertwine. The first theme arises from rules that Karl Barth and Karl Rahner established for rethinking the doctrine of the Trinity. If it were not for that rethinking, my interpretation of Thomas Aquinas would not have been possible; it is indebted to them. But it is also an apology for Thomas and his use of Augustine and Dionysius, suggesting that the errors Barth and Rahner identified were not as widespread as they, or those who came after them, anticipated. The crisis of metaphysics, like the twilight of the idols, "has been postponed."[3] If my interpretation is accepted, then the next three themes are unnecessary. They ask for radical revisions to the traditional answer based on what was perceived as an epidemic, when in fact it was a localized outbreak that could be remedied by less drastic measures. This chapter goes through the four themes, seeking to understand why so many contemporary theologians draw on them to revise the doctrine of God in order to assess their strengths and weaknesses.

The Ordering of and Basis for Divine Knowledge

Two theologians, Karl Barth and Karl Rahner, posed important questions to the traditional answer by asking whether it adequately incorporated the divine economy into the doctrine of God. Karl Barth laid out a rule for statements about God in the first volume of his *Church Dogmatics*: "statements about the divine modes of being in themselves cannot be different in content from those that are to be made about their reality in revelation."[4] What we can say about the Trinity should be ruled by what we know from the divine economy.

Rahner's Rule

Karl Rahner offers a rule similar to Barth's. His well-known, and much-

---

3. See Mark Lilla, *The Stillborn God: Religion, Politics and the Modern West* (New York: Vintage Books, 2008), 3.
4. *CD* I/1, 479. Cited in Bruce McCormack, "The Lord and Giver of Life: A 'Barthian' Defense of the *Filioque*," in Robert J. Wozniak and Giulio Maspero, eds., *Rethinking Trinitarian Theology* (London: T&T Clark International, 2012), 230.

debated, "basic thesis" states: *"The 'economic' Trinity is the 'immanent' Trinity and the 'immanent' Trinity is the 'economic' Trinity."*[5] What Rahner opposed with his thesis is clearer than what he affirmed. He opposed the "school theology" that divided the treatises on God between the *de deo uno* and the *de deo trino*. This division meant that all the real work was done once the divine essence was set forth, and the Triune persons offered little that affected the existential situation of the believer.[6] Rahner set theology the task of finding the existential usefulness of the doctrine of the Trinity, and many theologians, Catholic and Protestant, took up that task. The reason the Trinity lacked existential significance was due to Augustine; his emphasis on the divine essence originates the mistake in the doctrine of God (a version of analysis 2). But, according to Rahner, it is Thomas who first advocates that the divine essence rather than Father should be the "first topic under study." The result was a division between the *de deo uno* and the *de deo trino*. This division became problematic for three reasons. First, "It looks as if everything which matters for us in God has already been said in the treatise *On the One God*."[7] Second, "metaphysical properties" become more determinative for the doctrine of God than "salvation history."[8] Third, these metaphysical properties misname God. Rahner states, "Even these statements, however, refer only to a Trinity which is absolutely locked within itself—one which is not, in its reality, open to anything distinct from it."[9] Rahner has identified a significant error—dividing Thomas's teaching into two treatises and reading them in opposition. His first point must always be kept in mind. Any teaching on the Trinity that begins with the divine essence could "look as if" all that needs to be said has been said. Appearances in this case, however, are deceiving. We do not need to read divine simplicity, perfection,

---

5. Karl Rahner, *The Trinity*, trans. Joseph Donceel (London: Burns and Oates, 2001), 21–22.
6. Rahner asks about the Trinity, "Or is our awareness of this mystery merely the knowledge of something purely extrinsic, which, as such, remains as isolated from all existential knowledge about ourselves as in our present theology the treatise on the Trinity is isolated from other dogmatic treatises telling us something about ourselves conducive to our real salvation?" (ibid., 15).
7. Ibid., 17.
8. Ibid., 18.
9. Ibid.

eternity, etc. as "metaphysical properties" if we understand the treatise *de Deo* as integrated. Rahner himself permits such an interpretation. If it is correct, then his third reason overstates his case. What is a possibility, misnaming God as perfectly simple without Trinity, misnames what those terms do—the very opposite that Rahner identified; they prevent conceiving the Trinity as "absolutely locked within itself."

Rahner's correction to the division between the *de deo uno* and *de deo trino* depends on his judgment that the incarnation was irrelevant to the traditional teaching on the Trinity because who-God-is was already determined in the *de deo uno* without reference to this most basic Christian doctrine. Augustine, Lombard, and Aquinas also taught that the divine essence could have been incarnate in any of the persons. For Rahner, this is "proof" that essential positions on the Trinity had been established before attending to the divine economy.

Barth's Perfections

Karl Barth also found the traditional ordering of the unitary essence and three persons to be misleading. In *CD* II/1 and II/2 he makes the incarnation essential for knowledge of God and the doctrine of the Trinity. Barth did not read simplicity as a prolegomena to the Triune God but as essential to it.[10] The *de deo uno* and *de deo trino* were read together. In his reordered teaching on God, Barth prefers the term *perfections* to either *attributes* or *names*, although he uses both *attributes* and *perfections*. His initial thesis to §29 on "The Perfections of God" shows both his concerns about, and affirmation of, divine simplicity. Barth writes, "God lives His perfect life in the abundance of many individual and distinct perfections. Each of these is perfect in itself

---

10. His reordering of the doctrine of God had tremendous influence on Hans Urs von Balthasar, prompting him to meet with Barth and express his gratitude. In 1941 Barth invited Balthasar to sit in on his summer semester seminar on the Council of Trent. He told his students that Balthasar "tows especially II/1 in his briefcase around like a cat her youth." See D. Stephen Long, *Saving Karl Barth: Hans Urs von Balthasar's Preoccupation* (Minneapolis: Fortress Press, 2014), 130–45, for a fuller discussion of Balthasar's interpretation and appreciation of Barth's reordering doctrinal loci. See Manfred Lochbrunner, *Hans Urs von Balthasar und seine Theologenkollegen: Sechs Beziehungsgeschichten* (Würzburg: Echter, 2009), 279.

and in combination with all the others. For whether it is a form of love in which God is free, or a form of freedom in which God loves, it is nothing else but God Himself, His one, simple, distinctive being."[11] The perfections characterize God in God's own life, not God in relation to creation. For this reason, Barth worries that divine simplicity can contribute to a nominalism in which God's essence is a "bare essence" (*nuda essentia*) devoid of the rich fullness of divine glory. If the perfections are understood as only logical relations to creation and not the fullness of the divine life, then, he fears, we never speak of God but either our subjective conceptions of God or God's relation to us.

Barth accuses Eunomius, Ockham, Gabriel Biel, and Schleiermacher of a strict nominalism in which "all individual and distinct statements about the being of God have no other value than that of purely subjective ideas and descriptions (*conceptus, nomina*)."[12] He finds the "main stream of theological tradition" preferable to this strict nominalism, for it interprets the "multiplicity of perfections" more positively as "statements expressing our vision of God." Irenaeus and Aquinas are his examples of the mainstream tradition; he cites the *Summa Theologiae* on the question of divine simplicity, in which Thomas argues that the multiple attributes of God are diverse in our intellect but not in God, for God is simple.[13] Barth still finds Thomas prone to a tacit seminominalism because simplicity does not refer to the richness of the divine life, but only its logical relation to us. He never cites Thomas's use of simplicity with respect to the divine processions (*ST* I 27), which is unfortunate, for if he had he could have made a case

---

11. *CD* II/1, 322.
12. Ibid., 327. Radde-Gallwitz's historical work on Eunomius shows that Barth's interpretation lacks important nuances. Eunomius denied the Son's consubstantiality with the Father because of simplicity, but not because it was a bare name. It was because he equated the ingenerate Father with the being of God in its fullness that he could not fathom a "generated" Second Person as also the divine "being." Eunomius opposed Origen's "conceptualization" of divine names and sought a more direct knowledge of the divine name not mediated by human concepts. He argued that the term *ungenerate* was neither a concept nor a privation but a "true notion." Radde-Gallwitz writes, "In Eunomius we are dealing with a hyper-realism, by which I mean a view that language and concepts map directly onto the ontological sphere to such an extent that semantic diversity by itself implies ontological diversity"; Andrew Radde-Gallwitz, *Basil of Caesarea, Gregory of Nyssa and the Transformation of Divine Simplicity* (Oxford: Oxford University Press, 2009), 98–112, quotations from 112.
13. *CD* II/1, 328.

that Thomas's more "positive" reading of simplicity allows for the multiplicity and fullness Barth rightly worried nominalism rejected. Barth's reordering would not be a doctrinal revolution but a retrieval.

Barth interprets the perfections within his understanding of divine freedom not as a willfulness emanating from a bare essence, a concern he also had about nominalism, but as the freedom to love. The result is an unmistakable affirmation of divine simplicity, as we saw above in his statement beginning §29. God's perfections are, for Barth, "nothing else but God Himself, His one, simple, distinctive being." Much as we saw Thomas use simplicity, Barth uses it to argue that the perfections of God are not relations to creation but manifestations of the richness of the divine life; it is not bare but gloriously full. However, these perfections, even in their multiplicity, do not constitute divisions in God. Barth is a traditional theologian. The multiple attributes cannot be really distinct. He cites Augustine affirmatively against what he takes to be a nominalist or seminominalist interpretation of them: "As a result it was impossible to make proper use of what Augustine had so happily indicated with his phrase *multiplex simplicitas* or *simplex multiplicitas*: the triumphal unity in God of the Lord with glory and of glory with the Lord."[14]

When Barth begins his positive account of the perfections, he sets the context for doing so through three statements: (1) "The multiplicity, individuality and diversity of the divine perfections are those of the one divine being and therefore not those of another divine nature allied to it." (2) "The multiplicity, individuality and diversity of the perfections of God are those of His simple being, which is not therefore divided and then put together again." (3) "The multiplicity, individuality and diversity of God's perfections are rooted in His own being and not in His participation in the character of other beings."[15] The third is a clear statement of what Hegel and Aristotle meant by *substance*. God's being is "in itself" and not in another. Simplicity and unity are affirmed in each of these statements. Barth then develops

14. Ibid., 329.
15. Ibid., 331–33.

"perfections of the divine loving"—grace and holiness, mercy and righteousness, patience and wisdom, followed by "perfections of the divine freedom"—unity and omnipresence, constancy and omnipotence, eternity and glory.[16] Throughout his discussion of the divine perfections, Barth makes reference to the Trinity. However, he is never as explicit as Thomas that the multiplicity of the perfections that are the divine simplicity find their life in the divine processions.

Barth, like Rahner, correctly identified a difficulty in the ordering of the doctrine of God once the *de deo uno* was not read in tandem with the *de deo trino*. For Rahner, Augustine created the problem, and Aquinas accentuated it. For Barth, nominalism created the problem, and Thomas had not done enough to prevent it. Much of the criticism of this ordering fails to take note of anything beyond question 13 of Thomas's *Summa*. It acts as if Thomas said all that needed to be said in the first thirteen questions of the *Summa* and does not attend to how beginning with question 27 Thomas provides a fuller interpretation of the divine attributes.

Rahner acknowledged that there is a way to read Thomas that does not require this troubling division. He faults Thomas for the division: "It is not as easy to distinguish these two treatises as was thought after St. Thomas and under the influence of his example."[17] Yet he also acknowledges, "Things do not necessarily have to be this way every time the two treatises On the One God and On the Triune God are separated and studied in the usual sequence."[18] He affirmed two starting points in teaching the Trinity:

> A *double starting point* is possible: we may, with scriptural theology, the older creeds, and Eastern theology, start with the one God who is, and insofar as he is the Father. Or we may, as with later official explanations by the Church start from the Trinity, that is, from the *one* God whose *one* essence subsists in three persons. We prefer the former starting point for reasons which should be stated now and developed later more systematically.[19]

16. Ibid., 351–679.
17. Rahner, *Trinity*, 45.
18. Ibid., 20.
19. Ibid., 58.

Rahner was not as revisionary as Rahnerians tend to be.

Barth's Diagnosis

Like Thomas, although Barth did not acknowledge it, Barth coupled simplicity and perfection. Simplicity without perfection was not divine simplicity. Barth also identified problematic interpretations of divine simplicity. Eunomius, like other Arians, so emphasized simplicity that he found no way to affirm the unity of divine processions. Nominalism turned the perfections into concepts or names that said nothing about God but only about our conception of God, thus evacuating God of fullness, of the divine perfection(s). Speculative theology was emptied out into practical theology. Schleiermacher's inordinate emphasis on divine causality and its relation to our consciousness likewise turned the attributes into nothing but our concepts of them. What Barth is concerned about is a worthy concern. His worry is that once the attributes are understood along these lines, ruled by an account of simplicity that is only heuristic for us, then the consequence (citing Thomasius) "imperils God's independence of the world."[20] Yet having diagnosed a malady, Barth then finds an epidemic. Impatient in his reading of Thomas, he fails to see him as the ally he was. In fact, he fails to see that Thomas had already accomplished more fully what Barth attempted. Divine simplicity must be affirmed not as a bare essence but as the fullness of divine life (perfection, holiness, and glory) that only the Triune processions helped secure. The generative multiplicity of God emanates from the simple divine unity that processes without change and acts without potential, diffusing the divine goodness via the two processions to that which is not God, creation. Having rightly identified a malady but wrongly finding a contagion, Barth set the stage for Barthians to reject more and more of the traditional answer, calling for more and more revision. Despite Barth's approval of Augustine, not even he will be spared from quarantine.

Barth and Rahner were in many ways traditional theologians. They

20. *CD* II/1, 330.

themselves did not fundamentally call into question the traditional answer, but they reconfigured it, showing us how to think past the fateful division between *de deo uno* and *de deo trino*. But their rule spawned theological projects seeking to rethink the doctrine of God by refusing to begin with the divine essence and then speak of the divine persons. These projects, unfortunately, still assume that division and seek to overcome it by dispensing with the *de deo uno* altogether, something neither Barth nor Rahner did. The next step would be to renarrate the "essence" altogether. Once the divine economy is incorporated into the doctrine of the Trinity, then a real relation is conceived between God and creation. It requires changes to simplicity, impassibility, immutability, and eternity.

Catherine LaCugna (analysis 2) takes up Rahner's theological task and argues that his basic thesis has now found "wide agreement in Catholic and Protestant Theology." LaCugna finds the separation between the treatises *On the One God* and *On the Triune God* in Catholic theology a mistake because the separation "produces a nonbiblical and problematic separation between person and nature."[21] The problem begins with Augustine's theology, a problem Thomas accentuated, in which the divine essence precedes relation.[22] Once this occurs, it establishes a "breach between *oikonomia* and *theologia*" from which Latin theology will suffer.

Her judgment about its "wide agreement" is warranted. Eberhard Jüngel gives Rahner's thesis "unqualified agreement" and finds a version of it present as early as Melanchthon.[23] Pannenberg notes the similarity between Barth's rule and Rahner's, but he finds Barth failing to follow through with his own rule.[24] Rahner was more successful, but even he has not done what theology needs to do. Both Jüngel and

---

21. Catherine LaCugna, *God for Us: The Trinity & Christian Life* (New York: HarperCollins, 1993), 215.
22. Ibid., 89.
23. Eberhard Jüngel, *God as the Mystery of the World: On the Foundation of the Theology of the Crucified One in the Dispute between Theism and Atheism* (Grand Rapids: Eerdmans, 1983), 370, 348.
24. "Karl Barth demanded that we base the doctrine of the Trinity on the revelation of God in Jesus Christ. He did not succeed in meeting his own demand, but Karl Rahner has taken it up and sharpened it with his thesis of an identity between the immanent and the economic Trinity"; Wolfhart Pannenberg, *Systematic Theology*, trans. Geoffrey W. Bromiley (Grand Rapids: Eerdmans, 1991), 1:327–28.

Pannenberg seek to fulfill the project that began with this rule but has not yet been accomplished.

These projects do not interpret Rahner and Barth's rule unanimously. LaCugna, following the counsel of Piet Schoonenberg, Yves Congar, and Walter Kasper, affirms more asymmetry between the immanent and economic Trinity than Rahner's rule suggests.[25] She does so, however, by a new interpretation of what is meant by the "immanent" Trinity. In "revising the framework of Trinitarian theology," she writes,

> An immanent theology of the Trinity therefore is not, properly speaking, a theology of an intra-divine Trinity of persons unrelated to the world. An immanent theology of God is not concerned with a purely intra-divine self-communication. As Rahner's theology shows, there is only *one* self-communication of God, one begetting of the Son, one breathing forth of the Spirit, with both eternal and temporal aspects.[26]

What is meant by this statement is unclear, but it seems to suggest there is no God who is a "purely intra-divine self-communication." This position is nearly identical to Bruce McCormack's interpretation of Barth's rule. God is always God as already related to creation through the incarnation. The problem, then, is that by beginning with the divine essence, God is conceived apart from God's communication to creation. The problem begins with Augustine.

The Problem with Augustine,
or On Not Beginning with the Divine Essence

Theologians across ecclesial divides have followed Rahner's rule, finding the source of the problem in the doctrine of God to begin with Augustine. What unites them is the assumption that Augustine and Aquinas misled us. They failed to incorporate the incarnation into the doctrine of God. Jüngel, Moltmann, Pannenberg, and others extend this analysis by seeing the failure in incorporating not only the incarnation but even more the crucifixion. The result is almost always an

25. LaCugna, *God for Us*, 217.
26. Ibid., 224.

affirmation of a "social" trinitarianism against the perceived weaknesses of a "psychological" Trinity. The call for a renewed social Trinity works with the assumption that the doctrine of the Trinity was lost to the West after the eighteenth century and now needs to be retrieved.

Beginning with the Divine Economy

LaCugna notes that the "proof" for Rahner's thesis is the incarnation.[27] As we saw above, Rahner argued that the problem with the traditional teaching on the Trinity was that it was not normed by the incarnation. The error resided in Augustine's teaching that any of the persons could have been incarnate; he was then followed by Lombard and Aquinas. Rahner wrote, "No wonder, since starting from Augustine, and as opposed to the older tradition, it has been among theologians a more or less foregone conclusion that each of the divine persons (if God freely so decided) could have become man, so that the incarnation of precisely this person can tell us nothing about the peculiar features of *this* person with the divinity."[28] If any of the persons could be incarnate, then the economy of God gives us little knowledge about God in God's own being. LaCugna agrees. "After Augustine," she writes, "in the period of scholasticism, the eternal ontological relationships among Father, Son, and Holy Spirit would be viewed largely independently of the Incarnation and sending of the Spirit."[29] She too sets the Cappadocians against Augustine and finds the remedy for the twin Western errors of beginning with the essence and neglecting the incarnation to be found in the Eastern tradition. The Cappadocians provide a preferable alternative because they develop *theologia* from the *oikonomia*. It is not the essence but the Father who constitutes the unity of the Trinity.

Rather than the incarnation, Jüngel argues that the crucifixion must norm our doctrine of God; it alone leads to a proper understanding

27. Ibid., 211–12.
28. Rahner, *Trinity*, 11.
29. LaCugna, *God for Us*, 81.

of the Trinity consistent with Rahner's rule. Although Jüngel cautions his readers against a "contemporary arrogance" toward the "tradition" that is based on a "dreadful caricature," he finds serious problems with the traditional teaching on the divine essence. It did not permit any contact by God with the reality of the temporal and mortal. In fact, he writes, "*What* tradition has understood by 'God' is what has become a problem." The Reformation should have addressed this problem, but it was Hegel who did so.[30] We must rethink the Trinity in terms of the death of God.

Jürgen Moltmann takes up Barth's task of reordering the traditional teaching on God and does so by way of Jüngel's incorporation of the death of God into theology. He also criticizes Thomas's distinction between the *de deo uno* and *de deo trino*, but he adds something to the criticism: "One cannot first describe the unity of the nature of God and then distinguish between the three divine persons or hypostases, as in that case one is essentially dealing with four beings."[31] If we start with the essence, then we will have posited a "fourth" entity behind the persons. The result will be something akin to modalism; we have a divine essence that is gradually revealed through the persons. Moltmann does not show us where in Augustine and Aquinas this occurs, and neither does he examine their explicit objection to such an interpretation. Divine simplicity, of course, is one way both Augustine and Aquinas thwart this objection. Moltmann is not convinced the Western tradition can avoid such a consequence if it begins with the essence. The difficulty in the Western doctrine is the metaphysics of substance that since Tertullian, into Augustine, and through Aquinas prevented the "theology of revelation" from having its proper place. Instead, the "natural theology" of metaphysics does all the work. It provides the framework for the *de deo uno* in which the *de deo trino* must be rendered intelligible.[32] Once again, the incarnation of the Son

---

30. Jüngel, *God as the Mystery of the World*, 100–102.
31. Jürgen Moltmann, *The Crucified God: The Cross of Christ as the Foundation and Criticism of Christian Theology*, trans. R. A. Wilson and John Bowden (New York: Harper & Row, 1974), 239–40.
32. Jürgen Moltmann, *Trinity and the Kingdom: The Doctrine of God*, trans. Margaret Kohl (San Francisco: Harper & Row, 1981), 16–17.

is thought not to do sufficient work in the doctrine of God. Once it does, significant revisions will be necessary.

Augustinian Errors, Cappadocian Corrections

Moltmann, like LaCugna, sets the Cappadocians against Augustine. There have always been two analogies for the Trinity, he suggests, "the category of the individual person, and the category of community." Augustine represents the former with his "psychological doctrine" of the Trinity; the Cappadocians represent the latter. Although he affirms both analogies, he finds the need at present for a social doctrine of the Trinity. Its loss, he asserts, "has made room for the development of individualism, and especially 'possessive individualism,' in the Western world."[33] The disease has political consequences.

Pannenberg "extends" Rahner's rule so that "creation is brought into the relations of the trinitarian persons and participates in them."[34] He acknowledges that making creation central to the divine essence was first brought about by Jüngel and Moltmann.[35] Rahner's rule is extended by Pannenberg, however, by way of eschatology. Who God is depends on what God does in creation to bring about the kingdom Christ proclaimed. God becomes an event. As we shall see, this eschatological move will have revisionary implications for the traditional answer.

Colin Gunton also defines Western Trinitarian theology as diseased, but he finds Eastern theology as problematic (analysis 3). Gunton was a devoted Barthian and adept Reformed theologian who looked to Barth for a development of the attributes that corrected the traditional answer: "That is to reverse the order found in so much of the history of the topic, where the a priori, abstract and impersonal—attributes deriving from the analogy of causality—provide a foundation—an essentially contradictory one, as it has turned out—for the personal."[36]

---

33. Ibid., 199.
34. Pannenberg, *Systematic Theology*, 1:328.
35. "The dependence of the deity of the Father upon the course of events in the world of creation was first worked out by Jüngel and then by Moltmann, who illustrated it by the crucifixion of Jesus"; Pannenberg, *Systematic Theology*, 1:329.

His argument here is identical to Pannenberg's. Both interpret Thomas as deriving "all his statements about what God is from the proof of his mere existence as the first cause of the world." Gunton's analysis assumes Pannenberg's interpretation of Thomas that his entire theology of the divine essence and attributes are logical deductions, via analogy, from causality. Thomas's teaching on God is less a pilgrimage and more like solving a mathematical problem, but this sets up a too-easy caricature in which the "essence" will now be impersonal and the attributes a list of things derived solely from God as first cause. This logical deduction from causality, states Pannenberg, then defines Latin Scholasticism[37] and leads to the "decay" of the doctrine of the Trinity because it did not have an adequate "inner systematic connection between the trinitarian statements and the divine unity."[38] Both Pannenberg and Gunton find Trinitarian retrieval and revision necessary because of the assumption that theology lost the doctrine of the Trinity in the late medieval/early modern era.

Gunton also finds it scandalous that the tradition taught that any of the persons could have become incarnate; he categorically rejects this teaching.[39] He traces it to Augustine, who taught "the principle of *opera ad extra trinitatis sunt indivisa*." It is the tradition's "chief pitfall."[40] Here too he follows Pannenberg, who argued that "the "rule" of "the indivisibility of the outward works of the Trinity" is in "need of revision."[41] Trinitarian theology should draw the differences among the persons more starkly.

Gunton found Augustine's theology deeply problematic because of its residual Neoplatonism, but unlike LaCugna and Moltmann he did not turn to the Greeks for a better Trinitarian theology. For Gunton, their work was just as flawed. (Gunton's analysis fits well 3c and 4 above.) He refers to the problem created by the tradition of the divine

---

36. Colin E. Gunton, *Act & Being: Towards a Theology of the Divine Attributes* (Grand Rapids: Eerdmans, 2002), 100.
37. Pannenberg, *Systematic Theology*, 1:348.
38. Ibid., 1:291.
39. Gunton, *Act & Being*, 143.
40. Ibid., 139.
41. Pannenberg, *Systematic Theology*, 1:326.

names, analogical predication, and negative theology as a "disease."[42] He finds symptoms of it more widespread than even Barth did. Although Augustine is particularly singled out as the cause for the disease, Dionysius and the Eastern tradition of negative theology receive equal blame. Aquinas's theology is also afflicted with the "depressing syndrome."[43] He rejects the teaching in both Dionysius and Augustine, and taken up by Thomas, that the essence of God cannot be known. Such a teaching, he suggests, fails to take seriously that God has revealed himself to us. It fails to incorporate the divine economy into Trinitarian theology and depends on a metaphysics of being that unnecessarily restricts divine action and thus sets forth the divine attributes improperly.[44] The Reformation began to put things back together, but it too created a "hybrid deity"; the Reformers should have "derived" the doctrine of God from the "biblical narrative," but they too polluted it with Greek metaphysics.[45] Gunton attempts to follow through with a process of de-Hellenization.

Robert Jenson offers a more complicated affirmation and critique of the traditional teaching. Nonetheless, he also argues that the traditional teaching went awry with St. Augustine. (Pannenberg cites Jenson's critique approvingly.)[46] Augustine rejected the "temporal differentiation" of God found in Athanasius and the Cappadocians because Greek metaphysics misled him, not Aristotle this time but Plato.

> The reason he did not [affirm temporal differentiation] is apparent throughout his writings: unquestioning commitment to the axiom of antecedent Platonic theology, that God is metaphysically "simple," that *no* sort of self-differentiation can really be true of him. He assumed as a priori truth that temporal distinctions are simply nonexistent for God, so there can be no real narrative differentiations of any kind in God, not even among the identities [Jenson's word for the Triune persons].[47]

42. Gunton, *Act & Being*, 15.
43. "Aquinas's treatment [in the *prima pars*] is shaped by the depressing syndrome that we have met so far" (ibid., 50).
44. Ibid., 23.
45. Ibid., 2.
46. Pannenberg, *Systematic Theology*, 1:323.
47. Robert Jenson, *Systematic Theology* (New York: Oxford University Press, 1997), 1:111. "What in this way undoes trinitarianism in Augustine's thinking is the old dissonance between the

The problem is the attribution of "identity" between the divine essence and persons rather than "equality," which leads to the common Western assumption that any of the persons could have hypothetically been incarnate. "Most disastrously," he writes, Peter Lombard inherits from Augustine the teaching that any of the persons could be incarnate. Jenson cites Lombard, "'As the Son was made man, so the Father or the Holy Spirit could have been and could be now.'"[48] The difficulty for Jenson is that Augustine's "supposition" violates the theological soundness of Barth's rule. "The Augustinian supposition that there is no necessary connection between what differentiates the triune identities in God and the structure of God's work in time bankrupts the doctrine of the Trinity cognitively, for it detaches language about the triune identities from the only thing that made such language meaningful in the first place: the biblical narrative."[49] If we assume, as Augustine, Lombard, and Thomas did, that any of the persons could have been incarnate, then the doctrine of the Trinity loses its intelligibility. It becomes divorced from Scripture.

Evangelical theologians Olson and Hall agree that beginning with the divine unity is a problem that stems in the West from Augustine and Anselm (analysis 2). They ask whether Aquinas took "a step beyond the Augustinian-Anselmian emphasis on the unity of the divine being or did he also contribute to the *operational modalism* that plagues so much Western Christian thought?" Like Moltmann, they see operational modalism in the decision to begin with the essence and exhibit it through the persons. It assumed that, contrary to their explicit denial of such a position, Augustine and Aquinas posited a god behind the persons. Their answer is that Aquinas "seemed to deepen the problems of trinitarian theology in the West."[50] Notice once again the language of plague. The Western theology of the Trinity is a disease in need of

---

metaphysical principles of the Greeks and the storytelling of the gospel" (ibid., 112). Likewise, he states, "The Augustinian supposition that there is no necessary connection between what differentiates the triune identities and the structure of God's work in time bankrupts the doctrine of the Trinity cognitively, for it detaches language about the triune identities from the only thing that made such language meaningful in the first place: the biblical narrative."

48. Ibid.
49. Ibid.
50. Roger E. Olson and Christopher A. Hall, *The Trinity* (Grand Rapids: Eerdmans, 2002), 64.

remedy. Like many others who raise the metaphysical question, they find Luther and Barth to be the antidote. Barth "was revolutionizing so-called 'classical Christian theism' along trinitarian lines" because he viewed God's being as "historical."[51] Luther was not as radical; he was not yet a "social Trinitarian," but he was also not "locked into the Augustinian psychological analogy that tended to reduce the persons of God to mere relations of origin."[52] He avoided "over-rationalistic speculation" and emphasized the "three different persons."

Lutheran theologian Paul Hinlicky suggests something similar (analysis 2). He does not reject the importance of identifying the divine essence; he does reject conceiving it as other than "social." He writes,

> None of this then is to deny divine nature or substance, as Western theology almost reflexively fears, but rather to conceive of immaterial substance not on the analogy of mental operations of a private mind, but rather as the public life of a society. It is thus rather rigorously to discover divine substance in and not apart from the trinitarian existence of God by the event of the coming of His kingdom.[53]

This statement succinctly sets forth much that is present in those who raise the metaphysical question: a social Trinity is set against a psychological Trinity; the latter begins with the essence understood as substance apart from the divine persons. To counter it, God is conceived of as an event who will be really related to history such that the event God is takes place in the future. God's being is in becoming.

(Ana)baptist theologian James McClendon (a version of analysis 3a) offers a nuanced criticism of the traditional answer, one that affirms much in Thomas, but in the end he also replaces being with history. He does so in order to incorporate not only the incarnation, crucifixion, and the coming kingdom into the doctrine of God but also the importance of Christian discipleship. It is the latter that provides access to our knowledge of God, and once it is incorporated, it revises what we thought we knew of God.

---

51. Ibid., 97.
52. Ibid., 69.
53. Paul Hinlicky, *Divine Complexity: The Rise of Creedal Christianity* (Minneapolis: Fortress Press, 2011), 210.

Righting Wrongs?

All the above theologians draw on some version of Rahner or Barth's rule. They share three assumptions that guide their analysis and calls for revision: (1) the Trinity was lost in the later Middle Ages and early modern era and needed to be retrieved; (2) it was lost because it did not incorporate the incarnation; and (3) Augustine was responsible for the seeds that led to its loss by beginning with the essence in a psychological analogy. Given the rather remarkable revision they ask us to make to the traditional answer, it is important to ask, Are these assumptions sound?

Much of the rethinking of Trinitarian theology assumes the divorce between the divine economy and Trinity began in "Scholasticism" and culminated in the eighteenth century, especially in Schleiermacher. On the one hand, Schleiermacher found the Trinity to be the "coping stone" of Christian redemption. On the other, he found its "dualism" of "unity of Essence and trinity of Persons" to be inadequate. Schleiermacher leaned more toward the importance of the divine unity than the persons for existential reasons. Positing real distinctions in the Trinity did not arise from "an utterance concerning the religious consciousness."[54] The Trinity had not yet been thought through based on its practical, soteriological relevance. The doctrine had not been reformed by the Protestants, and that meant there was work to be done: "We have the less reason to regard this doctrine as finally settled since it did not receive any fresh treatment when the Evangelical (Protestant) Church was set up; and so there must be still in store for it a transformation which will go back to its very beginnings."[55]

The need to retrieve and reform the doctrine assumes that something had gone terribly wrong. The assumption is that the Trinity mattered little in the development of Scholastic/early modern theology, and thus the calls for revision are a corrective to what had been lost. But this assumption needs to be challenged, which the third

---

54. Friedrich Schleiermacher, *The Christian Faith*, trans. and ed. H. R. Mackintosh and J. S. Stewart (Edinburgh: T&T Clark, 1986), 739.
55. Ibid., 747.

chapter above attempted to do. The assumption gives too much influence to a few early modern German theologians and their debates. We have already seen that there was a strong tradition of making the Trinity central to Christian life and practice in the sixteenth to eighteenth centuries. Arminius, John Owen, John Wesley, Richard Hooker, and many others not only affirmed it but made it central in theology. Nor did they imagine they needed to revise it because it had somehow become useless or out of date. In fact, they were worried about the extent of the revisions to which the Protestant theologian Biddle was willing to go, based in his interpretation that, by not reforming the doctrine of God, especially by de-Hellenizing it and reading it only biblically, the Reformation was incomplete. The early modern opponents to Biddle defended it not because it was existentially useful, relevant to cultural critics, or in need of reform; for them it was true. We need not have the anxiety about the doctrine that underlies much of the modern calls for revision, an anxiety often based on a fear that if we do not revise the doctrine of God we cannot answer atheism. Lose that anxiety, and the call for revision is less compelling.

The above critique is not meant to disregard the important correction Rahner and Barth's rule brought. Insofar as a strong distinction between *de deo uno* and *de deo trino* was presented in Scholastic theology, and that distinction was supposedly grounded on a sharp distinction between philosophy and theology or nature and grace, a distinction not known to the Fathers, Thomas, or the Protestant Scholastics, then it is essential to be reminded, as Barth and Rahner did, that the Trinity is only intelligible and meaningful from the biblical narrative. The only way for Christians to engage in the core practice of worshiping Jesus as God without violating the commandment not to make a graven image and worship a creature was the doctrine of the incarnation. Once Jesus is affirmed as fully divine and fully human, then the doctrine of the Trinity must follow if Christians are to remain faithful to Judaism. But must there be such a strong identity between Jesus' mission and the divine processions? One cannot help but see a bit too much "Hegeling" occurring in that move.

Rahner united the immanent and economic more so than LaCugna. Rahner acknowledges that it was the affirmation of divine freedom that led previous Christian theologians to the hypothetical possibility that any of the persons could be incarnate. If God could only relate to creation in one way, then God would be locked up within the economy. It would become necessary for God to act in this singular way in order for God not only to create and redeem but for God to be God. But he is not convinced this poses any significant threat to divine freedom. In fact, Rahner concludes that God *must* act in the way the divine economy reveals. "We suppose that, when God freely steps outside of himself in *self*-communication (not merely through creation, positing other realities which are not himself), it is and must be the Son who appears historically in the flesh as man."[56] Rahner takes this further: "If God wishes to step freely outside of himself, he must create man."[57] In order to "prove" his basic thesis, the incarnation ties God to the economy such that it is difficult to see how God could be God without it. We have already seen how Pannenberg extends Rahner's rule to make creation a real relation to the divine essence. Jüngel offers a similar judgment. He too, like Rahner and Pannenberg, insists on the distinction between God and creation, but the strong version of Rahner's rule he affirms makes it difficult to see how we can sustain the claim that God could be God without being ordered toward creation. He states that in the death of Jesus, "God himself was the event which happened."[58] This statement, for all its powerful resonances as a preached word, leaves many questions. How is God an event? How can God be an event that happens in time? What was God prior to this event, not only in eternity but in salvation history? Why could we not say God was the event that happened in giving Torah to Moses, or a house to David? As we shall see, Jüngel will draw from his teaching on God as an event that happens radical revisions to the traditional answer.

But surely we can learn much from the incarnation without positing

---

56. Rahner, *Trinity*, 86.
57. Ibid., 89–90.
58. Jüngel, *God as the Mystery of the World*, 363.

a real relation between God and creation? That God in God's fullness can freely enter into that which is not God, both in the incarnation and crucifixion, without ceasing to be God, shows us something about the "immanent" Trinity, or what the Fathers called *theologia*. But does the relationship between the incarnation and the immanent Trinity need to be bound up with Rahner's language of "must"? If each person is the essence, and the person of Christ expresses the divine essence in the incarnation, then from the historical datum of the incarnation can we not likewise affirm that each of the persons *could* become incarnate? We would not have known this if we did not know the incarnation, so it is incorrect to think the incarnation has not normed the doctrine of the Trinity with this teaching. It is *only* because of the incarnation that Augustine, Lombard, and Aquinas could have ventured such a daring, kataphatic teaching. It was also because the God incarnate in Jesus was the same God who gave Torah to Moses that they had to affirm divine unity. It is the insistence on divine unity that permits speculation that any of the persons could have been incarnate. Such a hypothetical incarnation would have looked different from the economy we have, but this hypothesis only ensures that God's relation to the world (practical theology) is not identical to God's real relations in God's self (speculative theology). Creation is not a divine hypostasis. We have learned something profound from the incarnation—we have learned that God is Trinity and in that Trinity there is a deep and mysterious unity unlike any unity we know in created reality. We can affirm this and say, with Aquinas, although it is not necessary for God to become incarnate only in the Son, it is more fitting—*convenientia*.[59] We know it is more fitting because it is how God worked. We do not then need to say that God must create humanity in order to "step outside himself."

---

59. Thomas makes a distinction in the incarnation between the act of God assuming (*actum assumentis*) human nature and the end of what is assumed (*terminum assumptionis*) (*ST* III 3. art. 1, 2, 4, 5). The act of assuming occurs from the common power of the divine nature. The end is in the Second Person. He acknowledges that natures do not act. Nature is not a principle that acts (*ST* III 3.2 obj. 3). However, due to divine simplicity in God the that by which something acts and the acting person are the same, so the nature and the person act (*ST* III 3.2 resp.). For this reason it is possible that any of the divine persons could have been incarnate, but it is more "fitting" that it is the Son as the Word (*ST* III 3.8 resp.).

That language is clearly metaphorical, but it is difficult to know what it might mean.

The common move in contemporary Trinitarian theology to set a psychological Western Trinitarian theology against an Eastern social one has been subjected to serious criticism by historians. Michel Barnes notes how it is indebted to the work of Théodore de Régnon, who did not affirm it to the extent those indebted to him did.[60] Lewis Ayres has shown how Gregory of Nyssa's "fundamental" Trinitarian theology does not provide an analogy beginning with plurality rather than unity.[61] Philipp Gabriel Renczes points out that the Cappadocians had a stronger distinction between *oikonomia* and *theologia* than Rahner or LaCugna suggests, equating the former with a kataphatic and the latter an apophatic theology.[62] Renczes denies that the distinction between them is indebted more to Neoplatonism than Scripture, citing Matt. 11:27 as support, "All things have been handed over to me by my Father. No one knows the Son except the Father, and no one knows the Father except the Son and anyone to whom the Son wishes to reveal him."[63] Renczes concludes that Rahner's "intuitive association of his thesis with Greek thought proved simultaneously true and false, while his polarization with respect to Augustinian theology has not held up."[64] The initial intuition of many modern theologians that the perceived problem with Augustine could be fixed with the Cappadocians has not held up under historical scrutiny. It should be abandoned.

---

60. See M. R. Barnes, "Augustine in Contemporary Trinitarian Theology," *Theological Studies* 56 (1995): 237–50; and "De Régnon Reconsidered," *Augustinian Studies* 26 (1995): 51–79. See also Sarah Coakley, ed., *Rethinking Gregory of Nyssa* (London: Wiley-Blackwell, 2003).
61. Lewis Ayres, "On Not Three People: The Fundamental Themes of Gregory of Nyssa's Trinitarian Theology as Seen in *To Ablabius: On Not Three Gods*," *Modern Theology* 18, no. 4 (2002): 445–74.
62. Renczes notes that the distinction between *theologia* and *oikonomia* is as early as Origen. He then states, "To meet the challenge of the neo-Arian Eunomius, who adopted the Gnostic idea that the human being disposes of a basic and all-encompassing knowledge of God, the Cappadocians made precise the extent of what *theologia* and *oikonomia* must mean. They identified the first with God's nature/essence (οὐσία) and the second with God's (saving) action (ἐνέργεια), and went on to couple this distinction with the concepts of 'cataphatic' and 'apophatic' theology"; Philipp Gabriel Renczes, "The Scope of Rahner's Fundamental Axiom in the Patristic Perspective: A Dialogue of Systematic and Historical Theology," in Wozniak and Maspero, *Rethinking Trinitarian Theology*, 260.
63. Ibid., 265.
64. Ibid., 288.

Two trinities do not exist. Barth and Rahner's rule is unavoidable; it should be affirmed. However, a second unavoidable rule in Trinitarian theology is that the terms used to express the real relations that constitute the divine persons cannot be equated with the relation between God and creation. Although there is only one Trinity, and the Trinity revealed in the economy should give theologians boldness to confess that this Trinity is God, creation is not necessary for God to be God. All sound theologians should also affirm this principle. It is in the call for revisions to the traditional answer that the second rule seems to be sacrificed to the first. Before examining those revisions, two other reasons for them will be noted, Luther's revolution and the call for de-Hellenization.

Luther's (or Hegel's) Revolution: The Crisis of Metaphysics

The meaning of Barth's rule, like Rahner's, is contested among theologians. It could mean, as Bruce McCormack notes, that God just is his modes of being. In that sense, it is a restatement of divine simplicity. The divine persons are nothing other than the divine essence, but McCormack finds more to it than that. He finds it overturning errors in the tradition: "What has happened here is that the logic of divine *subjectivity* has supplanted the ancient logic of substance metaphysics by which the choice between essence and 'persons' was traditionally made possible."[65] This shift from substance to subject has its precursor in Hegel. Barth's rule revolutionizes a "metaphysics of substance"; the revolution is fortuitous because it fits well the crisis of metaphysics that occurred in the modern era.

Many of the theologians who raise the metaphysical question either explicitly or implicitly assume the crisis of metaphysics now defines our historical context, a context that makes it impossible to think God and contributes to modern atheism. Eberhard Jüngel writes, "At the end of the history of metaphysics, God appears to have become unthinkable."[66] Jüngel assumes metaphysics has come to an end; he

---

65. McCormack, "Lord and Giver of Life," 235.
66. Jüngel, *God as the Mystery of the World*, vii.

seeks to develop a way to think God in our new context. The role of the theologian is "constantly" to think God "anew," and that means thinking God with and against Hegel.[67] What must be rethought is the divine "essence." McCormack argues something similar. He interprets the traditional answer as requiring a choice between essence and person. For both Jüngel and McCormack, Barth speaks best to our modern, historical context because his rule shifts the discussion of God from substance to subject and refuses to divide the divine essence from the divine modes of being (Barth's term for what were previously called *persons*). The result is the beginning of a revolution in the doctrine of God that will require significant dogmatic revisions.

As we saw in chapter 3, Luther argued that the doctrine of God was not an issue between Protestants and Catholics. He did not argue for God as a "subject" rather than a "substance." Nor did he historicize the being of God. His late disputations reveal how thoroughly he affirmed the traditional answer, especially divine simplicity. Moreover, David Luy shows that Luther also affirmed divine impassibility despite the "divergence" narrative that reads him as challenging it. Why has it become conventional wisdom that Luther calls for significant revisions to the doctrine of God?[68] One reason is that, post-Hegel, Luther gets read through Hegelian philosophy. Hegel's philosophy undoubtedly requires revisions to the traditional answer. If he is viewed as a consistent development from Luther, then reading Luther through Hegel will likewise entail revision.

From Substance to Subject

As we have already noted, Hegel is responsible for the argument that in the history of Spirit, Spirit moves from substance to subject. This move was central to the *Phenomenology of Spirit*; Hegel notes it in his preface,

---

67. "God can be thought only as something constantly to be thought anew" (ibid., 227).

68. I repeated this common wisdom in *Speaking of God* when I stated, "Luther's theology of the cross began a trend in theology that emptied God of the divine names." I was dependent on Hans Urs von Balthasar's critique of Luther that had been influenced by Theobald Beer (D. Stephen Long, *Speaking of God: Theology, Language and Truth* [Grand Rapids: Eerdmans, 2009], 180–81 and 44–47). David Luy convinced me I was wrong. For his critique of Beer see Luy, *Dominus Mortis: Martin Luther on the Incorruptibility of God in Christ* (Minneapolis: Fortress Press, 2014), 22–27.

"In my view, which can be justified only by the exposition of the system itself, everything turns on grasping and expressing the True, not only as *Substance*, but equally as *Subject*."[69] Substance is the "in-itself." It is, in one form, immediate self-consciousness. As substance it is only self-aware and thus not yet being for another. Only through the negation of itself as substance can it become subject and then return to itself. The history of Spirit is the history of this movement.

For Hegel, the cross is the quintessential act of negation in which God becomes being for others and thus at the same time returns to himself. In his *Lectures on the Philosophy of Religion* Hegel explained his point.

> Death, the negative, is the mediating term through which the original majesty is posited as now achieved. The history of the resurrection and the ascension of Christ to the right hand of God begins at the point where this history receives a spiritual interpretation. That is when it came about that the little community achieved the certainty that God has appeared as a human being. But this humanity in God—and indeed the most abstract form of humanity, the greatest dependence, the ultimate weakness, the utmost fragility—is natural death. "God himself is dead," it says in a Lutheran hymn, expressing an awareness that the human, the finite, the fragile, the weak, the negative are themselves a moment of the divine, that they are within God himself, that finitude, negativity, otherness are not outside of God and do not, as otherness, hinder unity with God. Otherness, the negative, is known to be a moment of the divine nature itself.[70]

Through this negation, God moves from substance to subject, returning to himself as substance but now also always as subject.

One would be hard-pressed to find such a thought in Luther. Of course he speaks of the cross and the death of God, as did the tradition before him, but negation as mediating from substance to subject is not Luther's language; it is Hegel's. Some theologians who make a similar move, finding Luther as a source for revision, explicitly draw on Hegel.

---

69. G. W. F. Hegel, *Phenomenology of Spirit*, trans. A. V. Miller (Oxford: Oxford University Press, 1977), 9.
70. G. W. F. Hegel, *Lectures on the Philosophy of Religion*, trans. R. F. Brown, P. C. Hodgson, and J. M. Stewart (Berkeley: University of California Press, 1988), 468.

Others seek some distance from Hegel, but this distancing is not always convincing.

Luther-Hegel-Barth Trajectories

Jüngel is forthright in finding the source for his revisions not only in Luther but also in Hegel. He writes, "It is fascinating to see in Hegel's exposition how Luther's dogmatic insights are made hermeneutically fruitful. The 'theology of the cross' (*theologia crucis*) asserts its material insights hermeneutically at this point. The crucifixion of Jesus Christ is regarded not only as *the decisive event of his life* but also as *the criterion for the proper understanding* of his being."[71] Jüngel's interpretation of Hegel reveals much. First we see that God is understood as "event." Second, the cross now sets forth God's identity, but it sets it forth such that it calls into question metaphysical accounts of God's nature. Hegel's fruitful hermeneutical insight raises for Jüngel the question of God's "essence." Traditional teaching on the divine essence raised an aporia that brought Western metaphysics to an end; it led to its crisis.[72] The aporia is this: "The *perfection* of God required by the law of metaphysics forbade imagining God as suffering or even thinking of him together with one who was dead."[73] Metaphysical perfection prevents theology from identifying God with death, but the Christian faith requires this identification. Hegel, drawing on Luther, resolves the aporia. Jüngel also sees the "older Barth" following "the path which had been opened up by Luther and Hegel."[74] Jüngel is helpful in tracing a trajectory that calls for revision that begins with Luther, goes through Hegel, and concludes in Barth.

Evangelical theologian Veli-Matti Kärkkäinen stands in the Luther-Barth trajectory. While not dismissive of the traditional answer, he

---

71. Jüngel, *God as the Mystery of the World*, 92. Jüngel also affirmed Hegel in *God's Being Is in Becoming: The Trinitarian Being of God in the Theology of Karl Barth*, trans. John Webster (London: Bloomsbury, 2014), 127–29. Of course, Jüngel does not affirm everything in Hegel's system, but he does find that "Hegel drew attention to the centre of the Christian faith as it is understood in the reformation tradition much more effectively than many of his theological contemporaries and very many of our own" (127).

72. Jüngel, *God as the Mystery of the World*, 100.

73. Ibid., 39.

74. Ibid., 40.

acknowledges that "classical theism" is "under attack" in contemporary theology. "Classical theism," he states, "denotes those post-biblical developments of early Christian theology as it sought to express faith in the biblical God with the help of Greco-Roman philosophical categories." He cites Donald Bloesch to explain why it has come under attack: "Here God is depicted as immutable, self-contained, all-sufficient, impassible, supremely detached from the world of pain and suffering."[75] The term *self-contained* is perplexing; in the traditional answer God is not finite, so God is not *in* a category, even of God's own being. Divine simplicity rules out such a possibility. *Self-contained* is not a term that either Augustine or Aquinas could have used. Such a term would seem to be similar to Hegel's substance, whether it is explicitly being drawn on or not. Kärkkäinen affirms Bloesch's criticism and argues that every generation must develop theology within its own philosophical context; the postbiblical developments that produced "classical theism" accomplished one such philosophical synthesis, but he raises questions about its appropriateness in our post-Enlightenment context.[76] A new synthesis may be necessary. It is necessary because Luther and Barth put things into place that call for it.

For Kärkkäinen, Barth and Luther represent two crucial historical developments beyond classical theism that must now be taken into account. Barth introduced "historicity" into the Trinitarian God, and Luther, along with other Protestant theologians, "almost turned the tables with their dynamic view of God." Luther's doctrine of God cannot cohere with the classical theism of Anselm and the Scholastics.[77] Although Kärkkäinen discusses Hegel's Trinitarian theology, unlike Jüngel, he does not relate it to Luther and Barth.

---

75. Veli-Matti Kärkkäinen, *The Doctrine of God: A Global Introduction* (Grand Rapids: Baker Academic, 2004), 10–11. Kärkkäinen finds that the "energy" for the "contemporary resurgence" in the doctrine of God "has its source in the desire to radically revise the classical approach" (11).

76. He writes, "The fathers took the biblical witness seriously and tried to make sense of it for their times. They also took seriously the contemporary philosophies and the challenges of syncretistic, polytheistic religions. Employing the categories of Greek thought to shape the dynamic biblical view of God into a more coherent, rational and apologetic system made sense in their environment. It was but another way of contextualizing the gospel" (ibid., 81).

77. Ibid., 120–22, 128.

Although he is not a Lutheran theologian, Jürgen Moltmann also stands in the Luther-Hegel-Barth trajectory. He makes a Lutheran theology of the cross the center of theology. Moltmann assumes that the crucial question in modern theology is a dialectic between identity and relevance. The more theologians seek relevance, "the more deeply they are drawn into the crisis of their own Christian identity." The more they "assert their identity in traditional dogmas, rights and moral notions, the more irrelevant and unbelievable they become."[78] In response to this "double crisis," Moltmann begins with Luther's "lapidary statement: *Crux probat omnia* [The cross demonstrates/makes credible everything]." Luther's theology helps Moltmann address the double crisis of modernity because on the one hand, the cross can never be fashionable; it cannot be loved. It avoids the temptation to side with relevance at the expense of identity. On the other hand, the cross calls the past into question. It challenges traditional dogmas and thus avoids the temptation of identity at the expense of relevance.

Moltmann's indebtedness to Luther is explicit. He affirms Luther against Thomas's analogical theology and against Schleiermacher and Hegel's "*theology as a science* under the conditions of the modern age." Luther's theology of the cross turns against both of these possibilities; Jesus, who died "abandoned by God," calls all such theologies into question.[79] Moltmann calls for revisions similar if not identical to Jüngel's, despite objections to him, objections Jüngel admits he does not understand.[80] Both seek to think the "death of God" in the crucifixion and use it to critique and revise the metaphysical tradition. In order to do so, Jüngel does not flinch from his indebtedness to Hegel; Moltmann is more circumspect. He acknowledges that with Hegel we move from Aquinas's God as "supreme substance" to God as "absolute subject." The latter is preferable, but it is too bourgeois. It was "the archetype of the free, reasonable, sovereign person, who has complete disposal over himself" in the modern era.[81] He does not claim Hegel as a

---

78. Moltmann, *Crucified God*, 7.
79. Ibid., 67–69.
80. See ibid., 217; and Jüngel, *God as the Mystery of the World*, 220n65.
81. Moltmann, *Trinity and the Kingdom*, 15.

precedent for his Trinitarian theology, as he does Luther, but nor does he reject Hegel. When he contrasts the "God of theism," who is "poor" and "cannot love nor can he suffer," with how we should conceive of God, he too calls on Hegel. As we saw with Jüngel, for Moltmann God is "event," and as we shall see with Pannenberg, God as "event" is future oriented. Explaining what Hegel offers theology, Moltmann writes, "For eschatological faith, the Trinitarian God-event on the cross becomes the history of God which is open to the future and which opens up the future."[82]

Robert Jenson has a complex relationship to the Luther-Hegel-Barth trajectory. He does not work with an identity-relevance dialectic nor assume theology must be expressed through the cultural or philosophical lens available to it in each generation. He is less "modern" in his theological approach than many of the others. He explicitly criticizes theologians who think it is the task of each generation to revise the tradition based on their philosophical context. Jenson writes, "It is a particular and particularly baneful instance of an error . . . that theology, when it has acknowledged its own claim to universal scope, has sometimes nevertheless thought it must achieve this by finding the 'right' metaphysics among those offered by officially designated philosophers."[83] Process theologians do so with Whitehead, "epigones of Bultmann" with Heidegger. Invoking Thomas's relationship to Aristotle as justification for such a move, he rightly notes, is unconvincing. Thomas did the opposite. "He *conversed* with Aristotle, and in the conversation was stimulated and helped to his own metaphysical positions, the key items of which could hardly be less Aristotelian."[84] Barth did the same with the philosophers. He neither adopted them nor rejected them; he conversed with them and in so doing created what can be considered as "the first truly major system of Western metaphysics since the collapse of Hegelianism."[85]

---

82. Moltmann, *Crucified God*, 254–55.
83. Jenson, *Systematic Theology*, 1:21.
84. Ibid.
85. Ibid.

Barth is not in a Luther-Hegel trajectory; Barth steps in when Hegelianism failed.

Jenson does not think metaphysics per se has come to an end, but the metaphysics on which the traditional answer drew has become problematic. His dissertation was on Barth, and in that work, which Barth himself affirmed, Jenson distanced Barth's doctrine of God from the traditional answer.[86] Its metaphysics no longer constitutes a "framework" in which we live.[87] God is not atemporal, but "God's being is an event" and "not the static peace of pure 'isness' which theologians have often described," because for Barth "the incarnation happened in eternity before all time."[88]

"God according to the Gospel"

Jenson affirms Barth more so than Luther. On the one hand, he recognizes how traditional Luther was. His teaching on God's "hiddenness" was consistent with the tradition that upheld divine "invisibility, intangibility, and ineffability," a tradition Jenson criticizes. On the other hand, Luther affirmed something like Barth and Rahner's rule—"we may not seek to rise above the temporal revelation of God." God's hiddenness is not because of a "metaphysical distance," but it is God's own act.[89] Luther did not accomplish what Barth did; God is not an "event," but Jenson finds only Luther as "rigorously" as Barth perceiving "the difference between the Hellenic quest for God . . . and the gospel's proclamation that Jesus is God's quest for us."[90] Jenson makes a similar argument in his later work, critiquing doctrines of predestination that forget God is Trinity and instead adopting a theology of a "monadic Majesty." Jenson writes, "Barth found only

86. For Jenson's account of Barth's affirmation of his work see Robert Jenson, "D. Stephen Long's *Saving Karl Barth*: An Agent's Perspective," *Pro Ecclesia* XXIV, no. 2 (Spring 2015): 132. *Alpha and Omega* is the revised version of the dissertation, "The Election of Jesus Christ in the Theology of Karl Barth." Jenson finds this to be "dispositive" evidence that my reading of Barth is incorrect. See my response in that same volume of *Pro Ecclesia*, 157.
87. Robert W. Jenson, *Alpha and Omega: A Study in the Theology of Karl Barth* (Eugene, OR: Wipf & Stock, 2002), 15.
88. Ibid., 69, 67.
89. Robert Jenson, *The Triune Identity: God according to the Gospel* (Philadelphia: Fortress Press, 1982), 27.
90. Ibid., 137.

Luther as a predecessor."[91] Jenson reads Luther and Barth as engaging in the same project; it is a worthwhile project consistent with the subtitle of his *Triune Identity*—"God according to the Gospel." It is his desire to be faithful to the gospel that animates Jenson's theology, which is also true for LaCugna, Jüngel, Moltmann, Pannenberg, and Kärkkäinen.

If revisions to the doctrine of God emerge only from Luther, Barth, or Hegel's idiosyncratic teachings, such revisions should be treated with indifference. But if they are required by the gospel, then of course they should be heeded. The inheritors of the Luther-Barth (and sometimes Hegel) trajectory in modern theology seek to be rigorous in presenting God according to the gospel. Many of the revisions they call for approach those of the analytic theologians, open theists, and on occasion process theologians. Moltmann's theology in particular had profound influence among liberation theologies. Jon Sobrino offers a powerful defense of a revision all the above theologians call for—a revision to divine impassibility—by recalling the story of what occurred when the Jesuits in El Salvador were murdered in 1989:

> If we do not forget those who are being crucified today, it will be more difficult to forget the crucified Jesus. But if we keep him in mind, of necessity we must ask about God. And, although the formulation, like all formulations, is limited, and is open to questioning, I think there is no substitute for calling this God "the crucified God." Allow me to say this with a very personal experience. On 16 November 1989, when the Jesuits of the Central American University were murdered outside their house, the body of Juan Ramón Moreno was dragged inside the residence into one of the rooms, mine. In the movement one book from the bookcase in the room fell on to the floor and became soaked in Juan Ramón's blood. That book was *The Crucified God*. It is a symbol, of course, but it expresses God's real participation in the passion of the world.[92]

Such a powerful testimony expresses well the positive reason many have called for revisions to the doctrine of God. Did the traditional

91. Robert Jenson, *America's Theology: A Recommendation of Jonathan Edwards* (Oxford: Oxford University Press, 1988), 106.
92. Jon Sobrino, *Jesus the Liberator: Historical-Theological Reading of Jesus of Nazareth* (Maryknoll, NY: Orbis, 1993), 235.

answer "express God's real participation in the passion of the world"? Here is where the metaphysical question and questions of liberation unite. This unity has advanced our understanding of God. The question is whether it requires bringing out and developing what was latent in the traditional answer, looking at it again to see whether we saw all that was there, or does it require rejection and revision?

Many of the above theologians will argue that something missing from the traditional answer is God's holiness. I will take up that important argument below. Moltmann and Sobrino's theology of the crucified God expresses divine holiness in the midst of the suffering and crucified in history. If the traditional answer has no means to express this holiness as well, then it should be revised.

The Constantinian Shift and De-Hellenization

The call to "de-Hellenize" Christian doctrine emerges from diverse sources. One such source is the liberal Protestantism of Adolf von Harnack. His "essence of Christianity" sought to de-Hellenize a Christianity he thought had been wrongly Hellenized in the fourth and fifth centuries. The history of religions school took up this task of de-Hellenization, looking for the source of Christianity in a Palestinian Judaism purified of Hellenistic influence. It has been widely acknowledged as a failed search. De-Hellenization is not the sole province of Harnack or the history of religions school; as we have seen above, another source is Martin Luther's more biblical mode of theology, which (so it is argued) makes doctrinal revisions central to Protestantism, especially revisiting traditional teachings on simplicity and impassibility. Jenson found Luther and Barth working together to distance theology from the "Hellenic quest for God." De-Hellenization has also become a project for theologians influenced by Heidegger who find "ontotheology" to be the major threat to a faithful articulation of Christian teaching. These diverse sources share little else in common, but they share in the project of de-Hellenization. Merold Westphal explains the project: "Within Christian history, the critique of onto-theology belongs to a tradition of dehellenizing repristination.

Heidegger explicitly links his critique with Luther, and thus, by implication, with a tradition that looks back to Augustine and ahead to Pascal, Kierkegaard, and Barth."[93] The diverse sources contributing to the project of de-Hellenization led several generations of theologians to affirm it. That project has now been questioned.

Distinguishing a putative, static Hellenism from a dynamic Judaism is an exaggeration, if not caricature, of both. As Robert Wilken has put it, "The notion that the development of early Christian thought represented a Hellenization of Christianity has outlived its usefulness."[94] Wilken's historical analysis shows how the spirit of early Christian thought was much more a Christianization of Hellenism than vice versa. This analysis should free theologians to engage once again with the intersections among Judaism, Christianity, and Greek thought without the burden of purifying either Judaism or Christianity from a putatively corrupting Greek influence. Insofar as calls for revision assume Christianity must be purified from that influence, those calls should now fall on deaf ears.

A sign that some version of de-Hellenization still lingers in theologians can be found in the invocation and dismissal of "substance metaphysics." There is, however, another version of the Hellenization thesis that is less concerned with metaphysics and more concerned with politics. We already saw this in Catherine Keller's critique of the traditional answer. The static, aloof God of Greek metaphysics becomes the support for empire. Another version of this critique can be found in the theology from the Radical Reformation. Most of the Radical Reformers, like their counterparts among the Reformers, did not challenge the doctrine of God.[95] However, as we saw with modern Protestant theologians, some contemporary Radical Reformation theologians think the baptist vision of theology requires more revision than can be found among the Radical Reformers. The emperor

---

93. Westphal, *Overcoming Ontotheology*, 18.
94. Robert Wilken, *The Spirit of Early Christianity* (New Haven, CT: Yale University Press, 2003), xvi.
95. See Thomas Finger, *A Contemporary Anabaptist Theology* (Downers Grove, IL: InterVarsity, 2004), 408–64. Finger disagrees with McClendon that baptist theology should replace ontological categories with historical ones.

Constantine enabled doctrinal orthodoxy via the use of imperial power. If that is true, then it casts a shadow over the dogmatic results. If practices such as infant Baptism and transubstantiation should be called into question, as the Radical Reformers did, then so should the "metaphysics of substance" that undergirds them. That metaphysics inclines us to look away from what matters most, the lived practice of the Christian life, as if doctrine were only a matter of correct cognitive content.

Although significantly different from Keller's critique of Christian doctrine, James McClendon, a small-*b* baptist theologian, offers an important call for revision. McClendon was not only influenced by the Radical Reformers; he was also influenced by Barth. Like Barth, McClendon reorders the traditional teaching, but he does so with an important difference. He does not integrate the *de deo uno* with the *de deo trino*; instead, he begins explicitly with ethics as practical theology and then moves to doctrine. His calls for revision are based not so much on the usual de-Hellenization project but more on the political concerns about Constantinianism. It signals "the dissolving of Christian faith into culture."[96] This dissolution involves practice more so than theory. Constantinianism occurs when Christians accommodate their teaching to an alien culture for the sake of ruling, or holding power over, others. Although McClendon does not directly correlate specific doctrinal teachings with such accommodation, he does suggest that doctrine, especially dogma, can disengage with questions of discipleship. When it does so, it distracts from what matters most—the practice of the Christian life, which is more like a culture than a set of beliefs.

McClendon acknowledges that there is no pure Christian culture separated from its mediation by the cultures it always already

---

96. James McClendon, *Systematic Theology: Doctrine* (Nashville: Abingdon, 1994), 391. McClendon has a three-volume systematic theology. The first is *Systematic Theology: Ethics* (Nashville: Abingdon, 1986). The second is *Doctrine*, and the third is *Systematic Theology: Witness* (Nashville: Abingdon, 2000). In his final volume McClendon explains what each contributed. "While *Ethics* asked how the church must live to be the church, and *Doctrine*, what it must teach to be the church, *Witness*, the present volume, has asked how in order to be itself the church must relate to the world outside the church."

inhabits.[97] For instance, he does not fault Augustine for setting Christianity forth in terms of Neoplatonism, nor Thomas with Aristotelianism. Nor does he argue that these philosophies are the basis for Constantinianism. McClendon is no Platonist, nor Aristotelian; nor is he a fideist who rejects the role of philosophy for a purely biblical theology. He examines three moments in the Christian use of philosophy that he finds illuminating. The first is the philosophy used in the Trinitarian controversies. The second is in Thomas's "theism," and the third is "modern subjectivist" philosophies. Following David Burrell, McClendon argues that turning Thomas's discussion of God into "attributes" as the basis for a theism was a mistake. "Yet if David Burrell and others are correct, these latter-day heirs of Thomas Aquinas have missed the Angelic Doctor's point, which was not to describe the Aristotelian God afresh, but to use the concept of a limiting source of all else in order to *establish the limits* of what Christians could say about the God they knew to be 'the beginning and end of all things.'"[98] Thomas, and Burrell, teach that God's existence is a "different *kind* of existence"; it cannot be known simply through philosophical reason alone. Knowledge of such a unique existence requires conversion. For this reason, McClendon redefines metaphysics. It is "essentially a historical task; it is precisely the discovery of the absolute presuppositions of a preceding era."[99] Metaphysics is not about content but context. It does not abstract from history in a quest for transcendentals such as truth, goodness, and being; instead, it is a historical discipline that reflects on the presuppositions of diverse cultures.

McClendon compares and contrasts his baptist approach to both a Catholic and a Protestant one. He finds evidence that Catholic and Protestant doctrines have arisen organically from Christian life and affirms them for it. He does not reject everything present in these other approaches, but he critiques them from the perspective of the baptist vision. The Catholic approach understands "doctrine" as

97. McClendon, *Systematic Theology: Witness*, 195.
98. McClendon, *Systematic Theology: Doctrine*, 301.
99. McClendon, *Systematic Theology: Witness*, 189.

"revealed truth imparted to the church." Its weakness is its inflexibility and nonbiblical teaching on the "magisterium" and on "doctrine (or dogma) itself."[100] What Catholics mean by dogma cannot find its basis in the Bible. One version of the Protestant approach shares the Catholic understanding of doctrine as "received truth." A second, originating with Schleiermacher, places doctrine "on a completely new footing." Some view this new foundation as a reduction of doctrine to anthropology, while others see it as making "room for affective faith."[101] McClendon does not reject these Protestant and Catholic approaches, but he supplements them with "the baptist vision."[102] Their conviction that doctrine emerges from "God's authority in Jesus Christ," that all doctrine is limited, grounded in community, and is a "regular practice" of the church is consistent with the baptist vision, but more is still needed.[103] The more is this:

> The baptist vision is the way the Bible is read by those who (1) accept the plain sense of Scripture as its dominant sense and recognize their continuity with the story it tells, and who (2) acknowledge that finding the point of that story leads them to its application, and who also (3) see past and present and future linked by a "this is that" and "then is now" vision, a trope of mystical identity binding the story now to the story then, and the story then and now to God's future yet to come.[104]

The baptist vision finds God in biblical narrative and seeks doctrines consistent with it. These narratives will be self-involving; the continuity between the past and future (eschatology) in the present engages the disciple in living practices of faithfulness. There is no doctrine without conversion. Doctrine names the history of God's interaction with creatures through Israel, Jesus, and the church.

This emphasis on history leads McClendon to challenge the "metaphysics of substance," but he does so by way of the ethical significance of the Eucharist as a meal of reconciliation more so than any explicit critique of metaphysics per se. He asks whether the

100. McClendon, *Systematic Theology: Doctrine*, 25–27; McClendon, *Systematic Theology: Witness*, 410.
101. McClendon, *Systematic Theology: Doctrine*, 26–27.
102. Ibid., 28–29.
103. Ibid., 27–28.
104. Ibid., 45.

traditional answer is capable of rendering intelligible that the Lord's Supper is an act of reconciliation. If it can, then no objections are necessary. If it cannot, then the metaphysics dissolves Christian discipleship into a bland Christian culture that makes little difference in everyday life. If doctrine's purpose is to "establish the limits" of what can be said of God, then all such language will have a practical import. If it does not demonstrate its practical import, it can be subject to revision. For this reason, McClendon replaces *being* with *narrative*, and God's *nature* with God's *identity*. Systematic theology does not define God or resolve logical problems; it uses language so that the God who acts in history can be identified as God and in turn convert persons into disciples. McClendon states, "Yet 'God' has not been defined here, or God's essence described, apart from the Israel-Jesus-church story itself."[105] For this reason, he agrees with the above analyses and finds that the traditional metaphysics now requires doctrinal revisions. The problem was not Thomas, for he did not seek "diversion from the biblical story," but those who came after him "generated the diverted theism of the following centuries . . . , a cluster of detached philosophical propositions supposed to be self-authenticating apart from Scripture."[106] Once those stand-alone theistic propositions were deconstructed in the modern era, atheism arose. The god that was destroyed, however, was not the God of biblical faith, but a hollowed-out theism built up from putatively philosophical reason alone. The proper response to both this theism and its rejection is to relate the doctrine of God directly to history and practice. It is in "witness," not in metaphysical speculation, that the doctrine of God is demonstrated. For this reason, McClendon concludes his trilogy with a "theology of witness."

Revisions of Divine Attributes

The previous sections sought the reasons why influential contemporary theologians raise the metaphysical question. It prepares

---

105. Ibid., 294.
106. Ibid., 310, emphasis original.

us now to undertake what revisions they call for. Although the reasons for the revisions differ from the process, open, analytic, and liberation theologians, the content bears a family resemblance. McClendon either dismisses or redescribes divine impassibility, immutability, and the teaching that there is no real relation between God and creation. His "comprehensive view" of God's relationship to creation requires "four elements." First, "For God to continue to be God, there must be that about God which is utterly reliable." It is "creative love." McClendon ignores discussions of divine simplicity or eternity in favor of "creative love." This first point requires no revisions to the traditional answer. His second element does; it is "reciprocity." God brings about "changed circumstances" with creation, but creation also implies change for God. As he puts it, "God-who-has-created is other than God-who-only-might-create."[107] Creation appears to add something to God. This second point requires further revisions. The real, reciprocal relation between God and creation entails a third element, God's suffering. He agrees with Moltmann and others that "to love is to suffer." However, God's suffering is different, and this difference makes for the fourth element, that God suffers "creatively."[108] What we say of God should be consistent with these four elements.

McClendon's revisions are marked less by his commitment to the Radical Reformation and more by ecumenical moves current in modern theology that draw on Barth and Rahner's rules to tie the doctrine of God indissolubly to the divine economy. Theologians have done so by making the incarnation, the crucifixion, or the practice of Christian life central to the doctrine of God. The result has been an emphasis on practical theology, and a suspicion against speculative theology. Different sources are drawn on for this practical theology, but the calls for revision are similar. Divine simplicity, eternity, impassibility, and immutability are accused of distorting faithful Christian doctrine. Along with revisions to them, the relationship between God and creation must be reconceived. That these two forms

---

107. McClendon, *Systematic Theology: Witness*, 171.
108. Ibid.

of revision are related is telling. Deny simplicity and its correlates and God and creation will inevitably be really related, resulting in a newly conceived relationship between God and creation.

Simplicity

Given his dissatisfaction with both Augustine and the Greek Fathers, one would expect Gunton to call for revisions as radical as the process theologians. He does not; in fact, he calls for fewer revisions than many Barthians. He acknowledges it has become "fashionable" to reject simplicity, but he finds that, short-sighted, "This will not do if we wish to hold on to the doctrine of the unity and coherence of the divine being."[109] Although he affirms a version of divine simplicity, he rejects any identity among the divine attributes (what analytic theologians call "property-property identity"). The divine simplicity that gets affirmed is qualified by a diversity of attributes.[110]

Along with simplicity, he affirms immutability and impassibility, but only after they are excised of their pagan accretions. He summarizes the results: "Aseity provides a necessary defence of God's ontological self-sufficiency; simplicity a defence of the indivisibility of his action, immutability of his utter constancy and consistency, impassibility of the indefectibility of his purposes for the perfection of his creation and omnipotence of the guarantee that what God began in creation he will complete."[111] In truth, he hardly challenges the traditional answer. If readers can see past the rhetoric and uncharitable reading of the tradition, one finds that Gunton, like Barth, has provided a retrieval of the tradition more so than a revision within it. His most convincing revision is one we also saw in Arminius; holiness gets emphasized as a divine attribute.

Gunton finds holiness first emerging in "Hodge's list of divine attributes" and states, "It is the presence in the list of holiness which marks a departure, for, as we saw, it did not appear in Aquinas's

---

109. Gunton, *Act & Being*, 32.
110. Ibid., 123.
111. Ibid., 133.

treatment of the attributes. There seems to be little doubt that its presence is the result of Reformation, and particularly Calvin's emphasis on the doctrine of sanctification."[112] Gunton, like analytic theologians, wrongly identifies what Thomas is doing in the *prima pars* as a "list" of attributes. Thomas is not providing a list, and although Gunton is correct that holiness does not play an adequate role in the journey Thomas takes us on, he is incorrect to suggest it is not present. Perfection is another way of expressing holiness. Moreover, Thomas makes an explicit reference to love and holiness in question 36, in a discussion on the name "Holy Spirit," suggesting that they come together to make sense of the name and the Spirit's role in creation and redemption: "holiness is attributed to those things that are ordered to God" (*ST* I 36.1, rep. obj. 1). Gunton, like Barth, restricted his analysis of Thomas to the first thirteen questions and missed how they were used in the *de Deo*. Thomas also makes a case that God is "Holy Love."[113]

Despite Gunton's polemics against the common teaching that we cannot know God's essence, he is inconsistent in his critique. After arguing strenuously that we do know the divine essence, he then qualifies his claim by stating that we do not have an "inside view of the being of God"; it is reserved for the beatific vision.[114] If that is the case, how much of a departure has Gunton actually made from the traditional answer? Many of the revisions called for are less revisions but refinements and restatements of the traditional answer that respond to caricatures rather than the nuanced arguments set forth by theologians such as Thomas.

Gunton affirms divine simplicity for the sake of unity but rejects the teaching that the operations of the persons in the economy are "undivided." He seeks a stronger division among the persons. He also rejects beginning with the essence, and despite his rejection of much of the Eastern tradition, he nonetheless finds the unity of the Trinity in the Father. He sets forth this principle for divine agency, a principle reminiscent of one set forth by LaCugna: "all divine action . . . begins

112. Ibid., 88.
113. Ibid., 121–22.
114. Ibid., 111.

with the Father, takes shape through the Son and reaches its completion in the Spirit."[115] Because Gunton does not affirm an unknown essence and derives our knowledge of the divine essence from the economy, it is unclear whether this statement applies to God's relation to creation or to the Triune relations. He seems to suggest both, for before setting forth this principle he states, "God's being is known in and through his action, his triune action." Is Gunton suggesting that the divine action we know in God's relation to us is the same as God's self-relation? If so, then does it follow that God "reaches completion in the Spirit"? It is unclear that Gunton would affirm that statement as a reference to the immanent Trinity; it is also unclear that he would not. If he did, it would require something like Hegel, something like "being is becoming." This ontology has been significant for post-Barthian theologians.

Hinlicky and Jenson ask us to consider deeper revisions to the traditional answer than does Gunton. They too base their criticism on the metaphysics underlying that teaching and counter it by correlating all knowledge of God with the doctrine of the Trinity. Thinking God consistently with this rule requires "disentangling" theology from much of Greek metaphysics. Hinlicky writes,

> To think "God" this way today entails disentangling the fateful but peculiar alliance of Christian theology with the cosmo-theological scheme of Greek metaphysical theology (thinking of God as the highest link or supreme cause *within* the cosmic chain of being), and more insidiously by means of the Platonic "axiom of impassibility" (God is not what everything else is), otherwise known as the doctrine of divine simplicity (taken not as a rule for reverent speech but as an insight into the being of God).[116]

Hinlicky does not reject divine simplicity, as long as it is understood as a "rule of reverent speech," but if it is used to express a "positive account of God's being," then it goes too far. Hinlicky finds it misused

---

115. Gunton, *Act & Being*, 113.
116. Paul Hinlicky, *Divine Complexity: The Rise of Creedal Christianity* (Minneapolis: Fortress Press, 2011), 19. Hinlicky has a forthcoming book on simplicity, *Divine Simplicity: Christ the Crisis of Metaphysics* (Grand Rapids: Baker Academic, 2016). It will be interesting to see if it qualifies any of his previous critiques of simplicity. I have not had access to it at the time of this publication.

for this purpose in what he calls "the more or less traditional notion that God is God as a timeless, spaceless, incommunicable, self-identical nature, especially when such divine essence is actually thought of as a 'fourth' reality over against the Father and the Son in the Spirit."[117] To avoid this error, Hinlicky complements simplicity with "divine complexity," in which God's being is "*esse deum dare*, that is, that for God to be God is to give." God gives to us out of God's future, out of the "event of the coming of His kingdom."[118] Hinlicky puts this baldly: "God *happens* or God *is* not; God *comes* and *becomes* our God or God is—really—dead."[119] The becoming or happening of God also entails a rejection of divine impassibility.[120]

Impassibility

Apart from Gunton, Barth, and Rahner, all the theologians who raise the metaphysical question challenge divine impassibility. In some sense, they assert, God suffers. It is insufficient to affirm with our theological forebears that God suffers in the humanity of Jesus, taking that suffering into God's being and healing it. Once Barth and Rahner's rules are worked out more fully, then God must suffer in divinity. In explaining how "divine complexity" must complement simplicity Hinlicky states, "This ontology of charity is what I designate the *complexity* of divine life, in complement, not contradiction, of 'simplicity'—rightly understood—that is, as qualifying the suffering of the man Christ as a divine suffering, 'impassible passibility.'" Like many of the revisions Hinlicky calls for, it is unclear how radical this revision is. Is he stating that God suffers by taking on himself the "suffering of the man Christ," which would be similar to Cyril of Alexandria's traditional claim that in the crucifixion the impassible suffers impassibly? Or is he stating something more along the lines of Hegel, Jüngel, and Moltmann in which God suffers not in the humanity

---

117. Ibid., xi. Whether any theologian ever thought of God's essence as a "fourth reality" is certainly something that needs to be proven and not just asserted.
118. Ibid., 210.
119. Ibid., 220.
120. Ibid., xi.

of Jesus but in the divinity, and this suffering somehow counters modern atheism? In the crucifixion, does God encounter and even contradict God?

Jüngel acknowledges that the contemporary rejection of the traditional answer is often based on caricatures and warns against such facile rejections of the hard-fought wisdom of the church's teaching.[121] Nonetheless, he finds a "danger" in the traditional answer, one that McClendon also found. Theology fell "under the *dictatorship* of metaphysics, rather than using its language *critically*." Once this happened, it opened itself to atheism, for when that metaphysics came to an end, so did God. One important reason why he finds the crisis of metaphysics leads to an inability to think God is divine impassibility.[122] It is in thinking God with death that Hegel becomes helpful, because he helps us affirm divine passibility. Jüngel does not merely repeat Hegel's philosophical theology without remainder; theology pushes back against it. He does, however, affirm Hegel's thinking of the Trinity through Jesus' death, and he allows Hegel to pose the question that the end of metaphysics raises, "Where is God?"[123] The result is that God can no longer be thought without the world, and this is a new form of "speculative thought," a "speculative Good Friday." To think this new "speculative thought" is to think God as encountering God in the crucifixion.

> In that God differentiates himself and *thus*, in unity with the crucified Jesus, suffers as God the Son being forsaken by God the Father, he is God the Reconciler. God reconciles the world with himself in that in the death of Jesus he encounters himself as *God the Father* and *God the Son* without becoming disunited in himself. On the contrary, in the encounter of God and God, of Father and Son, God reveals himself as the one who he is. He is God the Spirit, who lets Father and Son be one in the death of Jesus, in true distinction in this encounter.[124]

---

121. He states, "We must in fact emphatically warn against the common contemporary arrogance with regard to the tradition, and especially against the wholesale rejection of the traditional thought of God. Usually the object of such criticism is nothing more than a dreadful caricature"; Jüngel, *God as the Mystery of the World*, 9.
122. Ibid., vii.
123. Jüngel, *God as the Mystery of the World*, 94. Jüngel's primary criticism is that Hegel's theology is a restoration of deification (94).
124. Ibid., 368.

What God encounters, and confronts, in the crucifixion is less a sinful, recalcitrant creation and more God's own self.

Moltmann is well known for building on Jüngel's divine passibility. He stipulates that love necessarily entails suffering. "Were God incapable of suffering in any respect, and therefore in an absolute sense, then he would also be incapable of love."[125] However, exactly what divine passibility signifies is not readily apparent in Moltmann or any theologian who affirms it. For human creatures, suffering leads to change, and change involves decay and death. In whatever way God suffers, no theologian affirms that. The content of divine suffering is always left undeveloped because, in the final analysis, it makes little sense. Moltmann comes the closest to explaining it. He explicitly rejects patripassianism. We cannot say the Father "suffered and died." What we can say is this: "The Son suffers dying, the Father suffers the death of the Son." Divine suffering means that on the cross there is "a deep division in God himself."[126] God is not dead, but death is "in" God.[127]

Jüngel and Moltmann are apologists. Key to their concern is their diagnosis of the causes of atheism. If metaphysical theism led to atheism, then once the former disappears, so too will the protest atheism it spawned. If God suffers in God's divinity, God is no longer the distant, aloof monarch impassible to the suffering and death in the world. God intimately knows it. Moltmann states, "The only way past protest atheism is through a theology of the cross which understands God as the suffering God in the suffering of Christ and which cries out with the godforsaken God, 'My God, why have you forsaken me?'"[128] Psalm 22 is no longer a cry of God's vindication for a righteous Jew; it has become a cry of dereliction and abandonment.

Immutability

If God is passible, then in some sense, God must change. Theologians

125. Moltmann, *Crucified God*, 230.
126. Ibid., 243–44.
127. Ibid., 207.
128. Ibid., 227.

THE METAPHYSICAL QUESTION

must be careful in revising impassibility and immutability unless they present God's being as a rotting existence that, like all that lives, fades away. God's suffering and change cannot lead to this result unless theology is theologically assisted deicide. As we saw in every theological movement that affirms divine mutability except process theism, one way to avoid that unpalatable conclusion is to argue that God's suffering and change is unlike ours. We cannot but suffer and change. Most of us do not willingly suffer; it happens by accident. Events occur in life over which we have no control, leading to suffering and death; such inescapable, temporal, finite events are what it means for us to suffer and change. Christian theologians who affirm divine mutability use it other than that. Often, they affirm that God voluntarily changes; it is not a necessity of the divine nature. Moltmann writes, "If God is not passively changeable by some things like other creatures, this does not mean that he is not free to change himself, or even free to allow himself to be changed by others of his own free will."[129] Both the incarnation and crucifixion raise the question of divine immutability. If God "becomes" human, as the incarnation suggests, then surely that seems to imply mutability? The church's creeds refused to abandon divine immutability, and for Moltmann the result is a "mild Docetism."[130] Divinity and humanity have been insufficiently united in the person of Jesus. Yet no one explains how a God who does not need to change is related to a God who changes voluntarily. If voluntary change now defines God, then is it the case that once God changes, the God who does not need to change is constrained by the divine will that voluntarily changes? Of course, a god who voluntarily changes from what god was prior to the change entails temporality.

Eternity

If God is in some sense mutable, then God will bear some kind of temporality. Jenson, like Sanders, sets the Cappadocians against

129. Ibid., 229.
130. Moltmann, *Crucified God*, 89.

Augustine and finds them preferable. Nevertheless, they left three unfinished issues. First, they maintained impassibility. Second, they did not recover "a biblical understanding of the *Logos* as God's *speech*." Third, their recognition of "only relations of *origin* as constitutive for the divine life" failed to incorporate "the *eschatological* character of God's scriptural history."[131] Jenson seeks to correct the errors lingering from their problematic metaphysics. The three errors lose the temporal differentiation of the Trinity and its significance for both the missions and processions. Jenson writes, "*At this precise point*, the Western tradition must simply be corrected."[132] The correction will occur through becoming more aware of the "gospel's religious oddity and so also of its metaphysical oddity." Jenson sets forth what this requires:

> It is time and past time for Western theology to move on from its effectively pre-Nicene doctrine of God's relation to creatures. An authentically trinitarian teaching about the *opera ad extra* would be something like the following: The occurrence and plot of the life of God's people with God depends as a whole upon the occurrence and plot of the life of God with his people. It does so precisely as this one life is in both aspects constituted in the Father's originating, the Spirit's perfecting, and the Son's mediating of the two, and as it is the whole reality of God on the one hand and of the creature on the other.[133]

Exactly what this means is not readily apparent. It could mean nothing more than the noncontroversial claim that the economy of the Triune persons is consistent with the Triune missions. But two claims Jenson sets forth make it more than that. First, he states, "The distinction between the triune story as it is about God and as it is about creatures is not a distinction between the simplicity of timelessness and the differentiations of temporality: eventful differentiation is real on both sides."[134] As we saw with John Sanders, eternity now becomes ever-lastingness, and simplicity must be abandoned. The result, as it was for Sanders, is that God has a future, which is the second controversial

131. Jenson, *Systematic Theology*, 1:108.
132. Ibid., 113.
133. Ibid., 114.
134. Ibid., 113.

claim Jenson makes. "The biblical God's eternity is his temporal infinity."[135] He takes this insight beyond Barth. God "is *temporally* infinite because 'source' and 'goal' are present *and* asymmetrical in him, because he is primarily future to himself and only thereupon past and present for himself."[136] God has a present, past, and future, and it is the latter that allows for the revised ontology of being as becoming.

Pannenberg makes a similar judgment. He writes, "Today we see that differentiating the eternal Trinity from all temporal change makes trinitarian theology one-sided and detaches it from its biblical basis. The situation obviously calls for revision."[137] The problem emerged from Augustine, who was influenced by Plato rather than Plotinus, and for whom eternity is only the negative of time.[138] Unlike many of those who call for revision, Pannenberg affirms Boethius's definition of eternity and finds in it something more like Plotinian eternity as unlimited duration. It allows us to conceive God as "intrinsically differentiated unity."[139] But the Plotinian-Boethian eternity does not go far enough. It did not combine eternity with New Testament "eschatology."[140] Once combined, then we can make the daring affirmation of divine temporality.

> If eternity and time coincide only in the eschatological consummation of history, then from the standpoint of the history of God that moves toward this consummation there is room for becoming in God himself, namely, in the relation of the immanent and economic Trinity, and in this frame it is possible to say of God that he himself became something that he previously was not because of his Son.[141]

Relation between God and Creation

A consequence of the revisions to the divine attributes is a reconception of the relationship between God and creation. If God is

---

135. Ibid., 217.
136. Ibid.
137. Pannenberg, *Systematic Theology*, 1:333.
138. Ibid., 404.
139. Ibid., 407.
140. Ibid., 408.
141. Ibid., 438.

not simple, is in some sense temporal, and can in fact change and suffer, then of course creation will have some kind of affect on God. Moltmann, like McClendon, conceives of the relationship as real. "[T]he relationship between God and the world has a *reciprocal* character, because this relationship must be seen as a living one."[142] Pannenberg follows suit: "The divine essence can no longer be thought of as an unrelated identity outside the world. It has to be recognized that an idea of this kind is contradictory because the idea of transcendence itself expresses a relation."[143] If God is transcendent, then God transcends something. Whatever it is that God transcends implies a relation to it. Pannenberg distances his concept of relation from Spinoza, Hegel, or Whitehead but then states, "Nevertheless, theological thinking now faces the task of revising traditional ideas of God. It cannot escape this challenge if it is to remain in intellectual dialogue with modern criticism of the traditional doctrine of God and with atheism, and if it is not to fall back upon loose symbolical language in its statements about God."[144] Theology addresses the challenge by introducing "relation" into "substance." Clearly Pannenberg knew this had already been done from Nicea through Aquinas; he mentions as much throughout his work. So what could it mean that introducing relation into substance will be a revision of traditional ideas? It is relation to creation that is now meant. "The relational structure of the concept also includes God's relations with the world. In trinitarian theology, the principle of the unity of the immanent and economic Trinity in the doctrine of God embraces these relations."[145]

Conclusion

Barth and Rahner's rules challenged any sharp division between *de deo uno* and *de deo trino*. They offered a much-needed correction to late Scholastic manuals on the doctrine of God. That division, however, was not found in Thomas or prior to him. Thomas's treatise *de deo*

---

142. Moltmann, *Trinity and the Kingdom*, 98.
143. Pannenberg, *Systematic Theology*, 1:367.
144. Ibid.
145. Ibid.

was divided in its first two parts, based on the grammar of the Nicene Creed, "On the essence of God," and "On the processions." He did not present a list of divine attributes or properties known by reason alone, followed by a separate treatise on the Trinity only available to revelation. The two treatises were always about the Holy Trinity. Once that is recognized, Barth and Rahner's rules are not that revolutionary. They do not require the deep revisions found among those who raise the metaphysical question.

The theologians in this chapter share in common with those of previous chapters a dissatisfaction with their forebears' discussion of the divine essence and attributes. A common thread uniting all of them is that modern theology must overcome a metaphysics of substance. As we have seen, the critique has become so common that many theologians set it forth without argumentation as to what a substance metaphysics is, why it is a problem, and who in the tradition taught it. We have also seen that the critique is indebted to Hegel.

Jüngel does not engage Hegel as to whether or not he has adequately set up the question of the end of metaphysics. He does not ask whether Aristotle's "substances" were indeed essential to the Christian tradition. He assumes Hegel's accuracy, especially in the terms used by the Fathers at the first ecumenical councils.[146] Pannenberg also assumes Hegel's analysis (similar to analysis 1 above), arguing that modern science and philosophy require the rejection of "substance." He writes, "The dissolving of solids into pure relations, as in modern science, helps us to understand Kant's view of things as pure phenomena. Hegel went further along the same path. For him it was part of the concept of essence to be self-related to something else."[147] That modern science could decide metaphysical matters would be a category mistake. For all of its accomplishments, its method is not equipped to make such judgments. That Hegel requires us to abandon "substance" because essence is now always related to something is also problematic. It assumes God is no exception to Hegel's metaphysical

---

146. Jüngel, *God as the Mystery of the World*, 82.
147. Pannenberg, *Systematic Theology*, 1:365–66.

framework. If this is the case, then the Hegelian reason for revision is not far from the one we saw above with Whitehead.

Barry Smith argues from within an analytic approach that both analytic philosophers who deny simplicity and others who defend it depend on a substance metaphysics. He states, "What both sides of the debate have in common is the assumption that God is a substance who has attributes, or to use more modern terminology, a concrete object, i.e., individual, that exemplifies properties, which are abstract objects."[148] Some reject it; others affirm it. This shared presupposition, he suggests, "should be called into question."[149] If it is, he argues, then we can neither be for nor against simplicity. Smith acknowledges that St. Augustine explicitly taught that Christian theology should not affirm Aristotle's substances, but it makes no difference in his critique. Simplicity, despite Augustine, requires Aristotle's substances, to which properties are predicated. But he is incorrect. The argument is not over Aristotle's "substance." It is modern theologians who turn it into one overarching "thing" and make it something to be overcome.

How "substance" functions in metaphysics had no consensus among ancient philosophers or early church fathers. Some thought it was appropriate to attribute it to divinity; others were less convinced. Radde-Gallwitz notes that for Plotinus "of Aristotle's ten categories, the nine nonsubstance categories, including relation, only apply within the sensible world, and substance in the sensible world is only analogically related to true substance in the intelligible."[150] No one seems to have thought that substance could have been applied to God as a substrate to which the other categories are then attributed as properties.

Aristotle's ten categories seek to explain the meaning of every "uncombined word or expression." A combined expression would be "man runs" or "tree blooms." His most basic category, one that stands by and for itself without being for anything else, is substance. The substance is "that which is neither asserted of nor can be found in a

---

148. Barry Smith, *The Oneness and Simplicity of God* (Eugene, OR: Pickwick, 2014), 121.
149. Ibid., 122.
150. Radde-Gallwitz, *Basil of Caesarea, Gregory of Nyssa and the Transformation of Divine Simplicity*, 115.

subject."[151] Running can be found in a human being like blossoming can be found in a tree, but neither human being nor tree can be found in something more basic to it. Being human is not "in" running any more than being a tree is in a house. The substance of the tree must change for it to become house. Of course, the incarnation will qualify the particulars of the human substance; humanity is now found in divinity, but in order to be surprised by that, we must first recognize that it is unusual. Aristotle's substance alone never sufficed for Christian doctrine. The other categories—quality, quantity, relation, place, time, posture, state or condition, action or affection—are found in, of, or for substances. Relation is "of some other thing" so that relation appears to be less basic than substance.[152] Aristotle has not given us a metaphysics with his categories but an analysis of language. This analysis of language is related to his metaphysics, but the latter is much less precise than the former.

As is well known, the term *metaphysics* originated from Aristotle's librarian, who placed what Aristotle called "first philosophy" after his physics because it did not fit within the science of physics. Metaphysics, in its most general meaning, is the science of being. It purports to tell us what "is." More precisely, according to Aristotle, it explains the "first principles" for what is. It is not a science that categorizes "what is" like biology or botany. It does not merely indicate, pointing to existing objects and placing them within intelligible categories. It is not physics. Physics shows what is available in nature qua nature [φύσις]. Metaphysics is its possibility and not the other way around. Aristotle defined it as "the theory [θεωρητικός] of first principles [ἀρχή] and explanations [αἰτία] among which is the good or the where-for [τὸ οὖ ἕνεκα]." It is a science, he stated, that originates from "wonder."[153] It is also a "divine science," he writes, "in a double

---

151. Aristotle, *Categories*, trans. Harold P. Cooke (Cambridge, MA: Harvard University Press, 1983), 19.
152. Ibid., 47. Aristotle does state, "The view that no substance is relative—a view that is commonly held—would appear to be open to question" (ibid., 59).
153. Aristotle, *Metaphysics*, trans. Richard Hope (Ann Arbor: University of Michigan Press, 1990), 7 (i.2 982b 8–10).

sense." God is "one of the reasons for all things," and "first philosophy" would be the only kind of science God would have.[154]

Aristotle's answers to the questions posed by the wonder first philosophy generated were often found in his categories of substance and accidents. Such answers differed from Plato's insistence on participation and relationality, drawing on his theory of the "ideas." Philosophers and theologians have debated those answers and their compatibility with Christianity and have never come to consensus how best to answer the question of "being" that originates from wonder. In that sense, metaphysics has never been an uncontested science. It is a tradition of debate. To be against metaphysics, to seek to overcome it or bring it to an end, could then mean one of two things. It could find an end either to its answers or its questions. First, it could mean metaphysics fails to give definitive or convincing *answers* to the question of being, and its failure entails its exhaustion. Second, it could mean "do not ask those *questions*." "Do not engage in that debate." "Know the limits of what your language can do and live within them." Both meanings are, however, unconvincing. The first asks metaphysics to achieve what its sober practitioners would have avoided, a science of being based on certitude, more like a modern understanding of science, and then accuses it for having failed in such an achievement. One cannot help but see in this analysis a lingering effect of the failed project of logical positivism and its principle of verification. The second is less a criticism of metaphysics and more a materialist program that takes the wonder out of existence. Perhaps these attempts to bring metaphysics to an end get it wrong because they do something antimetaphysical; they ask for a definitive answer to the question "What is metaphysics?"

St. Augustine also reflected on being from the perspective of wonder, but he did not find the answer in Aristotle's categories. Much as Aquinas rejected any use of language for God that considered God composed of substance and accidents, so did Augustine. Simplicity served the function of blocking this possibility. In his *Confessions*,

---

154. Ibid. (i.2 983a 5–10).

Augustine explains Aristotle's *Categories* and then asks, "What profit did this study bring me?" He answers,

> None. In fact it made difficulties for me because I thought that everything that existed could be reduced to these ten categories, and I therefore attempted to understand you, my God, in all your wonderful immutable simplicity, in these same terms, as though you too were substance and greatness and beauty were your attributes in the same way that a body has attributes by which it is defined. But your greatness and beauty are your own self: whereas a body is not great or beautiful simply because it is a body.[155]

Augustine rejects Aristotle's "substance metaphysics" because of divine simplicity; it taught him not to think of God in terms of the category of substance. For any modern theologian or philosopher to argue that simplicity requires a metaphysics of substance in Aristotle's terms is patently misguided.

If substance is interpreted outside the framework of the ten categories, if it is only understood in the minimal sense as that which exists in itself and not for another, then one wonders why it would be inappropriate for God. It would only restate the ancient wisdom that God is *a se* ("from himself") and not *ab alio* ("from others"). To deny this truth would be to be speaking about an entity other than what the Jewish, Christian, and Islamic tradition means by *God*. Christianity, however, made relation as basic an ontological category as substance as early as Nicea.

If the critique of substance metaphysics is that Aristotle's categories cannot help us understand the perfectly simple Triune God, the Christian tradition would largely be in agreement. Metropolitan John Zizioulas argues that once "hypostasis" became associated with person rather than "substance," as it did in the fourth century, then a "revolution" occurred in Greek metaphysics. Rather than substance as primary and relation as secondary, relation became primary.[156] Gisbert Greshake finds Thomas Aquinas's development of "subsistent

---

155. Augustine, *Confessions* (London: Penguin Classics, 1961), 88.
156. See Gisbert Greshake, "Trinity as 'Commuio,'" in Wozniak and Maspero, *Rethinking Trinitarian Theology*, 333.

relations" to build on that revolution.[157] As we saw above in the discussion on simplicity in the *Summa*, Thomas explicitly rejected thinking of God in terms of substance and accidents. He asks, "Is there composition of substance and accidents" in God (*ST* I 3.6)? Thomas categorically denies this possibility. For a substance to be open to accidents, it must have potentiality. Divine simplicity rules out potentiality, so God cannot be conceived of as a substance with accidents. Ironically, theologians who argue God has a potentiality that can be actualized make an argument that thinks God as a substance in Aristotle's terms more so than do either Augustine or Aquinas.

The new theological projects noted above ask us, at some level, to dispense with the traditional answer. Some of them look to Luther and a crucicentric theology in order to revise it. Others look to the incarnation to do so. Still others to Christian practice. Most of these projects have affirmed a "social" Trinity supposedly found among the Eastern Orthodox Fathers against a "psychological" Trinity found in the West. Almost all of them assume that the doctrine of the Trinity errs when it begins with the divine essence. Perhaps this assumption was a necessary correction, given the counters to the Reformation and modernity that led to the sharp distinction between the *de deo uno* and *trino*. But like most course corrections, once taken too far, they create new difficulties. Theology seldom advances by reacting against something. It flourishes best when it knows what it is about, not what it is against. Because of these new theological projects, modern theology often lacks the ability to speak well of God's unity. The basic confession that God is one will always be essential for Trinitarian theology. Perhaps another course correction is now needed?

157. "In this regard, Thomas Aquinas expresses a thought of defining importance for the following era, and which before him had never been so radically expressed when he says that in God, the persons are constituted by the very same divine relations: Personhood in God is a subsistent relation and thus communication. Before the time of St. Thomas Aquinas, this thought was considered impossible. This was because—it was assumed—'relation' is just an (accidental!) connection between one independent being and another" (ibid., 336–37).

9

Conclusion: A Retrieval of the Traditional Answer Attending to Its Critics

The previous five chapters leave us with a very different answer to the question "Who is God?" from where we began. Despite the vastly different reasons for the revision, and the disparate, if not contradictory, philosophies, metaphysics, and theologies underlying the calls, the results of each of these challenges are remarkably the same. A common thread that unites them is their opposition to a "metaphysics of substance," and with that comes a rejection of simplicity. Only the term *perfection* remains standing; none of the theologians we have examined argues for divine imperfection. The perfect God, however, has gone through some drastic changes. God is not simple and possibly complex, mutable, and passible, and has temporal differentiation. The real relations that constitute the divine processions include a real relation with creation. Most of the theologians above would reject any suggestion that they have equated the divine-creation relation with the relations that are the Father, Son, and Spirit. Yet the distinction between these relations has not been a pressing concern; they have not provided a language that can allow us to speak about the Triune relations without also always speaking of the divine-creation relation. Practical theology has rendered speculative theology mute. This condition has existed for so long that it has become commonplace. The perfect God has also been supplemented with terms the traditional answer did not deny but did not always emphasize, especially holiness and God's love for the poor and dispossessed. Although many of the theologians argued for divine love against what they perceived was its neglect in the traditional answer, we have seen how the assumption that it made God aloof, static, and unloving was a caricature.

The reasons for the revisions are many. Each reason emerges from perceived weaknesses the traditional answer either could not or did not address. The revised teaching solves the theoretical problem of evil and the dilemma of divine and human freedom. The God conceived by it is better equipped to challenge oppression and stand in solidarity with the dispossessed. It is more logically rigorous and minimizes the incoherencies that divine simplicity produces with its property-property identity and property-nature identity. It is more faithful to the gospel, integrating what became divided in medieval theology—the teaching on God's unity and Trinity. It incorporates the divine economy fully into the doctrine of God via Barth or Rahner's rule through attending to the importance of the incarnation, crucifixion, eschatology, and/or Christian practice for our knowledge of God.

Given these laudable reasons for calls for revision, and the remarkable harmony they produce for a revised teaching on God, why should those concerned with teaching or preaching not heed their summons? Good reasons exist to attend to the critiques. We must not make God the author of evil. We must not deny divine or human freedom. We must not continue a doctrinal tradition that makes God a tyrant, neglects the poor, or legitimates political conquest. Any adequate doctrine of God should incorporate prophetic voices that remind us God is on the side of the dispossessed and affirm that theology is always produced in and out of historical contexts. It should also incorporate more fully the divine economy into the doctrine of God. These "oughts" should guide teaching and preaching. Yet has the case been made that the perfectly simple Triune God is incapable of satisfying these demands? Do these revisions gain clarity, or do they leave us more confused than before, asking us to abandon confessional and dogmatic traditions, something that should not be the role of the theologian? I find them leaving us more confused and less able to affirm that the God we worship today bears similarities to the God our forebears worshiped and less able of providing an ecumenical consensus diachronically and synchronically on who God is. If I am correct about this, it should cause significant concern. However, the point of this exercise has not been to defend the "traditional" answer because it is traditional. Progress in the development of the doctrine of God has been achieved. I will conclude with three theologians who provide a way of affirming what is good and right about the traditional answer without denying the progress that has been made. They show us a way forward.

Moving Forward: Affirming the Good in the Traditional Answer and Modern Developments

Three important contemporary theologians—Kathryn Tanner, Katherine Sonderegger, and Sarah Coakley—in different but compatible ways have begun to challenge the calls for revision without repristinating some putatively premodern theological ideal. Tanner offers formal rules in which to think and speak about the God-creation relationship that dissolve the divine-human freedom dilemma. Sonderegger retrieves the oneness of God as essential for the Trinity. She invites further reflections on how we speak of the relationship between God and creation. Sarah Coakley challenges univocal approaches to theology that implicitly or explicitly make God a being among beings. She encourages theologians to an "unmastery" of theology that takes up mystical experiences of desire and reinvigorates a speculative or contemplative theology. She offers a new way to begin with speculative theology without setting it against practical theology or vice versa. Each of these theologians makes possible bringing forth the traditional answer without positioning it against the significant gains of modern theologians, especially the historical situatedness of our knowledge and language, the place of the cultural and political questions, the significance of conversion and discipleship, and the importance of the divine economy for the doctrine of the Trinity.

Kathryn Tanner does not offer a systematic treatise on the doctrine of God,[1] as do Coakley and Sonderegger; she sets forth "rules" for speaking about God's relation to creation that offer wise counsel in passing on the best in the traditional answer without reacting against important modern developments. Tanner acknowledges that "these ruled relations have generally undergone a radical transformation during the last five centuries." She also notes that the radical transformation has had "deleterious effects" for "traditional theological claims."[2] For modern theology, the traditional claims have become "unintelligible." Tanner draws on the historical situatedness of these "modern assumptions" in order to call them into question. Two of those modern assumptions are "preference for explanations that remain within the natural order, and high esteem for the self-determining character of human action."[3] Such assumptions, she argues, do not need to conflict with traditional claims once the ruled relations between God and creation are set forth.

The seeming incoherence between modern assumptions and traditional claims can be found in two Christian teachings that seem to conflict: "God's power in creating and governing the world is unconditional and unlimited" and creatures act "on their own" and are "free and therefore responsible for the character of their lives."[4] We have seen process theology, open theism, and analytic theology argue that these two claims cannot be sustained by the traditional answer. The divine-human freedom dilemma requires doctrinal revisions.

1. Though Kathryn Tanner does provide some "sketches" of such in her *Jesus, Humanity, and the Trinity* (Minneapolis: Fortress Press, 2001).
2. Kathryn Tanner, *God and Creation in Christian Theology: Tyranny or Empowerment* (Minneapolis: Fortress Press, 2005), 5.
3. Ibid., 7.
4. Ibid., 1–2.

Tanner is less convinced; she finds the dilemma disappearing if we have the proper understanding of divine transcendence. It is too often assumed to be "contrastive." In other words, God and creation are viewed in opposition. In order to view them as such, it is first necessary to place God and creatures "within a single order."[5] Then God either becomes a transcendent power over creation or one being among others who is affected by what those beings do. If God's transcendence is viewed "non-contrastively," however, the seeming incoherencies of transcendence are dissolved.

Tanner formulates two important rules in speaking about the relation between God and creation to block any sense of a contrastive transcendence. First, "avoid both a simple univocal attribution of predicates to God and world and a simple contrast of divine and non-divine predicates." Second, "avoid in talk about God's creative agency all suggestions of limitation in scope or manner."[6] The two rules mutually reinforce each other. If we avoid univocal and contrastive predicates, then divine and human agency will not need to be conceived as competitive. The first rule restates what theologians mean by *analogy*. Terms applied to God cannot be assumed to be univocally applied, for univocation will assume that God and creation are within a "single order," and that is a sign we have lost transcendence altogether; God becomes a being among beings. Nor can terms applied to God simply be contrasted or negated. Although Tanner would allow for more apophaticism than the analytic theologians or a Barthian like Gunton, terms applied to God cannot simply be contrasts—God is not *x*—for that views transcendence as contrastive.

The second rule prohibits conceiving divine agency in competition with other agencies. God is free to do what God does consistent with God's nature. Because God and creation are not contrasted or in competition, God acts directly in creation. Tanner offers an implication of her rule: "God must not be said to be at work to a limited extent on or

---

5. Ibid., 45.
6. Ibid., 47.

with what pre-exists it. God must not be talked about as only indirectly efficacious of the whole in virtue of intermediate agencies. In either case God would take on the character of a finite agent; the rule for talk of God as transcendent would thereby be violated."[7]

Tanner affirms simplicity over compositeness as a "heuristic device" because it reminds us that all our finite terms are inapplicable to God. Immutability is affirmed for a similar reason. These terms are not a list of attributes, nor a definition or description of God, but a "meta-level articulation" of how to speak about God. They have a formal character, which should be respected. Her rules are "formal directives" and not "material proposals." But can the formal and material be so easily divided? Her formal directives bring with them material content that many of the theologians examined above would question and Tanner does not always seem to own. As we shall see, Katherine Sonderegger is willing to take such rules one step further. They offer an answer not only to God's "identity" but to God's "*quiddity*" or "whatness."

Tanner's rules do not prescribe what must be said about God, but how it should be said if we are to speak about the same God Christians have traditionally spoken about. They are immensely helpful in achieving that end, if the presupposition is shared that we should be speaking about the same God. This presupposition is not universally shared among theologians who call into question the traditional answer. They would ask whether these rules assist us in addressing the problem of evil. Have they simply asserted the compatibility of divine and human freedom? Is analogy logically coherent? Tanner has an answer for the question of divine and human freedom more so than the other questions that modern theologians have raised. She specifies another rule for that purpose: "Talk of the creature's power and efficacy is compatible with talk about God's universal and immediate agency if the theologian follows a rule according to which divinity is said to exercise its power in founding rather than suppressing created being, and created being is said to maintain and fulfill itself, not independently of such agency, but in essential

---

7. Ibid., 82.

dependence upon it."[8] This rule entails metaphysical commitments of "two orders," one on a "'horizontal' plane" ruled by "created causes and effects," and another on a "'vertical' plane." It is the "order whereby God founds the former." These two orders require different kinds of predication.[9] They exist harmoniously because God is not a "power" that evacuates the horizontal of its proper creaturely agency. God is the donating source who makes it possible.

Tanner's rules clarify the God-creation relation in response to some of the searching criticisms of it that arise from faulty interpretations of divine transcendence such as we saw in Aquinas's teaching on predestination. The rules ameliorate its tyrannical implications without abdicating divine sovereignty or making creation necessary for, or competitive with, God. Our earlier discussion of Rowan Williams's defense of *creatio ex nihilo* attempted to make a similar point, showing how God is misconstrued as a sovereign power over the created order. As we saw, for Thomas "power" is not an "internal operation," for God does not exercise power over himself. It is an "external operation." On this point, Thomas could have more carefully expressed how God is a causal power consistent with the divine essence and processions that he argued were necessary to understand creation well (*ST* I 32). He lost sight of that and often presented God as a monadic, causal force, as Jenson rightly critiques in doctrines of predestination. Williams offers an understanding of divine "power" as a causal agent more consistent with Thomas's best insights. Creation, recall, "is not an exercise of divine *power* . . . because it is not exercised *on* anything."[10] God is not causal power per se but the donating source of being. Hinlicky named this well; it is an expression we also saw in Aquinas. God is *esse deum dare*. But there is no reason to reject simplicity in order to affirm this account of divine agency.

Tanner's rules do not require the radical revisions modern theologians have called for. If we understand God's noncontrastive transcendence, then we do not need to resolve the divine-human

8. Ibid., 85.
9. Ibid.; see 92.
10. Rowan Williams, *On Christian Theology* (Oxford: Blackwell, 2000), 68–69.

freedom dilemma; the dilemma disappears. It only exists because of faulty understandings of transcendence, divine power, freedom, and divine-human competition. Her rules also allow us to incorporate the divine economy into the doctrine of God without requiring mutability or passibility. God can be affected by something other than God only if that something other is within a single order that contains both God and creatures. Rather than asking Jüngel's question, "Where is God?" these rules lead us to ask "Where is creation?" If God is infinite—without limits—and creates without change, then where does creation exist? It cannot exist outside God, for there is no "outside" to which God goes except in a metaphoric sense. Jenson implicitly poses this question in the final section to his first volume of a systematic theology, "Our Place in God." He uses two highly evocative images. First he tells us God does have a body, and it is Jesus. How Jesus' body now functions in God is left undeveloped, but he also presents God as a "great fugue" who is capacious.[11] It is a beautiful image and one that helps make sense of the relationship between infinity and simplicity as Thomas developed them. To add creation's voice to God's polyphonous perfectly simple Triune existence need not take away or add to what is already a beautiful harmony. It does not change God, for God is in no need of change. Hans Urs von Balthasar suggests something similar when he locates creation at the Second Hypostasis of the Trinity.[12] We are "in" God without any hint of pantheism or panentheism. The divine procession that eternally generates the real relation to the Son makes possible a space for a different relation, a temporal one, the logical relation of creation. It adds nothing to God, for finitude added to infinity makes no increase to infinity. It likewise offers no "composition," because God plus creation is not greater than God alone.[13] Locating creation at the Second Hypostasis, but as a different kind of relation, allows for the procession and mission

11. Robert Jenson, *Systematic Theology* (New York: Oxford University Press, 1997), 1:229, 236.
12. Hans Urs von Balthasar, *Theodrama II: The Dramatis Personae: Man in God,* trans. Graham Harrison (San Francisco: Ignatius Press, 1990), 260.
13. See Robert Sokolowski, *The God of Faith and Reason: Foundations of Christian Theology* (Washington, DC: Catholic University of America Press, 1995).

of the Son to have an identity without collapsing the temporal mission into the eternal procession and thus failing to distinguish the Triune relations of the persons from the God-creation relation. The legitimate concerns of the metaphysical questions are answered *because* of simplicity, eternity, immutability, and impassibility.

We can supplement Tanner's rules with a few others that help answer several of the questions and challenges posed in the preceding five chapters. Her first two rules should be affirmed: (1) "avoid both a simple univocal attribution of predicates to God and world and a simple contrast of divine and non-divine predicates"; and (2) "avoid in talk about God's creative agency all suggestions of limitation in scope or manner." The following three are further exemplifications of these two rules. They both adopt and qualify the reasons for the calls for revision. (3) Avoid depicting God such that God is not an agent who acts in the world, whose actions would be inconsistent with divine love and holiness. (4) Observe Rahner and Barth's rule, but do so mindful that the divine relations cannot be equated with God's relation to creation. The difference between these relations must be maintained in speech and writing. (5) "Power" should not be used in speaking of the relations of the Triune persons.[14] When it is used, as it should be used, use it to make sense of the God-creation relation. Do not make it a causal source of "power over" but a donating source of being. Nothing in the traditional answer as I presented it in the first two chapters violates these rules. In fact, understood at its best, it assists us in maintaining them.

Tanner's ruled relation helps us answer some of the questions raised above. The rules, however, remain at a formal, narrative level. They do not yet provide a doctrine of God as robust as one finds in Augustine, Dionysius, Thomas Aquinas, Zanchi, Arminius, or John Owen. More needs to be said.[15] Theology should recover its speculative task; it must

---

14. By *power* here is meant a monadic, causal force that acts on something to make it something it otherwise would not seek to be. It is not a denial of divine *potentia* if it is understood consistent with simplicity, perfection, immutability, and impassibility.
15. This is not intended as a critique of Tanner. No single work can do all that needs to be done. Only if the rules would somehow exclude a work like Sonderegger's would it be a criticism. I do not see how their two theological projects, different as they are, conflict.

take as its subject matter something more than humans-as-they-speak-about-God. It must speak of God.

Simplicity is a rule of theological grammar. It lets us know what cannot be said, and inasmuch as we know what cannot, it also helps us know what can and should be said. As Thomas explicitly noted, we must know something about who God is before we can know who God is not. Barth worried that simplicity would become a bare name, doing nothing more than relating God to us and not expressing the fullness of the divine life. There is a certain irony to this, because critics of "Barthian story" theology find Barth contributing to this very problem. Katherine Sonderegger identifies the problem well:

> In some modern movements within biblical studies, the doctrine of God is confined and determined by the words of Scripture itself, without remainder or qualification, so that the very Being of God comes to bear the historical, finite, and human traits of the biblical text itself. In some "narrative readings" of Scripture, for example, the Invisible Lord becomes *visible* with a concreteness unimaginable to the orthodox. God Almighty becomes a "character" in the "drama of Scripture."[16]

The problem occurs when Barth's rule goes bad, when the doctrine of God takes on the finite cadences of Scripture without attending to the metaphysics or theology that makes sense of the fact that God is the author of Scripture, not its main character. Rather than making God the author of the story, God becomes subordinate to it.

Francesca Murphy makes a similar argument to Sonderegger's. She worries that Barthian story theology and grammatical Thomism treat *story* as if it could stand in for the reality, especially the being, of God. God begins to look like a character in a story—temporal, passible, mutable, composite. *Story* becomes either the "foundation upon which God stands" or the category within which God is conceived.[17] Because narrative and grammar are finite historical creations dependent on human minds, the result for the doctrine of God is deleterious. "The 'God' of narrative theology is not self-subsistent being, *Ipsum esse*

16. Katherine Sonderegger, *Systematic Theology*, vol. 1, *God* (Minneapolis: Fortress Press, 2015), 1:551–52.
17. Francesca Murphy, *God Is Not a Story* (Oxford: Oxford University Press, 2007), 93.

Subsistens, but a being which is in its essence related to human minds. And this is thus a contingent existence, dependent upon a language-using other for its reality."[18] She asks why we have abandoned language such as *ousia* for that of *story*, as if *story* is somehow "less pagan or any more biblical."[19] Although one could quibble with Murphy's interpretation of numerous figures who represent Barthian story theology or grammatical Thomism, the fact that many of the revisions examined above depict God as such a character suggests there is something to her critique.

Narrative and metaphysics need not be an either-or, even if theologians and philosophers seek to make it such.[20] Murphy acknowledges as much. She worries about setting metaphysics against temporality. "Since Aristotle's *Metaphysics*," she notes, "all authentic philosophies have begun in *wonder*." Unfortunately, they too often have presupposed "the perspective of an adult male" who seeks to overcome historical contingency for certainty. Thus philosophers "detemporalize it."[21] Murphy seeks an "objectively given truth" that captivates the subject, rather than a subject who captures an object through a narrative grid that functions like a Kantian transcendental.[22] To do so, metaphysics does not bracket out history but attends more intensely to it. Metaphysics goes wrong when it confuses wonder with the wonderer and "forgets about what is inspiring the wonder."[23] She does not return to something like the neo-Thomist metaphysics of objectivity; instead, her metaphysics or authentic philosophy takes its cue from von Balthasar. Objectivity is found in the "amazed delight in existing" a mother's smile elicits from a child. She writes, "The

---

18. Ibid., 121.
19. "It is not easy to see how the idea of story as such is any less pagan or any more biblical than, say, that of *ousia*" (ibid., 294).
20. Murphy quotes Hans Frei's words to show how it was made an either-or. "We can sum up the previous discussion like this. Story Barthianism is, in Hans Frei's words, 'inquiring into the shape of a story and what it tells about a man, in contrast to metaphysical explanations that would tell us what sorts of things are or are not real and on what principles they cohere'" (ibid., 70).
21. Ibid., 221.
22. Ibid., 50. Tanner is less worried than Murphy about Kant's "transcendental analysis of subjective structures of consciousness." She finds such structures capable of working within her rules as much as previous metaphysical categories; Tanner, *God and Creation in Christian Theology*, 62–80. She brings Barth and Thomas together in this section.
23. Murphy, *God Is Not a Story*, 199.

principle which we have tried to express in many of our criticisms of a fictive God is that only a real, objectively given truth can make personal subjects of us; 'because of the "objectivity" of the mother's smile, the child's "subjectivity" is guaranteed.'"[24] The objective comes prior to the subjective, and it is the delight and fascination of the latter for the former that makes it a subject at all.

Murphy's objectivity finds common cause with Katherine Sonderegger's important course correction in contemporary theology. She acknowledges our situation. "Perhaps nothing so marks out the modern in systematic theology as the aversion to the scholastic treatise, *De Deo Uno*."[25] She finds this aversion mistaken and challenges it by reversing the order of modern theology that has become normative since the predominance of Rahner and Barth's rule. She dares to begin theology with "The One God." Kathryn Tanner has made a similar move, questioning modern theologians' preoccupation with finding a correlation between a proper Trinitarian theology, usually a "social trinitarianism," and a proper politics, as well as finding divine unity the problem that needs to be overcome. She asks, "can monotheism and Trinitarianism, for example, be this easily distinguished?"[26] Tanner and Sonderegger remind us of a simple fact, one I tried to emphasize in interpreting Thomas—God's unity is *essential* for any proper teaching of the Trinity.[27] To argue that beginning with divine unity is somehow not to begin with Trinity is already to have abandoned the teaching of the Trinity.

A cursory reading of Sonderegger's doctrine of God's oneness could lead one to think she has adopted the very position Rahner and Barth rejected. Not only does she reverse their order, but she states: "Not all is Trinity! The Unique One relates toward His creatures in His own Nature; that is His Power. These Divine Realities, the Nature and the Persons, are not *reducible,* One to the Other, but rather both are real,

---

24. Ibid., 310. See also 221.
25. Sonderegger, *Systematic Theology*, 1:xiv.
26. Kathryn Tanner, "Social Trinitarianism and Its Critics," in Robert J. Wozniak and Giulio Maspero, eds., *Rethinking Trinitarian Theology* (London: T&T Clark International, 2012), 371.
27. Sonderegger states, "we need only say that the Oneness of God comes under heavy threat in the world that Barth and Rahner have made"; Sonderegger, *Systematic Theology*, 1:9.

alive, distinct."[28] To state "Not all is Trinity" is nothing short of scandalous among modern theologians. She will repeat the same refrain with respect to Christology: "Not all is Christology!" For someone influenced by Barth (as Sonderegger is) to make this kind of statement seems to require not a revision to but a rejection of Barth's theological project.

To defend God's essence or nature and begin with "The One God" requires explanation. Has she posited a divine essence behind the persons who works independently of them? Has she made the nature or essence really distinct from the persons? It seems as though she has when she writes, "not all relations of God to the world are the Acts of the Persons! God relates to the world through His Nature as well."[29] So do we have numerous God-creation relations—Father-creation, Son-creation, Spirit-creation, and essence-creation? I think not. What we have is something much more profound, something that must be normed by her further commentary: "Not yet have we scaled the heights of Trinity, the dogma of Divine Mystery as Tripersonal, but we are never outside this Mystery, even or especially in the Divine Unity."[30] She reminds us of what we have lost sight in modern theology. God as Trinity is *one* in three. If we did not have the one God, if we did not have the Jewish and Christian prayer "Hear, O Israel, the Lord our God is one," then we would not have Trinity. The proper knowledge of God does not logically begin with Jesus revealed in the divine economy but with God who speaks to Moses, giving him an unmistakable image of his oneness.[31] If this were not the case, then when the apostle Thomas confesses before the resurrected Christ, "My Lord and my God" (John 20:28), or when the women after the Resurrection "took hold of his feet, and worshiped him" (Matt. 28:9), they would have been rejecting rather than reaffirming their Judaism with its "exclusive monotheism." Jesus must be Jewish because Jews were given the name, image, and theophanic manifestation of the one

28. Ibid., 1:268.
29. Ibid., 1:418.
30. Ibid., 1:247.
31. Sonderegger states, "Moses is the 'proper home of the knowledge of God'" (ibid., 1:405).

God. Had they been unable to identify that same manifestation in Jesus, then the event of the resurrection would have been nothing more than a Roman polytheistic encounter, and the teaching on the Trinity would have never emerged.

The oneness of God gives the biblical story its dramatic character. This oneness also allows for the event of the incarnation (an event that always includes Jesus' life, teachings, crucifixion, resurrection, ascension, and promised return) to present a new creation-God relation (practical theology 2) without compromising God's simplicity, perfection, holiness, or love. God does not change in the event of the incarnation. God's immutable, perfect simplicity is the ground that makes possible a change in the relation of creation to God, and not vice versa. So Sonderegger states, "Christ's Person manifests a fresh *relatio* in the cosmos, and so, in Christian doctrine. When we say so often, Not all is Christology!, we aim to preserve this very freshness."[32] If God has real relations with creation, there is no need for the incarnation. It brings nothing new but only exemplifies what always was. Creation and redemption are the same act. If it is a "fresh relation," then who is changed? If God is composite or mutable, then it signifies a transformation not of creation's relation to God but of God himself. If the incarnation changes God, then we must ask, why did God need to change? If God needed to change, even voluntarily, could the God who was in need of change be trusted? Was that pretransformational God not the God of perfect, holy love? Might that God return?

Sonderegger, if I understand her correctly, does not begin with "the One God" because we must first have a defensible metaphysical demonstration of God's existence by reason alone—as if such existed. She neither endorses the *analogia entis* nor the natural knowledge from Vatican I that putatively demonstrates God's existence with certainty, and under which Roman Catholic theology has labored since it was promulgated.[33] Her overriding concern is the unique Subject of Holy Scripture. Like Murphy, this Subject is not discovered by reading into

---

32. Ibid., 1:417.
33. Ibid., 1:441.

God's being the narrative structure within which those actions are presented but by catching a glimpse of what is withheld. "A proper doctrine of Scripture," Sonderegger states, "recognizes in the holy books a unique form, means and presence of the One Lord who dwells openly, yes, but also invisibly, secretly, within its pages."[34] It is the oddness of the Subject of Holy Scripture who also makes himself Object for our gaze and contemplation that animates her to begin with "the One God." The divine "nature" that relates to creation, then, is not a nature that exists apart from the three persons, but it is the one nature that is always expressed in and through the persons, a nature that communicates to creation even as the object of our speculative theology.[35]

Sonderegger returns us to the task of speculative theology. It is not an identical repetition of the traditional answer; without rejecting it, she nonetheless adds much to it.[36] This is as it should be. The traditional answer was only for beginners. It initiates a journey. It is not a list of attributes, a description, or a definition. It is never the final answer, for no final answer exists in theology. What she adds is a better account of divine power than one often finds in the tradition. She acknowledges that the emphasis on God as causal power is more indebted to Schleiermacher than Aquinas, but it nonetheless needs more careful articulation than Thomas himself provided. In discussing divine omnipotence, she "quietly sets aside the notion of *cause* as central to the doctrine of God, especially in the relation of God to the world, *ad extra*."[37] She presents the one divine power consistent with the Triune persons in a way Thomas suggested but seldom executed. Divine power is "a form of Goodness itself." It is that God is "the One for Others," as the "Lowly One." This power is divine holiness.[38]

---

34. Ibid., 1:521.
35. She writes, "God just is His own Relations, His own Subject in Object" (ibid., 1:268).
36. See ibid., 1:390, for the ways she "builds from the ground up" on the traditional answer.
37. Ibid., 1:78.
38. Ibid., 1:143, 151. She states, "in our day, we must say that Divine Omnipotence, the Lord's Holy Humility, must be removed from the category *cause* altogether. This radical break with the tradition—at least we must say with the early modern tradition, and its vigilance about causality—is warranted, I believe, by the aching demand in our day to view, to praise, and to accept once again the Reality, the Majesty, and the Goodness of Divine Power itself" (1:177).

If I were to follow this work up with a treatise on the doctrine of God, it would be similar to Sonderegger's. The fact that she has done it means I do not need to. I would question some things. Given what she has stated about divine power and holiness, I want to know more why she also states the following:

> The Attributes are identical to the Divine Nature; true. And indeed they just are Deity, the one surpassing and superabundant God. But they are not for all that identical to one another, nor ordered in such a way that the foundational Goodness of the Lord, say, measures and constricts the Reality and Act of Divine Power. Rather, the Divine Attributes are incommunicable in the One God; communicable to the world that the One Lord has made: just this is the surpassing Mystery of the Utterly, Unique God.[39]

What would it mean to say the attributes are "incommunicable" in the One God and yet "communicable" to the world? How does this fit with her important summons for theology always to be ordered toward divine perfection? "The doctrine of Divine Perfections must be the sum and summit of theology, and all we do hereafter must be nothing more than an outworking of this doctrine, a return to it so that everything—really everything—is bathed in its Light."[40] Given her opposition to divine composition, more yet needs to be said. But that is always the case with the perfectly simple, infinite, and eternal Triune God.

Sonderegger, like others, rightly raises the question of the identity of the divine attributes. As we have seen, analytic philosophers have posed this in terms of two different accounts of divine simplicity based on property-nature identity or property-property identity. The first states that each of the properties is identical with the divine nature, the second that each of the properties is identical with each other. The conclusion of the last chapter suggested that the language of substance (or nature) with properties is itself inappropriate; the language of property-property or property-nature identity is likewise too

---

39. Ibid., 1:163. I would also ask why she appears to oppose analogy and opts for Scotus's formal distinction.
40. Ibid., 1:394–95.

truncated, too simplistic to express the "transformation" divine simplicity went through in the patristic and the medieval eras. It is an analytic proposition laid over a much more nuanced discussion found in the tradition that requires hermeneutic attentiveness.

The discussion of relations in a perfectly simple God is without a doubt tricky. As Richard Muller notes, "Against Islamic and Jewish philosophy, the medieval scholastic theologians were pressed to argue that the distinctions between the persons were not divisions of the divine essence."[41] If God is simple, then it would seem to entail God has no real distinctions. We have already seen that Thomas argued it does not entail this conclusion. He was not being innovative; he was working with the consistent "transformation" of simplicity required by the doctrine of the Trinity.[42] If the persons are real distinctions in a simple divine essence, then to assume that attributes are also really distinct would be to proliferate persons excessively. But this did not mean Thomas and others only taught that the diverse attributes have a strict identity to a bare existence. Dolezal points out that the distinctions among the attributes could take different forms. They could, per Ockham, be purely conceptual, per Scotus formal, or per Aquinas "virtual." Aquinas's virtual distinction is "a distinction of reason with an extramental foundation in its object."[43] Exactly what that "extramental foundation" is we do not know; it is beyond us via the way of eminence. It is not a real distinction, however, or it would be a procession, and that is not possible. Nor is it a strict identity in which the appearance of divine wisdom or mercy is all reducible to nothing but existence. Christopher Hughes has critiqued Thomas along these lines. He finds simplicity teaching that God's essence is

---

41. Richard A. Muller, *Post-Reformation Reformed Dogmatics*, vol. 3, *The Divine Essence and Attributes* (Grand Rapids: Baker Academic, 2003), 50.

42. See Andrew Radde-Gallwitz, *Basil of Caesarea, Gregory of Nyssa and the Transformation of Divine Simplicity* (Oxford: Oxford University Press, 2009). Radde-Gallwitz's excellent history of simplicity in Basil and Gregory assumes that Plantinga properly identifies Aquinas's teaching on simplicity as the "identity thesis." He then distances Basil and Gregory from it. He is successful, however, only if Plantinga adequately presents Thomas's teaching. See Lawrence Dewan, "Saint Thomas, Alvin Plantinga, and the Divine Simplicity," *The Modern Schoolman* 66 (1989): 141–51, for an argument that he has not.

43. James Dolezal, *God without Parts: Divine Simplicity and the Metaphysics of God's Absoluteness* (Eugene, OR: Pickwick, 2011), 133.

existence and denying that there is more to God than existence. He states, "it does not follow that there is nothing more to God's essence than His existence." He seems to think that this is what Thomas's teaching on simplicity suggests. As we saw above, Thomas himself raised this possibility when he asked whether we should add "life" to *esse* in the doctrine of God and argued that we should. It is always possible that Thomas was inconsistent, but his teaching on simplicity simply does not do what Hughes thinks it must do. Hughes himself acknowledges as much. It could be that Hughes has laid a reductive grid over Thomas from his analytic method that lacks the hermeneutic richness to discern how simplicity is being used.[44] The traditional answer is content with a level of apophaticism and metaphor that much of modern philosophy and theology is not.[45] A richer hermeneutical approach is necessary if we are to make sense of the perfectly simple Triune God.

Sarah Coakley's *théologie totale* points in such a direction. She addresses the questions posed by analytic theology and in response opens a way for a more speculative or contemplative theology. She affirms analytic theology's logical rigor but questions its "hemeneutical blindness."[46] Its methodological desire for precision prevents it from discerning the heart of mystical practices. She does not reject the analytic approach but supplements it with a hermeneutic richness that has space for the traditional answer.

For Coakley, the analytic approach moves in a salutary direction because it acknowledges the collapse of classic foundationalism and in so doing offers new resources for theology. Michael Rea argues

---

44. See Christopher Hughes, *On a Complex Theory of a Simple God: An Investigation in Aquinas's Philosophical Theology* (Ithaca, NY: Cornell University Press, 1989), 55.

45. Muller notes, "To argue that a rational distinction can have a basis in the properties of a thing presses the question of the relationship between logical being and real being: Aquinas's notion of a rational distinction founded in the thing assumes that our attributions reflect actual properties and are not merely rational distinctions made for the convenience of the human knower. What Aquinas does not do, at least not to the satisfaction of later scholastics, is make clear precisely what kind of distinction there may be in the thing that is reflected in the distinctions made by reason concerning the thing"; Muller, *Post-Reformation Reformed Dogmatics*, 3:56.

46. Sarah Coakley, "Dark Contemplation and Epistemic Transformation: The Analytic Theologian Re-Meets Theresa of Avila," in Oliver D. Crisp and Michael C. Rea, eds., *Analytic Theology: New Essays in the Philosophy of Theology* (Oxford: Oxford University Press, 2009), 280.

that after this collapse there are still two forms of "foundationalism" possible—doxastic and source. Doxastic foundationalism does not claim a universal foundation available to all right-thinking people based on the intellect qua intellect, but it holds that some beliefs are "properly basic," and once those beliefs are established they can provide a foundation for an adequate knowledge of God. Source foundationalism differs from both doxastic and classical foundationalism in that it argues certain sources have a reliability to them unless evidence is provided to the contrary. It is then irrational "to rely on other sources of evidence unless they are somehow 'certified' by the privileged sources."[47] Coakley affirms the analytic approach for the correlative emphases on testimony, credulity, religious experience, and mysticism that it opens up. She suggests it is an unconscious wrestling with the feminine. However, analytic theologians miss the hermeneutic import of mystical texts, especially in their "excess" and apophaticism.[48] She does not put it this way, but the point seems to be that analytic fascination with propositions seeks to clarify what often exceeds its methodological constraints. More so than many analytic theologians, she recognizes God is not a being among beings. "God, being God, is unlike *any* Other, and thus by definition is not to be 'perceived' in a way straightforwardly akin to any other item in the universe (which is his own creation, after all). Should we not then positively expect an 'experience' of God in contemplation to be epistemically unique, even bizarre?"[49] Her point fits well both with Tanner's rules and Sonderegger's journey into the oneness of God. God's uniqueness opens up new epistemic possibilities, especially a rapprochement with mysticism. Reason is informed by desire, the body, and the mystical experience of "darkness." Coakley suggests that we find this richer, hermeneutically informed theology in a mystic such as Teresa of Àvila, for in her teaching on God, "in a way impossible to describe clearly (or at least not without metaphorical stretching and apophatic reminders) the sensual, the apophatic, and

---

47. Rea, "Introduction," in Crisp and Rea, *Analytic Theology*, 13.
48. Coakley, "Dark Contemplation and Epistemic Transformation," 285.
49. Ibid., 306.

the intellectual are now all one, and Christ is all in all."[50] For this mystical experience, "reason" and "perception" have been transformed. "Here we do not so much grasp or 'perceive' God, but more truly God grasps us—if at any rate we over time have fostered the special epistemic passivity that is the condition for the possibility of this graced contemplative occurrence."[51]

Coakley's "new venture" in the doctrine of the Trinity is unusual in that she takes desire and prayer as central to theology, appealing to both "ascetic transformation" and "ascetic fidelity" for a contemplative theology that "keeps ethics, doctrine and spiritual practice tightly wound together."[52] She avoids any reactionary antimodern theology that takes refuge in "revelatory or magisterial authority," a "new theological meta-narrative" that has a nostalgia for the premodern, or a liberal feminist/liberation theology found "in certain forms of post-Kantian American liberal theology," in which "'God' is freely reconceived to fit with pragmatist feminist goals."[53] Instead of these possible approaches, she adopts a "*théologie totale*."

Théologie totale begins in contemplation by "radical attention to the Real." Contemplation is not "speculative" in the sense so many modern theologians have come to deride—an abstract metaphysics that detaches from everyday life. It is a practice of "primary ascetical submission to the divine demanded by revelation, and the link to the creative source of life for which it continually returns." Speculative theology should be a form of contemplative prayer that includes an apophatic element, not as a counter to ontotheology or obedience to Kantian restrictions on transcendental illusions, but as an emptying, coming to know what God is not, so it can also be a filling, knowing who God is. For that reason, theology will also be an "interruption of the Spirit." It is also always *in via*. As a journey, it includes all the sciences available to it without granting them an autonomy founded on a "pure nature." It seeks orthodoxy not as a foundation but as a goal.

---

50. Ibid., 296.
51. Ibid., 300.
52. Sarah Coakley, *God, Sexuality, and the Self* (Cambridge: Cambridge University Press, 2013), 87.
53. Ibid., 75.

It acknowledges "social location," but not the untenable claim that because our knowledge is always socially located it can also be limited to its social situation. It takes "desire" as its "constellating theological category," and attends to "aesthetic expression." It also resists the many bifurcations of modern theology such as belief/practice and practical/systematic. Finally, it does not discount or reject the classical loci but enriches them.[54] What we find in Coakley's approach to the doctrine of the Trinity is a retrieval without nostalgic return, an expansion without rejection or reaction. She shows how to move out of the domination of "practical" theology and begin in contemplation/speculation without losing the importance of practice. In so doing, God is not tied to creation by our mastery of theology; instead, creation is taken up by the Spirit into the divine life. The necessary distinctions, and relations, among God's triune relations, God's relation to creation, and creation's relation to God are preserved.

The Simple, Perfect Triune God Revisited

Tanner's rules, Sonderegger's doctrine of God's oneness, and Coakley's *théologie totale* bring the traditional answer forward into modern advancements in the doctrine of God without some of the ruptures or radical revisions that the antimetaphysical, liberation, analytic, open theist, and process theology's questioners called for.

The perfectly simple Triune God should be presented so that the divine economy is integrated into the teaching of the Trinity. It does not need to be set forward in terms of two treatises, one on the divine essence and the other on the procession of the persons; both are necessary. But if we do not have a way of naming the divine essence, then we do not have a doctrine of the Trinity. The names Thomas uses are first and foremost names. As Janet Soskice reminds us, "When Aquinas dealt with such predicates as 'eternal,' 'One,' and 'simple,' he stood in a tradition of reflections *de nominibus dei* going back to Denys the Areopagite and beyond—a theological and mystical as well as a

---

54. Ibid., 88–92.

philosophical tradition." However, once metaphysics and philosophy become independent disciplines in the later Middle Ages and into early modernity, then a confidence in reason alone displaces this tradition of the divine names. Soskice continues,

> Locke's confidence that not only God's existence but also God's qualities could be spelled out apart from revelation and through rational reflection alone is new, or rather was new in Descartes, whom Locke follows here. Apellations that had been distinctively theological became with Descartes the terminology of rational analysis and metaphysics alone. With Descartes the "divine names" have become the "classical attributes."[55]

What should concern contemporary theologians is that the tradition of the divine names, a mystical and liturgical tradition, has been reduced to metaphysical properties known in the same way all other properties can be known. The unique object and subject God is then enmeshed in a single order in which God can only be an object among other objects.

The metaphysical question raises the legitimate concern how the divine economy is fully integrated into the doctrine of God. Those who raise this question often accept a narrative that imagines a Trinitarian renaissance occurred some time after the Reformation. Seeds were set in place that led to furthering the Reformation beyond the limited concerns of the early Reformers themselves, seeds that came to fruition in the nineteenth and twentieth centuries. Luther or Hegel or Barth, or some combination thereof, are given credit for this renaissance. As Olson and Hall put it, the twentieth century "turned slowly but inexorably into a tidal wave of Christian rediscovery of and new reflection on the Trinity."[56] A more modest claim is possible. The twentieth century neither "rediscovered" the Trinity, as if it had been lost outside the narrow confines of a few modern Protestant theologians, nor did it offer something new. Too much credit has been given Hegel for preserving the doctrine of the Trinity. His narrative of the transition of Spirit from Substance to Subject, while intriguing

---

55. Janet Soskice, "Naming God: A Study in Faith and Reason," in Paul Griffiths and Reinhard Hütter, *Reason and the Reasons of Faith* (New York: Continuum, 2005), 247.
56. Roger E. Olson and Christopher A. Hall, *The Trinity* (Grand Rapids: Eerdmans, 2002), 96.

and perhaps a proper correction to some teachings on God, has had too much influence on modern theology. Although what Hegel taught is, and will be, contested, one result has been a tendency for modern theologians to construe God's relations to creation as a real relationship. Once that occurs, then in creation God encounters God's self. God suffers in order to *become* God for us. Theogony replaces theology. The divine economy itself has become as much about God redeeming God's self as it is about God redeeming creation.

This revised economy has had too much of a hold on modern theology. The need to be "modern" is part of the problem, when the "modern" is understood as a never-ending apocalyptic moment in which everything we have done up until this moment does not prepare us for the "now" that is about to arrive but never does. Everything must be revised; everything must be new. There has been a modern, apocalyptic anxiety about theology that seeks calls for revision and is fated to continue to do so, each call for revision trying to be more apocalyptic and historical than the previous one. The historical situatedness of this assumption need not hold us captive. To challenge this modern anxiety is not to wax nostalgic for premodernity.

How far modern theology must go in revising the traditional answer will depend on whether Barth and Rahner identified a local malady or an epidemic. Many of the theologians find an epidemic that plays into a hypermodern, apocalyptic anxiety. It makes one wonder where divine providence was if theology so thoroughly lost sight of its core constitutive practice, the worship of God. There was a local malady that needed to be addressed. What was necessary, and happened, was a rejection of the sharp division between two treatises *de deo uno* and *de deo trino*, a division that was marked by the "counters" from the Council of Trent, through Vatican I and into Leo XIII's 1879 encyclical *Aeterni patris*. Barth's theology, taken up by its eloquent Roman Catholic interlocutors, united those two treatises into the unity in which they belonged from the patristic into the early medieval teachings on the Trinity. God's simple perfection found its rightful place in the Triune processions. Unfortunately, the necessary revision let loose a flurry of revisions that nearly abandoned the oneness of God and focused on divine identity rather than the divine essence or nature.

The traditional answer has not adequately addressed the questions raised by liberation and/or postcolonial theology. Those questions will inevitably highlight practical theology and focus less on speculative theology. As Coakley notes, these two should not be opposed. Theology cannot be reduced to practice, but speculation without practice only advances the "scholastic disposition" Jennings and Carter warn against. Both speculative and practical theology are always necessary if God is to be the object of theology. If God is only what God is because of what God has done for us, then God becomes an instrumental good. Walter Kasper finds this reduction to be a perennial temptation for Protestant theology. It begins, he suggests, with Luther's stress on the *pro me* emphasis in Christ and accentuated by Melanchthon's "one sided emphasis" on this principle. It reduces Christology, and we could add, the doctrine of God, to soteriology.[57] All that we know of God is what God is for us. There is a secular correlate to this so-called Melanchthonian epistemology that is found among the left-wing Hegelians.

Luce Irigaray's work illustrates this secular correlate well; she remains on the Nietzschean quest and tells us, "A female god is still to come." The pressing question is, "How is our God to be imagined?" The answer for "Divine Women" is, oddly enough, found in Feuerbach:

> Do we possess a quality that can reverse the predicate to the subject, as Feuerbach does for *God* and *man* in the analysis of *The Essence of Christianity*? If there is no one quality, which of the many would we choose to conceive our becoming perfect women? This is not a luxury but a necessity, the need for a finalized, theoretical, and practical activity that would be both speculative and moral. Every man (according to Feuerbach) and every woman who is not fated to remain a slave to the logic of the essence of man, must imagine a God, an objective-subjective place or path whereby the self could be coalesced in space and time. . . . God alone can save us, keep us safe. The feeling or experience of a positive, objective, glorious existence, the feeling of subjectivity, is essential for us. Just like a God who helps us and leads us in the path of becoming, who keeps track

57. Walter Kasper, *Jesus the Christ* (London: Burns & Oates, 1976), 22.

of our limits and our infinite possibilities—as women—who inspires our projects. These might include not just *opposition to, criticism of,* but also *positing new values* that would be essentially divine.[58]

Irigaray has a space for "God" in the emancipatory journey that will make women divine and perfect her subjectivity; what opens up this space for divine women is Feuerbach's philosophy and Nietzsche's quest. Theology's task is the a-theologian's projection of divinity for the sake of my, or our, subjectivity. Although such a subjectivity is essential to the theological vocation, more is needed than what she allows; the more is a speculative theology irreducible to practical theology.

Kasper suggests that what prevents the reduction of theology to soteriology, sacred or secular, is the fact that "[a] Christian is so to speak compelled to become a metaphysician on the account of his faith."[59] As we saw above, Gutiérrez made a similar claim. What is needed for liberation is not just how God is for us, but "an authentic deep sense of God," a proper view of God's transcendence. He cites Cone to remind us of the need for a speculative theology: "God is always more than our experience of him."[60] To express this "more," and to express that it cannot exhaustively be expressed, is the task of speculative theology. It is to wonder, to refuse the reduction of God to a logical puzzle set forth in propositions. It is to pray and be caught up in the Spirit.

Speculative theology matters for liberation and postcolonial theology because it reminds us that God is other than a "power-over." The powerful have a stake in maintaining God as power, for it serves their interests. An epistemology rooted in a social context affirming that all our knowledge is a claim to power has little prospect for political transformation. As Bernard Williams notes, "The hard-pressed chairman of an English department once confessed to me that, faced with a group of faculty accusing him of being an agent of the hegemonic power structure, he would have liked to say, 'You're right,

---

58. Luce Irigaray, *Sexes and Genealogies* (New York: Columbia University Press, 1993), 67.
59. Kasper, *Jesus the Christ*, 21.
60. Gustavo Gutiérrez, *The God of Life* (Maryknoll, NY: Orbis, 1996), 27.

and you're fired.'"[61] There is a theological correlate. If theology is only about the power to name God from our context for the sake of our liberation, then those who have traditionally held the power to name God will have no motivation to consider how our naming of God could be other than what it is. If, however, theology has a speculative dimension that is not ensconced in power-over, then such considerations must be heard. Sarah Coakley accomplishes this reconsideration of our images for God when she juxtaposes what the tradition says theoretically about God—divine simplicity entails that God is not male—with its artistic expressions.[62] They universally say something other. If speculative theology is true, then artistic and liturgical expressions need to be open to change.

Chapter 3 attempted to show that Kasper is wrong about Luther and Melanchthon. Neither of them reduced theology to the practical task of soteriology. The fact that they maintained the perfectly, simple God and argued for it demonstrates as much. The political importance of divine simplicity is its utter uselessness. This uselessness can be seen if we bring to mind again the three relationships about which theology is concerned—God in God's self (speculative theology), God's relation to creation (practical theology 1), and creation's relationship to God (practical theology 2). Practical theology 1 and 2 always face the temptation of making God useful, turning God into a utilitarian, pragmatic, or instrumental value. In an era in which nearly everything can be given a value, placed on a continuum, and traded based on formal equivalence, having a useless God may be the most useful aspect of theology. God is not there to secure our politics, our nation, our future, our knowledge, our religion, our economy, our family, our souls, or our way of life. God is not a foundation for anything, for there is nothing that can be built on an infinite, perfectly simple God. God is there to be enjoyed, to become enraptured with, to take us out of ourselves (*ekstasis*) and into that which is other than us solely because God is beautiful perfection, good, wise, and holy. In God these names

---

61. Bernard Williams, *Truth and Truthfulness* (Princeton, NJ: Princeton University Press, 2004), 8.
62. See Sarah Coakley, "Seeing God: Trinitarian Thought through Iconography," in *God, Sexuality, and the Self*, 190–206.

are not competitive or even "parts" that can be used by us for some instrumental gain. They are meant to be enjoyed. Speculative theology is not the entirety of theology, and we have no access to it apart from practical theology, but without it "God" will too easily become an instrumental good. Theology is more than soteriology, sacred or secular.

Analytic theology trains our language to be precise, and that is an important gain. Because God delights, as Sonderegger notes, in being not only an unsublatable Subject but also an object for our gaze, we need not fear the logical quest for God. Reason and logic have a necessary place, especially when they draw on testimony, desire, witness, and belief. But if we must adopt univocal terms in order to exact precision, the cost is too much. John Milbank has been critiqued for his interpretation of Duns Scotus, and I will leave it to Scotus scholars to argue over the particulars, but the way Scotus and univocity are used by analytic theology and others who seek revision to the traditional answer demonstrates Milbank is not wrong in the reception of Scotus among contemporary theologians. It is insufficient to argue Scotus is only giving us a conceptual or linguistic theory of predication when the results demand such thoroughgoing revisions to metaphysics and the traditional answer. Analytic theology will need to use its method to better effect before its large claims to supplant the continental tradition, and even contemporary theology, can be believed. The doctrine of God it often presents is so confused that even those working with the method find it objectionable. Its effort to treat theology as problems and dilemmas to be resolved poses constant temptations to secularize theology and treat it as a mathematical equation rather than a mystery to be lived. Of course, as noted above, its soberer practitioners resist this temptation.

Open theism seeks the laudable goal of preserving divine and human freedom, but it too asks too high a price. The traditional answer handled this much better by attending to Tanner's rules. Only if modern, libertarian freedom must define both God and creatures are its radical revisions necessary, but then have we not conceived something greater than God—libertarian freedom? Open theists are also deeply influenced by a doctrine of univocity similar to process theology.

These theologians find illogical Aquinas's claim that God can be the primary "cause" of all that is, and yet human creatures have a "secondary causality" that is free and makes a difference in creaturely existence. Aquinas uses the metaphor of God as artisan to explain this by drawing on Aristotle's distinction between practical and speculative knowledge. Aquinas writes, "The knowledge of God is the cause of all things. For the knowledge of God is to all creatures what the knowledge of the artificer is to things made by his art. Now the knowledge of the artificer is the cause of the things made by his art from the fact that the artificer works through his intellect" (ST I 14.8 resp.). Burrell explains this, "Taking a cue from Aquinas's strategy regarding God's knowledge of singulars, we must say that divine knowledge extends as far as divine activity, for God does not work mindlessly."[63] Milbank and Pickstock refer to the image of God's knowledge of creatures as akin to that of a "rusticus" or "country bumpkin." This knowledge is even more material than that of an "artisan," for it goes beyond knowledge of the form and extends to the material itself, to the singular.[64] God knows not just in general, or the universal cause; God knows all singulars, even "future contingents." God knows them like the artisan because God makes them. God knows them like the *rusticus* because God is intimately present to them in their singularity. God knows this by knowing God's self: "for He sees all things other than Himself in Himself, and He knows Himself speculatively; and so in the speculative knowledge of Himself; He possesses both speculative and practical

---

63. David Burrell, "Act of Creation with Its Theological Consequences," in *Aquinas on Doctrine*, ed. Thomas G. Weinandy, Daniel Keating, and John Yocum (New York: T&T Clark, 2004), 30.

64. "Aquinas suggests that God is much more of a country bumpkin (*rusticus*) capable of a brutal direct unreflective intuition of cloddish earth, bleared and smeared with toil. For God's mind, although immaterial, is (in a mysterious way) commensurate with matter, since God creates matter. Because he can *make* matter, so also he can *know* it. This does not mean that He receives matter into Himself; He does not receive forms or species either. Rather, He knows by the one species which is His essence, and knows things outside Himself entirely by His productive capacity—form and matter alike—for both are fundamentally existence. At this point, one might note how very far Aquinas has moved from Aristotle"; Catherine Pickstock and John Milbank, *Truth in Aquinas* (London: Routledge, 2001), 14.

knowledge of all other things" (*ST* I 14.16 ad 3). It is the most intimate form of love; perhaps a good metaphor for it is the one McFague used—a divine Mother who intimately knows the creation within her.

God's knowledge of all things "in Himself" such that they are "other things" fits well Tanner's two orders. God's artistic expression through creation makes creaturely freedom possible. God and creation do not occupy the same ontological "space." Therefore no competition exists between God and creatures. God's knowledge predestines all that God makes, including possible future contingents (which would not be future to God but only to us). Our will nevertheless freely causes what it causes without being determined to do so by God's knowledge. The two "causes" do not compete in a monocausal ontological plane. It would be illogical if we accept any kind of logical positivism or doctrine of univocity as the condition for making truthful and meaningful utterances. That just "fixes the game" before we start. It flattens out the mystery and reduces God's creation to an immanence that knows no proper, noncontrastive transcendence.

We moderns are preoccupied with the problem of evil. If God's knowledge is the cause of all things, then we are thrust into David Hume's intractable either-or, either God is good but not omniscient/omnipotent or God is omniscient/omnipotent but evil. Aquinas, like Augustine, does not find himself caught on the horns of this dilemma because he does not make "evil" a thing that can be known. God's knowledge of evil then cannot cause it, for what God knows is the "perfection" and goodness of all things. God's knowledge of evil is only in the "degree" to which evil is the "privation of good" (*ST* I 14.10 resp.). God's knowledge of evil is not "speculative," for speculative knowledge "is the consideration of truth," and there is no truth in evil. God's "practical" knowledge extends only to the things God makes. Evil is not something God makes, and so we would expect that Aquinas would also reject a practical knowledge of evil for God. This is not the case. God does not cause evil, but God nevertheless has a practical knowledge of it because in knowing the good God creates, God also knows the failures of human creatures to attain that good and their resultant evil. God only knows evil because God creates the good, which thereby permits evil. God knows it as God heals it. "And as regards evil things, although they are not operable by Him, yet they fall under His practical knowledge, as also do good things, inasmuch as He permits, or impedes, or directs them; just as sicknesses fall under the practical knowledge of the physician, inasmuch as he cures them by his art" (ST I 14.16 resp.).

If this does not render "evil" intelligible, then all the better for it. Thomas's teaching goes awry when he offers a theoretical resolution to evil in his teaching on predestination. Christian theology should never make evil intelligible or seek to justify it; it always remains unintelligible, unknowable—a surd that is surprising and ultimately not to be made into a thing because it is nothing. The problem with process theology is that it thinks it has accomplished something positive by solving the theoretical problem of evil; in so doing it renders evil intelligible and thus gives it being. I find more wisdom in the position Aquinas and Augustine shared (in their better moments). St. Augustine puts it this way, "The movement away from God does not come from God, so where does it come from? If you put the question like that, I must reply that I do not know. That may sadden you, but my answer is still right. There can be no knowledge of what is nothing."[65] Aquinas's (and Augustine's) answers may not satisfy all inquiring minds. They do not answer all the questions about God's freedom and human freedom, or about the questions of evil. But then, Aquinas never intended to provide such a complete system. Who could? Perhaps the temptation to offer such a complete system leads to the practical theologies that tie God to creation, ontologize evil, and make God and creation competing causes located in the same space and time. The result is not a God that loves, but a god who loves like we do, which, given our track record, may not be that reassuring. Only a God can save us, but it must be a God who is more than the god who is nothing but the god who saves us.

---

65. Quoted in Hans Urs von Balthasar, *The Glory of the Lord: A Theological Aesthetics, II: Studies in Theological Style: Clerical Styles* (San Francisco: Ignatius, 1984), 105.

Appendix

The following table lists the number of explicit references Thomas makes to each of the books of the Old Testament.

Genesis	8
Exodus	8
Leviticus	0
Numbers	3
Deuteronomy	7
Joshua	0
Judges	0
Ruth	0
1 Samuel	1
2 Samuel	0
1 Kings	1
2 Kings	1
1 Chronicles	0
2 Chronicles	0
Ezra	0
Nehemiah	0
Esther	0
Job	11
Psalms	40

Proverbs	8
Ecclesiastes	2
Song of Solomon	0
Isaiah	14
Jeremiah	7
Lamentations	2
Ezekiel	0
Daniel	1
Hosea	1
Joel	1
Amos	1
Obadiah	0
Jonah	0
Micah	2
Nahum	0
Habakkuk	0
Zephaniah	0
Haggai	0
Zechariah	1
Malachi	1
Tobit	0
Judith	0
1 Maccabees	0
2 Maccabees	1
Wisdom	16
Ecclesiasticus	10
Baruch	0
Total	**148**

New Testament Citations:

Matthew	18
Mark	0
Luke	5
John	39
Acts of the Apostles	3
Romans	35
1 Corinthians	25
2 Corinthians	5
Galatians	2
Ephesians	9
Philippians	3
Colossians	3
1 Thessalonians	1
2 Thessalonians	1
1 Timothy	7
2 Timothy	5
Titus	2
Philemon	0
Hebrews	12
James	5
1 Peter	0
2 Peter	2
1 John	9
2 John	0
3 John	0
Jude	0
Revelation	0
Total	**191**

Below is a table of the sources Aquinas assumed were from Augustine.

Not all of them are considered written by Augustine. They are ordered by their appearance in the *Summa*.

Source	Total Citations	Citations in First Treatise	Citations in Second Treatise
De Trinitate	81	19	62
Confessiones	7	4	3
Contra Vicentium Donatistam	1	1	0
Enchiridion	9	9	0
De Verbis Domini	2	1	1
De Civitas Dei	22	20	2
De Doctrina Christiana	4	4	0
Super Genesim ad Litteram	14	14	0
De Natura Boni	3	3	0
De diversis quaestionibus LXXXIII	20	15	5
Ad Volusianum	1	1	0
De Videndo Deum ad Paulinam	6	6	0
De Vera Religione	8	6	2
Soliloquia	6	6	0
Retractationes	1	1	0
De Libero Arbitrio	3	3	0
Super Ioannem	5	2	3
Praedestinatio Sanctorum	3	3	0
De Correptione et Gratia	1	1	0
Contra Faustum	1	1	0
Contra Maximinum	8	1	7
De Fide ad Petrum	7	0	7
De Haeresibus	2	0	2
Ad Orosium	2	0	2
No specific reference	30	20	10
Totals	**247**	**141**	**106**

Finding the quotation in Augustine's *De Trinitate* that Augustine cites is not always easy, as we will see below. This table lists the places in *De Trinitate* that Aquinas cites.

Thomas's Citations of Augustine's *De Trinitate*	Number of Citations	Location in prima pars
Book 1	5	6.2, 12.12, 31.2, 32.4, 39.4, 39.5
Book 2	4	43.4, 43.7, 43.7, 43.8
Book 3	2	19.5, 43.7
Book 4	11	33.1, 38.2, 39.5, 43.3, 43.3, 43.4, 43.5, 43.6, 43.6, 43.6, 43.8
Book 5	8	13.7, 13.7, 28.2, 33.4, 36.4, 40.3, 40.3, 41.1
Book 6	13	8.4, 12.12, 31.3, 31.3, 31.4, 34.2, 34.2, 35.2, 37.2, 37.2, 42.1, 42.1, 42.1
Book 7	21	3.7, 6.4, 14.4, 28.3, 28.2, 29.4, 29.4, 29.4, 30.2, 30.4, 31.2, 34.1, 34.1, 34.1, 36.1, 37.2, 39.1, 39.2, 39.5, 39.7
Book 8	0	
Book 9	2	12.2, 43.5
Book 10	0	
Book 11	0	
Book 12	1	1.6
Book 13	0	
Book 14	1	1.2
Book 15	17	10.3, 12.2, 12.2, 12.10, 14.7, 14.8, 34.1, 36.1, 37.1, 37.1, 37.2, 38.1, 38.1, 38.2, 41.3, 43.3, 43.8
No book mentioned	2	34.1, 39.8

Bibliography

Alston, William P. "Substance and the Trinity." In *The Trinity*, edited by Stephen Davis, Daniel Kendall, and Gerald O'Collins, 179–203. Oxford: Oxford University Press, 1999.

Aquinas, Thomas. *On Being and Essence*. Translated by Armand Mauer. Toronto: Pontifical Institute of Mediaeval Studies, 1983.

_____. *Opusculum de Ente et Essentia*. 3rd edition. Torino: Marietti, 1957.

_____. *Summa Theologiae*. Textum Leonimum Romanum. www.corpus thomisticum.org.

_____. *Summa Theologiae*. Translated by Alfred J. Freddoso. December 23, 2014. Accessed at http://www3.nd.edu/~afreddos/summa-translation/TOC.htm.

Aristotle. *Posterior Analytics*. In *The Works of Aristotle*, translated by G. R. G. Mure, edited by W. D. Ross and J. A. Smith. Oxford: Clarendon Press, 1928.

Arminius, Jacobus. *Works*. Translated by James Nichols and William Bagnall. Grand Rapids: Baker, 1977.

Asselt, Willem J. van, and Eef Dekker, editors. *Reformation and Scholasticism: An Ecumenical Enterprise*. Grand Rapids: Baker Academic, 2001.

Augustine. *Confessions*. Translated by R. S. Pine-Coffin. London: Penguin Classics, 1961.

_____. *De Trinitate*. In *Corpus Christianorum, Series Latina*. Edited by W. J. Mountain, F. Glorie. Turnhout, Belgium: Brepols, 1968.

_____. *The Trinity*. Translated by Stephen McKenna, CSSR. Washington, DC: Catholic University of America Press, 1970.

Ayres, Lewis. *Augustine and the Trinity*. Cambridge: Cambridge University Press, 2010.

____. "Into the Cloud of Witnesses: Catholic Trinitarian Theology beyond and before Its Modern 'Revivals.'" In *Rethinking Trinitarian Theology*, edited by Robert J. Wozniak and Giulio Maspero, 3–26. London: T&T Clark International, 2012.

____. *Nicaea and Its Legacy: An Approach to Fourth-Century Trinitarian Theology*. Oxford: Oxford University Press, 2004.

____. "On Not Three People: The Fundamental Themes of Gregory of Nyssa's Trinitarian Theology as Seen in *To Ablabius: On Not Three Gods*." *Modern Theology* 18, no. 4 (2002): 445–74.

Balthasar, Hans Urs von. *The Glory of the Lord: A Theological Aesthetics, II: Studies in Theological Style: Clerical Styles*. Translated by Andrew Louth, Francis McDonagh, and Brian McNeil, CRV. San Francisco: Ignatius, 1984.

____. *Theo-Drama*, vol. II: *The Dramatis Personae: Man in God*. Translated by Graham Harrison. San Francisco: Ignatius Press, 1990.

Barnes, M. R. "Augustine in Contemporary Trinitarian Theology." *Theological Studies* 56 (1995): 237–50.

____. "De Régnon Reconsidered." *Augustinian Studies* 26 (1995): 51–79.

Barth, Karl. *Church Dogmatics*. 4 parts in 14 vols. Translated by Geoffrey W. Bromiley. Edited by G. W. Bromiley and T. F. Torrance. 2nd ed. Edinburgh: T&T Clark, 1956–75.

Bauerschmidt, Frederick. *Thomas Aquinas: Faith, Reason and Following Christ*. Oxford: Oxford University Press, 2013.

Bergmann, M., and J. Brower. "A Theistic Argument against Platonism and in Support of Truthmakers and Divine Simplicity." *Oxford Studies in Metaphysics* 2 (2006): 357–86.

Biddle, John. *A Twofold Catechism: The One Simply called A Scripture Catechism; The Other A brief Scripture-Catechism for Children*. London: printed by J. Cottrel, 1654.

Bielfeldt, Dennis, Mickey L. Mattox, and Paul R. Hinlicky. *The Substance of the Faith: Luther's Doctrinal Theology for Today*. Minneapolis: Fortress Press, 2008.

Boyd, Gregory. *God of the Possible*. Grand Rapids: Baker Books, 2000.

Boyd, R. H. S. *India and the Latin Captivity of the Church*. London: Cambridge University Press, 1974.

Brian, Rustin E. *Jakob Arminius: The Man from Oudewater*. Eugene, OR: Cascade, 2015.

Brower, Jeffrey E. "Simplicity and Aseity." In *The Oxford Handbook of Philosophical Theology*, edited by Thomas P. Flint and Michael Rea, 105–29. Oxford: Oxford University Press, 2011.

Burrell, David. "Act of Creation with Its Theological Consequences." In *Aquinas on Doctrine*, edited by Daniel Keating, John Yocum, and Thomas G. Weinandy, 27–44. New York: T&T Clark, 2004.

_____. *Aquinas: God & Action*. London: Routledge & Kegan Paul, 1979.

_____. *Knowing the Unknowable God: Ibn Sina, Maimonides, Aquinas*. South Bend, IN: University of Notre Dame Press, 1992.

Calvin, John. *Commentarii in Quatuor Reliquos Libros Mosis*. Amsterdam: Apud viduam Ioannis Iacobi Schipperi, 1671. Accessed at Digital Library of Classic Protestant Texts, http://solomon.tcpt.alexanderstreet.com.

_____. *Institutes of the Christian Religion*. Translated by Ford Lewis Battles. Edited by John T. McNeill. Philadelphia: Westminster, 1960.

Carter, J. Kameron. *Race: A Theological Account*. Oxford: Oxford University Press, 2008.

Chesteron, G. K. *Orthodoxy*. Charleston, SC: Bibliobazar, 2007.

Clayton, Phillip. *The Problem of God in Modern Thought*. Grand Rapids: Eerdmans, 2000.

Cleveland, Christopher. *Thomism in John Owen*. Burlington, VT: Ashgate, 2013.

Coakley, Sarah. *God, Sexuality, and the Self*. Cambridge: Cambridge University Press, 2013.

_____. *Rethinking Gregory of Nyssa*. London: Wiley-Blackwell, 2003.

Cobb, John, and David Ray Griffin. *Process Theology: An Introductory Exposition*. Philadelphia: Westminster, 1976.

Colón-Emeric, Edgardo A. *Wesley, Aquinas & Christian Perfection: An Ecumenical Dialogue*. Waco, TX: Baylor University Press, 2009.

Cone, James. *Black Theology and Black Power*. Maryknoll, NY: Orbis, 1997.

_____. *A Black Theology of Liberation*. Maryknoll, NY: Orbis, 1993.

_____. *The Cross and the Lynching Tree*. Maryknoll, NY: Orbis, 2011.

THE PERFECTLY SIMPLE TRIUNE GOD

_____. *God of the Oppressed.* Maryknoll, NY: Orbis, 1997.

Cottret, Bernard. *Calvin: A Biography.* Translated by M. Wallace McDonald. Edinburgh: T&T Clark, 2000.

Craig, William Lane. *The Only Wise God: The Compatibility of Divine Foreknowledge and Human Freedom.* Eugene, OR: Wipf and Stock, 2000.

_____. *The Problem of Divine Foreknowledge and Future Contingents from Aristotle to Suarez.* Leiden: Brill, 1988.

_____. *Time and Eternity: Exploring God's Relationship to Time.* Wheaton, IL: Crossway, 2001.

Crisp, Oliver D., and Michael C. Rea, editors. *Analytic Theology: New Essays in the Philosophy of Theology.* Oxford: Oxford University Press, 2009.

Critchley, Simon. *Continental Philosophy: A Very Short Introduction.* Oxford: Oxford University Press, 2001.

Cross, Richard. "Medieval Trinitarianism and Modern Theology." In *Rethinking Trinitarian Theology,* edited by Giulio Maspero and Robert J. Wozniak, 26–44. London: T&T Clark International, 2012.

Daly, Mary. *Beyond God the Father.* Boston: Beacon, 1972.

Dauphinais, Michael, Barry David, and Matthew Levering. *Aquinas the Augustinian.* Washington, DC: Catholic University of America Press, 2007.

Dauphinais, Michael, and Matthew Levering. *Reading John with St. Thomas Aquinas.* Washington, DC: Catholic University of America Press, 2005.

Desmond, William. *God and the Between.* Oxford: Blackwell, 2008.

Dewan, Lawrence. "Saint Thomas, Alvin Plantinga, and the Divine Simplicity." *The Modern Schoolman* 66 (1989): 141–51.

Dionysius. *Pseudo-Dionysius: The Complete Works.* Translated by Colm Luibheid. New York: Paulist, 1987.

Dolezal, James. *God without Parts: Divine Simplicity and the Metaphysics of God's Absoluteness.* Eugene, OR: Pickwick, 2011.

Donnelly, John Patrick, SJ. *Calvinism and Scholasticism in Vermigli's Doctrine of Man and Grace.* Leiden: Brill, 1976.

_____, editor. *The Peter Martyr Reader.* Kirksville, MO: Truman State University Press, 1999.

Dorrien, Gary. *Kantian Reason and the Hegelian Spirit.* Oxford: Wiley-Blackwell, 2012.

_____. *Social Ethics in the Making: Interpreting an American Tradition.* Oxford: Wiley-Blackwell, 2011.

Emery, Gilles. *Trinity in Aquinas.* Ypsilanti, MI: Sapientia Press of Ave Maria College, 2003.

Feser, Edward. *Scholastic Metaphysics: A Contemporary Introduction.* Neunkirchen-Seelscheid, Germany: Editiones scholasticae, 2014.

Finger, Thomas. *A Contemporary Anabaptist Theology.* Downers Grove, IL: InterVarsity, 2004.

Gillespie, Michael. *Nihilism before Nietzsche.* Chicago: University of Chicago Press, 1995.

Gilson, Etienne. *The Christian Philosophy of St. Thomas Aquinas.* South Bend, IN: University of Notre Dame Press, 1994.

Golitzen, Alexander. *Mystagogy: A Monastic Reading of Dionysius Areopagita.* Edited by Bodgan G. Bucur. Collegeville, MN: Liturgical Press, 2010.

Goris, Harm J. M. J. *Free Creatures of an Eternal God: Thomas Aquinas on God's Infallible Foreknowledge and Irresistible Will.* Nijmegen: Stichting Thomasfonds, 1996.

Grant, Jacqueline. *White Women's Christ and Black Women's Jesus.* Atlanta: Scholars Press, 1989.

Griffin, David Ray. *God, Power and Evil: A Process Theodicy.* Philadelphia: Westminster, 1976.

Gunton, Colin E. *Act & Being: Towards a Theology of the Divine Attributes.* Grand Rapids: Eerdmans, 2002.

Gutiérrez, Gustavo. *The God of Life.* Maryknoll, NY: Orbis, 1996.

_____. *The Power of the Poor in History.* Maryknoll, NY: Orbis, 1983.

_____. *A Theology of Liberation.* Maryknoll, NY: Orbis, 1988.

Haldane, John. Review of Richard Swinburne, *The Christian God. Religious Studies* 32 (1996): 281–83.

Hankey, Wayne. *God in Himself: Aquinas' Doctrine of God as Expounded in the Summa Theologiae.* Oxford: Oxford University Press, 1987.

Hart, David. *The Beauty of the Infinite: The Aesthetics of Christian Truth.* Grand Rapids: Eerdmans, 2004.

_____. "No Enduring City: The Gospel Both Created and Destroyed

Christendom." *First Things*, August 2013. www.firstthings.com/article/ 2013/08/no-enduring-city.

____. "Providence and Causality: On Divine Innocence." In *Providence of God: Deus Habet Consilium*, edited by Francesca Murphy and Philip Ziegler, 34–57. London: T&T Clark, 2009.

Harvey, Van. *Feuerbach and the Interpretation of Religion*. Cambridge: Cambridge University Press, 1997.

Hasker, William. *God, Time, and Knowledge*. Ithaca, NY, and London: Cornell University Press, 1989.

Hector, Kevin. *Theology without Metaphysics: God, Language and the Spirit of Recognition.* Cambridge: Cambridge University Press, 2011.

Hegel, G. W. F. *Lectures on the Philosophy of Religion*. Translated by R. F. Brown, P. C. Hodgson, and J. M. Stewart. Berkeley: University of California Press, 1988.

____. *Phenomenology of Spirit*. Translated by A. V. Miller. Oxford: Oxford University Press, 1977.

____. *Science of Logic*. Translated by A. V. Miller. Amherst, NY: Humanity Books, 1969.

Heidegger, Martin. *Identity and Difference*. Translated by Joan Stambaugh. New York: Harper & Row, 1969.

Helmer, Christine. *The Trinity and Martin Luther: A Study on the Relationship between Genre, Language and the Trinity in Luther's Works (1523–1546)*. Mainz: Verlag Philipp von Zabern, 1999.

Hinlicky, Paul. *Divine Complexity: The Rise of Creedal Christianity*. Minneapolis: Fortress Press, 2011.

Hooker, Richard. *Of the Laws of Ecclesiastical Polity*. Edited by Arthur Stephen McGrade. Cambridge: Cambridge University Press, 1989.

Hughes, Christopher. *On a Complex Theory of a Simple God: An Investigation in Aquinas' Philosophical Theology*. Ithaca, NY: Cornell University Press, 1989.

Hyppolite, Jean. *Genesis and Structure of Hegel's Phenomenology of Spirit*. Translated by Samuel Cherniak and John Heckman. Evanston, IL: Northwestern University Press, 1974.

Insole, Christopher J. *Kant and the Creation of Freedom: A Theological Problem*. Oxford: Oxford University Press, 2013.

Irigaray, Luce. *Sexes and Genealogies*. New York: Columbia University Press, 1993.

Isasi-Díaz, Ada Maria. *Mujerista Theology*. Maryknoll, NY: Orbis, 1996.

Jennings, Willie James. *The Christian Imagination: Theology and the Origins of Race*. New Haven, CT: Yale University Press, 2010.

Jenson, Robert. *Alpha and Omega: A Study in the Theology of Karl Barth*. Eugene, OR: Wipf & Stock, 2002.

____. *America's Theology: A Recommendation of Jonathan Edwards*. Oxford: Oxford University Press, 1988.

____. *Systematic Theology*. Volume 1. New York: Oxford University Press, 1997.

____. *The Triune Identity: God according to the Gospel*. Philadelphia: Fortress Press, 1982.

Johnson, Elizabeth, *She Who Is*. New York: Crossroad, 1996.

Jordan, Mark. "The Competition of Authoritative Languages and Aquinas's Theological Rhetoric." *Medieval Philosophy and Theology* 4 (1994): 71–90.

____. *Rewritten Theology*. Oxford: Wiley-Blackwell, 2005.

Jüngel, Eberhard. *God as the Mystery of the World: On the Foundation of the Theology of the Crucified One in the Dispute between Theism and Atheism*. Grand Rapids: Eerdmans, 1983.

____ *God's Being Is in Becoming: The Trinitarian Being of God in the Theology of Karl Barth*. Translated by John Webster. London: Bloomsbury, 2014.

Kant, Immanuel. *Foundations of the Metaphysics of Morals*. Translated by Lewis White Beck. New York: Macmillan, 1987.

Kärkkäinen, Veli-Matti. *The Doctrine of God: A Global Introduction*. Grand Rapids: Baker Academic, 2004.

Kasper, Walter. *Jesus the Christ*. London: Burns & Oates, 1976.

Keating, James F., and Thomas Joseph White, OP, editors. *Divine Impassibility and the Mystery of Human Suffering*. Grand Rapids: Eerdmans, 2009.

Keller, Catherine. *Faces of the Deep: A Theology of Becoming*. London: Routledge, 2003.

____. *On the Mystery: Discerning Divinity in Process*. Minneapolis: Fortress Press, 2008.

Kerr, Fergus. "A Different Word: Neoscholasticism and Its Discontents." *International Journal of Systematic Theology* 8 (2006): 128–48.

LaCugna, Catherine. *God for Us: The Trinity & Christian Life*. New York: HarperCollins, 1993.

Leftow, Brian. *Time and Eternity*. Ithaca, NY: Cornell University Press, 1991.

Levering, Matthew. *Predestination: Biblical and Theological Paths*. Oxford: Oxford University Press, 2011.

Lilla, Mark. *The Stillborn God: Religion, Politics and the Modern West*. New York: Vintage Books, 2008.

Lochbrunner, Manfred. *Hans Urs von Balthasar und seine Theologenkollegen: Sechs Beziehungsgeschichten*. Würzburg: Echter, 2009.

Lodahl, Michael. *The Story of God*. Kansas City, MO: Beacon Hill, 2008.

Lombard, Peter. *The Sentences: Book 1: The Mystery of the Trinity*. Translated by Giulio Silano. Toronto: Pontifical Institute of Mediaeval Studies, 2007.

Long, D. Stephen. *Divine Economy: Theology and the Market*. London: Routledge, 2000.

_____. *John Wesley's Moral Theology: The Quest for God and Goodness*. Nashville: Kingswood Books, 2005.

_____. *Saving Karl Barth: Hans Urs von Balthasar's Preoccupation*. Minneapolis: Fortress Press, 2014.

Long, D. Stephen, and George Kalantzis. *The Sovereignty of God Debate*. Eugene, OR: Cascade Books, 2009.

Louth, Andrew. *Denys the Areopagite*. London: Continuum, 1989.

Luther, Martin. "Pagan Servitude of the Church." In *Martin Luther: Selections from His Writings*, translated and edited by John Dillenberger, 249–363. Garden City, NY: Doubleday, 1961.

_____. *The Schmalkald Articles*. Translated by William R. Russell. Minneapolis: Fortress Press, 1995.

Luy, David. *Dominus Mortis: Martin Luther on the Incorruptibility of God in Christ*. Minneapolis: Fortress Press, 2014.

McAdoo, H. R. *The Structure of Caroline Moral Theology*. London: Longmans, Green, 1949.

McCabe, Herbert, OP. *God Matters*. Springfield, IL: Templegate, 1991.

McClendon, James. *Systematic Theology: Doctrine*. Nashville: Abingdon, 1994.

_____. *Systematic Theology: Ethics*. Nashville: Abingdon, 1986.

_____. *Systematic Theology: Witness*. Nashville: Abingdon, 2000.

McClintock Fulkerson, Mary. *Changing the Subject: Women's Discourses and Feminist Theology*. Minneapolis: Fortress Press, 1994.

McCord Adams, Marilyn. *Christ and Horrors*. Cambridge: Cambridge University Press, 2006.

_____. *Horrendous Evils and the Goodness of God*. Ithaca, NY, and London: Cornell University Press, 1999.

McFague, Sallie. *The Body of God: An Ecological Theology*. Minneapolis: Fortress Press, 1993.

_____. *Models of God*. Minneapolis: Fortress Press, 1987.

_____. *Super, Natural Christians*. Minneapolis: Fortress Press, 2000.

McInerny, Ralph. *Aquinas and Analogy*. Washington, DC: Catholic University of America Press, 1996.

Melanchthon, Philipp. *On Christian Doctrine, Loci Communes 1555*. Translated and edited by Clyde L. Manschreck. New York: Oxford University Press, 1965.

Merriell, D. Juvenal. *To the Image of the Trinity: A Study in the Development of Aquinas' Teaching*. Toronto: Pontifical Institute of Mediaeval Studies, 1990.

Milbank, John, and Catherine Pickstock. *Truth in Aquinas*. London: Routledge, 2001.

Moltmann, Jürgen. *The Crucified God: The Cross of Christ as the Foundation and Criticism of Christian Theology*. Translated by R. A. Wilson and John Bowden. New York: Harper & Row, 1974.

_____. *Das Kommen Gottes*. Gütersloh: Gütersloher Verlagshaus, 1995.

_____. *Trinity and the Kingdom: The Doctrine of God*. Translated by Margaret Kohl. San Francisco: Harper & Row, 1981.

Muller, Richard A. *Christ and the Decree*. Durham, NC: Labyrinth, 1986.

_____. *God, Creation, and Providence in the Thought of Jacobus Arminius*. Grand Rapids: Baker Book House, 1991.

_____. *Post-Reformation Reformed Dogmatics*, vol. 1, *Prolegomena to Theology*. 2nd ed. Grand Rapids: Baker Academic, 2003.

_____. *Post-Reformation Reformed Dogmatics*, vol. 3, *The Divine Essence and Attributes*. Grand Rapids: Baker Academic, 2003.

_____. *The Unaccommodated Calvin*. New York: Oxford University Press, 2000.

Murphy, Francesca. *God Is Not a Story*. Oxford: Oxford University Press, 2007.

Murphy, Francesca, and Philip Ziegler. *Providence of God: Deus Habet Consilium.* London: T&T Clark, 2009.

Norris, John. *Reason and Religion; or, The Grounds and Measures of Devotion Considered from the Nature of God and the Nature of Man in Several Contemplations.* 2nd ed. London: Samuel Manship, 1693.

Olson, Roger E., and Christopher A. Hall. *The Trinity.* Grand Rapids: Eerdmans, 2002.

Oord, Thomas Jay. *Defining Love: A Philosophical, Scientific, and Theological Engagement.* Grand Rapids: Brazos, 2010.

Oppy, Graham. "The Devilish Complexities of Divine Simplicity." *Philo* 6 (2003): 10–22.

O'Regan, Cyril. *The Anatomy of Misremembering: Von Balthasar's Response to Philosophical Modernity*, vol. 1, *Hegel.* New York: Herder & Herder, 2014.

O'Rourke, Fran. *Pseudo-Dionysius and the Metaphysics of Aquinas.* Leiden: Brill, 1992.

Owen, John. *A Display of Arminianism.* London: printed by J. L. for Phil Stephens, 1643.

_____. *Vindiciae Evangelicae.* In *The Works of John Owen*, vol. XII, edited by William H. Goold. Carlisle, PA: Banner of Truth Trust, 1976.

Pannenberg, Wolfhart. *Systematic Theology.* Volume 1. Translated by Geoffrey W. Bromiley. Grand Rapids: Eerdmans, 1991.

Pasnau, Robert. *Thomas Aquinas on Human Nature.* Cambridge: Cambridge University Press, 2002.

Pesch, Otto Hermann, OP. *The God Question in Thomas Aquinas and Martin Luther.* Translated by Gottfried G. Krodel. Philadelphia: Fortress Press, 1972.

Pippin, Robert. *Idealism as Modernism: Hegelian Variations.* Cambridge: Cambridge University Press, 1997.

Plantinga, Alvin. *Does God Have a Nature?* Milwaukee: Marquette University Press, 1980.

_____. "The Free Will Defense." In *The Analytic Theist: An Alvin Plantinga Reader*, edited by James F. Sennett, 22–50. Grand Rapids: Eerdmans, 1998.

Platt, John. *Reformed Thought and Scholasticism: The Arguments for the Existence of God in Dutch Theology, 1575–1650.* Leiden: Brill, 1982.

Preller, Victor. *Divine Science and the Science of God: A Reformulation of Thomas Aquinas*. Princeton, NJ: Princeton University Press, 1967.

Proclus. *The Elements of Theology*. Translated by E. R. Dodds. Oxford: Clarendon Press, 1933.

Pruss, Alexander R. "On Two Problems of Divine Simplicity." In *Oxford Studies in Philosophy of Religion*, vol. 1, edited by Jonathan Kvanvig, 150–68. Oxford: Oxford University Press, 2008.

Rad, Gerhard von. *Old Testament Theology*. Volume 1. New York: Harper & Row, 1962.

Radde-Gallwitz, Andrew. *Basil of Caesarea, Gregory of Nyssa and the Transformation of Divine Simplicity*. Oxford: Oxford University Press, 2009.

Rahner, Karl. *The Trinity*. Translated by Joseph Donceel. London: Burns and Oates, 2001.

Rauser, Randall. "Theology as a Bull Session." In *Analytic Theology: New Essays in the Philosophy of Theology*, edited by Oliver D. Crisp and Michael C. Rea, 70–87. Oxford: Oxford University Press, 2009.

Redding, Paul. *Analytic Philosophy and the Return of Hegelian Thought*. Cambridge: Cambridge University Press, 2007.

Rousseau, Jean-Jacques. *Emile or On Education*. Translated by Allan Bloom. New York: Basic Books, 1979.

Rummel, Erika. *The Humanist-Scholastic Debate in the Renaissance and Reformation*. Cambridge, MA: Harvard University Press, 1995.

Sanders, John. "Divine Suffering in an Openness of God Perspective" and "Response." In *The Sovereignty of God Debate*, edited by D. Stephen Long and George Kalantzis, 155–64. Eugene, OR: Cascade Books, 2009.

_____. *The God Who Risks*. Downers Grove, IL: InterVarsity, 2007.

Schleiermacher, Friedrich. *The Christian Faith*. Translated and edited by H. R. Mackintosh and J. S. Stewart. Edinburgh: T&T Clark, 1986.

Sennett, James F., ed. *The Analytic Theist: An Alvin Plantinga Reader*. Grand Rapids: Eerdmans, 1998.

Smith, Barry D. *The Oneness and Simplicity of God*. Eugene, OR: Pickwick, 2014.

Smith, Timothy L. *Thomas Aquinas' Trinitarian Theology: A Study in Theological Method*. Washington, DC: Catholic University of America Press, 2003.

Sobrino, Jon. *Jesus the Liberator: Historical-Theological Reading of Jesus of Nazareth*. Maryknoll, NY: Orbis, 1993.

Sokolowski, Robert. *The God of Faith and Reason: Foundations of Christian Theology*. Washington, DC: Catholic University of America Press, 1995.

Sonderegger, Katherine. *Systematic Theology*, vol. 1, *God*. Minneapolis: Fortress Press, 2015.

Song, Choan-Seng. *Third-Eye Theology: Theology in Formation in Asian Settings*. Eugene, OR: Wipf & Stock, 1979.

Soskice, Janet. "Aquinas and Augustine on Creation and God as 'Eternal Being.'" *New Blackfriars* 95, no. 1056 (2014): 190–207.

_____. "Naming God: A Study in Faith and Reason." In *Reason and the Reasons of Faith*, edited by Paul Griffiths and Reinhard Hütter, 241–54. New York: Continuum, 2005.

Stump, Eleonore. *Aquinas*. London: Routledge, 2003.

Stump, Eleonore, and Norman Kretzmann. "Eternity." *The Journal of Philosophy* 78, no. 8 (August 1981): 429–58.

Swinburne, Richard. *The Christian God*. Oxford: Oxford University Press, 1994.

_____. *The Coherence of Theism*. Oxford: Clarendon Press, 1977.

_____. *The Existence of God*. 2nd ed. Oxford: Clarendon Press, 2004.

_____. *Faith and Reason*. Oxford: Oxford University Press, 1981.

Tanner, Kathryn. *God and Creation in Christian Theology: Tyranny or Empowerment*. Minneapolis: Fortress Press, 2005.

Taylor, Charles. *Hegel*. Cambridge: Cambridge University Press, 1975.

Torrell, Jean-Pierre, OP. *Saint Thomas Aquinas*, vol. 1, *The Person and His Work*. Translated by Robert Royal. Washington, DC: Catholic University of America Press, 1996.

Trueman, Carl R. *John Owen: Reformed Catholic, Renaissance Man*. Aldershot, UK: Ashgate, 2007.

Turner, Denys. *Faith, Reason and the Existence of God*. Cambridge: Cambridge University Press, 2004.

Vermigli, Peter Martyr. *Loci Communes*. London: Ex typographia Ioannis Kyngstoni, 1576. Accessed at the Digital Library of Classic Protestant Texts, http://solomon.tcpt.alexanderstreet.com.

____. *Predestination and Justification.* Translated and edited by Frank A. James III. Kirksville, MO: Truman State University Press, 2003.

Vos, Arvin. *Aquinas, Calvin and Contemporary Protestant Thought: A Critique of Protestant Views on the Thought of Thomas Aquinas.* Washington, DC: Christian University Press, 1985.

Wear, Sarah, and John Dillon. *Dionysius the Areopagite and the Neoplatonist Tradition.* Aldershot, UK: Ashgate, 2007.

Weigel, Peter. *Aquinas on Simplicity: An Investigation into the Foundations of His Philosophical Theology.* Oxford: Peter Lang, 2008.

Weinandy, Thomas G. "The Marvel of the Incarnation." In *Aquinas on Doctrine,* edited by Daniel Keating, John Yocum, and Thomas G. Weinandy, 67–84. New York: T&T Clark, 2004.

Weitz, Morris. "Philosophical Analysis." In *The Encyclopedia of Philosophy,* edited by Paul Edwards, 1:97–105. London: Collier Macmillan, 1967.

Wesley, John. "Address to the Clergy." In *Works of John Wesley,* edited by Thomas Jackson (New York: Carlton & Porter, 1872), 10:481–500.

____. "Catholic Spirit." In *The Works of John Wesley,* edited by Albert Outler, 2: 82–94. Nashville: Abingdon, 1985.

Westphal, Merold. *Overcoming Ontotheology: Toward a Postmodern Christian Faith.* New York: Fordham University Press, 2001.

White, Graham. *Luther as Nominalist.* Helsinki: Luther-Agricola-Society, 1994.

Whitehead, Alfred North. *Process and Reality.* New York: Free Press, 1978.

Wilken, Robert. *The Spirit of Early Christianity.* New Haven, CT: Yale University Press, 2003.

Williams, Bernard. *Truth and Truthfulness.* Princeton, NJ: Princeton University Press, 2004.

Williams, Rowan. *On Christian Theology.* Oxford: Blackwell, 2000.

Wippel, John F. *Metaphysical Themes in Thomas Aquinas.* Washington, DC: Catholic University of America Press, 1984.

Wittgenstein, Ludwig. *Philosophical Investigations.* Translated by G. E. M. Anscombe. New York: Macmillan, 1968.

Wolterstorff, Nicholas. *Divine Discourse.* Cambridge: Cambridge University Press, 1995.

____. *Justice.* Princeton, NJ: Princeton University Press, 2010.

Wozniak, Robert J., and Giulio Maspero, eds. *Rethinking Trinitarian Theology.* London: T&T Clark International, 2012.

Zagzebski, Linda Trinkaus. *The Dilemma of Freedom and Foreknowledge.* New York: Oxford University Press, 1991.

_____. *Divine Motivation Theory.* Cambridge: Cambridge University Press, 2004.

Zanchi, Girolamo. *De natura Dei, seu de divinis attributis, libri V. Ad illustrissimum principem Ioannem Casimirum, comitem Palatinum ad Rhenum: Bavariae ducem, & c. Nunc emendatè & diligenter recusi.* Neustadt an der Weinstrasse: Typis Matthaei Harnisii, 1590. Accessed at the Digital Library of Classic Protestant Texts.

Index